the Unofficial Guide™ to College Admissions

Shannon Turlington

IDG Books Worldwide, Inc.

First Edition

IDG Books Worldwide, Inc.
An International Data Group Company
919 E. Hillsdale Boulevard
Suite 400
Foster City, CA 94404

An Arco Book

 The IDG Books Worldwide logo is a registered trademark under exclusive license to IDG Books Worldwide, Inc., from International Data Group, Inc.

For general information on IDG Books Worldwide's books in the U.S., please call our Consumer Customer Service department at 800-762-2974. For reseller information, including discounts and premium sales, please call our Reseller Customer Service department at 800-434-3422.

ISBN: 0-02-863547-7

Library of Congress Number information available upon request

Manufactured in the United States of America

10 9 8 7 6 5 4 3 2 1

Acknowledgments

The work of many people went into this book. I would like to particularly thank my agent, Martha Kaufman-Amitay, and all the people at Arco who helped make this book a reality, including Lorna Gentry, Dave Henthorn, and Karen Reinisch. I would also like to thank all of the college admissions officers who took the time to provide advice and insight.

Contents

Why "Unofficial"? The *Unofficial Guide* Declaration of
Independence xv

I Start Your College Search 1

1 Choosing the Right College...................................3
Getting Started 3

All-Important Academics 4
  Kinds of Schools 5
  What's Your Learning Style? 7
  Judging a College's Overall Academic Quality 8
  Judging the Strength of Individual Departments........9
  Important Extras 9

Considering Cost..10

Location, Location, Location 11
  The Big City 11
  Out in the Country 12
  Small-Town America..12

Size Matters..13
  Big and Diverse..13
  Small and Personal...14
  Somewhere in Between 14

Your Fellow Students 14
  Looking for Diversity 15
  Finding an Affiliation...15

The Social Scene..16
  What to Do After Class 16
  The Living Situation 17
  The Important "Others" 19

How Not to Choose a College...19
  Follow Your Friends..19
  Let Mom and Dad Choose for You 20
  Go for the Designer Label 20
  Rely on Rankings..21

Putting Together Your List of Final Choices..................21

Just the Facts 25

2 Making the Most of the Campus Visit **27**

Getting Ready for the Visit...27
  When to Go..*28*
  Scheduling Your Visit *28*
  What to Bring..*30*

What to See on the Campus Tour 30

Questions You Should Ask 32
  Questions About Academics..................................*32*
  Questions About Life on Campus..........................*34*
  Questions About Social Life..................................*34*
  Even More Questions...*35*

Other Things to Do While You're There 36

Keeping Your Parents Busy 37

If You Can't Visit 38

Just the Facts 39

3 What Admissions Committees Are Looking For **41**

How the Admissions Process Works.............................41

How Selective Should Your Schools Be?.......................42
  Selectivity Levels..*43*
  Course Requirements...*44*
  Matching Yourself to Admission Standards *44*

What Admissions Committees Are Looking For.............46
  *The Ideal Candidate (According to the
    Admissions Committee)*....................................*47*
  The Academic Record *48*
  Extracurricular Activities *49*
  *Other Qualities That Admissions Committees
    Look For*..*49*
  Need-Blind and Need-Aware Admissions..................*50*
  *Making an Impression on the Admissions
    Committee*...*51*

Improving Your Chances for Admission.......................51

Using the Interview to Help You Get In 53
  Preparing for the Interview *54*
  Interviewing Tips...*56*

Just the Facts 56

II When and How to Apply **59**

4 The Lowdown on the Application Process **61**

A College Countdown Calendar...................................61

Saving Time with the Common Application 62

Fast and Easy Electronic Applications 62
   Electronic Application Services..............................*68*
   Colleges That Accept Electronic Applications...........*68*
   What If You Don't Have a Computer?......................*68*
Just the Facts 70

5 Application Options—Playing It Smart **71**
Understanding Your Admissions Options 71
   Rolling Admission...*72*
   Open Admission *72*
   Deferred Admission...*73*
   Early Admission or Early Entrance.......................*73*
   Early Action *74*
   Early Decision...*74*
Choosing the *Right* Option 79
   Advantages of Applying Early *79*
   Disadvantages of Applying Early..........................*80*
   When Should You Apply Early?.............................*81*
Meeting and Beating Deadlines: What
Your Strategy Should Be 81
Just the Facts 82

6 Application Tips for International Students **85**
How to Apply to College in the United States..............85
   Choosing Where to Apply *86*
   Getting Started *90*
   Admission Requirements...................................*90*
   Other Parts of the Application *91*
What You Need to Know About Test Requirements 92
   Test of English as a Foreign Language....................*92*
   The Michigan English Language Assessment
      Battery *95*
   The SAT I or ACT *95*
Getting a Student Visa 96
Paying Your Way 97
Improving Your English Once You Get Here 100
Dealing with American Culture 102
Where to Turn for Help 102
   Help from the Schools....................................*103*
   Organizations for International Students *104*
   Internet Resources..*105*
Just the Facts 106

III Put Together Your Application Package 107

7 Creating an Exceptional Application Package..........109
Getting Organized 109
   Obtaining Application Forms..............................*109*
   Keeping Track of Applications *110*
Creating a Personal Profile.......................................113
Application Dos and Don'ts.......................................116
Getting Recommendations That Really Sell You..........118
Submitting High School Transcripts 120
Submitting Essays, Portfolios, and Other
Supplemental Application Materials 120
Application Packages from Homeschooled
and Alternative School Students...............................121
   Can Homeschoolers Go to College?........................*122*
   Demonstrating Your Academic Achievements...........*124*
   Presenting Yourself as a Desirable
     Nontraditional Student..................................*125*
Just the Facts 127

8 Writing Essays That Impact....................................129
Why the Essay Is So Important 129
Kinds of Essay Questions..130
   Telling Colleges About Yourself.............................*130*
   Telling Colleges Why You Want to
     Attend That School......................................*131*
   Showing Your Creative Side *132*
Choosing an Essay Topic...133
   Coming Up with Topic Ideas *133*
   Narrowing the List..*134*
   What You Shouldn't Write About...........................*136*
   Focusing Your Essay *138*
Essay-Writing Dos and Don'ts (Mostly Don'ts).............139
Just the Facts 141

IV Maximize Your Test Scores 143

9 The Unofficial Story on Standardized Tests.............145
How Important Are Standardized Test Scores
to Colleges? 145
The Standardized Test Controversy 147
Getting Ready for the Tests 150
   Printed Study Materials *151*
   Test-Prep Software..*152*

Video and Audio Test-Prep Packages......................*152*
Online Resources *152*
Other Proven Ways to Prepare *153*

Should You Take a Test-Prep Course? 153
Individual Tutoring *154*
School-Based Programs......................................*155*
Local Commercial Courses..................................*155*
National Commercial Courses *156*
Choosing a Test-Prep Course *157*

When Test Day Arrives 157

Test-Taking Strategies That Work Every Time 159

Just the Facts 160

10 Doing Your Best on the SAT I or ACT......................**161**
Which Test Should You Take? 161

Deciding When to Take the Test 165
Registering for the SAT I...................................*165*
Registering for the ACT *166*

Taking a Preliminary Test 167

Finding Your Way Around the SAT I 168
Strategies for Answering Verbal Questions *169*
Strategies for Answering Math Questions................*172*
A General Guessing Strategy *175*
*You Don't Need to Answer Every Question to
Get a Good Score* *176*

Finding Your Way Around the ACT 177
Strategies for Answering English Questions.............*177*
Strategies for Answering Reading Questions............*178*
Strategies for Answering Math Questions................*179*
*Strategies for Answering Science Reasoning
Questions* *181*
A General Guessing Strategy *181*

Finding Free Study Materials and Sample Tests 182

Just the Facts 183

11 Taking SAT II, AP, and CLEP Exams..........................**185**
Why You Should Take More Tests..............................185

Understanding SAT II Subject Tests..........................187
English SAT II Subject Tests...............................*187*
History SAT II Subject Tests...............................*188*
Foreign Language SAT II Subject Tests...................*189*
Math SAT II Subject Tests..................................*190*
Science SAT II Subject Tests *191*

Deciding Which SAT II Subject Tests to Take 193
Preparing for the SAT II Subject Tests 194

Understanding AP Exams 195
Types of AP Courses and Exams...........................196
Tackling the Free-Response Section 199
Strategies for Math and Science AP Exams 200
Preparing for Foreign Language APs......................201

Understanding CLEP Exams 201
Deciding Whether to Take a CLEP Exam..................202
Types of CLEP Exams 202
Registering for a CLEP Exam 204

Getting More Information......................................204

Just the Facts 205

12 After the Tests..207
Understanding Your Score Report...........................207
The SAT I Score Report 208
SAT II Subject Tests Score Reports 211
The ACT Score Report 212
AP Grade Reports..214

Deciding Whether to Cancel Your Scores 214

Deciding Whether to Retest 217
Help with Retaking the SAT I...............................218
Help with Retaking the ACT 219

Disputing Your Score 219
Requesting Hand Scoring 219
Challenging a Test Question or Procedure...............220

If You're Accused of Cheating 221

Just the Facts 222

V The Ins and Outs of Financial Aid 223

13 How Financial Aid Works 225
What College Really Costs......................................225
Tuition and Fees...227
Books and Supplies..227
Room and Board 227
Transportation and Personal Expenses 228
Miscellaneous Expenses......................................229

Basic Types of Financial Aid...................................229

How Much Aid Will You Get? 230
Are You Eligible? 230

Determining Dependent or Independent Student Status 231
Calculating Your Financial Need...........................231
Maximizing Your Financial Need 233
What If You Don't Qualify?.................................233
Why You Should Apply for Financial Aid.....................234
A Financial Aid Timetable.......................................236
How to Apply for Financial Aid................................238
The Three Commandments of Applying for Financial Aid 238
The Financial Aid Forms......................................240
Should You Hire a Financial Aid Consultant?.............244
Just the Facts 246

14 Understanding Your Financial Aid Award 247
What Happens After You Apply for Financial Aid 247
Federal Sources of Financial Aid 249
Pell Grants 251
Campus-Based Programs 252
State Sources of Financial Aid.................................253
Need-Based Financial Aid from the States..............254
Non-Need-Based Financial Aid from the States........254
State-Administered Federal Aid Programs 255
Tuition Savings Plans 255
Aid from Your School..256
Grants and Scholarships......................................257
Loans..258
Tuition Payment Plans...258
Innovative Come-Ons...259
The Lowdown on Loans...261
Loans for Students..261
Loans for Parents 264
Negotiating for More Aid...265
Just the Facts 266

15 Searching for Scholarships 269
The Skinny on Scholarships 270
How to Maximize Scholarship Awards 271
The National Merit Scholarship Program.....................272
Getting Athletic Scholarships...................................273
NCAA Division Schools 273
NAIA Member Schools...274
Other Athletic Associations...................................274

Scholarships for Needed Professions..........................275
   Teaching...*275*
   Health Professions...*276*
   Scholarships from Professional Organizations..........*276*

Scholarships for Diverse Groups................................276
   Money for Minorities..*277*
   Money for Women...*278*
   Money for Disabled Students....................................*279*
   Money for Gays and Lesbians...................................*279*
   Money from Religious Organizations........................*280*
   Money from Ethnic Societies...................................*280*

Other Sources of Scholarships 280
   National Scholarship Programs..............................*281*
   Your Own Experiences and Interests.......................*281*
   Taking Advantage of Your Parents' Associates.........*283*
   Money from Local Sources......................................*284*
   Contests..*285*

Taking Advantage of Scholarship Search Services 285
   Beware of Scholarship Search Services That
     Charge a Fee..*286*

Avoiding Scholarship Scams.....................................286

Just the Facts 288

16 Looking Elsewhere for Aid 291
Working Your Way Through College 291
   Cooperative Education..*292*
   Employer Tuition Plans...*293*
   Starting a Side Business...*293*

Letting the Military Pay 294
   Service Academies..*294*
   ROTC Programs...*294*
   Joining Up...*296*

Taking Advantage of Federal Programs.......................296
   Department of Health and Human
     Services Programs...*296*
   Public Service *297*

Tax Breaks That Help Pay for College.......................298

Getting a Private Loan..300
   The Advantages of Federal Loans...........................*300*
   Kinds of Private Education Loans............................*301*
   Choosing a Lender...*302*
   Managing Student Loans...*304*

How Not to Pay for College................................305
    Working Yourself Too Hard.............................*305*
    Burying Yourself in Debt *305*
Just the Facts 306

VI Get Ready for College...................................307

17 When the Letters Come In 309
Choosing Where to Go....................................309
Conditional Acceptance—What It Means...................310
Getting Off the Wait List...............................310
If You're Rejected 312
If You Aren't Accepted Anywhere..........................312
    Applying Elsewhere *313*
    Starting at a Community College *313*
    Distance Learning *315*
Just the Facts 316

18 Surviving Freshman Year................................317
Getting Ready for College...............................317
    A Packing List......................................*318*
    Buying a Computer for College *321*
The Ins and Outs of Dorm Living 323
How to Choose Classes...................................325
Keeping Your Grades Up and Having a Social Life.......325
    Managing Time Wisely *326*
    Developing Good Study Skills *327*
    Creating a Study Space...............................*329*
Common Problems for College Students and
How to Deal with Them...................................330
    Dealing with Stress *331*
    The Freshman 15.....................................*332*
    Avoiding Problems with Drugs and Alcohol.............*332*
    Staying Safe...*334*
College on a Budget 335
    Developing a College Budget.........................*335*
    Getting a Checking Account *336*
    Getting a Credit Card...............................*338*
    Saving Money on Room and Board......................*338*
    Saving Money on Everything Else.....................*340*
Just the Facts 341

19 Going on to Graduate School.................................343
Why Get an Advanced Degree? 343
Your Graduate School Options 346
Getting a Master's or Ph.D...............................346
Going to Business School 348
Going to Law School 349
Going to Medical School.....................................349
Selecting a Pre-Grad School College 350
Planning Your Undergrad Curriculum with
Grad School in Mind 351
Preparing to Earn a Master's Degree or Ph.D..........351
Preparing for Business School 352
Preparing for Law School 353
Preparing for Medical School...............................354
Preparing for Nursing School...............................355
Entering Graduate School from the Workplace.............355
Choosing a Graduate School..................................356
Paying for Graduate School...................................357
Paying for a Master's or Ph.D...............................359
Paying for Business School..................................359
Paying for Law School.......................................359
Paying for Medical School 360
Just the Facts 360

A Glossary of College Admissions Terms.....................363

B College Admissions Resource Guide.......................381

C Recommended Reading.......................................387

D Important Addresses 395

**E Colleges and Universities That Accept Common
   or Electronic Applications...................................411**

The *Unofficial Guide*™
Declaration of Independence

So, you're thinking about going to college. What an exciting time! So many choices are open to you as you prepare to make the move out on your own for the first time.

But, let's face it. The entire prospect of applying to college can be confusing, stressful, even overwhelming. You may feel pressure from everyone around you—your parents, your teachers, your friends. And so much misinformation is floating around—about how colleges choose who to let in, about the standardized tests, about how you're going to pay for it all.

To survive the process—and to get into the college of your dreams—you need help.

You Need a Helpful Guide

This book is designed to help you make sense of it all. Inside, you won't find any misinformation or myths, only facts. And since this book is "unofficial," you can trust it to give you only the insider scoop—what admissions officers really look for in applicants, proven strategies that really do improve your test scores, how financial aid really works.

And this book is complete. It covers the entire process of applying to college, starting with helping you decide where to apply, all the way through to when you move into the dorm. You won't have to buy additional books for learning about applying for financial aid or how to write the application essay. This is the only guide you need.

Finally, this book will be a practical aid for you. It's bursting with uncensored strategies, tips, and facts that you can put to use right away, no matter which stage you've reached in the college application process. It's packed with tables, calendars, and worksheets to help you make decisions, stay organized, and get into the college of your dreams. And since this book is frequently updated, you'll get the straight scoop about the latest developments in college admissions—information you can trust.

So, get ready to have the entire process of getting into college demystified. By the time you're done with this book, you'll feel fully prepared to lauch your college career.

How This Book Is Organized

This book is divided into six parts, each one focusing on a new step in the college admissions process:

- *Part I: Start Your College Search* gets you started in the right direction— learn how to choose which colleges to apply to, how to get the most value out of the campus visit, and what admissions committees are looking for in applicants.

- *Part II: When and How to Apply* helps you prepare for submitting college applications—discover what your options are in terms of applying electronically and applying early, and find a handy calendar to help you keep track of all the things you have to do.

- *Part III: Put Together Your Application Package* takes you through every step of crafting a dynamite application—find out how to get teacher recommendations, put together application portfolios, and write an impressive essay.

- *Part IV: Maximize Your Test Scores* helps you do your best on the admissions tests—find strategies for acing the ACT, SAT I, SAT II Subject Tests, and AP exams.

- *Part V: The Ins and Outs of Financial Aid* explains in clear terms the process of getting aid—learn how to apply, how to negotiate for more money, and where to look for scholarships.

- *Part VI: Get Ready for College* helps you make the transition to college— find out what your options are when the acceptance letters come in, get a guide for surviving freshman year, and start thinking about graduate school.

Special Features

To help you get the most out of this book quickly and easily, the text is enhanced with the following special sidebars:

- "Timesaver": tips and shortcuts to save you time
- "Moneysaver": tips and hints to save you money
- "Watch Out!": cautions and warnings about pitfalls to avoid
- "Bright Idea:" strategies that offer an easier or smarter way to do something
- "Unofficially…": an insider's fact or anecdote
- "Quote": statements from real people that can give you valuable insights

You also need to have quick information at your fingertips. Thus, I have included the following helpful sections at the back of the book:

- A glossary of college admissions and financial aid terms

- A list of Internet, software, and video resources

- A bibliography of recommended college guides, scholarship guides, and other helpful books

- Useful addresses, including all the state financial aid agencies

- Web addresses of electronic applications you can submit over the Internet

My Pledge to You

You can trust me to give you only the straight scoop on how to get into college. I have no bias. I have no agenda, except to help you to get those acceptance letters. I'm not a professional college consultant with a college-prep service to sell, and I have no interest in making any particular school look good. I'm here to tell you the truth about how to get into college, to give you the information that the schools won't or can't, and to help you avoid pitfalls like myths and scams.

I don't have any reason to hide information from you. My only concern is to offer you the most efficient, accurate, and useful guidance for finding the best college for you and then getting admitted to that school. So, you can focus your time and energy on completing applications, meeting deadlines, and making yourself into the best possible applicant, worry-free.

That's why this book proudly bears the banner of the Unofficial Guides. Authorized and controlled by no one, I serve only one master—you, the reader.

Letters, Comments, and Questions from Readers

I've learned a great deal over the years from students like yourself. I've heard from many people just like you who have generously shared their stories with me—helpful tips, anecdotes about how they got into college, mistakes they made along the way, and approaches they'd recommend to high school students who are about to go through the same things they did. Many of the tips and suggestions scattered throughout the book have benefited from their input.

If you have questions, comments, suggestions, or ideas for future editions of this book, I'd like to hear from you. Write to the author at this address:

Shannon Turlington
The Unofficial Guide™ to College Admissions
IDG Books
1633 Broadway
New York, NY 10019–6785

Start Your College Search

PART I

GET THE SCOOP ON...
Determining your goals, interests, and needs ▪ Selecting academic programs ▪ Factoring in the price tag ▪ Looking at the location of potential colleges ▪ Determining the size of school that you want to attend ▪ Considering whether diversity is important to you ▪ Picking schools where you'll want to live and play ▪ Deciding which factors *not* to use when selecting a college ▪ Creating a final list of colleges

Choosing the Right College

College will be your home for the next four (or five, or even six) years. It's the place where you'll launch your career, make lifelong friends, and perhaps even meet your future spouse. Therefore, choosing a college is one of the most important decisions that you'll ever make. You should give a lot of time and consideration to the schools that you choose to apply to.

Probably the most important thing to look for in a potential college is a strong academic program that suits your abilities and interests. But college is more than just the classroom—it's where you'll sleep, eat, study, and party while earning a degree. Often personal factors, rather than academic ones, are what cause students to leave college. You don't want to discover too late that a small, quaint campus is too stifling or that you're lost in the crowd at a big university.

When deciding where to apply, select schools that fit you as closely as possible—not only your academic goals and talents, but also your outside interests, the kind of place you want to live, the kind of people you want to know, and even the kind of food you want to eat. After all, you're the one who's going to that college, not your parents or your friends.

Getting Started

The best way to start college-hunting is to ask questions about yourself. Examine your personal priorities, then select colleges that closely match those priorities. Above all, you should feel excited about the schools you're considering. Study after study shows that students who take an active part in searching for colleges and who are enthusiastic about their choices are much more likely to succeed at college.

You have many resources at your disposal to help you find colleges that match what you're looking for in a school. You can turn to a comprehensive college guide like Arco's *Field Guide to Colleges*, which lists all of the accredited colleges and universities in the United States, along with their important characteristics. Many college guides, including the *Field Guide*, come with a CD-ROM that makes searching easier. (See Appendix C, "Recommended Reading," for a selection of recommended college guides.) If you have Internet access, you'll find many websites where you can search for colleges; you simply select the ideal characteristics of a college in an interactive form, click a button, and get back a list of matching colleges and universities. (Turn to Appendix B, "College Admissions Resource Guide," for a selection of college search sites.) Finally, your guidance office or school library should have a wide selection of resources—books, brochures, and software programs—to help you find colleges that fit your goals and interests.

Begin the college search process in your sophomore year or, at least, early in your junior year of high school—the earlier the better. Plan to finalize the list of colleges you'll apply to by the beginning of your senior year, so you can devote that time to preparing the applications. This chapter will help you determine what qualities to look for in a potential school; at the end of the chapter, you'll put together a list of schools that you'll want to get to know better and possibly apply to.

All-Important Academics

Bright Idea
This is a good time to do a career search. Typical career search programs match your interests and talents with potential jobs. You might find career search software in the guidance office, or visit a career search website like http://www.collegeboard.org/career/bin/career.pl or http://www.EMBARK.com.

Obviously, one of the most important considerations when choosing a school is its academic strength. But many factors go into judging a school's academic worth. You can't just go by the school's overall reputation; each school has strong academic departments and weak ones.

If you already know what you want to do with the rest of your life, then you're ahead of the game. You can narrow your list to schools that have strong programs in your chosen field.

Most graduating high school seniors aren't that lucky—they have no idea what they want to do after college. And that's okay, too. Begin searching for schools by examining your interests and talents, and then looking for strong academic programs in that general area. Ask yourself what you like to study, what your strongest subjects are, and what skills you have. What do you do in your free time? Do you have a passion for any particular hobbies? Do you enjoy working with people, banging away on the computer, putting together models? The answers to any or all of these questions could lead you in the direction of your lifetime career.

Even if you are set on a particular field of study, you may change your mind once you get to college and discover the wide range of choices that are open to you. In fact, college students change majors an average of three times. So, don't focus too narrowly on one profession when selecting colleges. Rather, look for schools with diverse strengths and a variety of programs, so if you do end up changing your mind, you don't also have to change your school.

Kinds of Schools

Focusing on a specific kind of school that satisfies your academic needs can help you pare down your list of potential colleges. Most undergraduates attend either a liberal arts college or a university, but you can also look at technical schools, professional schools, and other specialized colleges.

College or University?

Most likely, your list of potential schools will include a mix of colleges and universities. Colleges focus on undergraduate education and generally award only Bachelor's degrees. These liberal arts schools don't prepare you for a specific career path; instead, students take a broad base of courses in the humanities, sciences, and social sciences. Despite what you may have heard about liberal arts graduates being "unemployable," many employers value this well rounded preparation. In addition, a liberal arts education is mandatory for entry to most graduate and professional schools, including medical school and law school.

Universities, by contrast, are often large institutions that include an undergraduate college, some professional schools, and several graduate programs. Universities run the gamut from those known for their scholarship and research (like Harvard and the University of California at Berkeley) to those known for their football or basketball teams. Most state-funded public schools tend to be large universities, as well.

Even if you do decide to attend a university, that doesn't mean that you'll miss out on a liberal arts education. In fact, the undergraduate college at most universities is a liberal arts college, one contained within the larger university setting.

The biggest difference between the typical liberal arts college and the typical university is where the attention of the professors is focused. At liberal arts colleges, the professors' primary job is teaching undergraduates, which generally results in smaller classes and more personal interaction with professors. At universities, the professors may be more concerned with research, publishing, or teaching graduate-level classes. As a result, undergraduate courses may be larger, or graduate students instead of full professors may teach classes.

The teaching role of graduate students at many large universities may be far greater than you realize. A typical university undergraduate course consists of two lectures and one discussion session, or seminar, a week. The entire class—perhaps hundreds of people—meets for the lecture, which is given by the professor. Then, the class breaks into small groups for the seminar, which is often led by a graduate student teaching assistant. Therefore, you may have little or no opportunity for interaction with the professors whose classes you take.

But because universities are often larger, they offer more academic choices and more extensive resources than the typical liberal arts college. You'll probably have a wider range of majors to choose from and a larger

Unofficially...
According to current college students, there are too many teaching assistants at several major universities throughout the U.S. Most schools will tell you what percentage of their courses are taught by TAs and the faculty-to-student ratio; ask the admissions office.

Bright Idea
The class size listed in college brochures is usually an *average* of all four years. It doesn't hurt to ask about the average class size for under-classmen and upper-classmen. Classes for juniors and seniors may be significantly smaller than for freshmen and sophomores, particu-larly at the large universities.

Bright Idea
You don't have to avoid universities to get that small col-lege experience. If you join a small department in a big university, you'll probably get the small classes and close interaction with your professors and fellow students that you'd find at a liberal arts college.

selection of classes to take within your discipline. (Most liberal arts colleges offer an average of 20 different majors, whereas universities may provide three times as many.) You're also more likely to get the opportunity to pursue research or fieldwork opportunities with professors at a university. You may even be able to take graduate-level classes to supplement your major.

Not all universities are huge and impersonal, though. For example, the University of Chicago, Johns Hopkins, and Princeton all have fewer than 10,000 students, including graduate students. Smaller universities are able to offer all the advantages of the university system, but also avoid some of the problems, such as relying on graduate students to teach undergraduate courses.

On the other hand, some liberal arts colleges are quite large, if you crave that kind of setting. Boston College, for example, has almost 9,000 students. In addition, many colleges now offer graduate-level courses.

You probably shouldn't eliminate any school from your list of "possibles" simply because it's a college or a university. A more important consideration is the strength of that particular school's academic programs in the fields that interest you. But if you crave the small college experience, focus your search on liberal arts colleges. If big and diverse is what you're after, then you'd do well to look primarily at universities.

Specialized Schools

A wide range of higher education institutes offer a more specialized education than liberal arts colleges and comprehensive universities do. The category of "specialized schools" includes such prestigious technical institutes as the Massachusetts Institute of Technology (MIT) and California Institute of Technology (Caltech), which train students in the sciences, mathematics, and technical fields. This category also encompasses art schools, engineering schools, business schools, nursing schools, vocational schools, and some agricultural and mechanical universities.

Unlike liberal arts colleges, these professional and technical schools emphasize a specific career path. Specialized schools are best suited to students who have already decided what they want to study and plan to stick to that decision. Unfortunately, if you change your mind later, you can't switch to an entirely different discipline without transferring to another school. A university with a strong program in the discipline that interests you might be a better choice. Most universities have specialized schools—Columbia University has an undergraduate school of engineering and applied science, for instance—and if you later decide to change majors, it's often easier to switch over to the university's undergraduate liberal arts college.

The following is a broad selection of specialized schools, which should give you a good idea of the wide range of choices in this category:

School	Discipline
Babson College (MA)	Business
California College of Arts and Crafts	Fine art, design, and crafts
College of Insurance (NY)	Insurance
Emerson College (MA)	Performing and communication arts
Fashion Institute of Technology (NY)	Fashion design and the fashion industry
Georgia Institute of Technology	Sciences, mathematics, and engineering
Harvey Mudd College (CA)	Sciences, mathematics, and engineering
Johnson and Wales University (RI)	Management, marketing, and the culinary arts
The Juilliard School (NY)	Performing arts
Mount Carmel College of Nursing (OH)	Nursing
Philadelphia College of Textiles and Sciences	Business, sciences, and fashion design
Rose-Hulman Institute of Technology (IN)	Engineering, mathematics, and the physical sciences
San Francisco Conservatory	Music
Savannah College of Art and Design (GA)	Fine art and design
Unity College (ME)	Environmental sciences and out-doors studies
University of the Arts (PA)	Fine art and performing arts
Wheelock College (MA)	Education and social work

What's Your Learning Style?

Every college and university has a unique educational mission. You'll succeed better at college if you determine how you learn best and then look for schools that match your personal profile. Some students benefit from a traditional, structured style of teaching. Others thrive under a more freestyle approach. Some learn best in lecture-style courses, while others prefer discussion and seminars. Which way do you learn best?

If you're a "color outside the lines" kind of person, you may prefer a school with a nontraditional curriculum. For example, St. John's College and Thomas Aquinas College both base their curriculums on the "great books" of Western civilization; all students take the same courses and read the same works. Other nontraditional schools include Hampshire College,

Anna Maria College, Franklin Pierce College, and Sarah Lawrence College. If you'd prefer a nontraditional course of study in a traditional setting, look for schools that enable you to design your own majors, such as Northwestern University, Brown University, and Smith College.

Another major difference among many colleges and universities is their academic calendars. Depending on your personal learning style, some academic calendars may suit you better than others. The most common kinds of academic calendars include the following:

- *Semester calendar:* This is the traditional academic calendar that most colleges and universities follow. The school year is divided into two long sessions, generally lasting between 15 and 18 weeks, with one or two shorter summer sessions. If you require a lengthy term to absorb class materials, the semester system will work best for you. It's also ideal for students who intend to use summers to work or travel.

- *Trimester and quarter calendars:* In the trimester system, the academic year is divided into three equal periods, generally 15 weeks long. In the quarter system, the academic year is divided into four equal periods of around 12 weeks each. Students who prefer to take fewer subjects at a time and who like to change class schedules frequently will thrive under these calendars. Year-round calendars are often more flexible for planning time off-campus, such as for internships or studying abroad.

- *4-1-4, 4-4-1, and January term calendars:* These plans offer two long and one short academic term each academic year. Students can take advantage of the short term to complete an intensive course, perform independent study, do an internship, or pursue a special-interest project. Some schools follow variations of this system.

- *Block plan:* Under this calendar, students study one course at a time, usually for around three-and-a-half weeks. This type of calendar works best for students who prefer to learn in short, intense bursts.

Judging a College's Overall Academic Quality

Ideally, you should select a school that will challenge you but won't overwhelm you, academically speaking. The following statistics will help you determine how strong the school is academically (this information can usually be found in general college guides and in school brochures):

- *Retention rate.* This is the percentage of entering freshmen who remain at the college, rather than dropping out or transferring to another school. A high retention rate indicates that students are satisfied with the academic offerings, social life, and financial systems of the school.

- *Graduation rate.* This is the percentage of entering freshmen who graduate within a reasonable amount of time—four or five years. High graduation rates indicate that the school meets the educational requirements of its students and that required courses are offered frequently enough for students to finish their degrees on time.

▪ *Class size.* Look at the school's student-to-faculty ratio and the typical sizes of classes to get an idea of how much personal attention you'll get from professors. But don't base your decision entirely on raw numbers. Some departments in a large university may have significantly smaller classes than others, or your classes may get smaller when you become an upperclassman. The best way to judge class size is to sit in on a class and to talk to students of the college.

Judging the Strength of Individual Departments

Most college guides indicate what a school's strongest or most well-known academic departments are. You may also have heard through word of mouth of schools that excel in the fields you want to study. These sources should only be a starting point when judging the strength of particular academic departments.

The best way to judge a school's academic department is to visit. Talk to professors and current students in the department; ask whether you'll have the opportunity to write papers, work closely on projects, or do research with professors. Check out the classrooms and other facilities, such as labs, art studios, performing spaces, or high-tech equipment. Look into special programs that the department offers, such as independent research projects, fieldwork, or internships at related companies.

Another good way to judge an academic department is to look at the success of graduates of that program. Ask the school's career or placement office how many graduates of the program found good jobs in their field and how many of them went on to become noted authorities. If you plan to go on to graduate school, find out how many students in the program went on to earn a higher degree, the percentage of applicants to graduate school who were accepted, and what graduate programs they attended. All of these factors should add up to a clear picture of whether the academic program is right for you.

Important Extras

While classroom experience will be the largest part of your academic life at college, it won't be the only part. Other academic programs may also be important to you. Depending on the fields that interest you, you may desire opportunities for research, fieldwork, or extensive lab work. If you're an arts major, the chance to perform or show your art can be crucial. For many students, internships are a vital part of the college experience. Or you may crave opportunities to study abroad or to spend a semester away from campus, such as in the Semester at Sea or the United Nations Semester programs. If any of these programs are particularly important to you, factor them into your college search.

You may want to consider other kinds of programs, as well. For example, an accelerated degree program can get you out of school faster, while a dual degree program enables you to earn a bachelor's degree in more than one

Bright Idea
Statistics alone can't give a complete picture of what a college is like. Also find out what the classes are like and how accessible professors are outside of class. The campus visit and application interview give you the ideal opportunities to get all your questions answered, so take advantage of them (you'll learn more in Chapters 2 and 3).

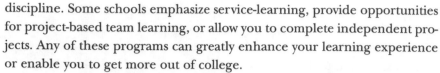

discipline. Some schools emphasize service-learning, provide opportunities for project-based team learning, or allow you to complete independent projects. Any of these programs can greatly enhance your learning experience or enable you to get more out of college.

It won't be difficult for you to find schools with study-abroad programs or that emphasize internships. But that doesn't mean that the programs will be easy to get into or offer exactly what you're looking for. When it comes to these academic "extras," some schools provide a broader range of opportunities and work more closely with you to ensure that you get the experience you want. For example, almost every college has a study-abroad program, but not every one lets you study in Japan or places you in international internships. It's important for you to get a good idea of what you might want out of these programs during the college search process.

Reading through college brochures, course catalogs, and college websites should give you a good idea of what opportunities for special programs will be available to you at different schools. An admissions officer at the school should also be able to answer your questions about these programs.

Considering Cost

For many students (and their parents), cost can be the most important factor when deciding on potential colleges. Although paying for college may be one of the most expensive purchases of your life—second only to buying a house for most families—it is also one of the best investments you'll ever make. Studies regularly show that college graduates earn more than those who don't attend. Fifteen years ago, college graduates made 38 percent more than workers with high school diplomas; now, they make 73 percent more.

You may be tempted to drop a school from your list because of its price tag, or to forego looking at private schools because they're just too expensive. But the truth is, with the convoluted financial aid process, you really don't know what you'll have to pay to attend any college until you apply. (You'll learn all about financial aid in Part 5 of this book.) Many of the more expensive private colleges give away a larger percentage of need-based financial aid than the lower-priced public universities, because they have a larger endowment and more monetary resources available for a smaller number of students. They may also offer more scholarships, particularly to students with strong academic records or special talents.

If you really can't afford a top-rated private college, don't despair. You can often get an equally good education at a lower-priced, in-state public university. Some public universities, like the University of North Carolina at Chapel Hill, the University of Virginia, and the University of California at Berkeley, are as highly regarded as the top private schools, and if you happen to live in one of those states, they're a real bargain.

To play it safe, apply to a mix of expensive, moderately priced, and low-priced schools, such as one or two public schools. Think of those low-priced schools as your financial "safety" schools, so you can still afford to go to college even if you don't receive much financial aid. But just as you shouldn't eliminate any school based solely on its high tuition, you also shouldn't put any school on your list just because it's cheap. The cheapest school still must meet your requirements for academic programs, size, location, social life, and other qualities, or you won't ever be happy there, despite all the money you save.

Location, Location, Location

What do you fantasize doing after class? Do you see yourself hanging out in a coffeehouse, touring a world-class museum, or hiking through the woods? Remember that the college you choose will be your home for the next several years, so select a setting where you'll thrive. Many students feel more comfortable when making a big transition like moving away from home if they go somewhere familiar, somewhere that's like their own hometown, but you may crave an entirely different experience.

Don't be afraid to look at schools that are far away from home. You may be well aware of all of the best schools in your home state or region of the country, because you've grown up hearing their names. But you may never have heard of good schools in different areas of the country, even though they may be perfect matches for you. This is the time to explore—don't limit yourself when making up your preliminary list.

Once you create a top-ten list of schools, visit as many as you can to get a firsthand impression of each school's setting. Seeing the school's location for yourself is the best (and fastest) way to decide whether you'll be happy there.

Your future college may be located in one of three broad kinds of settings: urban, rural, or suburban. Each has its own distinct advantages and disadvantages. One will be just right for you.

The Big City

Urban colleges are as different as the cities in which they are located. They include some of the nation's oldest and most respected colleges and some of the most modern universities. An urban school can be a collegiate island, separated from the city by a wall and a park-like campus. Or an urban school may sprawl over several city blocks. Some urban colleges only have a few hundred students, while others serve more than 30,000 undergraduates. Some provide dorms like any traditional college; others have no housing at all. There's just no such thing as the "typical" urban college.

In the city, you'll never run out of things to do—museums, theaters, sports, concerts, shopping, restaurants. And you won't need a car to get to them all. You'll have more opportunities for work, internships, and other experiences that supplement your education. And everywhere you go,

Watch Out!
Out-of-state tuition at a public university can be as high as or even higher than tuition at a private school. For instance, the University of Virginia's tuition is only $5,000 per year for in-state students, but it is a hefty $16,000 per year for out-of-state students.

Bright Idea
Many towns and cities have websites. Exploring a college town's website is a good way to find out what kinds of activities, shopping, and restaurants are available near the school.

you'll be surrounded by people, excitement, and an unimaginable variety of goings-on.

But the city isn't for everyone. Cities are crowded, noisy, and sometimes overwhelming if you're not used to them. Living in a city can be very expensive, and you'll have to take into account the higher cost of living when calculating the total cost of attending the college. All of the choices and activities could distract you from your schoolwork. Finally, there's the crime problem; cities have a well deserved reputation for being unsafe.

Out in the Country

Rural schools are located in very small towns or in no town at all. Many rural schools provide excellent opportunities for those who want to study science, agriculture, wildlife, forestry, geology, or any field that requires you to be outside most of the time. Some rural schools may have farms, arboretums, experimental forests, nature preserves, or lakes on campus. Often situated in the woods, in the mountains, or near lakes and rivers, rural schools provide the perfect setting for nature lovers and for those who relish outdoor sports.

Timesaver
It's gotten a lot easier to get a true picture of how much crime is on campus. Since 1990, all colleges have been required to keep track of a broad range of crimes, including robbery, rape, and murder; all you have to do is request the yearly statistics from campus security.

Rural schools tend to have a great sense of community, because the campus is usually entirely self-contained. But this can also be a disadvantage, since you have to completely rely on the school for all social and cultural activities. You'll probably need a car to make the most of the surrounding area, although some schools do provide transportation to nearby recreational areas. And resources are limited both on and off campus. You won't be able to run out for sushi every time you get a hankering or shop for the latest fashions. And you may be hours away from the nearest airport or train station. You might find such a limited atmosphere smothering.

On the other hand, you'll get to know your fellow students and your professors very well in such a small community. And rural schools are usually considered among the safest of college campuses. If you want a college that provides solitude, quiet, and few distractions from your studies, the rural campus may be the perfect fit for you.

Small-Town America

Actually, "small-town" schools are located in small towns, medium-sized towns, the suburbs, and even small cities. Generally, these schools offer the best of all worlds—they are usually within driving distance of an urban area, a rural area, or both, while remaining part of a small, close-knit community. Often, the college is situated in one of those cool college towns that you've heard so much about. The school may have more of a campus feel than an urban school, but you're not restricted to the campus for all of your activities, as you would be at a rural college.

You'll find these colleges throughout the country—within short driving distance of the beach, the mountains, resorts, or the big city. The small-town setting makes it easy to become a part of the college community, and you get to live among professors, alumni, and graduate students. And the close-knit community can help you feel safer. But life in a college town is anything but suburban. The college can draw such attractions as theater companies, art shows, and musicians, and local merchants often cater to the college crowd with food, entertainment, and recreational activities.

You may find the small-town atmosphere too stifling if you're a city guy or gal, or too crowded if you're a nature nut. And if you want to get to the city or the wilderness, you will most likely need a car (although many colleges will provide transportation to nearby activities). But the small-town college offers the best compromise for those who don't want to go to extremes.

Size Matters

The size of a school's total enrollment is a very important consideration when selecting a college—more than you might think at first. In fact, almost 45 percent of freshmen considered size a key factor in their decision about where to go to college, according to a study conducted by the University of California at Los Angeles. Whether you select a large, medium-sized, or small school depends on what you're looking for in a college experience and where you'll feel most comfortable.

Big and Diverse

Schools with a large number of undergraduates (anywhere from 10,000 to 35,000 students, depending on your definition of "large") have more of everything—more students, more activities, more clubs, more sports, more facilities, and more course choices. If you have a lot of specific needs—if you're looking for a school with a strong economics program, an intramural soccer team, and opportunities for internships with major companies, for example—you'll be more likely to find them all in one place at a large school. And if you're an independent person when it comes to studying or doing assignments, a large school may be tailor-made for you.

If you're unsure of what you want to do in life, you can sample several strong academic programs in diverse areas and take a wider variety of courses at a large university. It's much more likely that you'll discover a special subject that sparks your interest and that you'll be able to pursue it further. There may be significantly more course offerings within a department than at a smaller school, giving you more opportunity for diversity within your major. And on top of all those choices, the bigger schools offer more extracurricular activities—clubs, sports, arts, newspaper, fraternities, and sororities.

Large schools have plenty of drawbacks, though. You may start to feel like just a number. Your classes will be bigger and more impersonal. You may have to live in a dorm that's more like a high-rise apartment building, or you may not even be able to live on-campus. You could have trouble meeting people or gaining access to your teachers. There may be no real college "community" that you can participate in. While large schools offer

Watch Out!
Many students make campus visits in the spring, when the weather is best; but what about those hot and humid summers, or massive winter snowfalls? If your favorite outdoor activities require specific weather conditions, or if you are prone to health problems that can be affected by the weather, you need to include "climate" in your list of search criteria.

Bright Idea
You may want to consider a state university or a lower-ranked private school if it offers an honors program. The honors programs will get you into more challenging classes, which are often taught by professors rather than graduate students. Participating in the honors program is also a good way to get a more individualized education at a large university.

Watch Out!
Some schools—particularly large ones—have limited housing. Housing may not be available for upperclassmen or may be assigned by lottery.

more resources and classes, significantly more people are competing for them, and it's not unusual for freshmen and sophomores to find it impossible to get into popular—or even required—courses.

American universities with 30,000 or more undergraduate students include University of Texas (Austin), Ohio State (Columbus), Pennsylvania State (University Park), Texas A&M (College Station), Arizona State (Tempe), Michigan State (East Lansing), University of Minnesota (Twin Cities), and University of Florida (Gainesville).

Small and Personal

Schools with only a few hundred students offer more "community." The smaller campuses can be less threatening, the living arrangements are homier, and it's easier to get to know people. You'll get more personal attention with everything, from registering for classes to career counseling. And with the small class sizes, it's easier to form close relationships with professors.

The trade-off is a limited choice of academic majors; if you choose a small college because of its foreign languages program, you may not be able to switch to marine biology (without switching schools). Also, smaller schools may lack crucial resources, such as well equipped computer labs or a large research library. Finally, a small school is like a small town—everyone knows everything about everybody. If you're a private person, a small school can be a big pain.

American schools with fewer than 200 students include Hellenic College, the University of Judaism, Burlington College, and Sheldon Jackson College.

Somewhere in Between

Most college and university enrollments fall somewhere in between 2,000 to 10,000 students. These mid-range schools offer the best of both worlds. They provide more opportunities, social activities, and course offerings than the small schools do, but they lack the impersonal feel of the mega-university.

Visit a variety of different-sized colleges to get a good idea of what each is like. What seems too large on paper may be just the right size in person. Five thousand students may sound like a lot, but Yale University maintains a cozy community with just that number, for instance.

Your Fellow Students

For some, a school's demographic makeup is as important as the college's course offerings or its location. The student body is largely responsible for creating a college "culture," and much of your learning experience will come from studying, interacting, and working with other students, both in and out of the classroom. Not to mention that these people will be the people you hang out with, party with, and perhaps become lifelong friends with.

So, when considering what schools you want to apply to, don't forget to find out what kinds of students attend those schools.

Looking for Diversity

To succeed in a global society, you must develop skills in dealing with people from all walks of life. College may be your first real opportunity to work and socialize with others with widely different ethnic, cultural, and religious backgrounds.

The backlash against affirmative action has resulted in a sharp decline in minority applications to some large state school systems, such as in California and Texas. But at the same time, more private schools are making an effort to recruit minority students and create an ethnically mixed student body. In addition, many private schools recruit a sizeable number of foreign students, who contribute to the overall cultural diversity of the student body.

Gauging a school's diversity can be tricky. Just looking at a breakdown of the student population by ethnicity may not give you an accurate picture. Beyond the "numbers," a school's real diversity is exhibited by its demonstrated ability to provide opportunities for all students to interact.

One way to check diversity is to look at the school's course offerings— do you find a good mix of African-American, women's, religious, and gay studies? Find out if the residence halls tend to be integrated or segregated. Look for a variety of on-campus organizations catering to different ethnic and religious groups. Finally, talk with current students whose backgrounds are similar to yours to discover what their experiences have been like.

Finding an Affiliation

While some college applicants are searching for diversity, others are looking for a place where most of the student body is like them in some critical way. Colleges that cater to certain groups, such as African-Americans or women, offer opportunities that may not be as easy to get at other schools. Many affiliated schools provide expanded academic programs in subjects related to their affiliation. They also provide instant community that supports students during their transition between home and the "real world."

Women's colleges in particular are thriving right now. Women's colleges tend to have a larger number of female faculty and administrators than their coed counterparts, offer more opportunities for women in student leadership and organizations, and diminish the competitiveness that some women may have experienced in a mixed-gender environment. Of the 82 women's colleges in the US, many are considered among the best schools in the country, including Agnes Scott, Barnard, Bryn Mawr, Mount Holyoke, Smith, and Wellesley.

Guys who want to attend an all-male college don't have as many choices as the girls do, but there are a few. These include Hampden-Sydney College

Timesaver
Looking for "looks"? Don't waste time driving all over, searching for the most beautiful campuses at random. Trust the opinions of your fellow students, who liked the following campuses the best: Colby College, Colgate University, Furman University, Swarthmore College, Sweet Briar College, the University of Richmond, and Wellesley College.

Unofficially...
In a recent poll of college students, these schools were among those deemed "most diverse" around the nation: Boston University, Clark University, Columbia, Geneva College, Harvard, MIT, New York University, Occidental College, and Whittier College.

in Virginia, Morehouse College in Georgia, St. John's University in Minnesota, and Wabash College in Indiana.

The nation's 104 Historically Black Colleges and Universities (HCBUs) originated at the time when African-Americans were denied access to most other colleges and universities, and offer some of the strongest African-American studies programs in the nation. They hire committed faculty mentors who encourage students to set and attain the highest academic and professional goals. HBCUs include both highly rated private schools like Fisk University, Howard University, Spelman College, and Tuskegee University and good public schools like North Carolina Central University, Florida A&M University, and the University of Maryland at Eastern Shore.

Finally, many students choose a school based on its religious affiliation. Many religion-affiliated schools have small campuses and offer students a familiar environment, a strong sense of community, and an education that emphasizes religious studies and morality. Schools where religion is a central part of campus life can provide a nurturing atmosphere and can make the transition from home out into the "real world" an easier one. Students generally must agree to follow a strict code of conduct—too strict for some. Strongly religious schools include Augustana College (Lutheran), Baylor University (Baptist), Brigham Young University (Mormon), Calvin College (Christian Reformed Church), Grove City College (Presbyterian), Principia College (Christian Scientist), the University of Judaism, and the University of Notre Dame (Roman Catholic).

The Social Scene

You won't be studying 24 hours a day, seven days a week. Social life is an important part of college, too. When looking at colleges, measure what the social life is like against what you are like. If your idea of a good time is a poetry reading in a coffeehouse, you probably won't appreciate a "party school." If you don't plan to go home a lot, you don't want to wind up at a "suitcase school" that empties out on Friday afternoons. You get the idea.

It can be difficult to judge a school's social life unless you actually go there—and stay over the weekend. If you don't have the time to do this for all the colleges on your list, gauge what the social life is like by checking out the school's *and* the town's website, reading the campus and local newspapers, and asking current students what they do for fun. Also, find out what organizations, sports teams, and clubs the school supports (you can usually determine these from the college's brochure or website).

What to Do After Class

Whether it's sports or clubs or Greek life, many college students find that extracurricular activities fill the bulk of their time. So, select a school that offers plenty of activities that match your interests.

If you plan to join a fraternity or sorority, of course you'll search for schools that have an active Greek life. But what if you love theater but don't plan to major in drama—can you join an on-campus amateur company? Maybe chess is your hobby—is there a club for you on-campus? Does the school maintain a student radio or TV station, newspaper, or literary magazine where you can work? When reading through the college's promotional materials, look for organizations and clubs that you might want to participate in, so you can be sure that others who share your interests attend the school.

If you're a sports fan, you may just like to watch, or you may even want to join a team or two. From browsing through college brochures and from campus visits, you should be able to easily find out what the major sporting events on campus are. Check the campus website or ask the admissions officer or campus tour guide what intramural sports are available and how many students participate in team sports. Finally, while you're visiting, look for a golf course, tennis courts, lake, bike paths—whatever you need to satisfy your own interests.

So, what kind of a person are you? A jock? A hippie? A sorority girl? Table 1.1 lists a variety of college activities and some schools that strongly support those activities, so you can find a place where you'll feel right at home.

The Living Situation

Where you live will be a very important part of your life at college, so it's crucial that you check out the college's housing. Some schools don't even offer on-campus housing, while others don't permit you to live off-campus. Most fall somewhere in the middle—requiring you to live on-campus for one to three years.

Figure out what kind of living situation you want. Will you be miserable if you're stuck with three roommates? Do you need a cozy dorm with communal areas and lots of organized activities, or does the high-rise dorm appeal to you? Will you be unhappy if you can't live in a coed dorm? Will you want to live in a fraternity or sorority house as an upperclassman? Is it crucial that you keep your car on campus?

When thinking about housing, consider what other special arrangements are important to you. For example, many schools—but not all—provide special housing for disabled students. Others offer special housing for married couples, families, or single parents.

You should be able to find out what kind of housing is available from a college guide or by talking to the school's housing office. But keep in mind that not all dorms are created equal. Visiting campus is the only guaranteed way to tell if the dorms are palaces or dumps. A campus visit is also the best way to figure out what the college means by coed dorms, which can run the gamut from strictly segregated halls in the same building to sharing a bathroom with the opposite sex.

While you're checking out the housing, investigate the food situation and see what kinds of eating options are available. A meal at the cafeteria is

Bright Idea
If you're into drama and want to pursue your passion at college, consider one of these schools: Marlboro College, Sarah Lawrence College, Stephens College, and Wesleyan University.

Bright Idea
Some schools offer (usually to upperclassmen only) special kinds of housing, such as foreign-language halls, honors halls, international housing, and other theme-style housing that give you the opportunity to live with others who share your interests. If this type of living arrangement appeals to you, check your target schools for availability and restrictions.

TABLE 1.1: COLLEGES AND UNIVERSITIES AND THEIR NOTED EXTRACURRICULAR ACTIVITIES

Parties	Greek Life	Sports	Outdoor Life	Creativity	Activism
Florida State University	Birmingham-Southern College	Auburn University	Eastern Washington University	Bennington College	Bard College
Ohio State University	Bucknell University	Baylor University	Green Mountain College	College of Santa Fe	College of the Atlantic
Seton Hall University	Davidson College	Colgate University	Mesa State College	Eugene Lang College	Earlham College
SUNY at Albany	DePauw University	Hampden-Sydney College	Pacific Union College	Goddard College	Evergreen State College
University of Colorado at Boulder	Lehigh University	Randolph-Macon College	Sierra Nevada College	Hampshire College	George Washington University
University of Florida	Millsaps College	University of Florida	Simpson College	Ithaca College	Oberlin College
University of Georgia	Randolph-Macon College	University of Illinois at Urbana-Champaign	University of Idaho	New College of the University of South Florida	Reed College
University of Kansas	Southern Methodist University	Villanova University	University of Montana	Sarah Lawrence College	Swarthmore College
University of Vermont	Wabash College	Wabash College	University of North Carolina at Asheville	Skidmore College	Warren Wilson College
University of Wisconsin at Madison	Washington and Lee University	Wake Forest University	University of Utah	Smith College	Wesleyan University

an important part of the campus visit. Asking other students at the school about their experiences is also a good way to discover what the room and board situation is like.

The Important "Others"

The little things can turn a college into a home—or into a nightmare. So, don't leave out the "extras" when considering colleges. The following list contains some college characteristics that don't fit neatly into any other category. Some of these factors may be vitally important to you; others may not matter at all. You'll probably be able to come up with more important extras on your own.

- *The library:* Of course, every college has a library, but is it a library where you can work comfortably? When you visit, find out how many library resources are available and if there are quiet places to study.

- *Laboratories:* If you're a science major, lab resources are critical. Determine what resources will be available to you and if you'll have access to the labs when you need them.

- *Computers:* Some schools require you to purchase a computer or give you one when you arrive (included in the bill, of course). Others provide computer labs in the dorms, library, student union, and other public places. And what about computer connections and Internet access in the dorm rooms, library, and so on? This is the information age, so definitely investigate the computer resources available to you.

- *Health club:* Many colleges have replaced the old-fashioned gym with modern, fully equipped health clubs. Some even offer aerobics classes, racquetball courts, or a rock-climbing wall.

- *And everything else:* Snack bar, coffeehouse, movie theater, bowling alley, concert hall, arts center, childcare facilities—find out what amenities the schools offer that will make your life there more enjoyable.

Unofficially...
College students say that the best food can be found at Bowdoin College, Colby Collage, Cornell, Dartmouth, Dickinson College, and Gettysburg College. The worst food, on the other hand, is at Fisk University, Hampton University, Hiram College, Oglethorpe University, Tuskegee University, and the University of Massachusetts at Amherst.

How Not to Choose a College

There is no one right way to go about selecting a college. Whatever is important to you should be taken into consideration. There are some wrong ways to pick a college, however—and every one of them involves listening to someone else more than you listen to yourself. This section discusses some of the common mistakes that graduating high school students make when choosing a college.

Follow Your Friends

Having your friends around may seem like the best way to deal with the huge transition of moving away from home, but in fact, it an be a big mistake. Hanging with the old gang can keep you from making new friends, and if you all start to move in different directions (as so many of us tend to do during our college years), you may end up on your own, anyway.

An even worse mistake may be following your boyfriend or girlfriend to college. It's an unfortunate fact of life that your high school relationship probably won't survive the move to college, even if you go to the same school. At college, you will meet new people, develop new interests, and have lots of dating opportunities. It's only natural that you and your high school sweetheart will grow apart, and you don't want to be stuck at a school where you're unhappy to boot.

Let Mom and Dad Choose for You

Your parents will definitely have a strong opinion on which college you should attend. They may want you to go to their alma mater, choose a school closer to home, or consider either a more inexpensive state school or a more prestigious private college. And your parents' opinions matter—they're part of this process and may well be paying for some or all of your education.

Never decide to attend a college for the sole reason that it's your parents' first choice. Numerous studies have shown that students who make the final decision themselves are much more likely to succeed in college. They are also more likely to make friends quickly, enjoy their classes, participate in campus life, and have a more fruitful college experience.

Go for the Designer Label

It's a fact of life that some schools have name-brand recognition; most people would agree that a degree from Harvard or Yale carries a certain cachet. But how important is this name recognition when you start applying for jobs or to graduate school? Is it worth the potential costs and extreme academic pressure that often comes along with it?

Granted, many graduates of Duke, Stanford, and the Ivy League schools go on to highly successful graduate and career experiences, but so do many people who don't graduate from the Ivies. Even prestigious schools have some mediocre programs, and very few employers or graduate schools will accept an applicant based solely on an Ivy League degree. It's more important that you choose your school based on the strength of the academic department where you intend to major, rather than on the school's overall prestige. If you want to go on to graduate school, medical school, or law school, find out how many students the school sends to higher degree programs and in what fields.

Also, keep in mind that prestigious (and, therefore, selective) schools may admit only 10 to 30 percent of their applicants, which means that even if you scored 1500 on your SAT and have a 4.0 grade point average, you can't count on getting accepted. Only the top contenders—those with the best grades, the most challenging courses, the best-written essays, and the most impressive extracurriculars—get in. By all means, apply to a selective school or two, but don't limit your college choices to only the most prestigious schools—or you may not receive any acceptance letters at all in May.

Bright Idea
If you and your parents have very different ideas on where you should go to college, it's best to talk out those differences at the beginning of the college search process. Evaluate their school choices with the same process you use to evaluate all of your "possibles," so you can compare them fairly. And do your research to back up *your* choices—the more information you have about the schools that interest you, the better you can defend your choices.

Rely on Rankings

One of our favorite pastimes is making lists: the most beautiful people; the best movies; the top colleges and universities. Every year, *U.S.News & World Report, Princeton Review,* and *Money Magazine* come out with their annual college rankings, and those issues are always big sellers. Every year, parents and students try to use these rankings to figure out which colleges to apply to. But relying on rankings is a big mistake. Here are some reasons why:

- Rankings are almost always based on information provided by the schools themselves. The schools may have manipulated this information to present the college in the best possible light, or they may have omitted key facts in an attempt to improve their rankings. Therefore, rankings are based on biased information and can't objectively depict the colleges.

- Rankings are usually based on numerical statistics, such as retention rates, graduation rates, acceptance rates, the scores of accepted students, the number of professors who hold Ph.D.s, and so on. While these numbers give you a starting point for evaluating the school, they tell little or nothing about the strengths of a particular academic department, whether classes are challenging and engaging, what the social atmosphere of the school is like, what amenities are available, and other important details that should go into your decision.

- Rankings are homogenous—they aren't designed with you in mind. While Harvard may consistently rank number one, not everyone will thrive there. That's why it's so important to personalize the college search and look for schools that match your unique goals, interests, and priorities. If you choose a school simply because it received a high ranking, you're choosing blindly.

Putting Together Your List of Final Choices

Now that you've learned what kind of factors should influence your choice of colleges, it's time to put together your top-ten list (or top-twelve, or top-eight—it's not written in stone). These are the schools where you'll seriously consider applying.

The following worksheet will help you sort out exactly what you're looking for in a college. Under each category, select or write in the characteristic that's most important to you. If a particular category doesn't make a difference to you, skip it.

When you've finished filling out the worksheet, determine which of the characteristics you listed are *most* important to you. In the right column, rank these characteristics on a scale of 1–5. Characteristics ranked "1" are essentials; those ranked "5" are nice, but not necessary.

Unofficially...
A high ranking or household name doesn't necessarily mean you'll have a rewarding academic experience. Check out the schools that college students ranked among the best for overall academic experience: Carleton College, Brandeis University, Haverford College, New York University, Reed College, Washington and Lee University, and Williams College.

Unofficially...
Here's another problem with relying on rankings for your college search: There are over 3000 colleges and universities in the United States. Limiting your college search to only the top 10 or top 20 schools eliminates way too many of your choices. You'll have the most successful college search if you widen your scope instead of narrowing it. Search with an open mind and explore all the possibilities.

WORKSHEET FOR DETERMINING THE MOST
IMPORTANT QUALITIES IN A COLLEGE

College Characteristics	Rank

Academics

Major(s) or general area(s) of study: _____

Special programs: _____

Additional resources/facilities: _____

Curriculum: ☐ Traditional ☐ Nontraditional   _____

Calendar: ☐ Semester ☐ Trimester ☐ Quarter ☐ 4-1-4/4-4-1
☐ Block plan   _____

Class size: ☐ Large ☐ Small   _____

Cost per Year

☐ Expensive ($16,000+) ☐ Moderately expensive ($12,000–$16,000)
☐ Moderate ($8,000–$12,000) ☐ Moderately cheap ($5,000–$8,000)
☐ Cheap (less than $5,000)   _____

Size

☐ Gigantic (15,000+ students) ☐ Large (10,000–15,000)
☐ Medium (5,000-10,000) ☐ Small (1,000-5,000)
☐ Tiny (less than 1,000)   _____

Location

Setting: ☐ Big city ☐ Small town/small city ☐ Rural   _____

Nearby attractions: _____

Geographic area: _____

Weather: _____

Living arrangements

Housing: ☐ On-campus ☐ Off-campus ☐ Both   _____

Quality of housing: _____

Food: _____

☐ On-campus parking   _____

College Characteristics	Rank

Culture

Ethnic affiliation:	_____
Religious affiliation:	_____
☐ Coed ☐ All-male ☐ All-female	_____
☐ Diversity	_____
☐ Support for disabled students	_____
☐ Support for international students	_____
☐ Support for married students/students with children	_____

Social Life

Sports/recreation:	_____
Arts:	_____
Fraternities/sororities:	_____
Clubs/associations:	_____
Activities:	_____
Amenities:	_____

Other important qualities:

_____	___
_____	___
_____	___
_____	___
_____	___
_____	___
_____	___
_____	___
_____	___
_____	___

Timesaver
Once you create a
preliminary list of
schools, take the list
to your guidance
counselor. Your
counselor can help
pinpoint the best
schools for you and
provide advice on
whether your choices
are realistic, given
your academic
record.

Now, using a college guide or college search website, start looking for schools that match as many of your top-ranked characteristics as possible, with an emphasis on those characteristics that you gave a score of 1 or 2. (Appendices B and C list several recommended college search websites and college guide books.) On a separate sheet of paper, make a preliminary list of 20–25 of these schools, noting what most appealed to you about them. You may find it helpful to order this list with your favorite schools at the top.

Your preliminary list can include schools that you've always dreamed about, your parents' favorites, recommendations by your guidance counselor, schools that you learn about at college fairs, and colleges that friends or siblings have attended. Be open to schools you haven't heard of; upon further investigation, one of those colleges may turn out to be a perfect match for you.

Send off for the brochures of all the schools on your preliminary list, and visit their websites if you have access to the Internet. Use these materials to weed out some schools or to make additional notes about others. When you're done, rank the schools on your preliminary list. Pare down your list to the 8–12 schools that most appeal to you and match as many of your essential college characteristics as possible. The following worksheet will help you.

FINAL TOP-TEN LIST OF SCHOOLS

School	Notes
1. _____	_____
2. _____	_____
3. _____	_____
4. _____	_____
5. _____	_____
6. _____	_____
7. _____	_____
8. _____	_____
9. _____	_____
10. _____	_____

After creating your list, visit as many of the schools as possible, and use what you learn on the campus visits to weed the list down to a manageable number of applications—between four and six. Your list may be larger or smaller, but don't let it grow too big. Remember, you'll have to pay a fee for every application you send, as well as invest a lot of time in preparing the applications. Your high school may also limit the number of colleges where you can apply.

When creating your final list, try to include a good mix of schools. The majority of the schools on your list should be "mid-range" colleges—schools whose admission standards closely match your qualifications and whose tuition costs are within your reach (with the help of financial aid, of course). Also select one or two schools that present an admission challenge and perhaps a financial challenge as well; guidance counselors often call these schools "reaches." Finally, mark down a "safety" school or two, where your academic achievements exceed those of most students and you're well assured of getting in. Some schools on your list should also be easily affordable, such as in-state public universities.

Give as much thought to your mid-range and safety schools as you do to your reaches. Make certain that you will be happy at those schools and that they provide the academic programs, setting, and extracurricular activities that you want. You never know where you might end up, so don't apply to a school that you don't really want to attend.

Just the Facts

- The most important quality to look for in potential colleges is a strong academic program in the fields that most interest you.

- Look for schools in locations where you'll feel comfortable living and that provide the kind of community you want to be a part of.

- The size of your college can make a big difference—do you prefer big and diverse, small and cozy, or somewhere in between?

- Whether you prefer to go to college with students who are different from you or just like you can help determine where you'll apply.

- Social life is a big part of college life, so look for schools that offer extracurricular activities and amenities that match your interests and living arrangements where you'll feel comfortable.

- Don't let others—your parents, your friends, or some magazine—tell you which college to go to; you'll be happiest at the schools that you select yourself.

- When you finalize your list of colleges, make sure to include a mix of reaches, mid-range schools, and safety schools—and make sure that you'll be happy at each and every one.

Making the Most of the Campus Visit

Chapter 2

The campus visit is crucial for assessing a college's setting and community, discovering what social life on campus is like, checking out the dorms, cafeteria, and amenities, and touring the academic departments that interest you—as well as for just getting a "feel" for a school. The campus visit also gives you a chance to get your application interview out of the way and to talk face-to-face with students, professors, admissions officers, and financial aid officers.

Obviously, you won't be able to visit every college that makes it onto your preliminary list—maybe not even every school to which you're applying (especially if those schools are scattered across the country). But you should visit as many as possible, especially your top picks. Once you've pared your selections down to a manageable list of maybe 6 to 10 favorites, a campus visit can eliminate some schools and move others to the front of the pack.

In this chapter, you'll learn tried and true strategies for getting the most out of campus visits, so they won't turn into wasted trips. Asking the right questions and seeing the right places while you're actually on campus should ensure that you come away with enough data to determine which schools are the best fits for you.

Getting Ready for the Visit

By this time, you should have already completed the worksheet in Chapter 1 and decided what qualities are most important to you in a potential school. This preparation will serve you well during the campus visit. You already know what your priorities are, so you can zero in on what you want to see and who you want to talk to while you're visiting. Also prepare a list of questions beforehand that address your concerns and interests. And once you get there, you don't have to waste time touring areas of the school that don't interest you.

Once you decide which schools you want to visit, research them. Learn everything you can about the schools. Send off for their brochures and other promotional materials, and read them. If you have Internet access, visit the schools' websites. Make notes of any questions you have that the school's informational materials don't address—you can ask these questions during your tour or interview.

When to Go

Begin touring as early as possible—fall or spring of your junior year is a good time to start. To get a true sense of the day-to-day student life on any campus, try to avoid scheduling visits during breaks, during special events, right before exams, or at the very beginning of the semester. During any of these times, students (and some faculty) are likely to be pre-occupied, frazzled—or absent! You want to see what it's like at the school during the majority of the year, and you want an opportunity to observe and speak with as many people as possible.

If you have to visit during a school holiday or during the summer because that's the only time you can make the trip, then by all means do it. Even a campus tour in the dead of summer will be valuable in helping you make your decisions on where to go to college—at least, much more helpful than not visiting at all.

Scheduling Your Visit

It's very important that you plan ahead for the campus visit. If you schedule your visit with the admissions office well ahead of time, the visit will go more smoothly and you'll accomplish more while you're there. Pre-scheduling ensures that someone will be available to give you a tour and that you can talk with an admissions officer, a financial aid officer, coaches, and professors. It also means that you won't show up at a bad time for visits, such as during midterms or spring break. If you want to stay overnight or schedule an application interview, you may have to reserve space several weeks ahead of time, so call early.

Call the admissions office directly to schedule your visit. Alternatively, you can often schedule your visit through the school's website; the "admissions" section of the site often provides an e-mail form for scheduling a visit, plus more information about special visitation days and directions to the school.

When you call, the admissions office should be able to help you arrange appointments with a professor in the department you're interested in, coaches and other faculty members who you want to talk to, the financial aid office, and for your application interview, if one is required. Try to find out what's on the guided tour, so you can arrange for special tours, such as a dorm walk-through, if you need to. Ask to have driving directions and a parking permit (if necessary) sent to you. If you plan to spend the night on campus, get recommendations of hotels where your parents can stay.

Many schools don't require an interview, but you can usually schedule a one-on-one informational session with an admissions officer for your visit. Most schools also offer regularly scheduled group informational sessions during peak visit times, which don't require as much advance notice to attend. The informational session is a good time to ask about application requirements, the costs of attending the school, financial aid, and other general questions.

Colleges usually schedule one or two open houses for prospective students each semester, and you may plan your visit for one of these events. Open houses are more structured and may offer panel discussions with current students, group meetings with faculty in different academic departments, and group financial aid sessions. These events attract lots of students and their families, so you may find it more difficult to schedule one-on-one time with admissions and financial aid officers during them. And, with so many attendants and events scheduled especially for prospective students during an open house, it may be difficult to get a feel for what everyday life on campus is like.

Every college handles campus visits differently. Some may hold special open houses just for athletes, and some may have weekend programs, for instance. Some schools only host visits on certain days of the week, while others hold several guided tours and informational sessions each day. At some schools the visit may be very informal, while at others a lot of pre-planning is required. It's best to call or e-mail the admissions office and find out what options are available.

While visiting, plan to spend a good part of the day on campus. This should give you plenty of time to take the guided tour, interview with an admissions officer, sit in on a class, eat a meal in the cafeteria, check out the dorms, and wander around on your own. If you have the time, an overnight stay is ideal, because then you can find out what dorm and after-hours life is like at the college.

But don't sweat it if you can't stay overnight or eat a meal at every college you visit. Just do as much as you possibly can while you're there without exhausting yourself. What is most important is that you get a feel for the school, so even just a quick visit for the informational session and guided tour can be valuable. A three-hour stay should leave you enough time to meet with an admissions officer and take the tour, with a little free time to spare. Prioritize your visits, and plan to spend more time at your top choices. If you can only make time for one or two overnight visits, schedule them at the schools where you most want to go.

If you're traveling far from home, you may want to plan an itinerary that takes in several colleges during one trip. But don't overdo it; you may get a bad impression of a school simply because you were tired from traveling. Limit yourself to no more than two campus visits per day, and give yourself time to rest and regroup between visits.

Moneysaver
Some hotels near colleges offer reduced rates to school visitors, and some colleges allow visiting parents to stay in open dorm rooms at a low cost. When you call to arrange your campus visit, be sure to inquire about deals on accommodations.

Watch Out!
Always assume that it will take longer to find the campus, locate a legal parking space, and get to the admissions office than the directions or your contact in the admissions office led you to believe

Bright Idea
If you stay overnight, try to bunk with a sophomore. Sophomores are more familiar with the school than freshmen, but they're still fairly close to your age.

Perhaps you want to visit just one college in a geographic area far away from home. It may not seem worth the expense to travel that far to see only one school. In that case, use the trip to drop in on nearby colleges where you might not have considered applying. It won't be a waste of time. Every college you visit serves as a basis of comparison, and the more visits you make, the better you become at sizing up schools and recognizing what you want out of a college. Besides, you may just discover a college that you real-ly love but that you would never have considered applying to if you hadn't visited.

What to Bring

Be prepared to walk all over campus and perhaps all over the college town, as well. Bring comfortable shoes with you, and dress appropriately for the season (if the college is far away, check out what the weather is like ahead of time). Even if you don't plan to stay overnight, you might want to bring two sets of clothes—one for interviews and one for touring campus.

Bring a notebook or a handheld tape recorder, and take notes on your impressions to refer to later. Make your notes as specific as possible—you won't believe how everything runs together after seeing five or six colleges. Jot down the names of the dorms you visit and what you thought of them, the names of the professors and students you meet, and the name of the admissions officer who interviews you. It's also a good idea to take pictures, which you can later use to compare the college with the other schools you visit. When you get home or back on the road, write down your overall impressions of what you liked and didn't like about the school.

Many students benefit from creating their own college tour ratings lists. One is provided here that you can either use as a model for your own tour notebook or copy directly from this book and take along with you. By rating specific items from 1 to 10 (10 being closest to ideal), you have a very quick and logical way to compare schools on specific conditions or characteristics.

What to See on the Campus Tour

Probably the first thing you'll do during your campus visit is attend an infor-mational session at the admissions office and take a guided tour. This is the best opportunity to get a general overview of the college. The tour usually sticks to the basics—the library, the cafeteria, the student union, classroom buildings, a dorm—so reserve some free time afterward to wander around on your own and see what else the campus has to offer.

Guided tours usually take about an hour and are generally led by a stu-dent volunteer, who's a good source of information about student life at the school. But remember that your tour guide can't possibly know every detail about the college or about a particular academic department. To get all of your questions answered, talk to many other students besides the tour guide during your visit.

SCHOOL: _____ **DATE:** _____

Contact Name/#_____

Rating (1 lowest–10 highest)

Campus layout   _____

Campus "look"   _____

Campus security   _____

Library size and setup   _____

Classroom look and layout   _____

Professor accessibility   _____

Courses in potential major   _____

TA Involvement   _____

Look/layout of dorm rooms   _____

Distance from dorms to classes   _____

Computer connections   _____

Food quality and variety   _____

Quality of student union   _____

Quality/variety of weekend

Activities   _____

Weekend student population   _____

Access to town   _____

Town quality   _____

Access to stores   _____

Access to recreation   _____

Add and rate your own categories here:

_____   _____

_____   _____

_____   _____

_____   _____

_____   _____

While you take the tour, try to picture yourself in these surroundings as a student. The tour will also give you a good idea of how much walking you'll have to do as a student as you move between the dorms, the cafeteria, classes, the library, and the student union.

Take the time to explore during the guided tour. When you visit a dorm, don't just look in the rooms; also check out the laundry facilities, the bathrooms, and the common areas, and try to picture yourself living there. When you get to the library, wander around a bit—is it crowded? Quiet? Comfortable? The student union is another good place to spend a lot of time. You can meet other students there and find out what the recreational facilities are like. Be sure to read the notices on the bulletin boards, which will tell you about clubs, upcoming events, and other student activities.

Other stops that may or may not be on the tour include the computer labs, science labs, theaters, concert halls, arts facilities, and the athletic center. If you'd like to see a building that isn't on the tour, ask the guide to give you directions. Be sure to stop by the admissions, financial aid, and housing offices, and pick up all of the applications and informational materials you'll need. Definitely pick up a course catalog while you're on-campus. Course catalogs are not usually mailed out with college viewbooks and applications, and they'll give you the best idea of the kinds and number of courses that are available at the school.

Questions You Should Ask

The most important thing to do during the campus visit is to ask questions of everybody you meet: the tour guide, the admissions officer, the financial aid officer, professors, and students. You can find out facts like application due dates, graduation rates, and required test scores from the college's literature. Use this time to ask questions about the not-so-obvious—the things that you don't learn from the school brochure.

This is your best opportunity to find out what students really think of their school. Don't be shy. Most students will be happy to answer your questions. After all, they were in your shoes not so long ago (and think about how much more you'll like the school if you approach several students and find them all to be friendly). But don't get offended if someone you approach says they have a big paper due the next day and don't have time to talk to you, or if you meet one grumpy student who may just be having a bad day.

Before you arrive on campus, make a list of questions that you still have. This section suggests a lot of good questions to ask (and I'm sure you'll think of many more).

Questions About Academics

- *Majors:* What are the most popular majors? When do you have to declare a major? Can you take a double major or a minor? How easy is it to change your major? Can you design your own major?

> "
> It is important to remember that a tour guide is not always what the majority of students are like at that university. That is why it is important to talk to someone else in the university who may have similar interests.
> —Mandy, college tour guide
> "

- *Course load:* How many classes does the average student take per semester, trimester, or quarter? How long does it take for most students to complete the core requirements?

- *Registering for classes:* How easy is it to get the classes you want? Can you easily get into classes that are required for graduation or for your major? What are the most popular classes? How do you register—do you have to wait in long lines, or can you do it by mail, over the phone, or on the computer?

- *Classes:* What do you like or dislike about the classes? How big are the classes for freshmen and for upperclassmen? Are classes more likely to be taught lecture-style or in seminars? Are they taught by full profs or TAs? Are the classes challenging? Did you feel under-prepared or over-prepared? Is discussion encouraged? Are most of the tests essay or multiple-choice? Are many papers required?

- *Professor accessibility:* Can you easily meet with your professor? Do professors have scheduled office hours? Can you contact them at home or via e-mail? Do you ever get together socially with your professors? Do you get the opportunity to do research or write papers with your professors?

- *Graduate students (at universities):* Do professors or graduate students teach most of the classes? Do graduate students generally lead discussion sections?

- *Academic extras:* Are any special programs available to members of your department (such as fieldwork, internship placement, or experiential learning)? Are there departmental or other academic organizations, and how active are they? Can you do independent research or work on team projects? What are the study-abroad and semester-away options? Is there an honors program, and how do you get in? What kinds of facilities are available?

- *Academic support:* Is your advisor helpful and available? Do professors serve as advisors? Are tutoring or support services available? Does the school provide special services for students with learning disabilities? Is there a writing center where a student can have a paper looked over? Does the school offer study skills workshops? Are these support services free?

- *Computers:* Are students required to bring or purchase a computer? How hard is it to find an open computer during exams? Does the school provide popular software programs? Do students get e-mail accounts and access to the Internet? Can you connect your computer to the school's network in your dorm room? Do professors use computers in class or provide class materials on the Internet?

- *Studying:* How many hours a week do most students study? Is it quiet enough to study in the dorms? How about in the library? Are there any quiet policies during exam time? How late do libraries, labs, and computer labs stay open?

Questions About Life on Campus

Bright Idea
Try to see as many of the dorms as you can. Where I went to college, some of the dorms were quaint and cozy, and others were huge high-rises. You can't count on getting into the dorm of your choice, but you may be able to indicate a dorm preference on your housing application.

- *Living arrangements:* Do most students live on campus or off campus? Are students required to live in the dorm as a freshman? Is housing guaranteed, or is it limited? Are there alternate forms of on-campus housing, besides the dorms (such as student apartments or co-op houses)? Are there Greek houses on-campus? Is married-student or family housing available, and is childcare provided? How much does it cost to live off campus?

- *The dorms:* Which are the best dorms to live in? Are the dorms coed or single sex? If they are coed, do men and women live together on the same hall? Are there any special dorms, such as an honors hall or a language hall?

- *Dorm life:* Can you choose your own roommate? Are there any curfews or visitor restrictions? What are some of the dorm rules? Are the freshman dorms noisy or dirty? Are the resident advisors helpful? Can you choose to live on a quiet floor, in a wellness dorm, or on a substance-free hall?

- *Food:* Is the food any good? Are there a lot of choices? How do you pay for food? Are special options, like vegetarian or kosher meals, available? Are there snack bars or coffeehouses on campus, and how late are they open? Can you get a pizza delivered to your dorm room in the middle of the night? Are there many good, cheap restaurants near campus?

- *Cars:* Are freshmen allowed to have a car on campus? Do you have to pay for parking? How are parking spaces assigned?

- *Getting around:* Is public transportation available, and how much does it cost? Does the school provide transportation to nearby attractions or to the airport, train station, or bus station? Can you walk to the grocery store, local hangout, and other popular places off campus?

Moneysaver
Admissions offices often provide cafeteria vouchers to visitors who ask for them, so you won't have to pay for your meals while on campus.

- *Safety:* What security measures are used in the dorms? Do the students have any safety concerns? Is campus well lit at night? Are there emergency phones, and are they well placed? Does the school provide transportation or security escorts around campus at night? How much crime is there in the areas around campus?

Questions About Social Life

- *The students:* Does the school attract a particular kind of person (hippies, jocks, or artists, for example)? Is it easy to make friends? What's the dating situation like? Is there support for alternative lifestyles? Are most of the students from one state or one area of the country? Do students come from a diverse mix of cultural, ethnic, and geographic backgrounds? Is it easy to integrate with students from different backgrounds?

- *After class:* Where do students hang out? Are there any music clubs, dance clubs, or movie theaters near campus? Does the school host many lectures, concerts, plays, or art shows? What do students usually do on the weekends? Do many students go home every weekend? Are fraternities and sororities a big part of campus life? When is rush? What are the parties like? Is there a lot of drinking?

- *Extracurriculars:* What are the big activities on campus? Is it easy to join the orchestra, choral group, or drama company? Can I work for the newspaper, literary magazine, radio station, or TV station? Are there volunteer opportunities, and is community service required? Are religious activities important to the student body?

- *Sports:* What are the major sporting events? How is school spirit? Can students get free tickets to games? Do many students play team sports? Is it easy to join intramural teams? Is there an athletic center on campus, and do you have to pay a fee to use it? What about jogging trails, bike trails, basketball or tennis courts, a golf course, or a pool? What recreational areas are nearby?

Even More Questions

- *New students:* What is student orientation like? Can you place out of required classes by taking a test or getting college credits in high school? Is there a freshman dorm? Are there any special activities to help freshmen meet other students when they first arrive?

- *Expenses:* What are the costs beyond tuition? Do you have to pay lab fees, computer fees, or program fees? Are there any hidden costs? How much do books typically cost?

- *Health care:* Is there a student clinic on campus? Are there any health fees? Does the school provide a health plan for students? Can you get counseling if you experience personal problems? Does the school provide special services, residence options, or support for students with physical disabilities? Is there a nearby hospital?

- *Working during school:* Can you get a part-time or work-study job on campus? Are part-time jobs plentiful in the area? Will the school help you find internships or summer jobs?

- *After graduation:* How helpful are the job placement services? Do major companies interview on campus? Do most students go on to graduate school or get good jobs after graduation?

- *Overall impressions:* Has college lived up to your expectations? Were there any major disappointments or surprises in store when you came to this school? What is distinctive or unique about this school? Are there any tensions on campus? What issues have concerned students recently, and how did the administration react? Is there much bureaucracy? If you were to do it all over again, would you still pick this college?

Other Things to Do While You're There

So, you've attended the informational session at the admissions office, you've taken the guided tour, you've finished your interview, and you've met with financial aid. After all of these planned activities, leave yourself some free time. Depending on your interests and priorities, you'll probably want to do many things while you're visiting. Here are some suggestions:

- Sit in on a class, preferably in your intended major. This is one of the best ways to get a feel for academic life at the school. You'll find out what the students and professors are like in action. The admissions office can provide a class schedule and help you arrange a class visit.

- Visit the academic department where you intend to major. See if any professors or students are available to talk to you. Pick up a course list to learn what kinds of classes are given in your intended major. Check out related facilities, such as the labs, art studios, or computer equipment.

- If you want to play a sport while at college, attend a game or practice, and talk to the coach. If you want to enter a music or drama program, schedule any required auditions. If you need to complete a departmental or scholarship interview, get it out of the way.

- Visit various student services, such as the health clinic, the writing center, or the tutoring center. Talk to the people who work there to find out how helpful and pleasant they are.

- Eat in the cafeteria. But remember that colleges aren't generally known for their gourmet cooking, so don't be too judgmental.

- Attend a social event. Go to a party, a play, a dance, or a game. Sit in on a club meeting. Go off campus with some students to a club, a concert, or shopping.

- Spend the night in the dorm. Most colleges encourage overnight stays; make arrangements through the admissions office. Try to stay with someone who has interests similar to yours; for instance, if you want to join the basketball team, bunk with a player.

- Get a copy of the student newspaper to read later. When you read the paper, notice what the hot campus topics are and try to determine the main concerns of the student body—do these issues interest you? The paper often publishes announcements of upcoming events and activities—are these the kinds of events that you want to participate in?

- Go by the student store. Buy a T-shirt, and check out the prices of books. Find out if you can easily purchase essentials like toothpaste and shampoo.

Bright Idea
If you had an interview with an admissions officer or met with a professor or faculty member during your visit, take the time to write a thank-you note when you get home. It makes a great impression!

■ Check out the off-campus community. Get ideas for places to visit from your tour guide. Go to a restaurant, a hangout, local shops—anywhere that will give you a feel for the nearby town. Seeing the area surrounding campus is a vital part of the college visit; you may like the school a lot, but once you step off campus, you may feel unsafe or realize that there isn't a whole lot to do. If you don't have time to walk around the neighborhood, at least drive around for a few minutes when you leave the school.

Keeping Your Parents Busy

Many students take campus tours with their parents, and I think this is a good idea. After all, your parents are heavily involved in this decision and should get the chance to see what they'll be shelling out so much money for. They can also ask the tour guide the embarrassing questions that you don't want to bring up.

Parents and students definitely have different agendas during campus visits. Parents most often focus on practical issues like finances, campus safety, and academic quality, while students try to get a gut-level impression of the school and see if they can picture themselves living and learning there. For instance, when you visit the dorms, you may wonder if you can live with the people you meet there, while your parents are wondering when the bathroom was last cleaned.

Many admissions officers and tour guides note that parents ask all the questions, while students mostly stay silent. It's okay for your parents to ask questions, but don't let them dominate the conversation, especially during interviews with admissions officers, professors, and coaches. In fact, it's best if you attend these interviews by yourself; you'll make a better impression, and the interviewer can focus on you and your concerns, rather than your parents'. You may also want to reserve some time to explore the campus by yourself, so you can get a better idea of what it will be like to attend the college on your own and more easily talk to other students.

So, what do your parents do while you're off on your own? That's the ideal time for them to meet with the financial aid officer and get all of their pressing questions answered. They may also want to visit the housing office, so they can learn about the costs of room and board, meal plans, and similar details. They can drop by campus security to find out about crime at the college and safety measures that are in place on campus. They might also want to go by the health clinic and learn what medical facilities are available.

After you finish visiting colleges, sit down with your parents and talk over your experiences. Because you and your parents have different priorities, you're bound to come away with different impressions. Your parents may have noticed important details that you overlooked. For instance, while you were charmed by the quaint beauty of the campus (or by the cute coeds you

Watch Out!
You may be tempted to visit colleges with your friends or to stay with a sibling while you're there. Often, you'll end up spending more time partying than investigating the academic life of the school. If your parents are with you, you're more likely to stay on track.

saw during the tour), your parents may point out that the average temperature is 90 degrees and that the dorms had no air-conditioning. You never know what may factor into your final decision.

But don't be surprised if you and your parents complete the campus visits with very different ideas on where you should go to college. It can be difficult to explain to your parents that you just have a good feeling about a particular school, or that you thought the students seemed dull, or that you found the atmosphere too stifling. Despite what your parents say, don't discount nebulous impressions like these. While you shouldn't base your final decision entirely on your gut feelings, they are still an important factor to take into account.

If You Can't Visit

If it's just impossible to visit some of the colleges on your top-ten list, don't despair. There are still many ways to learn about the schools. Gather information from all of the sources suggested in this section to make the most informed decisions about where to apply. In fact, I suggest that you do all of these things even if you do visit the campus.

Checking out a college on the Web is probably the next-best thing to actually going there. You should have no trouble locating the websites of the colleges where you want to apply. Simply search for the school's name in Yahoo! (http://www.yahoo.com/) or check the huge list of colleges and universities at http://www.mit.edu:8001/people/cdemello/univ.html. Most college guides also list the school's website address.

On the school's website, you can look at pictures or videos of the campus, read the student newspaper, learn about course offerings and student clubs, and exchange e-mail messages with professors and other students. College websites also provide lots of valuable information about admissions, housing, financial aid, different academic departments, and special programs. An extended visit to the school's website may even help you cross some schools off your list before you go to the expense of actually traveling there.

Many college websites have "virtual tours," which take you on a guided tour of campus via your computer. A virtual tour can be as simple as a series of photographs and descriptions, but the best ones are full-blown, interactive tours with clickable maps, 360-degree panoramas, video, and sound. Some tours even include live pictures of campus. A virtual tour can certainly give you a good idea of what campus is like if you can't go there yourself. To find a particular school's virtual tour, go to http://www.campustours. com/; this site connects directly to the virtual tours at the websites of hundreds of colleges, as well as to interactive maps, photographs, videos, and even live pictures of the schools.

If you can't visit a particular college, the Collegiate Choice Walking Tours service at http://www.collegiatechoice.com/ is a great alternative. At

Unofficially...
A 1998 survey found that 78 percent of prospective college students logged on to college websites during their college search, and that 64 percent of high schoolers use the Internet to narrow their college choices.

this website, you can purchase non-promotional, unedited videos of guided campus tours and informational sessions for over 300 colleges universities, both in this country and abroad. The tapes cost only $15 each, and unlike the school's promotional videos, they really do present an unbiased view of the college.

Another good resource is the college fair. There, you'll get the chance to meet representatives from the admissions office face-to-face and get the answers to your most pressing questions. Try to attend all of the college fairs and College Nights in your area.

You can also get answers to your questions about the school by scheduling an application interview, even if one is not required. If you can't make it to campus, an alumnus who lives nearby usually will meet with you. The interview is the perfect opportunity to learn about academics and life on campus. (You'll learn more about the application interview in Chapter 3, "What Admissions Committees Are Looking For.")

Talk to as many people connected with the college as you can find. Get the e-mail addresses and phone numbers of current students and professors who'd be willing to answer your questions from the admissions office. If you have Internet access, college-oriented newsgroups like soc.college and college chat boards are great places to talk with a large number of college students and find out their impressions of the schools that you can't visit (you'll find a long list of college chat rooms at http://events.yahoo.com/Net_Events/Education/Colleges_and_Universities/Chat_Rooms/). Also contact graduates of your high school or your friends' siblings who attend the colleges that you're considering. And if any of your friends are able to visit the campus, grill them about their impressions.

While it's not always possible to visit every college where you'll apply, it's crucial that you make the trip to the schools where you're accepted, or at least your top two or three choices, before making your final decision. It's just impossible to make a decision this monumental without trying out the merchandise first.

Just the Facts

- Plan campus visits well in advance, so you can visit at the optimum times and fit in all necessary interviews.

- Use the guided tour to get a general impression of the college, but be sure to explore on your own as well.

- The college visit is the best time to get answers to all your questions; prepare questions beforehand, and talk to many different students while you're there.

- Make the most of your time on campus; use the visit to sit in on a class, stay overnight in the dorms, explore the college town, and otherwise try to find out what life at that school is really like.

Watch Out!
Don't count on the college's viewbook and promotional video for the most objective or accurate portrayals of life at that school. I can pretty much guarantee that the majority of classes at any college don't occur outdoors under big green trees next to a duck pond. These materials are the best sources of statistical information about the school, but don't rely on them to form your opinion of the school.

- It's a good idea to take your parents with you on campus visits, but recognize that they'll have different priorities than yours; spend some time apart, so your parents can get their pressing questions answered and you can find out what it's like living on your own at the school.

- You may not be able to visit all of the schools that you're considering; in that case, gather information about the school from as many other sources as possible, including the website, at college fairs, and from other students who have visited the school.

GET THE SCOOP ON...
How colleges make admissions decisions ▪ How to match yourself to
college admissions standards ▪ The most important qualities that
admissions committees look for in applicants ▪ How to boost your
chances for admission ▪ Taking advantage of the interview

What Admissions Committees Are Looking For

Getting into college is not an exact science. The results aren't predictable, but the decisions aren't random, either. While each school creates its own standards to measure applicants, two factors control the admissions policies at all colleges and universities: what the school wants its incoming freshman class to be like; and the size and quality of the applicant pool. Generally speaking, your overall academic record and how you present yourself in the application are the most influential factors in making the final decision.

In this chapter, you'll learn exactly what admissions committees at different kinds of colleges and universities look for in applicants. Then, you'll discover how to use this knowledge to make yourself a better candidate for admission.

How the Admissions Process Works

The process of deciding whom to admit and whom to reject is not some secret ritual carried out in the basement of the admissions building. Actually, most admissions officers are very open about the process they use when making admissions decisions and the criteria on which they judge applicants. They honestly want to help applicants present their best side to the admissions committees. They also want to help students decide early on in the admissions process whether they are truly qualified for that school, thus saving everyone some time and effort if they're not.

For these reasons, don't be afraid to ask questions about admissions procedures and standards at the colleges where you want to apply. In fact, it's a very good idea to contact an admissions officer at each college you're serious about. Then, if you do decide to apply to the school, the admissions officer is already familiar with you and with your interest in the college.

Timesaver
Do you have questions about the admissions process? If you have Internet access, drop in on the newsgroup soc.college.admissions. Many of the people who read this newsgroup are actual admissions officers, and they're happy to give you advice or answer your questions about any part of the process of getting into college.

At most schools, particularly private and highly selective colleges, a committee of admissions officers makes admissions decisions. The process for evaluating applications and deciding whom to admit may differ in the details, but the general process is basically the same at these schools.

Here's what happens when an application comes through the door:

1. Applications are read first as they come in. Generally, the first read is by the admissions officer for your area of the country, someone you may have already interviewed with during the campus visit or talked to on the phone. Generally, the admissions officer spends 20 to 30 minutes on the application file during the first reading.

2. Another admissions officer gives the application a second reading, spending five to ten minutes on the file. At this point, several applications may be rejected because grades or test scores don't measure up to the school's standards. The second pass may also result in several acceptances of students who are clearly admissible. The majority of applications land in the "maybe" pile.

3. A third reading focuses on borderline applications and factors in special circumstances: athletics or other activities; legacy status; transfer or international students; and so on.

4. The committee reviews both the overall patterns of decisions—the number of students placed into various decision categories as compared to previous years, the class academic profile, and the balance of extracurricular talents, diversity, and other goals—and the individual decisions. Admissions officers have one last chance to argue for a particular borderline applicant.

5. The committee as a whole, or in some cases just the dean of admissions, decides whom among the remaining applicants to accept, whom to wait-list, and whom to reject.

As you can see, most applications receive at least two or three reviews by different admissions officers, and an application may get as many as four to eight readings before the committee makes the final decision. At the most competitive schools, you can be sure that each qualified application receives careful attention, and each student's unique situation is evaluated individually.

"
The goal [of the admissions procedure] is to speed up the decision process for those who are clearly admissible and to focus on those students who would benefit from several readings.
—Todd Leahy, Admissions Counselor, Wofford College
"

How Selective Should Your Schools Be?

Throughout this book, and in every other college guide you pick up, you'll see one term bandied about—*selectivity*. But what exactly does it mean to say that a college is selective? What makes Harvard more selective than Hofstra, or the University of Virginia more selective than the University of Georgia? And why should you care?

Selectivity generally refers to the percentage of applicants accepted out of the pool of students who apply. At one extreme are open admission colleges, which select 100 percent of applicants on a first-come-first-served basis. At the other extreme are very competitive colleges that admit only 15 to 30 percent of applicants.

The most selective colleges—the ones that admit the smallest percentage of applicants—typically have long-established reputations as top-notch schools. Therefore, they receive a lot of applications each year, and they can afford to choose only the best applicants out of the pool. So, the standards for admission at these schools are very high. These colleges may consider only applicants with SAT I scores over 1300 and a B+ average, students who took the most challenging courses, achieved the most in their extracurricular activities, and won the most prestigious awards and honors. (Compare that with an open-admission school, which requires only a high school diploma for admittance.)

But don't become discouraged if you don't meet these high standards. There are over 3000 colleges and universities in this country, and it's almost surprising how many of them are truly good schools. You don't have to go to Harvard or Princeton or Yale to get a top-notch education. And the majority of colleges fall between the two extremes of open admission and super-selectivity, so you're bound to find several schools whose admissions standards match your academic and extracurricular achievements.

Selectivity Levels

There are five broad categories of college selectivity:

- *Not very selective:* These schools focus on whether applicants meet the minimum requirements, and they admit a large percentage of applicants (generally over 90 percent). Grades are important, but high school GPAs of applicants are typically low (C or below). The SAT I or ACT may be required, but a score below the national average is usually acceptable. Other factors might be considered, but they probably won't play a major part in admissions decisions. Schools that fit this definition include Huron University, Teikyo Post University, Burlington College, North Carolina A&T State University, and Johnson and Wales University.

- *Somewhat selective:* These schools have relatively low admissions standards: C or B- grade average; average or lower test scores; and minimum college-prep courseload. Only in rare cases are any qualifications beyond grades and test scores considered for admission. Schools in this category include Rider University, Fisk University, Colby-Sawyer College, Kent State University, and the Indiana Institute of Technology.

- *Moderately selective:* These schools mainly look at grades and standardized test scores when deciding whom to admit. Admissions standards match the typical "average" student: a B average; average test scores; and a rank in the top 50 percent of the high school class. Other aspects of the application become important only with borderline applications

Watch Out!
College guides often list schools' admissions standards, including test scores and GPAs. These are generally *averages*, not cutoffs—50 percent of the freshman class scored above those numbers, and 50 percent scored *below*. So, if your GPA is a few decimal points shy of what's listed for your favorite school in a college guide, don't let that alone discourage you from applying.

or when there are too many qualified applicants for the number of spaces available. Schools in this category include Howard University, Temple University, the College of Santa Fe, the University of Colorado at Boulder, and California State Polytechnic University at Pomona.

- *Very selective:* These schools consider coursework, grades, standardized test scores, extracurriculars, recommendations, and essays when making admissions decisions. Applicants are often rejected because of weak academic preparation, low grades (below a B average), or low test scores (below the national average), but other factors—no extracurriculars or a lack of interest in the school, for instance—make a big difference, as well. Very selective schools include Trinity University, Brandeis University, Oberlin College, the University of Illinois at Urbana-Champaign, and the Georgia Institute of Technology.

- *Highly selective:* These schools are highly competitive. Admissions committees carefully scrutinize every aspect of applicants' high school records and application packages. Challenging high school courses, a high grade point average (B+ to A), a class rank in the top 20 percent, and well-above-average standardized test scores are a must. Other factors are also quite important in making decisions, including extracurriculars, background and experiences, essays, and recommendations. Highly selective schools include Stanford University, Princeton University, Carleton College, the University of North Carolina at Chapel Hill, and the Massachusetts Institute of Technology.

Course Requirements

Most colleges and universities require their applicants to have taken a specific number and kinds of academic courses in high school, so that they are prepared for college work. Table 3.1 lists the minimum and recommended requirements of the average college or university; bear in mind that the minimum requirements for many schools exceed the ones listed in this table. Meeting or exceeding the recommendations and taking a large number of accelerated, honors, and Advanced Placement (AP) courses will make you much more desirable to the more selective schools.

Matching Yourself to Admission Standards

You don't necessarily need perfect grades or a 1600 on the SAT I to get into a good college. Although your high school transcript and standardized test scores are considered the most important elements of your college application, admissions committees also look for many other qualities when making their decision, as you'll learn later on in this chapter.

Still, the more selective schools will strongly consider your GPA and test scores when deciding whether to admit you. Admissions committees will also look at the content of your high school courses to determine whether you've taken a challenging courseload. When creating your top-ten list of

Watch Out!
If there's such a thing as a gatekeeper, math is it. Students are often limited in their college options because they didn't take enough math courses during high school. If you have to take two math courses during one school year to keep up, bite the bullet and do it.

TABLE 3.1: MINIMUM AND RECOMMENDED HIGH SCHOOL COURSES FOR COLLEGE PREPARATION

Subject	Minimum Years	Recommended Years	Types of Courses to Take
English	4 years	4 years	Composition; American, English, and world literature
Math	3 years	4+ years	Algebra I and II; geometry; trigonometry or pre-calculus; calculus
Science	2 years	3–4 years*	Earth science; biology; chemistry; physics; electives like physiology, biochemistry, and anatomy or advanced courses in the basic sciences
History/ social studies	2 years	3–4 years	Geography; civics; US history and government; world history and cultures
Foreign language	2 years	3–4 years	Concentrate in one language only
Visual/ performing arts	1 year	3+ years	Art; dance; drama; music
Computer science	None	1+ years	Becoming more and more important
Electives	1 year	3+ years	Academic rather than vocational or "easy" electives, such as economics, psychology, statistics, or communications

* at least 2 years should be a laboratory science

Unofficially...
Seventy percent of
college freshmen
indicated in a
national survey that
they're attending
their first-choice
college; another 20
percent said they're
attending their
second-choice
school.

schools, don't overreach and look only at colleges with admissions standards that don't mesh well with your academic achievements.

During the college search process, take a personal academic inventory, noting your GPA, your class rank, any advanced or honors classes you've taken, and your best SAT I or ACT scores, as well as the scores of any SAT II Subject Tests that you've taken. When considering schools, try to select colleges whose standards for admission are close to your academic inventory. But keep in mind that many schools will take your special talents and extracurricular achievements into account, so let the admission requirements be a guide rather than a rigid standard.

While it's true that many people tend to overestimate their talents and qualifications, I believe that many more tend to *underestimate* themselves. Don't fall into this trap and keep yourself from applying to a college just because you don't think you measure up to the standards. Make it one of your reach schools, and apply anyway—you never know if some of your special qualities will get you admitted. And if you don't get in, you'll have backed up your application with several mid-range and safety schools, as I advised in Chapter 1, "Choosing the Right College."

What Admissions Committees Are Looking For

Most schools use a range of criteria to judge an application and decide whether to admit the applicant. Grades, course content, class rank, standardized test scores, the essay, recommendations, the interview, extracurricular activities, special talents, and alumni consideration can all figure into deciding whether to accept or reject a particular applicant.

According to admissions officers from a variety of colleges and universities, the most important parts of the application, from most important to least, are the following:

1. *Your high school courseload:* Admissions committees look for a variety of challenging classes in several academic subjects. The best candidates exceed the minimum required courses set by the college. The admissions committee wants to see a good selection of AP, honors, or other advanced courses. They also look for "meaningful" electives, such as arts courses and non-required classes in the subjects that you've expressed an interest in pursuing in college.

2. *Your grades and GPA:* The most competitive colleges like to see students with an A or B+ average. Your grades and GPA are always considered in light of your course choices; if you take more challenging classes, then you can get away with slightly lower grades in some of those classes.

3. *Your class rank:* For most admissions committees, class rank is more revealing than a simple grade point average. Your class rank enables the admissions committee to compare you against other students at your high school, while a high GPA may only be the result of a too-easy courseload.

4. *Your SAT I or ACT scores:* Standardized test scores are another measure of an applicant's academic ability, but they usually aren't a primary factor in determining admissions unless they fall significantly below the average standardized test scores for students who attend the college. (You'll learn more about how colleges look at standardized test scores in Part IV of this book.)

Other parts of the application package are very important in making admissions decisions, but they're not crucial. Admissions committees generally use these items to make decisions about borderline or average applicants. They include all of the following elements:

- The essay or writing sample
- Letters of recommendation
- Extracurricular activities
- Leadership experience
- Special accomplishments, honors, and awards
- Volunteer and paid work experience
- The interview
- Personal factors—your cultural background, your religious background, your ethnicity, or where you live
- Your character and personal qualities
- The major or field you want to study
- Relationships with alumni of the school
- Your family's ability to pay

The Ideal Candidate (According to the Admissions Committee)

According to admissions officers at a variety of colleges and universities, the "ideal" candidate—one who would be admitted as soon as the admissions committee got a glimpse at the application—would possess all or most of the following qualities:

- Exceeds the admissions standards set by the school
- Has a love for learning
- Demonstrates academic motivation by taking the most challenging courses available
- Maintains above-average academic performance in classes and on standardized tests
- Is a good writer or communicator
- Is a leader in the school or community
- Participates in activities outside the classroom that contribute positively to the environment or community
- Shows a keen interest in the college, in its mission or environment, and in becoming involved in campus activities and organizations

Watch Out!
Even though you may submit your application too early for colleges to consider your senior-year grades, they will look closely at the *kinds* of classes you take your senior year, to see if you're continuing to challenge yourself and live up to your academic potential. So, don't slack off!

Sounds like you have to be Superman or Wonder Woman, doesn't it? Don't despair if you don't meet all of these standards. Consider these qualities to be the ultimate goals that you should always strive for throughout your high school career.

The Academic Record

Your academic record is definitely the most important part of your college application, no matter where you apply. Not having a strong enough record to match the school's admissions criteria is often enough reason to reject you. Your academic record includes your high school transcript listing your grades and course choices from the ninth grade through to the end of your junior year, your grade point average, your class rank, and the scores of all the standardized tests that you've taken. Of all of these, admissions committees give the high school transcript the most weight.

Admissions officers strongly consider the difficulty of the courses that you take in high school. Honors, AP, and other accelerated courses are much more impressive than electives or basic courses that are required to graduate from high school. Admissions committees are more prone to reject you if it seems like you've taken a lighter courseload than you can handle. And don't think you can slack off once you become a senior; virtually all colleges require your high school to update your transcript with a mid-year grade report, and they really do care about your first-semester senior grades.

This doesn't mean that you should load up on accelerated courses if they'll overwhelm you. Instead, choose courses based on your abilities. If you intend to pursue a science major in college, then take challenging science and math courses while in high school; but if history isn't your strong suit, then opt for an "easier" class where you'll be more likely to earn a higher grade. While admissions committees may consider a B in an accelerated class to be worth more than an A in an easier course, a D or F in any course will definitely count heavily against you.

Many students worry that if their high schools don't offer many accelerated classes, their chances for admission to selective schools will be diminished. Admissions officers realize that high school is not a level playing field; some high schools have more resources to offer their students than others.

Admissions officers are assigned to different regions of the country, so they can make themselves experts on the high schools in their regions. They consult high school profiles that list the courses offered and other school data to evaluate an applicant's courseload in the context of his or her high school. Therefore, each high school's overall quality is taken into account when class ranks and courseloads of applicants are evaluated.

Admissions committees may overlook a low grade or substandard test score if the applicant has other qualities that make up for the deficiency. But top grades don't necessarily mean automatic admission. Admissions officers, especially at the more selective schools, search for several qualities in an applicant other than just a strong academic record. They want to make certain that students who enroll at the college will make valuable contributions both in and out of the classroom.

Extracurricular Activities

Most colleges, particularly private colleges and the more selective schools, value a broad variety of skills, interests, and backgrounds in their students, so you should highlight all of your unique qualities in your application. Extracurricular activities are particularly noted because they show the admissions committee what you care about and what interests you have outside of the classroom. Extracurricular activities also indicate what kind of citizen you'll be in the college community.

It's a persistent myth that colleges look for "well-rounded" applicants. The truth is that colleges try to put together a well-rounded freshman class, made up of individuals who possess unique talents, life experiences, and character traits.

A laundry list of extracurricular activities, to which you gave only a limited amount of time, will not impress the committee. What admissions committees like to see on your application are one, two, or three activities that you dedicated a lot of time to, eventually rising to a leadership position or making a significant contribution. This shows the committee that you committed to something that you're passionate about and excelled in it—important qualities that colleges highly value in potential students.

Admissions committees are particularly interested in extracurriculars that complement your academic learning—working on the school newspaper or yearbook, developing your creativity or special talents, taking student government positions, or playing a sport. Other activities that impress the admissions committee include internships, travel, volunteering or social advocacy, and taking community-college courses. If you didn't participate in many outside activities because you held a part-time job, your self-discipline and sense of responsibility will also impress the committee.

Colleges love to see applicants with leadership experience. Being a leader doesn't necessarily mean being president of the student council or captain of the football team. Valuable leadership experience includes initiating or overseeing projects, organizing a special event or program, or editing a school newspaper or literary magazine, as well.

Other Qualities That Admissions Committees Look For

Other parts of the application package include the essay, teacher and counselor recommendations, and, in some cases, a personal interview. Of all of these, the essay is the most important. Your writing will be read carefully, and the essay can significantly help or hurt you. The more selective schools may even read your essay before looking at your grades. (The essay and the other components of the application package are discussed in more detail in Part III of this book.)

"
Being involved does not mean joining ten different clubs. Instead, it means finding a few activities that revolve around your interests, and making a contribution in those activities.
—Todd Leahy, Admissions Counselor, Wofford College
"

Watch Out!
Don't load up your application with a long list of extracurricular activities. Admissions officers know how many hours are in a day, and they don't want "serial joiners." Listing too many activities tells them that you probably didn't participate fully in those clubs, that you just joined to have something else to put down on your college application.

Sometimes, several applications may closely parallel each other, but there aren't enough spaces to admit all of the applicants. In this case, the admissions committee will look at "tippers"—items that don't by themselves determine admission or rejection, but that can tip the balance in close calls.

There's no way to predict what factors may be important to different schools. In close cases, colleges may give weight to factors that are part of the school's commitment or history, such as religious history, ethnicity, or loyalty to a particular geographic area. Colleges seeking greater diversity may consider gender, ethnicity, or cultural background when deciding close calls. If the school needs to fill a specific need, it may seek out qualified applicants from a particular region of the country, who plan to major in a particular department, who will fill a vacant seat in the orchestra, or who will round out the rugby team.

A demonstrated commitment to attend the college, usually through an early decision or early action application, can also tip the balance your way (you'll learn more about these admission plans in Chapter 5, " Application Options—Playing It Smart").

Alumni consideration doesn't mean an automatic "yes" for students whose parents or siblings graduated from the college. It plays an important role only if there are two applicants who are otherwise equal in grades and qualifications and the school has limited space; the student who is related to an alumnus or alumna will probably get alumni consideration for admission in this case. But if the applicant's grades or other qualities don't measure up to the school's standards, alumni consideration alone won't get the student admitted to the school.

Bright Idea
If you don't need the extra money, volunteering shows as much character—if not more—as a summer job. Choose volunteer work that's meaningful to you, and admissions committees will notice your commitment.

Need-Blind and Need-Aware Admissions

In the past, admissions policies reflected the ideal that every qualified applicant should be admitted to the college, regardless of ability to pay. This policy—called *need-blind admission*—simply means that an applicant's financial resources aren't taken into account when deciding whether to admit that applicant. Many private colleges, particularly the most well-endowed schools, still maintain this policy.

But as the cost of tuition has steadily risen, many colleges have begun to realize that they can't satisfy the financial needs of every student admitted to the school. These schools generally accept the strongest applicants first, without regard for financial need. But as financial aid resources start to run out, admissions committees evaluate less-qualified applicants for their families' ability to pay. It may sound unfair, but it's an effective way of coping with shrinking financial aid resources.

Other schools maintain a policy of meeting part of the financial need of every student who is accepted. This more equitable policy results in a certain portion of financial need being left unmet for all.

Unfortunately, applicants have no control over the financial aid policies of the schools where they apply or over how financial aid resources are allotted. If you require financial aid to pay for college—any college—consider the school's financial aid policies before applying there. Look for schools where you exceed the admissions standards—you're much more likely to receive a larger slice of the financial aid pie. (To learn more about financial aid, turn to Part V of this book.)

The following are examples of very selective colleges that do *not* have need-blind admissions policies:

- Boston College
- Brigham Young University
- Brown University
- Carleton College
- Colby College
- Harvey Mudd College
- Johns Hopkins University
- Tufts University
- University of California at San Diego
- Vassar College

Making an Impression on the Admissions Committee

The admissions committee wants to feel that you are a serious applicant who truly wants to attend the school, and every part of your application package will tell the committee if this is so. As I stressed in Chapter 1, all of the schools that you apply to, even your safety schools, should be schools that you really want to attend. If you've carefully chosen colleges to match your goals, interests, likes, and needs, and if you've visited the campus and really gotten to know the school, then it will show in your application.

Your respect for the school also comes through in the care that you give to filling out the application. Not following directions or application procedures, submitting an incomplete application, not writing neatly and concisely—all of these things tell the admissions officer that you just don't care.

Finally, a word to the wise about gimmicks—they don't impress. Flowers, gift baskets, and tins of cookies tend to detract from your application. If you really want to impress the admissions committee, follow directions and submit a neat, professional-looking application form.

Improving Your Chances for Admission

According to admissions officers, you can do several things to improve your chances for admission to your dream school if you don't feel that your academic record is quite up to snuff. Some steps you'll have to take early—before your senior year begins. Others you can complete just before you send in the application.

> 66
> Get in touch with the territory manager (admissions counselor) for your area. Let him/her know who you are before you send in an application. Meet with the territory manager while at the school, and keep in e-mail contact.
> —Lori Boatright, Admissions Counselor, Furman University
> 99

So, if you feel that your application lacks something, if you don't think you measure up to admission standards at your favorite school, or if you just want to seal the deal, consider taking one or more of the following steps:

- Work hard in your classes and show improvement in your grades over the course of your junior and senior years in high school. Consider hiring a tutor to help you with difficult subjects.

- Challenge yourself your senior year by taking several AP and honors courses. Continue taking advanced foreign language, math, and science courses during your last year in high school, even if they're not required for graduation.

- Throughout your application form, essay, and interview, show your interest in and commitment to the school. Learn a lot about the school, and demonstrate that knowledge to the admissions committee. Consider applying early, if that option is available.

- Schedule an interview with an admissions officer, even if it's not required. Use this opportunity to discuss any questionable spots on your record and to emphasize why you are a good candidate for admission.

- Visit the campus more than once, if possible. Talk with admissions officers each time you visit, so they can get to know you and see how interested you are in the school.

- Make a significant contribution in your extracurricular activities, such as becoming a team captain or producing the best yearbook your school has ever had.

- Highlight your academic talents and special interests in your application. If the admissions office encourages it, consider submitting class essays, independent research, or internship reports to show your academic achievements.

- Highlight a special talent in your application, such as an athletic, artistic, or musical talent. If the admissions office encourages it, consider submitting samples of your artwork, tapes of performances, or creative writing excerpts.

- If you have a special interest or talent, contact the appropriate department or club at the college. For instance, if you're an accomplished debater, get in touch with the president of the debate club. If you'd like to be a photojournalist, visit the journalism department and the editor of the school newspaper. The people you meet may be so impressed with you that they'll contact the admissions office to emphasize what a good addition you'd make to the campus.

- List unusual activities on your application, such as winning a chess championship, completing an internship at a computer company, living for three months in a foreign country, training seeing eye dogs, or tagging along with an archaeological expedition. Anything that helps you stand out from the crowd of applicants is worth mentioning.

- Inform the admissions officer of special circumstances that may explain a weak spot on your application. If your parents are first-generation immigrants, for example, that could explain why your essay isn't grammatically perfect. Or if you come from a single-parent, low-income family, that could explain why you spent your free time after school working rather than participating in a large number of extracurricular activities.

- Write a thoughtful, original essay. If you feel that your writing talent isn't up to the school's standards, inquire about submitting extra writing samples with your application, especially in-class samples with teachers' comments. If an essay isn't required, consider submitting a personal statement anyway.

- Get to know your guidance counselor. This is good advice anyway, but it can come in handy if your application is borderline. An admissions officer may call your guidance counselor to ask about you, and if your counselor knows you well, then he or she can help the admissions officer make a tough decision. Also, a counselor who knows you can write a detailed letter of recommendation that may help explain why your academic record suffered and what you're doing about it.

- Provide additional letters of recommendation from your teachers, your boss, a religious advisor (for colleges with strong religious affiliations), a club sponsor, or a mentor.

Using the Interview to Help You Get In

Of all the parts of the application package, the interview is probably the least important factor in deciding whether you're admitted to the college. It certainly isn't worth the stomach-churning and nerve-fraying it causes in some students. The majority of colleges and universities don't even require an interview. Small, private, selective, and nontraditional colleges most often use interviews, and even there, they are generally optional.

Still, interviews do make impressions, and if an interview is required, it will carry some weight with the admissions committee, particularly if you're a borderline or "maybe" application. The interview is your chance to show the admissions officer your personality and self-confidence. You'll want to appear bright, interested, mature, and at ease to make a good impression. A great interview can win over an admissions officer. But very few students are rejected because they bombed their interviews.

Even if the interview is only optional, strongly consider scheduling one. The interview provides the admissions committee with yet another piece of information with which to evaluate you. If at all possible, go to the school and interview with an admissions officer. If you can't travel to campus for the interview, an alumni volunteer who lives near your hometown will probably interview you, but that person's opinion won't carry as much weight with the admissions committee as the opinion of a member of the admissions staff.

Watch Out!
Before sending in anything that goes beyond what the application requests—such as additional recommendations, writing samples, or tapes—call the admissions office and ask if such materials will be appreciated and considered.

Unofficially...
The interview may be much more important to specialized schools. For instance, many art schools both require an interview and consider it a major factor in making admissions decisions. The service academies also place a great deal of weight on the interview.

Preparing for the Interview

The best way to make a good impression at the interview is to be prepared. Good preparation will boost your self-confidence and will make you appear more at ease and enthusiastic to the interviewer.

Be ready to answer several stock questions, including the following:

- What do you hope to gain from the college experience?
- Why do you want to go to this school?
- What first brought this school to your attention?
- What other colleges are you considering?
- What do you want to major in?
- What activities outside the classroom do you want to participate in at college?
- What do you want to do with your life?
- Where do you see yourself in five or ten years?
- How would your teachers describe you?
- What classes are you taking in high school?
- What is your greatest accomplishment?
- What is your strongest or weakest quality?
- What characteristics make you special or unique?
- What are your interests or activities?
- What is your family like?
- Who has most influenced you?
- What do you think about this recent news event?
- If you could meet any historical figure, who would it be and why?
- Who is your favorite author?
- What books have you read in the last year?

Watch Out!
Practice answering stock interview questions, but don't memorize stock answers. In the interview, you'll sound like you're reading from a script. Don't over-rehearse your answers, and leave room for improvisation.

Before the interview, think of general answers to these questions. You don't want your answers to sound glib and rehearsed, but you do want to have an intelligent and convincing response ready if these questions come up. If you haven't decided on a field of study or a future career, don't be afraid to say so, but be prepared to tell the interviewer why not.

Discuss your accomplishments honestly, avoiding both boasting and self-effacement. Feel free to talk about your achievements, concentrating on those that have been most important to you and discussing the reasons for their importance. But don't take a "shopping list" approach and talk about everything that you've ever done. Instead, focus on those few things that you feel most passionately about.

Don't be afraid to discuss the less positive aspects of your high school career. A willingness to discuss problems honestly, without looking for excuses or someone to blame, shows maturity. The interview is also a good opportunity to account for a spotty transcript, low test scores, or extenuating circumstances that you can't explain in the application.

Sometimes, interviewers will ask a strange question—"If you could be a tree, what kind of tree would you be?" Don't let it throw you. Just answer the question as best as you can. Grace under pressure is what will impress the interviewer in this case, not some "right" answer that the interviewer is searching for.

You will be expected to ask questions during the interview, as well as answer them. In a sense, you and the school are interviewing each other—the admissions officer wants to learn if you'll make a good addition to the college community, and you want to learn if the school is the right place for you.

Think of some smart questions before you go into the interview, ones that you truly want to learn the answers to and that aren't already answered in the college brochure. If you have several questions in mind when you go into the interview, you can always ask one if the conversation lags. You will also impress the interviewer if you already know a lot about the school and ask pertinent questions based on that knowledge. But don't ask any questions unless you really are interested in the answers.

Here are some examples of questions that you could ask:

- Why would you recommend this school?
- What is the school's greatest asset?
- What does the school need to improve on?
- What are the most popular or strongest academic departments?
- How do I compare academically with students already attending the school? (You may want to bring along an unofficial transcript if you intend to ask this question.)
- How would you describe the student body?
- What do students typically do immediately after graduation?
- What are the current student issues on campus?
- What are the most active extracurricular activities and organizations?

These are just some general suggestions. Any question is fair game, as long as it's not already addressed in the college literature. Obviously, the best questions are ones that are specific to your interests and to what you're looking for in a potential college. One caveat—it's generally a good idea to save questions about social life and living on-campus for the campus tour. (For more examples of questions you could ask, turn back to Chapter 2, "Making the Most of the Campus Visit.")

Practice makes perfect, so save the interviews for your favorite schools until last. You'll get more confident and develop better questions as you go along.

Bright Idea
If you have Internet access, you can practice interviewing at http://www. bergen.org/AAST/ Projects/CollegePrep/ interview.html. This "virtual" college interview asks you stock questions and then gives you feedback about your answers.

❝
While we do not require an on-campus interview, it certainly does help both the student and the admissions staff when they come to visit us. We can put a face with the name on the file, and they are indicating to us how interested they are by coming to campus.
—Todd Leahy, Admissions Counselor, Wofford College
❞

Interviewing Tips

Here are a few more tips to help you make the best impression in the interview:

- Plan to arrive about ten minutes early.

- Wear nice clothes (but not too formal), and dress conservatively.

- Don't chew gum, sit up straight, and maintain eye contact.

- Don't forget to smile.

- Be honest and sincere; don't tell the interviewer what you think he or she wants to hear.

- Speak naturally and confidently.

- Don't use too many slang terms.

- Avoid words like "um," "like," and "you know," as in, "Um, I'm going to, like, major in engineering, you know?"

- Try to keep from fidgeting, stuttering, or talking too quickly.

- Don't try to sneak your stellar SAT scores or grades into the conversation (unless the interviewer specifically asks you about them).

- Always follow up with a thank-you note.

The most important college interviewing "don't" is: Don't bring your parents with you. This never makes a good impression on the admissions officer. If you can, schedule an appointment for your parents with the financial aid office at the same time as your interview.

Some students are told that a sign of a good interview is that it lasts longer than the allotted time. Don't worry about this. Most colleges schedule interviews so tightly that it's impossible to let one run long without throwing off everyone. So, don't try to stretch out your interview by asking a lot of long-winded questions.

Bright Idea
Another way to practice interviewing is to meet and talk with college representatives as often as possible; attend as many college fairs as you can, for instance.

Just the Facts

- The admissions process allows for several thorough readings of each application, particularly at small, private, and selective colleges; this ensures that applicants are considered for all of their qualifications, not just for grades or test scores.

- You'll have a much better shot at being accepted if you search for and apply to colleges whose admissions standards are a good match with your own academic qualifications. However, don't become discouraged from applying to one or two "reach" schools—you never know what factors may contribute to your acceptance.

- Admissions committees look for applicants with strong academic qualifications who also have passionate interests and leadership experience outside of the classroom and who are truly committed to the college. The most important parts of the application package for making admission decisions are the applicant's high school courseload and grades, class rank, and standardized test scores.

- If you feel that you fall too far below the admissions standards at your favorite college to be accepted, you can take steps to improve your chances; the best ones are showing an improvement in your grades, taking more challenging courses and doing well in them, demonstrating leadership or creative abilities, showing a commitment to the school, and submitting extra application materials to present a more complete picture of who you are.

- The college interview is not usually an important factor in making admissions decisions, but it can cause a lot of anxiety nonetheless. To make a better impression, practice answering stock questions and prepare some thoughtful questions that *you* want the answers to.

When and How to Apply

PART II

GET THE SCOOP ON...
Important dates and deadlines in the college application process ▪
Using "universal" applications to save time when applying ▪
Using your computer or the Internet to apply to colleges
more quickly and easily

Chapter 4

The Lowdown on the Application Process

Once you decide where you want to apply, it's time to get down to the nitty-gritty of filling out those applications and sending them in. This chapter will help you get started. First, you'll find a calendar that outlines the entire college search and application process from start to finish and tells you everything you need to do and when you need to do it. No matter what stage you're at in the application process, it's a good idea to consult this calendar frequently— it will help you stay on track.

Also in this chapter, you'll learn about your options when it comes to what kinds of application forms to submit. Yes, you do have options. Most colleges and universities have entered the information age by publishing their applications in a variety of electronic formats, such as on computer disk and on the Internet. Also, many schools try to save the time of both admissions officers and applicants by using universal application forms— forms that you fill out only once and submit to a number of different schools. And you can generally submit these common applications on computer disk or over the Internet, as well.

Taking advantage of these application options can save you both time and money. But if you prefer to do things the old-fashioned way, you still can get a paper application form from any college.

A College Countdown Calendar

It's never too early to start thinking about and planning for college. Even freshmen in high school can start preparing themselves for college. In fact, it's best to start planning for college before your freshman year starts, so that you can take the right courses and participate in the best activities throughout high school.

It doesn't matter if you just started high school or if you're already a junior or senior when the college application process kicks into high gear.

Keeping up with everything that you have to do—all the tests you have to take, the campuses you have to visit, the recommendations you have to get, the forms you have to fill out—can be a nightmare. And if you forget something or miss a deadline, that could mean that you miss out on going to your favorite college.

Don't worry—help is here. Use the calendar in Table 4.1 to track your progress on all steps of the college application process, from the beginning of freshman year to the day you head off to college. It's a good idea to photocopy this calendar and tape it on your wall, so you can check off tasks as you complete them. (Give a copy to your parents, as well, so they can help you keep on track.)

Saving Time with the Common Application

A growing number of private colleges and universities allow you to apply using the *Common Application*. The Common Application, sponsored by the National Association of Secondary School Principals (NASSP), is a single generic application form that you can complete, photocopy, and send to each school that accepts it in lieu of the school's own application form. The school gives equal weight to the Common Application as to its own application form (and many schools only accept the Common Application).

The Common Application should be available in your high school guidance office, or you can request a copy on floppy disk directly from NASSP by calling 1-800-253-7746 (there is a $10 charge). If you have Internet access, you can download the Common Application for Windows or Mac at no charge from http://www.commonapp.org/. Several (but not all) of the schools that participate in the Common Application program accept the application electronically, over the Internet; at the same website, you can fill out and submit the electronic version of the Common Application.

Almost 200 private colleges and universities participate in the Common Application program. Appendix E, "Colleges and Universities That Accept Common or Electronic Applications," lists the schools that use the Common Application and indicates which schools accept the electronic version and which schools request a supplemental form in addition to the Common Application (you must obtain supplemental forms directly from the college—either request the form by mail or download it from the school's website).

Fast and Easy Electronic Applications

If you have a computer or Internet access, applying electronically has several advantages over the old-fashioned pen-and-paper method. Submitting electronic applications saves time, particularly if you use a service that enables you to complete several applications at once or to submit a universal application. It's easier to edit your application, because you don't have to rely on messy white-out or laboriously copy over rough drafts or try to line up application blanks on a typewriter.

TABLE 4.1: CALENDAR OF IMPORTANT DATES

When	What to Do
Freshman Year	
During the year…	Decide what courses to take throughout high school. Create a challenging but balanced course schedule that goes beyond the minimum college-prep requirements.
	Work on getting good grades from the day you start high school.
	Get involved in extracurricular activities that you intend to pursue all through high school.
	Begin developing a relationship with your guidance counselor.
	Start making plans with your parents for financing your college education.
Sophomore Year	
During the year…	Take PLAN to practice for the ACT (it's given in October through December).
	Consider taking the PSAT/NMSQT (it's given in October).
	Begin working toward a leadership position in your extracurricular activities; or do something innovative, like organizing a club or participating in a special project.
	Keep your grades up—aim for all A's and high B's.
	At the end of the school year, take SAT II Subject Tests or AP exams for the courses that you completed.
	Plan worthwhile summer activities.
	It's never too early to start thinking about where you want to go to college!

TABLE 4.1: CALENDAR OF IMPORTANT DATES (CONT.)

When	What to Do
Junior Year	
September	Sign up for challenging college-prep courses, and continue to maintain your grades.
	Begin thinking about career goals and college majors.
	Prepare for the PSAT/NMSQT.
	Get to know your favorite teachers, and start thinking about who you will ask to write recommendations for you.
	If you intend to seek an athletic scholarship, start contacting coaches at the schools that most interest you.
October	Take the PSAT/NMSQT.
	Meet with your guidance counselor to discuss college plans.
	Focus on extracurriculars; become a leader or continue to develop interests outside of school.
November	Begin developing a preliminary college list.
December	Evaluate your PSAT/NMSQT scores to determine which areas need further study.
	Register for the spring SAT I or ACT.
January-February	Begin preparing for the SAT I or ACT.
	Send for information about the colleges on your preliminary list.
March	Take the SAT I.
	Begin preparing for any AP exams and SAT II Subject Tests that you intend to take at the end of the school year.
	Finalize your list of top-ten schools.

When	What to Do
Junior Year (cont.)	
April	Take the ACT.
	Register for the late spring SAT I or ACT (if you haven't already taken them).
	Register for any SAT II Subject Tests you need to take.
	Begin visiting the colleges on your top-ten list.
	Plan worthwhile summer activities.
May	Take the SAT I (if you didn't take it in March).
	Take the SAT II Subject Tests and AP exams for courses that you completed this year.
	Sign up for challenging college-prep and AP courses for your senior year.
June	Take the ACT (if you didn't take it in April).
Summer	Get a job or internship, do community service work, take community college classes, or attend a summer program.
	Continue to make college visits.
	Finalize the list of colleges that you want to apply to, and request applications for them.
	Start working on your application essays.
	Start looking into scholarships that you qualify for. Make a list of deadlines and obtain applications.
Senior Year	
September	Meet with your guidance counselor to review your college plans.
	Register for the SAT I or ACT if you need to retake it.
	Register for the remaining SAT II Subject Tests that you need to take.
	Begin requesting teacher recommendations.
	Request that your transcript is sent to all schools where you're applying.

TABLE 4.1: CALENDAR OF IMPORTANT DATES (CONT.)

When	What to Do
Senior Year (cont.)	
September (cont.)	Register for the College Scholarship Service (CSS) Financial Aid Profile if any colleges on your list require it.
	Don't slack off in your classes!
October	Retake the SAT I or ACT, if necessary.
	If you decided to apply to a school under its early action or early decision plan, send in your application, transcript, and test scores.
November	Some early decision or early action applications may be due this month.
	Take any remaining SAT II Subject Tests.
	Obtain the Federal Application for Student Aid (FAFSA) and begin filling it out.
	Check with your guidance counselor to find out if a separate application is required to apply for state financial aid.
December	Early decision and early actions answers start coming in.
	Submit applications to the colleges where you're applying under the regular decision plan.
January	Mail in the FAFSA as soon after January 1 as possible (you can't submit it before January 1).
	Request that the transcript of your first-semester senior grades is sent to the colleges where you've applied.
	Concentrate on applying for outside scholarships while you wait to hear from the colleges.
February	Double-check that the colleges received all of your application materials and financial aid forms.
	Review the Student Aid Report (SAR) and correct any errors.
	Submit the SAR to all the colleges where you applied.

When	What to Do
Senior Year (cont.)	
March	Begin preparing for any AP exams that you plan to take.
April	College acceptances and financial aid decisions start to arrive; review all packages thoroughly.
	Contact financial aid officers with additional questions.
	Visit the campuses of the schools that accepted you if you're having problems making up your mind.
	Decide where you're going to go (the last date to make your decision is May 1)!
	Notify the colleges that you didn't choose.
May	Take any remaining AP exams.
	Follow up with the housing and financial aid offices at the college of your choice.
	Request that your high school send your final transcript to your chosen college.
	Send thank-you notes to teachers and counselors who made recommendations for you and to anyone else who helped you get in.
	Create a college budget and begin applying for additional student loans, if necessary.
Summer	Attend freshman orientation and start packing!

Watch Out!
Colleges always reject students found to have cheated on their essays or embellished their records on the application forms, and they usually notify the other schools where the student applied.

Timesaver
While the Common Application is the most "common" of the generic application forms, other groups of schools also use universal applications—you complete one copy and submit it to as many schools in the group as you like.

Watch Out!
Before you submit any application, proofread it carefully and check that you've filled out every blank and that you followed all the directions exactly. If Mom or Dad wants to help, they can proofread behind you—they might just catch something you missed.

The electronic application also arrives at the school faster and is often processed more quickly. You'll still have to mail in the application fee, though, as well as provide paper copies of your transcript and recommendations (but you'll save quite a bit in postage).

Electronic Application Services

A large number of colleges participate in electronic application services, offered by several different commercial websites. Many of these services, including CollegeEdge and CollegeLink, also allow you to complete and submit the Common Application over the Internet.

These services transfer the information that you enter into the computer to the application forms of the schools that you specify, and then forward the applications electronically or provide printouts that you can mail in, depending on the college's preferences. All of these services use standard Internet security measures to protect your private information. Best of all, most of these services are free!

Table 4.2 lists the most popular of these electronic application services.

Colleges That Accept Electronic Applications

More and more colleges now welcome electronic applications. Most will send the application form to you on a floppy disk if you request it. You can also fill out electronic applications on the school's website and submit them over the Internet, saving both time and postage. Some schools even let you pay the application fee over the Internet using a credit card.

Appendix E contains a directory that lists most of the colleges and universities that enable you to fill out and submit applications over the Internet, along with the Web addresses of their electronic applications. This list excludes schools that solely accept the electronic version of the Common Application (also in Appendix E) or that accept electronic applications only via one of the services listed in Table 4.1.

Keep in mind that most schools have a separate application for graduate and undergraduate programs. Make sure you find and fill out the correct application form. For the most part, the Web addresses in the listing in Appendix E link directly to the application for full-time, undergraduate admissions. If you're a graduate school applicant, a transfer student, an international student, a nontraditional student, or if you're applying for part-time admission, check for a different application form or special instructions. You should find all the information you need in the school website's "Admissions" or "For Prospective Students" section.

What If You Don't Have a Computer?

If you don't have access to a computer or the Internet, you may be able to apply electronically through your high school guidance office, public library, or community center, using either the ExPAN service or the College Connector service.

TABLE 4.2: ELECTRONIC APPLICATION SERVICES

Service	Website	Number of Schools Supported	Special Features
Apply!	http://www.weapply.com/	500+	Download free Apply! software so you don't have to fill out applications online.
Apply Yourself	http://www.applyyourself.com/	50+	Applications are linked directly to the schools' websites and are kept confidential.
AppZap	http://www.collegeview.com/appzap/	20+	Download customized electronic applications to your computer instead of filling them out online.
CollegeEdge	http://apply.collegeedge.com/WebApps/	400+	Checks applications for accuracy and completeness before submitting them.
CollegeLink	http://www.collegelink.com/	800+	The first application is free, but each additional application costs $5, and there is a charge for postage.
CollegeNET	http://www.collegenet.com/	250+	Allows you to apply to schools in Africa, Canada, Europe, and Mexico.
CollegeQuest	http://www.collegequest.com/	1,000+	Provides college profiles and a scholarship database.
Next Stop College	http://nextstopcollege.cbreston.org/	100+	Creates a personalized "desktop" to store personal information and manage applications.
Xap	http://www.xap.com/apply_online.html	100+	Provides applications for many schools in Massachusetts, Texas, and California.

Bright Idea
If you apply using an electronic application, print out a copy for your records before submitting it. Then, you'll have a copy on file in case there's a problem with the application or if you need to resubmit it.

Timesaver
Save time by printing applications from many schools' websites, instead of requesting them through the mail. Most colleges publish their applications on the Web in PDF format, so you'll need a program called Adobe Acrobat Reader to open and print them. You can download the program at no charge from http://www.adobe.com/prodindex/acrobat/readstep.html.

Moneysaver
Online applications not only save time, but they can also save money. Many schools waive the application fee if you apply using the electronic application form. Check with the schools where you want to apply to find out if they offer this bargain.

The College Board sponsors the ExPAN service. It lets you apply to over 1000 colleges. It also includes a database of college profiles, so that you can search for schools that match your criteria, and a database of scholarships. You can use the program to create an electronic profile of your personal, academic, and extracurricular information, as well as to complete college applications. You have to enter this information only once, and then transfer it to all of the application forms and college inquiries you plan to send.

College Connector, which American College Testing (ACT) sponsors, provides applications for 600 schools. It also has a college search, so that you can quickly identify schools that fit your specific needs. You can submit college applications electronically, and you only have to type in repetitive personal, academic, and extracurricular information once. There's even an interactive tool to help you predict how much financial aid you're likely to receive.

Ask your guidance officer whether one of these options is available in your school or community.

Just the Facts

- There's a lot that you have to do to get ready for applying to college, particularly in your junior and senior years of high school. Plan ahead and use an organizational checklist to make sure you get it all done on time.

- Many colleges and universities—including the most selective of the private schools—accept a generic application form called the Common Application. If two or more of your potential schools accept the Common Application, you can save time by completing the form once, photocopying it, and sending it to each school.

- Another way to save time when filling out application forms is to use a computerized application service that inserts repeated information into each school's application. You can also submit applications faster and save yourself some postage if you take advantage of electronic applications that you can submit over the Internet.

GET THE SCOOP ON...
The difference between early decision, early action, rolling
admission, and other kinds of admission plans ▪ Choosing the
right admissions plan for you ▪ Your best strategy for meeting
and beating application deadlines

Chapter 5

Application Options—
Playing It Smart

At every step of the college admissions process, you're faced with more choices. Choosing when to apply is no exception. Depending on the schools on your "apply" list, you can choose from multiple deadlines and multiple admissions programs, including the confusing "early" application plans.

It's all too easy to get carried away at this point. You may hear rumors that you won't get admitted to your first-choice school unless you apply early or that the Ivy League schools accept the majority of their freshman classes from the early decision pool. Every day, you're faced with a new piece of information, and it often contradicts what you last heard. How can you sort it all out and make the right decision for yourself when everyone around you is pressuring you to apply right now?

This chapter will help you sort it all out. You'll learn exactly what the colleges mean when they say "early decision," "early action," and other confusing terms. You'll also find out exactly what the advantages and disadvantages to applying early are, dispelling the rumors once and for all. Armed with this information, you should easily be able to choose the right admissions plan and make sound decisions about when to apply.

Understanding Your Admissions Options

There are four general types of admissions plans for high school seniors. The one that we're all familiar with is regular admission; that's when you submit several applications at once under the normal deadlines and then bite your fingernails until April, waiting for either the fat or thin envelopes to show up in your mailbox.

Two admissions plans—early decision and early action—enable you to apply before the regular application deadline and receive an early answer in return, essentially getting the whole thing out of the way before second semester starts. The fourth option, rolling admission, doesn't even have a set deadline for applications to come in. In this section, you'll learn more about these alternative admissions plans, as well as a couple of other plans that aren't so common, so you can best decide which way to apply.

Rolling Admission

Typically, it's the big state universities and the less competitive colleges that have rolling admissions policies. Under a rolling admissions policy, the school decides whether to accept you immediately after you submit all the components of your application; there are no application deadlines. The school's admissions office keeps accepting and rejecting students until the freshman class is filled.

Generally, the admissions office mails out an acceptance or rejection notice within two to three weeks of receiving every required part of your application. If you apply in October, the admissions committee will review your application in October, and you might receive an answer before Thanksgiving. Most students apply by February of their senior year.

The advantage to rolling admissions is that you generally receive a notification very quickly after you apply. You still have until the regular notification deadline in April or May to let the school know whether you accept an offer of admission.

If you want to apply to a school with a rolling admissions policy, it's in your best interest to get your application in as early as you can. The longer you wait, the more likely that the school will run out of space. Sending your application in early will also put you in the running for the best financial aid awards and the choice housing assignments. If you get your application in early in your second semester—by March 1 at the latest—you should be safe. But don't wait. Once the application is finished, go ahead and mail it in.

Open Admission

A few schools maintain an open admission policy. These schools accept every student who applies and who has a high school degree, without regard for test scores, grade point average, or class rank. Most two-year community colleges maintain open admission policies, but some four-year schools do as well. Sometimes, open admission is limited only to in-state students, or certain programs may be excluded from the open admissions policy, such as the school's nursing program. If you don't feel that your academic record is strong enough for admittance to a selective four-year school, consider applying to one or two open-admission schools as a backup.

The following are some of the four-year colleges and universities that maintain an open admission policy:

- Franklin University (Ohio)
- Lincoln University (Missouri residents only)
- Northwestern State University (Louisiana)

- Oklahoma Panhandle State University

- Shawnee State University (Ohio)

- Southeastern Louisiana University

- University of the District of Columbia

- University of Houston—Downtown

- Wichita State University (Kansas residents only)

Deferred Admission

Under a deferred admission plan, you apply to college following the normal deadlines and find out whether you were accepted in the spring along with everybody else. But you don't *start* college until up to a year after you apply. Most colleges and universities give high school senior applicants the option of deferring admission, although you may have to submit a separate special request to the admissions office to be considered for deferred admission.

Deferred admission is intended for students who can't start college right out of high school because of financial or personal reasons. For example, you may need to take a year off to work in order to pay for college, or you may have a medical problem that you need to address before you can start college. Or you may take the time off to take advantage of a special opportunity, such as travel abroad, a volunteer service program, or a special project. The one thing you can't do during your period of deferment is apply to or attend any other colleges.

Usually, you must explain your reasons for applying for deferment and provide proof of your situation in order to be considered for deferred admission. You will also be required to submit a nonrefundable "commitment deposit," to assure the college that you will enroll after your deferment period. Many schools don't guarantee housing and financial aid for students who defer admission.

Most colleges and universities offer deferment periods of one semester or one year, but deferment periods vary greatly from school to school. Where some schools may allow only a one-month deferment, others allow you to defer enrollment indefinitely. If you're interested in this enrollment option, ask an admissions officer about the deferment policies of the schools to which you're applying.

Early Admission or Early Entrance

Colleges have a variety of "early" plans, and every school may have its own way of defining and naming its processes. It's important that you understand the differences between all of the "early" plans, so that you don't inadvertently apply under the wrong plan. You learn about early decision and early action plans later in this chapter; this section discusses one more kind of "early" application plan—early admission or early entrance (the term varies depending on the school).

Unofficially...
If you are in an accelerated high school program where you graduate from high school in three years and then apply to college, you will be considered a candidate for regular admission, not early admission.

Only a very small percentage of college applicants apply for early admission/early entrance. These plans are aimed at students who want to enter college immediately after completing their junior year in high school. Students accepted under an early admission/early entrance plan receive their high school diplomas during their first year at college.

Generally, the academic and test score requirements for early admission/early entrance plans are stringent, and only the most exceptional and mature students qualify. The interview usually plays a much more important part in deciding whether the applicant is admitted, because admissions officers use the interview to determine whether the candidate is mature enough to start college early. Often, letters from your high school principal and guidance counselor that strongly support your candidacy are also required. A written statement from your parents indicating their approval may also be required.

Almost every four-year college and university has some kind of early admission program, but very few students are admitted under these programs each year.

Early Action

Under an early action admission plan, you apply to one school early (usually by December 1) and receive an answer early, generally by January or February. But—and this is an important point—you don't have to say "yes" or "no" until the regular deadline. You can still apply to several other colleges via regular admission, and you can compare offers and financial aid packages from all the schools where you apply.

Watch Out!
Not all schools use the same terminology to describe their early application plans. Some schools offer both early decision and early action plans, and some offer different versions of early decision plans. It's important to completely understand your options *before* you apply. Carefully read the school's description of its application processes. Contact an admissions officer if you have any questions at all.

Early action plans offer some obvious advantages to the student. While you get the security of knowing early in the year whether your favorite school accepted you, you can still compare offers from several schools and take a longer time to make your final decision. If you decide to apply early action at your favorite college, be sure to read the fine print carefully first. Every early action plan is slightly different, and some colleges who accept you under an early action plan may require a firm commitment or a non-refundable deposit before the spring.

Considerably fewer schools offer early action plans. For instance, Harvard and Brown are the only two Ivy League schools with an early action plan. Table 5.1 lists other colleges and universities that let you apply early action (note that this is not a complete list).

Early Decision

Applying early decision is much more restrictive than any other "early" plan. You can apply to only one college or university as an early decision applicant, and you apply by early November of your senior year. By December—January at the latest—you'll know if you're in. If you are accepted, and if the financial aid package is sufficient, you are obligated to enroll. If the school doesn't accept you as an early decision candidate, it can defer your application to the pool of regular applications, or it can reject you outright.

TABLE 5.1: COLLEGES THAT HAVE EARLY ACTION PLANS

School	Application Deadline	Notification Deadline
Bard College	December 1	February 1
Birmingham-Southern College	December 1	December 15
Boston College	October 1	December 25
Butler University	December 1	January 15
California Institute of Technology	November 1	December 20
Colorado College	November 15	December 31
DePaul University	December 1	December 31
Furman University	December 1	January 1
Georgetown University	November 1	December 15
Massachusetts Institute of Technology	November 1	December 20
Pepperdine University	November 15	December 15
Pitzer College	November 1	December 1
Spelman College	November 15	December 30
Southern Methodist University	November 1	December 30
Texas A&M University	December 4	January 31
Tulane University	November 1	December 15
United States Military Academy	December 1	January 15
University of Chicago	November 15	December 15
University of North Carolina at Chapel Hill	October 15	December 5
University of Notre Dame	November 1	December 20
Villanova University	December 1	January 1
Virginia Tech	November 1	December 15
Willamette University	December 1	January 15

Moneysaver
If you decide to apply early to any school, be sure to get your financial aid applications in as early as possible. See Chapter 13, "How Financial Aid Works," for more information about applying for financial aid.

There are two varieties of the early decision plan. The most common is the first-choice plan. Under this plan, you apply early decision to one school and apply regular decision to all the other schools on your final list; if the school where you applied early decision accepts you, and if the financial aid award is adequate, then you must withdraw all of the pending applications.

If you apply under this plan, it's a very good idea to go ahead and send in applications to all the other colleges on your final list under their regular admission plans, despite the possibility of having to withdraw those applications later if you are accepted early decision. That's a whole lot easier to do than scrambling to get applications in before the final deadlines if the school where you applied early decision rejects you or defers you into the regular admission pool.

The second type of early decision plan is the single-choice plan. Under this plan, you cannot apply to any other schools other than the one where you applied early decision. If the school doesn't accept you as an early decision candidate, then you can apply to the other colleges on your list under their regular admissions plans. Your application at the early decision school will be deferred into the regular admission pool, as well, and reconsidered without bias.

Applying to a school that follows the single-choice plan can put you at a big disadvantage, because if you are deferred, you'll have to scramble to submit the applications to the other schools on your list on time. On the other hand, the notification date is often much earlier than at schools with the first-choice plan, so you won't be left in the dark too long. My advice to you is to have those applications ready to mail out the second you receive the letter from the school where you applied early decision, just in case.

The single-choice plan is very uncommon—only a handful of schools employ it. So, it's unlikely that any college where you'd like to apply early decision has such a plan. Nevertheless, it's vitally important that you check all of the requirements and conditions of the early decision admissions plan at your favorite school before you decide to apply early.

To make it even more confusing, some schools offer two early decision deadlines—one slightly earlier than the second. For example, at Drew University you can apply by December 1 and get an answer by December 24, or you can apply by January 15 and get an answer by February 15. Smith College, Sarah Lawrence College, and Swarthmore College also have two sets of early decision deadlines and notification dates. The advantage for you is that you can wait a little longer before deciding if you want to apply early decision to your first-pick school. But keep in mind that even if you wait until the second date to apply, you are still legally obligated to attend that school if you are accepted.

Approximately 300 colleges and universities offer an early decision admissions plan. Table 5.2 lists several schools with early decision plans, including the application deadlines, the date the school notifies early decision applications whether they have been accepted, and the average

TABLE 5.2: COLLEGES AND UNIVERSITIES WITH EARLY DECISION PLANS

School	Application Deadline	Number of Early Decision Applicants	Percentage of Applicants Admitted
California State University at Sacramento	Nov. 30	2300	67%
California University of Pennsylvania	Nov. 1	520	94%
College of William and Mary	Nov. 1	619	68%
Columbia University	Nov. 1	890	41%
Cornell University	Nov. 10	2198	39%
Dartmouth College	Nov. 1	1317	30%
DePaul University	Nov. 15	2400	63%
Duke University	Nov. 1	1228	39%
Emory University	Nov. 1	514	66%
Flagler College	Jan. 15	568	72%
Furman University	Dec. 1	601	80%
Grove City College	Nov. 15	704	46%
Ithaca College	Nov. 1	659	42%
Miami University	Nov. 1	868	71%
Middlebury College	Nov. 15	629	32%
New York University	Nov. 15	1837	38%

TABLE 5.2: COLLEGES AND UNIVERSITIES WITH EARLY DECISION PLANS (CONT.)

School	Application Deadline	Number of Early Decision Applicants	Percentage of Applicants Admitted
Northwestern University	Nov. 1	833	45%
Pepperdine University	Nov. 15	614	66%
Princeton University	Nov. 1	1455	38%
Rochester Institute of Technology	Dec. 1	727	72%
Syracuse University	Nov. 15	504	77%
Tufts University	Nov. 15	939	48%
University of Delaware	Nov. 15	800	59%
University of Miami	Nov. 15	650	54%
University of Pennsylvania	Nov. 1	1828	51%
University of Virginia	Nov. 1	2297	34%
Virginia Tech	Nov. 1	1340	59%
Wake Forest University	Nov. 15	574	37%
Washington University in St. Louis	Nov. 15 and Jan. 1	571	53%
Wesleyan University	Nov. 15 and Jan. 1	571	53%
Yale University	Nov. 1	1262	37%

percentage of early decision applicants who are accepted. This should give you a good idea of how many students are accepted by selective schools under their early decision plans. (Note that this table is not a complete listing of schools that offer early decision plans.)

Choosing the *Right* Option

Applying early has become quite a fad in recent years, mostly due to the largely exaggerated idea that getting your application in early gives you an advantage over the applicants in the regular admission pool. When you're just sitting down to fill out several application forms and the entire application process looms before you, applying early may seem like a great idea. All your friends may be applying early decision or early action. Your parents may also pressure you to apply early. But before you decide whether to apply early decision or early action, you should understand exactly how these admissions plans work and the numerous disadvantages that they may pose to you.

Advantages of Applying Early

Early decision plans primarily benefit the school, rather than the applicant. For the most part, the applicants who apply early decision are the top candidates, the ones with the stellar grades and the highest standardized test scores. So, the most selective schools get a commitment from top-notch students early in the year, rather than waiting for the normal deadline. The schools also have to read fewer applications, because early decision acceptances take students off the college market who might otherwise have applied to several schools.

Early decision plans hold some advantages for the applicant, as well. If you get accepted, you'll usually find out before Christmas, taking the pressure off you for the rest of the school year. Knowing where you're going early also makes it easier to make financial decisions and to plan for the move. And you'll save the time and expense of submitting several college applications.

Some schools—but certainly not all—favor early decision applicants over regular admission applicants. These schools want to lock in as many candidates as possible during the early rounds. Typically, the less selective schools are the ones where an early decision application will increase your chances for admission. For example, Union College (NY), Dickinson College, and Franklin & Marshall all favor early decision applicants. Many high school guidance counselors know which schools look favorably upon early applicants.

At some schools, you may receive special perks for applying early and getting accepted. For instance, at Greensboro College, students accepted under the early action plan are given the best financial aid deals, they are invited to the earliest orientation programs, and they receive first choice

Bright Idea
Discuss your plans to apply early decision or early action with your guidance counselor *before* applying. Counselors have a lot of experience with different admissions plans, so they can give you good advice and warn you about the pitfalls.

Watch Out!
Before deciding to apply early, check the school's early application standards and make sure that you're not shooting yourself in the foot. Find out whether the school rejects early applicants outright or defers them into the regular pool and whether the school sets higher standards for early applicants.

Bright Idea
Some guidance counselors recommend enclosing a cover letter with your early application stating that the school is your first choice and why. The admissions committee may look more favorably on your application if they know that you have strongly committed to attending the school.

when it comes to residence hall rooms. At Franklin & Marshall, early decision applicants receive a discount in their first year's tuition and assurance they will receive full financial aid to meet their demonstrated need. It's in your best interests to check the early decision policies at your favorite schools to determine if applying early will put you at an advantage over the candidates who apply regular admission.

Disadvantages of Applying Early

Applying early can have significant disadvantages. The biggest is that applying early decision makes it nearly impossible to weigh financial aid offers among a variety of schools. Many schools see early decision applicants as motivated buyers, so they won't offer as much financial aid to an early decision applicant as they would to a top-notch student who they have to convince to attend. Financial aid set aside for members of minority groups also tends to be more generous for applicants accepted out of the regular admission pool. If you are counting on substantial financial aid to pay for college, you're much better off applying regular decision (unless your top choice is one of those few schools that promises to meet all the financial need of early applicants, like Franklin & Marshall).

Applying early decision also represents a serious commitment on the student's part. Many students don't understand when they apply early decision that they have committed to attending the school if they are accepted. In fact, most schools make you sign a legally binding contract to the effect that if accepted early, and if the financial aid award is adequate, you agree to attend that school. The only "out" you have is if you can prove that the financial aid package offered by the school does not meet your financial need and that attending the school would thus be a financial burden.

Some students think that they have a better chance of getting in if they apply early decision, because the acceptance rate of early decision applicants is usually higher than that for regular admission applicants. For example, at the University of Pennsylvania, the acceptance rate of early decision applicants is one-and-a-half times higher than that for regular admission applicants. But at most selective schools, the typical early decision candidate is much stronger than the typical regular admission candidate. Most legacies and students from private high schools also apply early decision. So, getting accepted when you apply early may actually be *harder*, because you're competing against better-qualified candidates, on average.

Applying early is definitely not a good idea if you're relying on your performance during your senior year to get into the better colleges. When making the decision to apply early, ask yourself if your application will look significantly better in January than it does now. Keep in mind that the extra time you'll get under a regular admission plan gives you more time to craft your application package, secure teacher recommendations, polish your essays, improve your GPA, and make yourself a more attractive applicant.

Finally, you need to be prepared to deal with an outright rejection early in your college application process. If the school does not accept you as an early decision candidate, they may defer you to the regular admission pool. However, they also may reject you outright. Receiving a single "no" in December, right before the holidays, can be downright depressing. On the other hand, if a college rejects you in April, it's usually balanced out by several "yes" responses.

When Should You Apply Early?

If you're absolutely certain of where you want to go to college—if one school is way ahead of the rest of the pack in your mind—then applying early is the best option. You get to find out quickly if your top choice wants you, and your early application demonstrates to the school how committed you are to going there.

If your first-pick school offers an early action plan, applying early isn't nearly as risky as it is under the typical early decision plan. If you're accepted, you've got an automatic safety school, but your choices aren't limited to that one school. You can still apply to as many other schools as you like and compare different financial aid packages.

Despite the temptation to apply early action, go this route only if the school where you're applying is clearly your first choice. Even though you're not obligated to attend the school if accepted, by applying early action you send the school a clear message that you have committed to going there.

Remember, no college or university completely fills its entire freshman class with early applicants. If you're a qualified applicant, you can still easily get admitted during regular admission.

Meeting and Beating Deadlines: What Your Strategy Should Be

Whether you decide to apply early decision, early action, or regular admission, try to beat the application deadline if you can. Keep in mind that most of your competitors wait until the final deadline to send in their applications, so getting your application in early makes a good impression at the admissions office and sends the message that you care about attending the school. Being early might even earn your application a more careful reading, since it won't go into the pile with hundreds of other applications that came in just under the wire. Many schools award financial aid on a "first come, first served" basis, so applying well before the final deadline may earn you a larger aid package. Also, being early gives you time to supply a missing document if the school didn't receive something.

On the other hand, you don't want to be *too* early. At the start of the admissions season, admissions committees are still determining the yardstick by which they'll measure candidates that year. They may also still be trying to get a sense of the applicant pool, since it varies from year to year. Therefore, the admissions committee often judges the first applications more stringently than applications that come in later, when there's a stronger basis of comparison among more applicants. Also, the admissions

Watch Out!
If you're accepted as an early decision candidate, avoid the all-too-common trap of "senioritis"—that tendency to slack off during second semester because you know you've already been accepted to college. Colleges have been known to rescind their early decision offers if a student's grades drop too drastically.

Unofficially...
A recent survey showed that when students ranked their college choices in October and again in April, the results were completely different; so, even if you think that you couldn't possibly change your mind about your first-choice school, you might.

Watch Out!
If you stay organized and start filling out college applications early, you shouldn't have to worry about missing any deadlines. But sometimes, you can't avoid a delay. If that's the case, plan to mail your application at least a week before the due date to ensure it reaches the admissions office on time. Applications that arrive in the admissions office after the final deadline may not be read at all.

Timesaver
Of course, every school has a different due date for applications. The more selective schools tend to have earlier application deadlines. Keep a chart on when applications are due at each school where you're applying, and adjust your strategy accordingly. You'll find a helpful organizational chart in Chapter 7, "Creating an Exceptional Application Package."

committee may be less likely to give you the benefit of the doubt if your qualifications aren't stellar. But at the end of the admissions season, the committee may be trying to fill empty class slots, and they'll have a better idea of what kinds of candidates they need to create a well rounded, diverse freshman class.

Your best strategy is to objectively evaluate your academic and extracurricular achievements and compare them against the typical applicant at the schools where you're applying. At some schools, you will likely be a very strong applicant, while at others, your chances for admission may be iffy. Plan to complete and submit applications to the schools where you are the strongest candidate first. Then, turn your attention to the mid-range schools on your list. Finally, send in the applications to your "reach" schools.

In every case, try to mail your application four to six weeks before the final due date. Try to time your applications to arrive at the middle of the admissions season. By then, the admissions committee has a good sense of what the applicant pool is like and is making consistent evaluations, but many open spaces are still available.

Obviously, this plan doesn't apply to schools with rolling admissions policies. These schools are often less competitive and have a set standard against which they measure applicants, which doesn't vary much from year to year. In those cases, go ahead and get your applications in as soon as possible, to ensure that space in the freshman class is still available. (Chances are, these applications will also be the easiest to complete, requiring fewer essays and extra materials).

Many schools with rolling admissions plans have a priority filing deadline. If you get your application in before the priority deadline—usually sometime in February or March 1 at the latest—you'll receive priority consideration for housing, financial aid, and scholarships if you're accepted. Although it's in your best interest to get your application in as early as possible, treat the priority deadline as the absolute last day to turn in your application.

Remember that the guidelines given in this section are simply that— guidelines. There are no hard and fast rules when it comes to deciding when to apply. Your first priority should be to prepare the best application that you can, even if that means delaying mailing in your application until closer to the final deadline.

Just the Facts

- Most colleges and universities offer multiple admission plans; but just because you have the choice of applying early decision or early action doesn't mean that you should.

- The disadvantages of applying early often outnumber the advantages; unless you're completely certain of your first-choice college and that you are an outstanding applicant for that school, you're better off waiting until regular admission to apply.

▪ Even if you choose not to apply early decision or early action, that doesn't mean you should wait until the day of the deadline to send in your application; mailing your application a few weeks before the deadline will probably earn a more careful reading and more thoughtful consideration.

GET THE SCOOP ON...
How to apply to American colleges and universities ▪ The test
requirements for foreign applicants ▪ How to obtain a student visa ▪
How to pay for college in the US ▪ Deciding whether to take an
intensive English program before starting your studies ▪ Dealing
with culture shock and homesickness ▪ Organizations and resources
that provide additional help

Application Tips for International Students

Chapter 6

In increasing numbers, students in foreign countries have ambitions to earn a college degree in the United States. Today, more than 400,000 non-US residents from almost every country in the world attend American colleges and universities. If you'd like to be one of those students, there's a lot you need to know about applying to and getting admitted to an American college.

The good news is that attending an American college or university may not be as difficult as you think. The US educational community values a diverse student body from a variety of backgrounds, and consequently, many American universities actively recruit international students. Even if you fear that your finances or command of English aren't adequate, there may be American colleges and universities that can accommodate you. And once you arrive, you're likely to find a long-established support network that will help you adjust to living and studying in a new culture.

Many parts of the college application process will be unfamiliar to you. For example, the most common US pre-college standardized tests—the SAT I and the ACT—aren't given to overseas students. But the process of selecting and getting admitted to a school that's right for *you* is the same as for any student, so you'll find value in every part of this book. You may find the glossary at the back of the book particularly helpful for understanding terms related to applying to college and financial aid (see Appendix A, "Glossary").

How to Apply to College in the United States

It's important that you start the college search and application process as early as possible, in case you must submit additional materials or complete

Moneysaver
Using the Internet will save a lot of money on airmail charges and long-distance telephone calls. You can research schools on the Web and then use e-mail to address questions to admissions officers. You may even be able to speed up the application process by submitting application materials electronically.

Bright Idea
You might feel right at home in an American city with a large ethnic community. For instance, Los Angeles has the largest Korean and Chinese communities in the US. It also has some very prestigious universities, including UCLA and the University of Southern California.

steps not required of American applicants. Because you have to send materials through the international postal system, the application process will take longer. I recommend that you start searching for the colleges where you want to apply 18–24 months before you plan to enter the academic program.

Choosing Where to Apply

Consider a wide range of schools. Don't just look at the universities that are well known internationally; these schools are highly competitive, and unless you are an exceptional candidate, your chances of being admitted are slim. There are over 3000 four-year colleges and universities in the United States, and a large number of them offer an excellent education. Use the techniques outlined in Chapter 1, "Choosing the Right College," to narrow your choices and select schools where you will be happy.

You need to be aware of one important difference between US universities and international universities. In the US, the government does not monitor the quality of institutes of higher learning. Instead, the U.S. Department of Education approves accrediting agencies, which review a school's academic program and certify that the program meets a minimum number of standards. It's important that you consider only accredited schools, since nonaccredited schools are likely to be of a lower quality. College guides and college search programs on the Internet should list the agencies that accredit each college and university in the guide.

When you research schools, find out the number of international students attending them. Colleges with a large number of international students are likely to have programs and services in place to help support those students.

So, which American colleges and universities are foreign students attending? Table 6.1 lists schools that have a large international student body from a wide number of countries.

TABLE 6.1: US COLLEGES AND UNIVERSITIES WITH LARGE NUMBERS OF INTERNATIONAL STUDENTS

School	Location	Most Represented Countries
American University	Washington, D.C.	Brazil, El Salvador, Japan, Saudi Arabia, South Korea, Spain
Andrews University	Berrien Springs, Michigan	Canada, Japan, Kenya, Korea, Malaysia, Taiwan
Arizona State University	Tempe, Arizona	Canada, Germany, Indonesia, Japan, Korea, Taiwan
Beloit College	Beloit, Wisconsin	Bahamas, Hungary, India, Indonesia, Japan, Malaysia
Bennington College	Bennington, Vermont	China, India, Pakistan, Nepal, United Kingdom, the former Yugoslavia

School	Location	Most Represented Countries
Bethany College	Bethany, West Virginia	Canada, Gambia, Germany, India, Sri Lanka, United Kingdom
Boston Univesity	Boston, Massachusetts	Brazil, China, Greece, India, Japan, United Kingdom
Brigham Young University	Provo, Utah	Brazil, Canada, China, Japan, Korea, Mexico
Bryn Mawr College	Bryn Mawr, Pennsylvania	India, Korea, Mexico, Pakistan, Philippines, Turkey
California Institute of Technology	Pasadena, California	Bulgaria, Canada, China, Romania, Singapore, the former Yugoslavia
California State University at Los Angeles	Los Angeles, California	China, El Salvador, Mexico, North Vietnam, Philippines, Taiwan
Carnegie Mellon University	Pittsburgh, Pennsylvania	China, India, Japan, South Korea, Taiwan, Turkey
City University of New York—Queens College	Flushing, New York	China, Columbia, Dominican Republic, Guyana, India, Russia
Clark University Massachusetts	Worcester,	China, India, Japan, Pakistan, Thailand, Turkey
College of Wooster	Wooster, Ohio	China, India, Malaysia, Pakistan, Sweden
Columbia University	New York, New York	Canada, China, France, Hong Kong, Taiwan, United Kingdom
Cornell University	Ithaca, New York	Bulgaria, China, India, Singapore, Switzerland, United Kingdom
Dartmouth College	Hanover, New Hampshire	Canada, China, India, Pakistan, South Korea, United Kingdom
Drexel University	Philadelphia, Pennsylvania	China, India, Japan, Malaysia, South Korea, Taiwan
Eckerd College	St. Petersburg, Florida	Brazil, India, Japan, Turkey, United Arab Emirates, Venezuela
Florida Institute of Technology	Melbourne, Florida	Barbados, France, India, Japan, Kuwait, United Kingdom
Georgetown University	Washington, D.C.	China, Germany, Japan, Korea, Mexico, United Kingdom
George Washington University	Washington, D.C.	Japan, Korea, Malaysia, Saudi Arabia, Turkey, United Arab Emirates
Grinnell College	Grinnell, Iowa	Bulgaria, China, India, Nepal, South Africa, South Korea

TABLE 6.1: US COLLEGES AND UNIVERSITIES WITH
LARGE NUMBERS OF INTERNATIONAL STUDENTS (CONT.)

School	Location	Most Represented Countries
Harvard University	Cambridge, Massachusetts	Canada, China, Germany, Poland, South Korea, United Kingdom
Howard University	Washington, D.C.	Bahamas, Bermuda, Canada, Jamaica, Nigeria, Trinidad/Tobago
Illinois Institute of Technology	Chicago, Illinois	China, Germany, India, South Korea, Taiwan, Thailand
Iowa State University	Ames, Iowa	China, India, Indonesia, Malaysia, South Korea, Taiwan
Knox College	Galesburg, Illinois	Bulgaria, Ghana, India, Japan, Thailand, Turkey
Macalester College	St. Paul, Minnesota	Cyprus, Jamaica, Japan, Sweden, Turkey, United Kingdom
Massachusetts Institute of Technology	Cambridge, Massachusetts	Canada, China, India, Japan, Korea, Mexico
Michigan State University	East Lansing, Michigan	Canada, Indonesia, Japan, Malaysia, South Korea, Taiwan
Middlebury College	Middlebury, Vermont	Canada, China, Germany, India, Jamaica, United Kingdom
Mount Holyoke College	South Hadley, Massachusetts	Bulgaria, China, India, Japan, Malaysia, Turkey
Northeastern University	Boston, Massachusetts	Canada, China, India, Indonesia, Japan, Turkey
Ohio State University	Columbus, Ohio	China, India, Indonesia, Japan, Korea, Taiwan
Ohio Wesleyan University	Delaware, Ohio	Bangladesh, Cyprus, India, Japan, Nepal, Pakistan
Pepperdine University	Malibu, California	Hong Kong, Indonesia, Japan, Mexico, United Arab Emirates, United Kingdom
Purdue University	West Lafayette, Indiana	India, Indonesia, Malaysia, Pakistan, South Korea, Turkey
Smith College	Northampton, Massachusetts	Canada, India, Japan, Pakistan, Singapore, South Korea
Southern Illinois University at Carbondale	Carbondale, Illinois	China, India, Japan, Malaysia, South Korea, Taiwan
St. Andrews Presbyterian College	Laurinburg, North Carolina	Canada, Costa Rica, Japan, Kenya, United Kingdom, Zimbabwe
Stanford University	Stanford, California	Canada, China, India, Japan, Korea, Singapore

School	Location	Most Represented Countries
Stevens Institute of Technology	Hoboken, New Jersey	Greece, India, Malaysia, Spain, Turkey, Zambia
Texas A&M University	College Station, Texas	China, India, Korea, Mexico, Taiwan
Tufts University	Medford, Massachusetts	Brazil, Canada, Greece, India, Japan, Korea
United States International University	San Diego, California	Indonesia, Japan, Korea, Taiwan, Thailand, Turkey
University of Denver	Denver, Colorado	Canada, Indonesia, Japan, Korea, Malaysia
University of the District of Columbia	Washington, D.C.	Cameroon, Ethiopia, Gambia, Kenya, Nigeria, Trinidad/Tobago
University of Georgia	Athens, Georgia	Canada, China, India, Japan, Korea, Taiwan
University of Houston	Houston, Texas	Hong Kong, India, Indonesia, Nigeria, Pakistan, Taiwan
University of Illinois at Urbana-Champaign	Urbana, Illinois	China, India, Japan, Korea, Taiwan, Thailand
University of Maryland	College Park, Maryland	India, Korea, Russia, Taiwan, Vietnam
University of Miami	Miami, Florida	Brazil, China, Colombia, India, Spain, Venezuela
University of Michigan	Ann Arbor, Michigan	China, India, Indonesia, Malaysia, Singapore, South Korea
University of Oregon	Eugene, Oregon	China, Indonesia, Japan, Korea, Malaysia, Taiwan
University of Pennsylvania	Philadelphia, Pennsylvania	Canada, Hong Kong, India, Korea, Singapore, Taiwan
University of San Francisco	San Francisco, California	China, Hong Kong, Indonesia, Japan, Korea, Taiwan
University of Southern California	Los Angeles, California	Canada, Hong Kong, Japan, Korea, Singapore, Taiwan
University of Texas	Austin, Texas	China, India, Indonesia, Korea, Mexico, Taiwan
University of Tulsa	Tulsa, Oklahoma	Angola, India, Malaysia, Saudi Arabia, United Arab Emirates, Venezuela
University of Wisconsin	Madison, Wisconsin	China, Hong Kong, Indonesia, Korea, Malaysia, Singapore
Washington College	Chestertown, Maryland	Bulgaria, India, Jamaica, Japan, Spain, Sri Lanka

Timesaver
Educational fairs
give you a valuable
opportunity to speak
directly to represen-
tatives of US univer-
sities and to get
brochures and appli-
cations. Watch for
American educational
fairs taking place in
major cities in your
country.

To get online information on these and other American colleges, visit the CollegeEdge website at http://www.collegeedge.com/. There, you can search through a large database of over 5,000 American schools to find those with the academic requirements and international student population that you want. You can also get direct access to every school's website from the CollegeEdge listings.

Getting Started

Start corresponding with the schools where you decided to apply at least one year in advance of the final application deadline. Because competition among international students for admittance to American schools is keen, I recommend that you apply to a large number of schools—between 8 and 15. If you plan to enter a highly competitive field like business, engineering, or computer science, definitely apply to a wide range of colleges.

To get started, contact the admissions office at the schools where you want to apply and find out what application materials international applicants must submit. Any good college guide will supply the admissions office mailing address and phone number (see Appendix C, "Recommended Reading," for some suggestions). If you have Internet access, it's best to connect directly to the college's website and find the contact information. Send all correspondence by airmail, and mail materials as far before the final deadlines as possible.

Some schools, such as the Massachusetts Institute of Technology, Yale University, and Amherst College, require international students to submit a preliminary application. The admissions officer uses this application to determine if you are compatible with the school. If the school requires a preliminary application, it will include one in the package of school information and application materials it sends to you. If the admissions officer feels that you are compatible with the school based on your preliminary application, you'll receive the final application, so return the preliminary application as quickly as possible to expedite the process.

Admission Requirements

Each college sets its own standards for admission—some schools are very selective and others are not. However, international students always face strong competition, because American colleges reserve a limited number of openings for international students. To gain admittance to an American school, you need a strong academic background, proficiency in the English language, and sufficient financial resources.

In general, the educational preparation required to attend a university in your own country will adequately prepare you for attending an American college or university. As a minimum standard, most American colleges require that applicants have completed 12 years of education, including the minimum course requirements outlined in Table 6.2. Some schools have more stringent entrance requirements, and you will be at a great advantage if you have taken courses that go well beyond the minimum requirements.

TABLE 6.2: MINIMUM HIGH SCHOOL COURSES REQUIRED FOR COLLEGE PREPARATION

Type of Course	Minimum Number of Years
English (grammar, writing, and literature)	4 years
Mathematics	2 years
Laboratory science (biology, chemistry, or physics)	2 years
Foreign language	2 years
History/social studies	2 years
Visual/performing arts	1 year
Electives	1 year

The American schools to which you apply will require that you submit your school report and a transcript of your academic record. The official in your school who is responsible for college placement should complete the school report form. The transcript should reflect your academic records for the past three or four years of school. Ask your school to include a guide with the transcript that explains the grading standards and ranking methods your school uses. If your academic records aren't in English, make sure that you send officially certified, literal English translations of all documents along with the official documents in the original language.

Other Parts of the Application

The college application often requests personal information—information about yourself, your abilities, goals, talents, and the reasons you want to attend that particular college. Most American colleges and universities seek the cultural and academic diversity that international students bring to the student population. As an international student, you will bring a unique experience to the school, so stress this in your application.

You may have to submit one or more letters of recommendation from your teachers. You may also have to write an essay on a specified topic. You'll find valuable information in Part III, "Put Together Your Application Package," about completing these application requirements. You will also need to include an application fee (in American currency), which covers the costs of processing your application.

There may be additional requirements as well, depending on the schools where you're applying and your home country. Most colleges require a certified Affidavit of Support from a bank proving that you have sufficient funds to pay the tuition and your living expenses (you'll learn more about financial aid available to international students later in this chapter). You may also need a physical exam form certified in English by a medical doctor. Check with each college to make certain that you understand exactly what documentation is required.

Timesaver
Many colleges will send you a school report form along with the application form for you to give to the official at your school responsible for college placement. If the official has questions, he or she can contact the admissions officer who recruits international students—this person's name and contact information is usually included with the application materials.

Bright Idea
If there's a national school-leaving certification examination at the end of secondary education in your country, such as British O- and A-Levels, have the official results sent to the colleges where you're applying. Some schools may use your scores to give you credit toward a college degree or exempt you from basic course requirements.

What You Need to Know About Test Requirements

All applicants to American colleges and universities must take standardized tests, and international applicants are no exceptions. Besides the tests required of all applicants to the college, you may also be required to take a test to demonstrate that your English speaking, comprehension, and writing skills are good enough for you to succeed at an American college. In this section, you'll learn about the different tests required by American colleges and universities, how to register for the tests, and what you can expect on test day.

Test of English as a Foreign Language

Almost all international students who apply to American colleges must take the Test of English as a Foreign Language (TOEFL) to demonstrate proficiency in English. There is no standard acceptable TOEFL score. Most colleges and universities require a minimum score between 450 and 550. A score of 600 or better is required for fields where English language proficiency is very important, such as journalism or literature, and at the more selective schools.

The Educational Testing Service (ETS) administers the TOEFL. A computerized version is given in most areas of the world, although the paper version of the test is still given in some countries in Asia. The computer-based test will completely replace the paper test by the year 2001. Taking the computer-based test costs US$100.

Don't worry if you don't have computer training or if you aren't familiar with using a computer. You won't need those skills to do well on the TOEFL. Before the test begins, you'll take several tutorials that show you how to use the computer equipment and software programs and how to answer the test questions. You also can get a copy of a TOEFL preparation book, such as ARCO's *TOEFL Test* book or the *Preparation for the TOEFL Test Kit*, that includes cassette recordings of the listening portion of the TOEFL exam (see Appendix C for more suggestions).

Schedule an appointment to take the TOEFL as soon as possible. Test centers fill up quickly, and you'll want to be sure that the colleges where you apply receive your scores in time to consider them with your application. To get started, order the appropriate Information Bulletin from ETS for the country or area in which you plan to take the test. This free publication tells you how to schedule an appointment to take the test, where testing centers are located, identification requirements, and everything else you need to know.

To order the bulletin, contact the local distribution office for your country or area:

- **Algeria, Kuwait, Oman, Qatar, Saudi Arabia, and United Arab Emirates:** AMIDEAST; Testing Programs; 1730 M St., NW, Suite 1100; Washington, D.C. 20036-4505, USA; 202-776-9600; testing@amideast.org

- **Australia, New Zealand, Papua New Guinea, Vanuatu, and the Solomon Islands:** Australian Council for Educational Research; ACER-ETS Administration Office; Private Bag 55; Camberwell, Victoria 3124, Australia; 61-3-9277-5555; aldous@acer.edu.au

- **Brazil:** Instituto Brasil-Estados Unidos (IBEU); Av. Nossa Senhora de Copacabana; 690 6th Floor; 22050-000 Rio de Janeiro, RJ, Brasil; 55-21-255-5830; mdavilla@ibeu.org.br

- **Egypt:** AMIDEAST/Cairo; 23, Mossadak Street; Dokki, Cairo, Egypt; 20-2-337-8265; egypt@amideast.org

- **Europe:** CITO-TOEFL; P.O. Box 1203; 6801 BE Arnhem, Netherlands; 31-26-32-1480; registration@cito.nl

- **Hong Kong:** Hong Kong Examinations Authority (HKEA); San Po Kong Sub-Office; 17 Tseuk Luk St.; San Po Kong; Kowloon, Hong Kong; 852-2328-0061 ext. 365

- **India and Bhutan:** Institute of Psychological and Educational Measurement (IPEM); Post Box No. 19; 119/25-A Mahatma Gandhi Marg; Allahabad, U.P. 211 001, India; 91-532-624988; ipem@nde.vsnl.net.in

- **Indonesia:** International Education Foundation (IEF); Menara Imperium, Lantai 28, Suite B; Metropolitan Kuningan Superblock Kav. 1; Jl. H.R. Rasuna Said; Jakarta Selatan 12980 Indonesia; 62-21-831-7304; ief@indo.net.id

- **Japan:** Council on International Educational Exchange; TOEFL Division; Cosmos Aoyama Bldg. B1; 5-53-67 Jinumae, Shibuya-ku; Tokyo 150-8355, Japan; 813-5467-5520; info@cieej.or.jp

- **Jordan:** AMIDEAST; P.O. Box 1249; Amman, Jordan; 962-6-286-2241; jordan@amideast.org

- **Korea:** Korean-American Educational Commission (KAEC); K.P.O. Box 643; Seoul 110-606, Korea; 822-732-7928/29; kooyh@fulbright.or.kr

- **Kuwait:** AMIDEAST; P.O. Box 44818; Hawalli 32063, Kuwait; 965-532-7794; kuwait@amideast.org

- **Lebanon:** AMIDEAST; P.O. Box 135-155; Ras Beirut, Lebanon; 961-1-345-341; lebanon@amideast.org

- **Malaysia and Singapore:** Malaysian-American Commission on Educational Exchange (MACEE); Testing Services; 8th Floor Menara John Hancock; Jalan Gelenggang; Damansara Heights; 50490 Kuala Lumpur, Malaysia; 6-03-253-8107; meena@macee.po.my

- **Mexico:** Institute of International Education (IIE); Londres No. 16, 2nd Floor; Apartado Postal 61-115; 06600 Mexico D.F., Mexico; 525-209-9100; iie@solar.sar.net

- **Morocco:** AMIDEAST; 15 rue Jabal El Ayachi Agdal; Rabat, Morocco; 212-7-67-50-81; morocco@amideast.org

Timesaver
If you have Internet access, you can order or download the Information Bulletin for your area directly from the TOEFL website at http://www.toefl.org/.

- **Pakistan:** World Learning Inc.; P.O. Box 13042; Karachi 75350, Pakistan; (92-21) 455-7166; toeflwl@digicom.net.pk

- **People's Republic of China:** China International Examinations Coordination Bureau (CIECB); 167 Haidian Rd.; Haidian District; 100080 Beijing, People's Republic of China; 86-10-6251-3994; neeaks@public.bta.net.cn

- **Puerto Rico:** Educational Testing Service; Suite 315; American International Plaza; 250 Munoz Rivera Ave.; Hato Rey, PR 00918; 787-753-6363

- **Syria:** AMIDEAST; P.O. Box 2313; Damascus, Syria; 963-11-333-4801; syria@amideast.org

- **Taiwan:** The Language Training & Testing Center (LTTC); P.O. Box 23-41; Taipei, Taiwan 106; 886-2-2362-6045; tfl@lttc.ntu.edu.tw

- **Thailand, Cambodia, and Laos:** Institute of International Education (IIE); G.P.O. Box 2050; Bangkok 10501, Thailand; 66-2-639-2700; iiethai@bkk.iie.org

- **Tunisia:** AMIDEAST; BP 351 Tunis-Cite Jardins 1002; Tunis-Belvedere, Tunisia; 216-1-790-559; tunisia@amideast.org

- **Vietnam:** Institute of International Education (IIE); City Gate Building; 104 Tran Hung Dao St.; Hanoi, Vietnam; 844-822-4093; iiehn@netnam.org.vn

- **Yemen:** AMIDEAST; P.O. Box 22347; Sana'a, Yemen; 967-1-216-975; yemen@amideast.org

Watch Out!
On the computer-based TOEFL, the questions at the beginning of the Listening and Structure sections affect your score more than the questions at the end, so focus on answering these questions correctly. The computer will determine your ability level by the number of correct answers you give to these initial questions.

- **All other countries:** TOEFL/TSE Services; PO Box 6151; Princeton, NJ 08541, USA; 1-800-468-6335; toefl@ets.org. (Allow up to eight weeks for delivery.)

The TOEFL lasts three hours and has four sections:

- *Listening:* This section measures your ability to understand English as it is spoken in the United States. You will listen to conversations and then answer questions based on those conversations.

- *Structure:* This section measures your ability to recognize standard written English. You will be given a sentence, and you will have to choose the word or phrase that best completes that sentence from the choices given.

- *Reading:* This section measures your ability to read and understand short passages. You will have to read passages and then answer questions based on what you have read.

- *Writing:* This section measures your ability to write in English. You will be given a topic on which you will have to write an essay.

Once you finish the test, your score on each section (except for the Writing section) and the range of your final overall score displays on the computer screen. You will only have the opportunity to cancel your scores *before* you view them. Once you look at your score, you may choose up to four schools to receive an official score report at no extra charge. Later, you can request that your score report be mailed to additional schools, if you want to apply to more than four schools.

Your chances for scoring well on the TOEFL will improve if you completely familiarize yourself with the content and format of the test before taking it. Also study and understand the directions for each question type.

The Information Bulletin will include some sample questions from each section of the TOEFL to help you prepare. You'll also find several sample questions, tutorials, and practice exercises on the TOEFL website (http://www.toefl.org/). If you have access to a computer, it's a good idea to order the TOEFL Sampler, a CD-ROM that simulates the actual test and contains interactive tutorials to help you prepare for the TOEFL. You can order the TOEFL Sampler and other preparation materials from your local distribution office or directly from ETS.

If your English proficiency isn't as strong as it should be, don't give up. Every school has its own requirements for English proficiency. Later in this chapter, the section "Improving Your English Once You Get Here" discusses some options that may be available to you.

The Michigan English Language Assessment Battery

A handful of American colleges and universities may require you to take the Michigan English Language Assessment Battery (MELAB) instead of the TOEFL. Many more schools will let you choose which test to take. Like the TOEFL, this test evaluates the English language competence of foreign students who want to attend college in the US. It was developed and is administered by the English Language Institute at the University of Michigan at Ann Arbor. The MELAB is given only at testing locations in the United States, Canada, and Iran.

If you are required to take the MELAB, order the free MELAB Bulletin, which enables you to register for the test and prepare by answering sample questions. To get the MELAB Bulletin and request more information about the test, write to English Language Institute, MELAB Testing, 3020 North University Building, University of Michigan, Ann Arbor, MI 48109-1057, or call 734-763-3452. You can also order the MELAB Bulletin through the MELAB website at http://www.lsa.umich.edu/eli/melab.htm.

The SAT I or ACT

Many US colleges and universities require all applicants to take either the Scholastic Aptitude Test (SAT) I or the American College Testing Assessment (ACT). The admissions officers at the universities where you're applying will tell you exactly what tests are required and what the minimum scores are for admittance.

Standardized tests may pose a problem for international applicants, because the context and format of these tests will be unfamiliar. Also, it may

Timesaver
You may not have to take the TOEFL if most of your formal schooling has been in English-speaking schools or if you completed your secondary education in an English-speaking country. Ask the admissions officers at the schools where you're applying if the TOEFL requirement can be waived for you.

be difficult to find a testing center close to where you live. If you need more information, contact either the College Board, which administers the SAT, or American College Testing, which administers the ACT. You'll find this contact information in Appendix D, "Important Addresses."

Don't get too anxious about these standardized tests. Admissions officers are aware of the difficulties they present to students outside the US or whose native language isn't English. Your academic record as a whole will be considered, and the results of any standardized tests will be placed in the proper context. Generally, greater weight is placed on the mathematics portion for international students. For more information about preparing for and doing well on the SAT I and ACT, turn to Chapter 10, "Doing Your Best on the SAT I or ACT."

ARCO, the publisher of this book, also offers study guides, such as *Master the ACT* and *Master the SAT*, to help you prepare for these standardized exams. If these guides aren't available in a bookstore near you, you can order them by telephone at 1-800-428-5331, or on our website at http://www.mgr.com/.

Bright Idea
Before leaving for the US, make a photocopy of the page in your passport that contains your photograph and passport number. If your passport is lost or stolen, it will be easier to replace.

Getting a Student Visa

Once an American college has accepted you, the school will issue you an I-20 Certificate of Eligibility. Take this form to the American Consulate in your country, along with your passport and proof that you can pay for your living and educational expenses, such as a certified Affidavit of Support from a bank. A certificate of health may also be required. A consular officer will review these documents and decide whether to issue you an F-1 Student Visa. If you have a spouse and children, the American Consulate will need to issue F-2 visas for them to accompany you to the United States.

The consular officer may request that you establish your intent to return to your home country once your studies are complete. To do this, you will have to demonstrate economic, personal, social, and cultural ties to your home country. The more proof you can provide—in the form of letters, deeds, records, and other documented sources—the better your chances of getting a student visa. Such proof can include any of the following:

- Names and addresses of close family members who are remaining at home

- Ownership of a family business

- Ownership of real estate in your own country

- Financial sponsorship of all or part of your education by your government or by a company based in your home country

- Evidence of job offers or job prospects in your home country that will take effect after receiving your degree

- The passports of siblings who studied in the United States and returned home afterward

- An explanation of why equivalent educational training is not available in your home country

Just because you've been accepted to college in the US doesn't guarantee that a student visa will be issued to you. The American Consulate must determine that your reasons for applying for the visa are genuine and that you'll return to your country once you complete your education. If your application for a student visa is rejected, contact the university that issued your I-20 right away. You can try to reapply for the student visa immediately, or you can wait until you've addressed the US consular officer's concerns before reapplying.

Once you have the visa, you can come to the US. Remember that your eligibility for opportunities like employment, transferring to a different university, or changing degree programs depends on you maintaining lawful visa status. To maintain lawful status, you must abide by the following rules:

- Remain enrolled full-time at the school you are authorized to attend (if you want to transfer to a different school, you will have to apply for admittance to the new school as a transfer student and obtain a new I-20 form from the school).

- Hold a valid, current I-20 ID.

- Maintain a passport that is valid for at least six months after the date you are supposed to complete your studies.

- Obtain the appropriate authorization for any employment that you pursue.

- Limit employment to only 20 hours per week while classes are in session.

- Don't leave the country without permission—you may not be allowed back in!

When you finish your studies, you will need to leave the US, get permission for practical training, or apply for another type of visa. If you have an F visa, you may apply to stay for up to one year of practical training in your field of study. If you can't complete your studies by the expiration date on your I-20 form, you'll have to apply to your school's international student advisor for an extension 30 days before the expiration date. Extensions are not difficult to get, so long as you haven't violated your visa status.

Paying Your Way

Attending college in the United States can be very expensive. The costs of education here tend to be greater than in other countries. The cost of living may also be higher than what you're used to. You must give a lot of thought to how you will pay for your education long before you apply. Many colleges and American Consulates require proof that you can pay for your entire period of study before you will be granted admission or a student visa. This helps prevent the all-too-common problem of international students

Watch Out!
It may be difficult for you to get a student visa if you have close relatives or financial interests in the United States, because the consular office may believe that you intend to immigrate to the US.

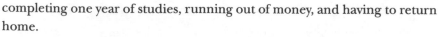

Timesaver
Devise a budget for the time you will spend attending school in the US. Plan the budget to cover the costs of your dorm room, cafeteria meals, books and supplies, miscellaneous personal and entertainment expenses, health insurance (approximately US$500 per year), and one trip home each year.

completing one year of studies, running out of money, and having to return home.

If you do need financial aid to study in the US, try first to obtain it in your own country. Your government, your parents' employers, your employer, or a religious organization may agree to sponsor you. Another source of funding is a direct exchange program between a university in your country and an American school; these programs may provide a full or partial waiver of tuition and fees. Ask your local university if such programs are available.

Private foundations and international agencies may also offer scholarships, grants, and financial aid to international students. These include the United Nations, the Organization of American States (OAS), AMIDEAST, the International Maritime Organization, the International Telecommunications Union, the League of Red Cross Societies, the Soros Foundation, the World Health Organization, and the World Council of Churches. Competition for these awards is very competitive, and many awards are limited to graduate students. Often, these scholarships require that you apply from your home country, so if you wait until after you arrive in the US to apply, you'll no longer be eligible.

If you want to seek financial assistance or scholarships from the school, you must submit the financial aid applications supplied by the school and documentation of your family's financial resources, such as a bank statement, to help the school determine your financial need. The deadline for submitting these forms may be as early as eight to nine months before classes begin, so it's important to start the process early.

Unofficially...
More than 60 percent of foreign students pay for their education themselves or with the help of their families. Another 15 percent receive financial aid from their governments.

Unfortunately, financial aid is usually very limited for international students, especially undergraduates, and it almost never covers all of your educational and living expenses. Schools are under a lot of pressure to allocate their limited financial aid funds to American students first. So, you must be prepared to pay part or all of the costs of attending college in the United States.

If financial aid is important to you, make sure that the schools where you apply offer aid to international students. Each college has a financial aid office, which can give you this information and tell you exactly how to apply for aid (your admissions officer will tell you how to get in touch with the financial aid office).

The following colleges and universities give financial aid to the most international students:

School	Number of International Students Who Receive Financial Aid Each Year
Florida International University	982
Louisiana State University and Agricultural and Mechanical College	506
California State University at Stanislaus	478

School	Number of International Students Who Receive Financial Aid Each Year
University of Nebraska at Lincoln	464
West Virginia University	450
University of Bridgeport	384
Drexel University	304
Arizona State University	298
University of Texas at Dallas	245
University of Southern Colorado	235
Massachusetts Institute of Technology	201
Illinois Institute of Technology	199
Ohio Wesleyan University	197
D'Youville College	195
Clark University	175
University of Hawaii at Manoa	170
Barry University	164
Iowa State University	164
Suffolk University	163
University of South Florida	162
Slippery Rock University of Pennsylvania	152
University of Pennsylvania	150
Michigan State University	145
University of Miami	143
Eckerd College	141
Luther College	140
Georgia Southern University	132
Florida Institute of Technology	129
Pace University	122
College of Wooster	115
Rensselaer Polytechnic Institute	115
Mercer University	110
American University	109
Smith College	104
Texas Christian University	102
Lawrence University	102

Student grants and loans from the US government are not available to foreign students. Some US governmental agencies provide funding in the form of assistantships, fellowships, and awards programs to students from specific countries. These funds are very limited, though; only two percent of all foreign students receive any funding from the US government. For more information, contact the American Consulate or U.S. Information Agency in your country.

International students with an F-1 Student Visa are permitted to work part-time on campus to help pay for tuition, but the money earned most likely won't completely cover your educational expenses, and you will still have to pay for living expenses. After you complete one year of study, you can apply for permission to work off campus. Off-campus employment requires approval by the U.S. Immigration and Naturalization Service and by the university's international student office, which isn't easy to get unless you can demonstrate special circumstances. Even if you do get permission to work off campus, the pay of a part-time job won't cover all of your expenses. And your spouse won't be allowed to work at all. So, don't expect to support yourself with a job while you study.

Finally, some commercial banks provide private loans to international students. Getting a private loan requires approval from your school's financial aid office and proof of your creditworthiness. You also must have a co-borrower, who must be a citizen or permanent resident of the US. These private student loans are very expensive. Obtain one only as a last resort.

Improving Your English Once You Get Here

Since the policies regarding English language proficiency vary from school to school, be sure to check the specific requirements of each school you're considering. If you know that your English-speaking ability is not up to acceptable standards, consider intensive study in an English as a Second Language (ESL) course before you apply. Some schools will accept students who score below the minimum required TOEFL score on the condition that those students complete an intensive English program before entering the academic program.

Even if your TOEFL score is good enough for you to be admitted, your English speaking and writing skills may still not be proficient enough for you to excel in classes at an American university. You will often have to give oral presentations and discuss materials in class, and you may have to write several papers for each class. If you need only a little help, the school's office for international student affairs or student services office can help you arrange to have a student tutor.

You may also benefit from attending an intensive English program before you start school. Generally, you take an intensive English program in the summer before you start your first academic term. ESL courses usually last 12–15 weeks, with 20–25 hours of classroom instruction per week.

Most American colleges and universities offer full-time intensive English programs. While attending the program, you'll live on campus and use the university facilities. One great advantage to these programs is that you'll have time to get used to American culture and college life before you start your regular studies. You'll also have the opportunity to meet other international students in the program and make new friends. Many intensive English programs organize after-class activities, such as trips to nearby cities, recreational attractions, or shopping. Participating in an intensive English program can be a great way to make the transition to living in the United States.

You can also choose to go to a private English language school. Private schools are often less expensive than those offered by colleges and universities, and the courses are shorter with more flexible schedules. But these schools are not always located near the campus of the university you will be attending. Many don't provide housing. So, you won't get as much support in making the transition to living in the United States.

If you decide to attend an intensive English program, look for programs that are members of the Consortium of University and College Intensive English Programs (UCIEP) or of the American Association of Intensive English Programs (AAIEP). Because a professional program accredits these programs, they maintain high standards of teaching and student services. Class sizes should be small—no more than 12 to 15 students in each classroom; in small classes, you'll receive more individualized instruction and develop closer relationships with the teachers and the other students.

It's also important to look for programs that will adequately prepare you for study at an American university. The program should teach a broad range of language skills, including how to take lecture notes, write term papers, take part in class discussion, and use a university library. Some programs are designed for students planning to enter a specialized field of study, such as business, engineering, or science.

Many intensive English programs offer valuable services outside the classroom to help you adjust to living in the US. For instance, they may provide housing or help you locate a place to live. They may offer an orientation program to help familiarize you with the town or city in which you'll be living. They may arrange for contacts with American families, so you can learn about American cultural life. Look for programs that offer the support services that you think you'll need.

The American Consulate frequently won't grant a student visa for admission to a US-based ESL program unless you have already received conditional admission to a full-time undergraduate program. You will have to produce a conditional acceptance letter from the university, which promises admission at a later date if you satisfactorily complete the ESL course. If you will attend an intensive English program before your regular college classes begin, the language school—not the university where you will be studying—will issue the I-20 form.

Moneysaver
Intensive English programs can cost hundreds of dollars. You will probably find that it's significantly less expensive to study English in your home country. But you'll miss out on the introduction to American culture and orientation to living in the US that many intensive English programs provide.

You can also choose to take part-time ESL classes while studying at the university. These classes are designed for international students who know enough English to attend university classes, but who want to improve their language skills.

Dealing with American Culture

Once you to get to the United States, it will take you some time to become accustomed to the different way of life here. You may have heard this transition referred to as "culture shock." You will have to get used to speaking English everywhere you go. You may find that the teachers and students you meet behave differently than in your home country. Little things like using the telephone can be unfamiliar and frustrating. You may even want to go home!

You're not alone. Everyone feels this way when they first go to a strange, new place. Even the American students at your school may feel homesick, even though they haven't left their home country.

Here are some tips for dealing with the culture shock and homesickness:

- Practice your English wherever you go. Your language skills will only get better with practice. Remember that it takes time to become comfortable with a new language, so don't get upset if you can't understand everyone right away.

- The American university setting, especially the classroom, may be more informal than what you're used to. Don't be afraid to speak up in class or to approach other students. You'll probably find both students and professors to be very friendly and helpful.

- Join in on activities, such as a sports team or a club. You'll meet new people, make friends, and get out of your room.

- Write about the new things that you encounter in a journal or in your letters home. Try to see the value of every new experience.

- If you experience problems—whether academic or personal—talk to someone, such as your academic advisor, an international student advisor, or someone at your church, temple, or synagogue. Don't be afraid to seek out help.

- Remember that all international students share in what you're going through. You're not alone. Join the international student organization on campus. Even if your new friends come from many different countries, you'll all have something in common and can help each other through the transition time.

❝
In class and out of class, English can be quite different. People don't necessarily use correct grammar, and they use many words you've never seen or heard before. You can check your dictionary over and over but still not understand the meaning. Eventually, you have to ask someone.
—Matt, a Taiwanese student at Eastern Washington University
❞

Where to Turn for Help

The process of applying to a university in the United States and then actually moving from your home to a strange new place where everyone speaks a different language can be a daunting one. International students who attend college abroad often experience culture shock. They miss their families, their friends, the food, and everything else that they're familiar with at home.

Fortunately, because American colleges and universities greatly encourage foreign students to attend, they have developed an extensive support network for students who are far from home. You won't have any problems finding someone on campus to answer all your questions and ease you through the transition. In addition, many private and US government organizations are dedicated to helping international students attend college in the US. These organizations can help you find the best school for you, guide you through the application and testing process, and help you locate financial aid. In this section, you'll discover resources in your home country, in the United States, and on the Internet that you can contact for help.

Help from the Schools

Most American colleges and universities have an office for international student affairs. Those offices counsel foreign students on all issues related to attending college in the United States, including obtaining student visas, orientation to life in the US, employment, off-campus social activities, personal and health concerns, general academic planning, and financial problems. The office for international student affairs is your best source of information both during the application process and after you arrive at the school; in fact, it should be your first stop after you arrive. You'll find the contact information for this office in the college's brochure or on the school's website, or ask the admissions office for more information.

The school's admissions office is another valuable resource for answering most—if not all—of your questions during the application process. Generally, one admissions officer works with all international applicants. This person will be most knowledgeable about what it's like for international students to attend the school and will be able to best help you through the application process.

The following are some questions to ask the admissions officer who represents international students:

- How many foreign students attend the school and which countries are represented?

- Is there an office for international student affairs on campus?

- Is there an orientation program for international students?

- What housing options are available?

- Does the school offer a health insurance plan for international students?

- What kinds of scholarships and financial aid options are available for international students?

- Can foreign students work on campus?

Bright Idea
Many universities with large numbers of international students have on-campus international houses, where international students live together and become a big "family," sharing cooking, shopping, cleaning, and social activities. Living in international housing can ease homesickness and make it easier to adjust to life in America.

- What are the special requirements for students from non-English-speaking countries?

- Does the school offer English as a second language (ESL) courses during the summer for students who want to improve their English-speaking skills before classes begin?

Organizations for International Students

The following organizations can provide valuable assistance to you during the process of applying to college in the United States:

- **Education International** publishes in-depth information about post-secondary study in the US, Canada, the United Kingdom, Australia, and New Zealand. This organization publishes a series of international study guides, including a guide to four-year colleges and universities in the US and a guide to ESL programs, which might be good places to start your college search. For more information or to order a guide, write to Education International Ltd., #205-5325 Cordova Bay Road, Victoria, BC, Canada V8Y 2L3, or visit the website at http://www.eiworldwide.com/.

- **The Institute of International Education** (IIE) publishes information on study opportunities in the US for international students. They also publish a very helpful guide for funding US studies. Write to IIE at 809 United Nations Plaza, New York, NY, USA, 10017-3580, or visit IIE's website at http://www.iie.org/.

- **The International Education Service** (IES) helps foreign students who want to study in the United States or Canada. This agency publishes a helpful guide to American colleges and universities for foreign students. It also provides a free placement service, which will help you find the right school based on your academic, financial, and geographic needs. Write to IES at 1512 11th St., Suite 201, Santa Monica, CA, 90401, USA, or visit the website at http://www.ies-ed.com/.

- **The United States Information Agency** promotes international educational exchanges, among other things. You may have a U.S. Information Service (USIS) post in the capital city of your country. These centers provide advising services and useful publications free of charge to prospective foreign students at American colleges and universities. To find out if a USIS post is located near you, contact the American Consulate in your country or write to United States Information Agency, Advising and Student Service Branch, Room 349, 301 4th St. SW, Washington, D.C. 20547, USA, or visit the website at http://e.usia.gov/education/advise/usadvis.htm.

- Every **American Consulate** has a small library of information about studying in the US. The Consulate is also the best source of accurate information about the procedures required for obtaining a student visa and the restrictions associated with the visa.

- If a **United States Education Foundation** (USEF) is located in your country, visit it. This office will provide helpful information as well as materials needed to prepare for the standardized tests. It may also provide counseling sessions.

Internet Resources

If you have Internet access, visit the following websites to find even more helpful information:

- The American Association of Intensive English Programs (AAIEP)— http://www.aaiep.org/: This organization works to increase awareness of opportunities to study English in the US. At the website, you can get help with choosing an English language or orientation program if you need to improve your English-speaking skills before starting your studies at an American college.

- eduPASS—http://www.edupass.org/: This complete guide to studying in the US provides information on just about every subject that will concern you, including admissions, learning English, getting a visa, paying for college, traveling to the US, cultural differences, and more. Definitely plan on spending a lot of time here.

- ESL Help Center—http://www.eslcafe.com/help/: If you need help with English, this is the site to come to. You can ask questions of actual ESL teachers 24 hours a day. This resource is particularly useful for getting help with vocabulary, grammar, idioms, slang, and the TOEFL.

- International Education Financial Aid—http://www.iefa.org/: This site provides a comprehensive database of grants, scholarships, and loan programs available to foreign students for study in the United States. Simply enter your country of origin and field of study in the form, and a list of awards appears that you might qualify for, complete with contact information and criteria for receiving the award.

- International Education Site—http://www.intstudy.com/: This website publishes a free guide to international education for all students who want to study abroad. You can search for a school, get help with choosing undergraduate courses, find valuable advice, and read articles from the leading journals of international education. You can even chat with other international students.

- Study in the USA—http://www.studyusa.com/: Here's another guide to studying in the US. This one provides information on American colleges and universities tailored especially to international students and written in a variety of languages. You can also choose an intensive English program or contact various admissions offices through this site.

- Tips for International Students—http://www.dartmouth.edu/admin/ acskills/intl.html: This short page provides valuable tips about how to participate in classes at American universities.

Bright Idea
Some American cities may have an International Visitors Council. This organization helps international visitors learn about American customs, gives tours of the city, matches international visitors with a host family, and hosts social events. After you arrive at your American college, look in the Yellow Pages telephone directory for such an organization near your school.

- U.S. Colleges for International Students—http://www.petersons.com/ac/: At this site, you can search for the US colleges and English-language programs that fit your needs and goals. You'll also find valuable information about preparing for the TOEFL, including sample questions and test-taking tips.

- U.S. Education Journal—http://www.usjournal.com/: At this Web publication for international students, you can learn more about the different college and English language programs available in the US and then request information directly from the school.

- U.S. State Department Foreign Student Visas—http://travel.state.gov/visa;foreignstuden.html: This is the official U.S. Department of State page that describes student visas.

Just the Facts

- International students who want to attend college in the United States should start searching for colleges early and set aside plenty of time to supply all of the required application materials in an acceptable format.

- If English isn't your first language, you will have to take the Test of English as a Foreign Language before applying to US colleges; your score on this test tells colleges how proficient you are in speaking and understanding English.

- Once an American college accepts you, you will have to get a student visa from the American Consulate in your country; you may have to prove that you have enough money to pay for all of your educational and living expenses and that you intend to return to your home country after receiving your degree.

- Financial aid for international students is limited, and you won't be able to work your way through school; the best sources of funds to help pay for your education are the government, companies, and foundations based in your home country.

- If you feel that you need to improve your English-speaking skills, consider taking an intensive English program; these programs may also help you meet new friends and help you get used to living in the US before you start your studies.

- It's normal for foreign students to experience culture shock when they first come to the US; international student organizations on campus can help you through this time of adjustment.

- Many sources of support exist for international students who attend college in the United States, including US government and private organizations, the office of international student affairs at your school, and informational websites.

Put Together Your Application Package

PART III

GET THE SCOOP ON...

Getting organized right from the start ▪ Putting together a personal profile ▪ Dos and don'ts for completing the application ▪ Gathering teacher recommendations ▪ Submitting high school transcripts ▪ Collecting items that might be required in the application package ▪ Putting together an application package if you come from a home school or nontraditional school

Creating an Exceptional Application Package

The application process is probably the most time-consuming, exhausting part of getting into college. There are so many steps, deadlines, and pieces of paper to keep track of and so many decisions to make along the way that you can easily become overwhelmed. But if you start early, go in prepared, and stay organized, you'll have a much easier time of it.

This chapter will help you sail through the college application process by going over what you need to do at each step along the way and outlining strategies for successfully accomplishing those tasks. You'll soon find that if you tackle each step of the college application process separately, you won't feel overwhelmed or have any trouble meeting deadlines.

Getting Organized

The process of submitting a college application has many separate steps, and you'll have to keep track of many different forms and other pieces of paper. Here's how to complete the application package:

- Obtain and complete the application form.
- Secure teacher recommendations.
- Send in your official high school transcripts.
- Send in official score reports of your standardized test scores.
- Write an essay or personal statement.
- Submit required financial aid materials.

Obtaining Application Forms

Request all of the application materials as soon as you finalize the list of four to six colleges to which you definitely want to apply. The summer between

109

your junior and senior year is the best time to start collecting application forms, so you can get an early start working on the essays.

To request an application, call the admissions office or send a postcard listing your name, address, and date of graduation and requesting an application. In many cases, you can also order or download the application directly from the school's website. Many schools accept the Common Application or another form of generic application, which you can get through your guidance office or on the Internet. (Turn back to Chapter 4, "The Lowdown on the Application Process," for more information.)

Keeping Track of Applications

Once you receive all of the application materials, take some time to get organized. Create a separate file for each school where you're applying, and keep all of the application materials and other correspondence for that school together in its file.

Make several photocopies of each application *before* you start filling it out. Use the copies to make rough drafts, and then copy the final draft neatly onto the original when you're ready to submit the application. Put the original in the school's file until you're ready to fill it out, so it will stay neat and won't get lost.

To help stay on track, photocopy the following worksheet, fill it out, and pin it up somewhere where you can consult it frequently. Be sure to note which application components each school requires and the deadlines for submitting them.

COLLEGE APPLICATION WORKSHEET

College Name	_____	_____	_____
Application Deadline	☐ Early ☐ Regular	☐ Early ☐ Regular	☐ Early ☐ Regular
	Deadline: __/__/__	Deadline: __/__/__	Deadline: __/__/__
Application			
Fee	$____ Sent ☐	$____ Sent ☐	$____ Sent ☐
Application Form Completed	☐ Date Sent: __/__/__	☐ Date Sent: __/__/__	☐ Date Sent: __/__/__
Essay	☐ Required Date completed: __/__/__	☐ Required Date completed: __/__/__	☐ Required Date completed: __/__/__
Follow-up with Admissions Office	☐ Date: __/__/__	☐ Date: __/__/__	☐ Date: __/__/__
Transcripts and Tests			
Transcript Requested	☐ Date: __/__/__	☐ Date: __/__/__	☐ Date: __/__/__

College Name	_____	_____	_____
	Transcripts and Tests (cont.)		
Midyear Report	☐ Required Date: __/__/__	☐ Required Date: __/__/__	☐ Required Date: __/__/__
SAT I/ACT Score Requested	☐ Required Date taken: __/__/__ ☐ Scores sent	☐ Required Date taken: __/__/__ ☐ Scores sent	☐ Required Date taken: __/__/__ ☐ Scores sent _
SAT II Subject Test 1	☐ Required Name of test: _____ Date taken: __/__/__ ☐ Score sent	☐ Required Name of test: _____ Date taken: __/__/__ ☐ Score sent	☐ Required Name of test: _____ Date taken: __/__/__ ☐ Score sent
SAT II Subject Test 2	☐ Required Name of test: _____ Date taken: __/__/__ ☐ Score sent	☐ Required Name of test: _____ Date taken: __/__/__ ☐ Score sent	☐ Required Name of test: _____ Date taken: __/__/__ ☐ Score sent
SAT II Subject Test 3	☐ Required Name of test: _____ Date taken: __/__/__ ☐ Score sent	☐ Required Name of test: _____ Date taken: __/__/__ ☐ Score sent	☐ Required Name of test: _____ Date taken: __/__/__ ☐ Score sent
Extra SAT II Subject Tests	Name of test: _____ Name of test: _____ Name of test: _____ ☐ Scores sent	Name of test: _____ Name of test: _____ Name of test: _____ ☐ Scores sent	Name of test: _____ Name of test: _____ Name of test: _____ ☐ Scores sent
AP Exams	Exam and score: _____ Exam and score: _____ Exam and score: _____ ☐ Scores sent	Exam and score: _____ Exam and score: _____ Exam and score: _____ ☐ Scores sent	Exam and score: _____ Exam and score: _____ Exam and score: _____ ☐ Scores sent
CLEP Exams	Exam and score: _____ Exam and score: _____ Exam and score: _____ ☐ Scores sent	Exam and score: _____ Exam and score: _____ Exam and score: _____ ☐ Scores sent	Exam and score: _____ Exam and score: _____ Exam and score: _____ ☐ Scores sent

COLLEGE APPLICATION WORKSHEET (CONT.)

College Name   _____   _____   _____

Recommendations

Recommen-dation 1	☐ Required Name: _____ Date requested: __/__/__ Date sent: __/__/__	☐ Required Name: _____ Date requested: __/__/__ Date sent: __/__/__	☐ Required Name: _____ Date requested: __/__/__ Date sent: __/__/__
Recommen-dation 2	☐ Required Name: _____ Date requested: __/__/__ Date sent: __/__/__	☐ Required Name: _____ Date requested: __/__/__ Date sent: __/__/__	☐ Required Name: _____ Date requested: __/__/__ Date sent: __/__/__
Recommen-dation 3	☐ Required Name: _____ Date requested: __/__/__ Date sent: __/__/__	☐ Required Name: _____ Date requested: __/__/__ Date sent: __/__/__	☐ Required Name: _____ Date requested: __/__/__ Date sent: __/__/__
Thank-You Notes Sent	☐ Date Sent: __/__/__	☐ Date Sent: __/__/__	☐ Date Sent: __/__/__

Financial Aid

FAFSA	☐ Required Deadline: __/__/__ Date sent: __/__/__	☐ Required Deadline: __/__/__ Deadline: __/__/__	☐ Required Deadline: __/__/__ Deadline: __/__/__
CSS/PROFILE	☐ Required Deadline: __/__/__ Date sent: __/__/__	☐ Required Deadline: __/__/__ Date sent: __/__/__	☐ Required Deadline: __/__/__ Date sent: __/__/__
School Fianancial Aid Form	☐ Required Deadline: __/__/__ Date sent: __/__/__	☐ Required Deadline: __/__/__ Date sent: __/__/__	☐ Required Deadline: __/__/__ Date sent: __/__/__
State Financial Aid Form	☐ Required Deadline: __/__/__ Date sent: __/__/__	☐ Required Deadline: __/__/__ Date sent: __/__/__	☐ Required Deadline: __/__/__ Date sent: __/__/__

College Name	_____	_____	_____
Other Requirements			

Interview	☐ Required ☐ Recommended Date: __/__/__ Interviewer's Name _____	☐ Required ☐ Recommended Date: __/__/__ Interviewer's Name _____	☐ Required ☐ Recommended Date: __/__/__ Interviewer's Name _____
Audition	☐ Required Date: __/__/__ Interviewer's Name _____	☐ Required Date: __/__/__ Interviewer's Name _____	☐ Required Date: __/__/__ Interviewer's Name _____
Writing/Art Samples	☐ Required Date sent: __/__/__	☐ Required Date sent: __/__/__	☐ Required Date sent: __/__/__
Other			

Creating a Personal Profile

You can streamline the application process by creating a personal profile—a list of facts about you—before you begin filling out application forms. The personal profile collects all of your biographical, academic, and extracurricular information in one place.

The personal profile is for your use only—you won't submit it with your college applications. Refer to it when completing application forms so that you don't omit some vital piece of information about yourself. When you start composing your application essays, the information in your personal profile can help you come up with essay topics. You will probably also consult your personal profile when preparing for interviews, applying for scholarships, and numerous other times during the college application process, so it's worth taking the time to create one first.

Take your time when creating your personal profile, and give it a lot of thought. Think about all of your achievements and the activities that you participated in during your high school years. Go back through your old class papers, and attach a few papers to your profile that you think admissions committees may want to see. That way, when you submit your application, you will remember to submit copies of these papers along with it.

Photocopy the following worksheet and use it to complete your personal profile:

Watch Out!
Some college guides recommend that you give your personal profile to teachers who write recommendations for you. Be careful—a recommendation that rehashes your academic and extracurricular achievements will not impress. A teacher who knows you well shouldn't need to see your personal profile and will probably write a better recommendation without it.

Full name: _____

Address: _____

_____

Phone number: _____ E-mail address: _____

Date of birth: _____ Place of birth: _____

Social Security number: _____ Citizenship: _____

Ethnicity: _____ Religion: _____

Foreign languages
spoken in your home: _____

Father's name: _____

Occupation: Employer:

College(s) attended
and degree(s) earned: _____

Mother's name: _____

Occupation: _____ Employer: _____

College(s) attended and
degree(s) earned: _____

Siblings: _____ Ages: _____-

_____ _____

Colleges attended: _____

Colleges where you're applying: _____

_____

Intended field(s) of study: _____

Academic Record

High School: _____

City/State: _____ CEEB CODE _____
(available from your counselor):

Type of School: ☐ Public ☐ Private ☐ Parochial

Date entered: _____ Date of graduation: _____

Guidance Counselor: _____

GPA: _____ Class rank: _____

AP courses: _____ _____

_____ _____

_____ _____

Honors courses: _____

College-level courses _____ _____
(courses you took at _____ _____
colleges/community colleges): _____ _____

Other courses: _____ _____
_____ _____
_____ _____

Academic awards (name of award, date received, and description):

_____ _____ _____
_____ _____ _____
_____ _____ _____
_____ _____ _____

Special programs (outside academic programs you completed, such as Governor's School or a summer program):

_____

Previous high school(s):   Dates attended:

_____ _____
_____ _____
_____ _____

Standardized Tests

PSAT Score: _____ National Merit Semifinalist/Finalist:

SAT I Score: _____ Math: _____ Verbal: _____

ACT Score: _____ Writing: _____ Reading: _____

 Math: _____ Science: _____

SAT II Subject Test: _____ Score: _____

SAT II Subject Test: _____ Score: _____

SAT II Subject Test: _____ Score: _____

SAT II Subject Test: _____ Score: _____

SAT II Subject Test: _____ Score: _____

SAT II Subject Test: _____ Score: _____

AP Exam: _____ Score: _____

AP Exam: _____ Score: _____

AP Exam: _____ Score: _____

AP Exam: _____ Score: _____

AP Exam: _____ Score: _____

CLEP Exam: _____ Score: _____

CLEP Exam: _____ Score: _____

CLEP Exam: _____ Score: _____

Also include information about your extracurricular activities, hobbies, and interests in your personal profile. Because all of this information may not be applicable to you, and because the amount of info within each category varies from student to student, I won't provide a photocopy model here. You can type your own version, including the categories and the amount of space that's right for you.

Employment—List employers, supervisors' names, dates of employment, the number of hours per week you worked, and a summary of your duties.

Unpaid internships—List employers, supervisors' names, dates of internships, and a summary of your duties.

Volunteer work—List organizations you volunteered for, supervisors' names, dates of service, and a summary of what you did.

Clubs/organizations—List in-school clubs and out-of-school organizations you joined, dates, descriptions, and any leadership positions.

Student government—List positions you've held and dates.

Military service—List the branch of service and dates of active service.

Sports—List sports you played, dates, coaches' names, and any special achievements.

Arts—List the areas you've studied, teachers, and any special achievements.

Travel—List any special trips.

Other—List any other activities, talents, or hobbies that you consider important.

Application Dos and Don'ts

Watch Out!
Don't assume that admissions committees automatically know what organizations and clubs are from their titles. On the application form, spell out acronyms and define each activity, as well as your role in it.

The application is the form that tells the college all the facts about you. On this form, you'll record your biographical information, your academic record, and your extracurricular activities. The application will probably ask you what major or majors you want to pursue at the school, what extracurricular activities you intend to participate in while in college, any special academic programs you plan to join, and what kind of housing you want. The application form may ask you whether any of your friends or relatives attended the college. Most schools also require a brief personal statement or essay; the next chapter covers the essay in more detail.

How you complete the application form tells the admission committee a lot about you. A neatly typed or handwritten application with no errors demonstrates that you're a careful, responsible person who respects the college. An incomplete, illegible, or sloppy application can easily earn you an automatic rejection.

Follow these simple tips to ensure that you turn in application forms that make the best possible impression:

- *Get started early.* Don't put off filling out the application. You'll feel a lot less stressed if you spread out the application process over a long period, instead of trying to get everything done at the last minute. Start with the applications for the schools with the earliest deadlines and with the applications for your top picks.

- *Follow directions exactly.* Before writing down anything, read through all the directions at least twice. Make certain that you understand everything that is asked of you. If you don't understand a question, contact the admissions office.

- *Be complete.* Every question on the application form is there for a reason, no matter how trivial it may seem to you. Thoroughly answer every question. If a question calls for a paragraph, respond with a paragraph, not with a sentence or a list. The only exceptions to this rule are questions marked "optional," such as questions of ethnicity, religion, gender, or marital status. Although you don't have to answer these questions, keep in mind that most colleges value a diverse freshman class, and your ethnicity or religious background may be seen as augmenting that diversity.

- *Be concise.* College application forms request exactly the amount of information that the admissions committee needs to fairly compare candidates. More is not necessarily better. Remember that one-paragraph question? Don't write more than a paragraph, no matter how tempting it may seem. A little more is fine, but a lot more is not. Try to fit all of your answers into the space provided (but attaching separate sheets is preferable to writing so small that the admissions officer can't read your application without a magnifying glass).

- *Be neat.* If you complete the application form by hand, use only blue or black ink, and make sure your handwriting is neat and legible (and no hearts over the i's). Don't use a lot of correction fluid, a pencil, or different colored pens. It's preferable to type. Pasting typed answers neatly into the designated areas is perfectly acceptable.

- *Proofread, proofread, and then proofread again.* Don't rely on a computer spellchecker or a grammar-checking program. It's always a good idea to have someone proofread your work behind you. This is where your parents or a helpful English teacher can really come in handy.

Note that before you start filling out college applications, you'll need a Social Security number, if you don't already have one. Colleges usually keep track of applicants using their Social Security numbers. Type or print this number on the top of each page of the application and on all other items that you send to the college. For instance, if you apply electronically and send your application fee in separately, it's important to write your Social Security number on the check so that it gets paired with the right application.

> **❝**
> An application that is littered with grammatical errors unfortunately leaves a bad impression with the admissions staff.
> —Todd Leahy, Admissions Counselor at Wofford College
> **❞**

When you're all done, double-check that you included everything that was required, including a check for the application fee—paperclip the check right in front. Application fees typically run around $25, although they can range from being completely free to costing $60 or more. The fee covers the cost of processing the application and is generally nonrefundable. If you can't afford the application fee, discuss your situation with the admissions officer at the college; the admissions officer may waive the fee if you can demonstrate financial need.

Before sending in the application (or mailing any other correspondence to the school), make a photocopy and put it in the school's file folder (the one you read about in the "Getting Organized" section of this chapter). That way, you won't be stuck if the application gets lost in the mail. To mail the application, use the envelope provided by the school, if there is one; otherwise, use a large manila envelope so you don't have to fold the application papers. Take the package to the post office to ensure that you attach the correct postage.

Some high schools prefer that you turn in your completed application forms to the guidance office, where transcripts and recommendations can be attached to the form and the entire package mailed at the same time. Find out early what the policy is at your high school. If your school has such a policy, turn in your completed application forms several weeks before the final due date to ensure that all materials are submitted on time.

The last step is to check that the admissions office received your application and all of the supporting materials. Wait a reasonable amount of time for the application to arrive and be processed—between two and three weeks. Then, call the admissions office and make sure that your application, transcript, test scores, and letters of recommendation arrived and that you don't have to submit any other materials to complete your application package.

Unofficially...
Unless the application form specifies otherwise, use the enclosed envelope to mail the form by U.S. Postal Service. Don't express-mail the application or send it via UPS or Federal Express. Colleges have their own systems for processing applications, which rely on applicants following directions. If you deviate, you'll just create more work for the admissions office.

Getting Recommendations That Really Sell You

Most colleges require two to three (or more) letters of recommendation. Colleges rely heavily on these letters of recommendation when making admissions decisions, so don't treat this step lightly.

Recommendations show the admissions committee how your classmates and teachers perceive you, how you fit into the high school community, and what leadership roles you have taken. Recommendations can also explain anomalies, such as a dip in your grades. While recommendations by themselves aren't usually a deciding factor in determining acceptance, a solid recommendation or two can help an admissions officer determine that you are the right person for that school.

Admissions officers don't want to see recommendations from public officials or local celebrities. Recommendations from teachers and guidance counselors carry a lot more weight, because they are familiar with your academic work and know you as a student. If you're an athlete seeking a scholarship, a recommendation from your coach is also a necessity.

Choose who will write your recommendations carefully, and pick people who you feel know you best. The people who recommend you should be familiar with your academic work and have a positive opinion of you as a person. Select teachers who taught you recently and who wrote detailed comments on your papers (if they're positive). A teacher who gave you a B in a class where you worked hard, showed consistent improvement, and participated often is a much better candidate for writing a recommendation than a teacher who gave you an easy A. Teachers who taught you in courses related to your potential major are also a good choice. Also consider teachers who both taught you in class and who served as faculty advisor on an internship or extracurricular activity you participated in; they should know you especially well.

Many colleges also require a letter of recommendation from your guidance counselor. If you spent time discussing your college plans with your counselor, as I suggested earlier in this book, then your guidance counselor should already have a good idea of who you are and what your college goals are—even if you're one of several hundred students who the counselor advises.

You don't have to submit letters of recommendation from only teachers and guidance counselors unless the application form specifies that you do so. For example, you might request a recommendation from your principal, your coach, your boss, an art, music, or dance teacher outside the high school, or a supervisor where you performed community service or completed an internship. But be aware that admissions committees most value recommendations from teachers and guidance counselors.

Start asking for recommendations early, at least two months before the application's due date. Set up a time to talk with potential letter-writers, rather than just catching them in the hall. At the appointment, discuss your activities and goals. Sometimes, it helps to share the college brochure with the letter-writer, so he or she has a general sense of what the school is looking for in an applicant; this is especially helpful if you're applying to a nontraditional school, such as an art school or "alternative" school. Finally, don't be afraid to ask whether the person feels comfortable writing a recommendation for you or whether the teacher has the time to write a strong recommendation; you want to select someone who is truly enthusiastic about recommending you.

Last but not least, be courteous. Give your letter-writers stamped envelopes addressed to the colleges where you're applying. Keep track of deadlines, and don't hesitate to follow up with your letter-writers to make sure that they meet them (teachers and guidance counselors tend to be very busy folks). Send the letter-writer a thank-you note a week or two before the application deadline to gently remind him or her to get on the stick. And

Watch Out!
You have the right to review everything in your college admissions folder, including letters of recommendation, once you have been accepted, but you should waive this right (you'll have to check a box on the application). This sends a signal to the admissions committee that recommendations are more candid and honest.

Timesaver
You don't have to select different letter-writers for each college that you apply to. Each letter-writer can write one recommendation and print out six copies, if need be, addressing each copy to a different school where you're applying. This ensures that each college receives an equally personal and thoughtful recommendation from a person who knows you well.

Watch Out!
If any teachers seem reluctant to give you a recommendation, provide an out (for instance, ask the teacher whether he is too busy or doesn't feel comfortable recommending you). A lukewarm recommendation can significantly hurt your chances, particularly at the more selective schools.

when you get accepted somewhere, let the people who recommended you know that they helped.

Submitting High School Transcripts

You must make certain that the colleges receive official reports of your standardized test scores and high school transcript. Colleges request grades beginning with the ninth grade. Three-and-a-half years' worth of grades gives admissions officers a good idea of your academic achievements and shows the pattern of your academic growth.

Don't leave this chore until the last minute (like everyone else). Give your registrar or guidance counselor at least a month's notice prior to the application deadline to make certain that your transcript arrives on time. Many high schools have transcript request forms.

Some colleges may request that you enclose the transcript with your application; in that case, just put the sealed envelope in the application package (but don't break the seal or your application won't be accepted). In addition, most schools require a midyear report to track your academic progress during the fall semester of your senior year; request these reports at the same time that you request your transcripts.

Most schools also require that you submit standardized test scores, typically the ACT or the SAT I. When you register to take these exams, you indicate on the registration form which schools are to receive the score results. The agency responsible for administering the exam forwards your results to those schools. If you need to send your scores to additional schools, contact ETS (for the SAT I and II and AP exams) or ACT directly; contact information is given in Appendix D, "Important Addresses."

Submitting Essays, Portfolios, and Other Supplemental Application Materials

Watch Out!
Some schools—particularly the large universities that receive a lot of applications and tend to make admissions decisions based on grades and test scores alone—don't want to see anything beyond what the application requests. It's always a good idea to ask your contact at the admissions office before sending in anything extra.

Many schools appreciate it when you submit a portfolio of extra materials that more clearly demonstrate your talents and interests than the application form alone can do. Selective schools in particular are relying more and more on these portfolios to help make admissions decisions.

What can you do that might make you sound appealing to the school? If you have an artistic talent, such as painting, photography, ceramics, or sculpture, submit slides of your work. If music is your forte, a short tape—no more than ten minutes—can help push your application into the "accepted" pile. And if you are a creative writer or journalist, attach extra writing samples to your application—articles, stories, or poems that were published in a forum outside your high school newspaper or literary magazine or that won in a contest are particularly impressive. Perhaps you're an aspiring filmmaker or television reporter; a short video sample—no more than 10 minutes long—might be the thing.

But you don't have to be an artist to create a supplementary portfolio for your application. Academic portfolios also impress admissions committees by showing them that you are passionate about a particular field of study, enough to complete extra work in that field. If science is your thing, a top-notch lab report or extra-credit experiment might make the grade. If you're a budding Internet expert, computer programmer, or graphic designer, think about submitting a sample of your work on CD-ROM or a floppy disk, or creating your own Web page to house your online portfolio. Use your imagination to come up with other ways that you can make your application stand out.

Some schools encourage applicants to submit an academic essay or writing sample, in addition to the essay that you will write expressly for that application (the application essay is covered in more detail in Chapter 8, "Writing Essays That Impact"). Colleges particularly value good writing skills, so including a well written paper or two with your application can only help your chances for admittance. There's no reason not to choose to send a school essay. Select a short paper on a not-too-esoteric topic that earned a strong grade—B+ or better. An illuminating essay on a short story, lab experience, or historic event is a good choice. If you can, send a paper that has a fair number of teacher comments; these show how hard you worked and how demanding your teachers are. It's okay to send the original paper, but if it's difficult to read, retype it.

If you do send in extra materials, make sure that they are not large or unwieldy. Cassettes, videos, slides, writing samples, and photographs are all good. Full-size artwork is not. Don't use overkill when submitting extra materials. The admissions committee may appreciate seeing a few samples of your work, but they don't want to see everything you've ever produced (unless that is specifically requested—when applying to an art school, for instance).

Note that you may be required to submit extra materials, particularly if you're a potential visual or performing arts student. At some colleges, applicants hoping to join the fine arts program must submit a portfolio of their work. If you want to join the dance, drama, or music department, you may have to audition. Some academic programs may have specific course requirements, such as extra science and math requirements for potential engineering students. And for entry into particularly competitive programs, such as a business, education, or nursing program, you may have to attend an interview or complete a supplemental application form that isn't required of other applicants to the college. Before applying, be sure that you understand exactly what's required; ask the admissions officer about special requirements for programs that interest you.

Application Packages from Homeschooled and Alternative School Students

Over the years, homeschooling has become an increasingly popular alternative to the public high school. Also, many students now attend alternative high schools that do not rely on traditional grading and ranking systems to

We have been impressed with students that have submitted with their applications slides of artwork or copies of musical performances if they happen to be talented in those areas. These applications stand out.
—Todd Leahy, Admissions Counselor at Wofford College

Bright Idea
If you're on the margin for admission, a strong recommendation from an alumnus can tip the balance in your favor.

judge students. Colleges recognize this trend and will certainly carefully consider applications coming from students schooled in these nontraditional environments.

Can Homeschoolers Go to College?

Don't make the mistake of thinking that you don't have a chance of getting into college just because you were homeschooled. On the contrary, many colleges consider homeschooled students more mature and more independent than students coming out of public schools. A rigorous homeschooling program demonstrates to a college that you are willing to challenge yourself academically and that you have developed the discipline and self-motivation to learn and excel on your own. Most admissions committees try to assemble freshman classes with a wide range of backgrounds and experiences, so being homeschooled or graduating from an alternative school may actually work in your favor.

Over 900 colleges have accepted homeschoolers, ranging from Harvard University to the United States Military Academy. The following colleges and universities have proven themselves to be particularly friendly to homeschoolers:

- Abilene Christian University (Abilene, TX)
- Antioch College (Yellow Springs, OH)
- Azusa Pacific University (Azusa, CA)
- Beaver College (Glenside, PA)
- Bennington College (Bennington, VT)
- Biola University (La Mirada, CA)
- Bryan College (Dayton, TN)
- Carson-Newman College (Jefferson City, TN)
- Colorado College (Colorado Springs, CO)
- Concordia University (River Forest, IL)
- Cumberland College (Williamsburg, KY)
- Dartmouth College (Hanover, NH)
- David Lipscomb University (Nashville, TN)
- Drake University (Des Moines, IA)
- Drexel University (Philadelphia, PA)
- Duquesne University (Pittsburgh, PA)
- Evangel University (Springfield, MO)
- Faulkner University (Montgomery, AL)
- Freed-Hardeman University (Henderson, TN)
- Geneva College (Beaver Falls, PA)
- Gordon College (Wenham, MA)
- Grove City College (Grove City, PA)

Timesaver
Some good sites for homeschoolers who want to go to college are the Colleges That Admit Homeschoolers FAQ at http://learninfreedom.org/colleges_4_hmsc.html and the Path from Home School to College at http://www.collegeboard.org/features/home/html/intro.html. You might also pick up a copy of *And What About College? How Homeschooling Leads to Admissions to the Best Colleges and Universities* by Cafi Cohen (Holt Associates, 1997).

- Hillsdale College (Hillsdale, MI)
- Houghton College (Houghton, NY)
- John Brown University (Siloam Springs, AR)
- Judson College (Elgin, IL)
- Juniata College (Huntingdon, PA)
- Kent State University (Kent, OH)
- King College (Bristol, TN)
- Lamar University (Beaumont, TX)
- Lebanon Valley College (Annville, PA)
- Lee University (Cleveland, TN)
- LeTourneau University (Longview, TX)
- Louisiana College (Pineville, LA)
- Lubbock Christian University (Lubbock, TX)
- Marlboro College (Marlboro, VT)
- The Master's College (Santa Clarita, CA)
- Messiah College (Grantham, PA)
- Nyack College (Nyack, NY)
- Occidental College (Los Angeles, CA)
- Richard Stockton College of New Jersey (Pomona, NJ)
- Rochester College (Rochester Hills, MI)
- Sarah Lawrence College (Bronxville, NY)
- Sheldon Jackson College (Sitka, AK)
- Simon's Rock College of Bard (Great Barrington, MA)
- Southern Nazarene University (Bethany, OK)
- Stanford University (Stanford, CA)
- Talladega College (Talladega, AL)
- Taylor University (Upland, IN)
- Thomas Aquinas College (Santa Paula, CA)
- Toccoa Falls College (Toccoa Falls, GA)
- Towson State University (Towson, MD)
- Union University (Jackson, TN)
- University of Bridgeport (Bridgeport, CT)
- University of Denver (Denver, CO)
- University of Missouri (Rolla, MO)
- University of Mobile (Mobile, AL)
- Vanderbilt University (Nashville, TN)
- Wesleyan University (Middletown, CT)

- Westmont College (Santa Barbara, CA)

- Wheaton College (Wheaton, IL)

As you can see from this list, homeschooled applicants are more attractive to and more heavily recruited by the private colleges and universities, and the more selective schools are much more open to admitting homeschooled applicants. Many colleges have developed special admissions guidelines or admissions procedures for homeschooled applicants. This enables the homeschooled applicant to better compete against other candidates in the applicant pool and ensures fair judging of all applicants.

On the other hand, certain schools—particularly large state universities who admit applicants based on a rigid formula—are not so conducive to admitting homeschooled students. Without the standard parts of the application package, especially the high school transcript, these universities don't know how to evaluate applicants. But as homeschooling has become more widely practiced, even the most bureaucratic universities have begun to adjust their admissions procedures.

Demonstrating Your Academic Achievements

Colleges depend on understanding each high school's curriculum and degree of difficulty in order to evaluate applicants from that high school. But admission committees won't intuitively know the content or scope of most homeschool curricula. Therefore, you must effectively communicate in the application package what you learned—the content of the courses you took and the tangible results you can demonstrate as an outcome of your participation in the course—rather than how you did, or the grades that you got. Take the initiative to explain your special circumstances. Provide a detailed description of your curriculum. It might also be helpful to write a letter explaining how and why the family chose homeschooling and the benefits you received from the experience.

Watch Out!
Colleges will carefully examine the balance of homeschooling curricula. Don't skimp on the basic requirements, especially math and foreign languages, when developing a homeschooling program.

Table 7.1 outlines the core requirements expected by most colleges; make certain that your homeschooling program adequately covers these subjects and that you can demonstrate your proficiency in them with papers and coursework, standardized test scores, and recommendations from outside the home.

Without a traditional high school transcript, colleges will look extra hard at your standardized test scores. Consider taking both the SAT and the ACT. Complete as many SAT II subject tests, AP exams, and CLEP exams that you feel comfortable taking, particularly in the core subjects required by nearly all colleges. Go beyond the college's minimum requirements for SAT II tests and AP exams if you can. Colleges will be able to objectively judge these scores and use them to figure out how academically advanced you are. (You'll find more help with preparing for standardized tests in Part IV, "Maximize Your Test Scores.")

Be sure to prepare well in advance for all standardized tests you take. Find out exactly what each test covers, and design a curriculum that

TABLE 7.1: CORE REQUIREMENTS FOR COLLEGE PREPARATION

Subject	Number of Years of Study	Course Material That Should Be Covered
Arts	1 or more years	Visual arts, music, dance, or drama
Computer Sciences	1 or more years	Computer applications or programming
English	4 years	American and English literature, writing, and speech
Foreign Languages	2–4 years	Intensive study in one language
Mathematics	3–4 years	Algebra, geometry, algebra II, and trigonometry; calculus recommended
Science	3 years	Biology, chemistry, and physics; lab experience is strongly recommended
Social Studies	3 years	US government, American history, and world history; economics and geography recommended

adequately covers that material. Take lots of practice tests under timed conditions to become accustomed to the formats of these tests.

Any way that you can stand out academically can help your cause. Attempt some coursework at a nearby college or community college to demonstrate that you have academic ability and are willing to push yourself academically; this will also show the admissions committee that you can succeed in the traditional classroom setting. Submitting a portfolio of your academic work, such as a few papers you have written in a variety of subjects, can help admissions committees understand what you have learned. You may also submit pages from a logbook of the hands-on learning activities you participated in, such as field trips, museum visits, lab work, and volunteer work, to show colleges the types of learning experiences you regularly had. Be creative in finding other ways to demonstrate your academic achievements.

Some homeschoolers do receive transcripts and grades from a home-based educational organization or from their local high school. In those cases, it's not so important to supplement your application with an academic portfolio. In any case, it's a good idea to write a letter describing your curriculum and how homeschooling has benefited you.

Presenting Yourself as a Desirable Nontraditional Student

Even though a common goal for homeschoolers is to have a unique educational experience and to excel in ways that differ greatly from the public school "norm," the reality is that you will be competing for admission with traditionally schooled students. Other parts of the application will serve as points of reference where the admissions officer can more easily compare you to other applicants. These include your level of involvement in the community and extracurricular activities, your essay, the interview, and letters of recommendation. You will need to be competitive in these areas. Pay special attention to the essay. Writing about yourself and your education will probably play a much more central role in your application than it would for the conventional high school student.

Even if the college does not require one, scheduling an interview is a good idea for homeschooled students and students from alternative schools. The interview gives you a chance to explain your alternative curriculum, describe the academic challenges that you met, and impress the admissions officer with your maturity. Try to schedule the interview on campus with an admissions officer, rather than with an alumni representative in your hometown. If you call far enough in advance, most colleges will accommodate you.

Letters of recommendation require some extra effort for many homeschoolers, because they don't have a large number of teachers to choose from. A letter from the parent who homeschooled you can explain the context and details of your educational experience, but a parent's recommendation obviously lacks objectivity, and your parent won't be able to compare you to other students when rating your performance. Therefore, you should submit two or more recommendation letters from people outside the home. If you take community college courses during your high school career or if you have a tutor outside the family as part of your homeschooling program, these teachers would be good sources of letters of recommendation. You can also request recommendations from employers, supervisors at an internship or community service program, art or music teachers, coaches, or club leaders.

Homeschooled applicants often don't participate in the same types of extracurricular activities that public school students do. Although the traditional sports teams, social clubs, school newspaper, and so on may not be part of your educational background, many homeschooled students actually have the benefit of a much richer variety of extracurricular activities. Community service, scouting, regional sports teams, religious activities, local theater companies and musical groups, local politics, and employment are all viable options. If you have a special talent, you can enter contests or seek publication. You may have the luxury of more extensive travel. Colleges find all of these activities to be assets, and they can easily compare activities like these to conventional high school extracurriculars.

Participating in clubs, religious activities, performing arts groups, and social organizations also demonstrates to admissions committees that the homeschooled student has a life outside the home and interests other than academic ones. This is especially important to help dispel the myth that homeschooled students lack in social skills. Remember to limit your extracurricular activities to those that you are truly passionate about and where you have the opportunity to excel. Don't overdo it simply because you're trying to impress admissions committees—the committee will see right through you.

If you are a homeschooled student or if you attended a nontraditional high school, it's particularly important that you discuss this with an admissions officer at each school where you're applying. Find out how you can better present yourself in the application and help the admissions committee compare you with other applicants. Be prepared to submit extra materials to supplement your application and demonstrate your academic standing.

Just the Facts

- The first thing to do before starting to fill out applications is get organized—make photocopies of all the application forms, fill out a chart tracking deadlines and required application materials, and create a file folder for each school to which you're applying.

- Before you get started, you can save time by completing a personal profile outlining your academic and extracurricular achievements; you can then use this information when completing application forms, writing essays, and applying for scholarships.

- How you complete the application form can make a big impression on the admissions committee; follow instructions exactly and turn in only a complete, professional-looking application.

- Teacher and guidance counselor recommendations are a very important part of the application package, so ask for recommendations from teachers who know you well and who can write an enthusiastic letter about you.

- Every college application requires a copy of your high school transcript; request transcripts early to avoid getting lost in the last-minute crunch.

- If you have a special academic or artistic talent, submitting extra materials like a high school paper, musical recording, or slides of your artwork may improve your chances for admission, but be sure to check with the college first to see whether they appreciate such extra submissions.

- Homeschooled students and students who attend nontraditional high schools make very attractive applicants to many colleges, but be prepared to submit extra materials and take more standardized tests in order to give the colleges enough information to evaluate you fairly.

Bright Idea
Homeschoolers should try to participate in extracurricular activities that supplement their education. While studying biology, volunteer at an animal shelter or a wildlife preserve. Get an internship at a computer company, a library, or a museum to supplement computer science, literature, or history studies. Hands-on academic experiences will impress admissions officers.

Writing Essays That Impact

The essay is an extremely important part of your college application. For many selective colleges, it can be the most important part. Therefore, you need to spend a great deal of time thinking about the essay topic, writing and rewriting, crafting the final draft, and proofreading for errors. The best time to start working on your college application essays is as soon as possible, preferably in the summer before your senior year.

Don't let the essay intimidate you. The essay provides your best opportunity to strut your stuff for the admissions committee and make yourself stand out in a crowd of applicants. Don't waste this opportunity—capitalize on it!

Why the Essay Is So Important

You may think that the most important part of your application package is your high school transcript, your standardized test scores, or your list of extracurriculars. You'd be wrong. At every college that does not rely on a formula when deciding who to admit, the essay is the single most important part of the application. One of the admissions committee's most important criteria for potential candidates is the ability to write, and the essay is how they find that out.

The essay is the only part of the application where the admissions officer can really get to know you—who you are, what you think, what your values are, what your personality is like. The essay can sell you to an admissions committee in a way that test scores and lists of courses and activities cannot.

You may have mediocre grades, an average SAT score, or ho-hum teacher recommendations. A strongly written essay—one that admissions officers will remember—can overcome any of these obstacles. Or your grades, test scores, recommendations, and extracurriculars may put you in the same category as hundreds of other applicants—the "maybe" category. A well written essay is the best way to stand out in the crowd. By the same

Chapter 8

129

Bright Idea
Read some good
writing before writ-
ing your own essay.
Read other essays—
not only successful
college application
essays, but also
essays by superb
writers like E.B.
White, Stephen Jay
Gould, and John
McPhee. Notice how
they tell a story and
draw in the reader.

token, a poorly written or unoriginal essay can quickly tip the balance toward rejection.

The essay is also important for determining whether the applicant and the school are a good fit for each other. Your essay can demonstrate your suitability for a college with a particular character or educational mission. It can describe an unusual background or experiences that the admissions committee may perceive as valuable in creating a more diverse freshman class.

The essay is also the most difficult part of the application package to complete, and it's the part you should spend the most time on. But at the same time, it's the one part of the application package that you have the most control over. By following the proven strategies outlined in this chapter, you can produce a dynamic essay that really captures the admissions officer's attention.

Kinds of Essay Questions

There is no limit to the kinds and number of essay questions found on college applications. Some schools request only one essay. Others want to see a combination of essays and short-answer themes. Some specify exactly what to write about. Others provide a vague topic and leave it up to you to supply the focus. Still others let you choose whatever topic you want.

Unless the essay question is entirely open-ended, essay questions on college applications typically fall into one of three broad categories:

- Tell us about yourself.

- Tell us why you want to come to our school.

- Show us the creative or imaginative side of your personality.

But within the confines of these generalized areas, it's entirely up to you to come up with a topic that grabs the reader and keeps him or her interested until the very last sentence.

No matter what kind of question is asked, you need to answer that question. You may write a brilliant essay, but if the question asks you to name the most influential person in your life and you don't, your essay won't be looked on favorably. Follow word limits and other instructions closely.

Telling Colleges About Yourself

Many applications ask for an essay specifically about you: "Tell us about yourself." The admissions officer wants to get to know you better and find out how you'll introduce yourself.

Unofficially...
Some college appli-
cations contain
mini-essays—
questions that you
only have a para-
graph in which to
answer. Approach
these questions with
the same care and
attention that you
give to the "big"
essay. Try to com-
pose a short but
vivid answer, and
never sacrifice
specifics.

Because this kind of essay question is so open-ended, you might feel like you have to tell everything that happened to you since the day you were born. Focus is the key. Make a list of the personal characteristics that you'd like to convey, pick the most important one, and then choose a specific event in your life that most effectively communicates that characteristic. Try to accentuate positive experiences rather than negative ones. If you do write about death, divorce, or illness, emphasize how you coped with the situation or what you learned from the experience, rather than dwelling on your bad luck.

The following are some examples of actual college application essay questions that require you to tell colleges about yourself:

- Discuss a teacher who has significantly influenced you in recent years. (Duquesne University)

- Explain a belief you held at one time and how you came to change your thinking about that belief. (Gonzaga University)

- Coping with a serious problem or challenge may help to establish a person's true moral or ethical character. Have you faced such a situation? What was the outcome? (Lynchburg College)

- Select some experience from which you have derived exceptional benefit and describe it, explaining its value to you. (St. John's College)

- Describe the most important experience with adversity you have encountered. Tell us about how you responded, coped, or triumphed. (University of Maryland at College Park)

Telling Colleges Why You Want to Attend That School

Another common essay question is one that asks you why you chose that college to apply to or why a particular career or major interests you. In this case, the admissions officer wants to learn about your educational direction and career goals. The admissions officer also wants to get an idea of how much you know about the school, how much research you put into choosing a college, and how serious your commitment is to this particular school.

If you went through the process of selecting schools as carefully and methodically as I suggested in Chapter 1, you should already be very familiar with your reasons for selecting the schools to which you're applying. But if you haven't researched the school thoroughly enough, this type of essay will definitely show it. The essay should contain factual knowledge of the college's programs and advantages; name specific course offerings, professors, and facilities. And be truthful about why you want to attend the school—this will produce a more sincere and enjoyable essay.

Reading the college brochure will be helpful when answering a "tell us why you want to come to our school" essay question. What's even more useful is personal experience, such as your experiences on the campus visit looking at the campus, meeting students, and talking with professors. Consult your notes on the campus visit before sitting down to write. Also look through the course catalog, read the school newspaper, and visit the school's website to pick up additional information about the school that may play a part in your essay.

The following are examples of this type of essay question taken from actual college applications:

- How do you think Bay State College will prepare you for the career you wish to pursue? (Bay State College)

- How will you connect with success at Cedar Crest? (Cedar Crest College)

- Clearly state the reasons you are seeking admission to Emerson College and what contribution you can make to the Emerson community. (Emerson College)

- Write your essay from the perspective of a Greensboro College senior. You are about to graduate from Greensboro College. Describe your experience in college. What did you do? What did you accomplish? Discuss all aspects of your college life—social, academic, spiritual, clubs and organizations, athletics, relationships with fellow students, faculty, and staff. (Greensboro College)

- Who or what most influenced you to apply to Jacksonville University? (Jacksonville University)

Showing Your Creative Side

The third most common college application essay topic is one that asks you to talk about some tangential item—a national issue, a famous person, what you would put in a time capsule, or a book that you've read, for instance. In this case, the admissions officer is judging your creativity and the breadth of your knowledge. The admissions officer may want to learn whether you're up on current events, discover what you've read and whether you've thought about it, or find out whether you can put yourself in an imaginary situation.

This type of essay tends to elicit a canned response—"someone I admire is Abraham Lincoln"—so try to think beyond the obvious. Your essay will be more effective if it surprises the reader. Although this type of essay calls for a more creative response, it also requires a serious, focused, thoughtful answer. And do your research; for instance, don't nominate Madeleine Albright for Woman of the Year if you don't have a clue about what she does.

The following are some examples of creative essay questions that you'll find on real college applications:

- If you could volunteer for any organization, anywhere, which would you choose and why? (Alaska Pacific University)

- Imagine that as a recent graduate, you have developed a new product, idea, or innovation. Describe your discovery, its merits, and your marketing strategy. (Alfred University)

- If you could have dinner with any one person, living or dead, who would it be? Why? (Assumption College)

- Discuss an issue of local, national, or international concern and why it is important to you. (Catholic University of America)

- If you could travel into the past or future, what time period would you select and why? What would you like to discover in that period? How would your discovery help us in the present? (Loyola University New Orleans)

- If you were chosen to host a new talk show, who would your first guests be and why? (Pitzer College)

- Develop a story involving dental floss, a cricket, and a tomato. Conclude your story with the phrase "and that is how I saved the world." (Rhodes College)

- Ask and answer the one important question that you wished we had asked. (Transylvania University)

- Imagine your 25-year college class reunion. Among your former classmates are several millionaires, the US President, a best-selling novelist, and the discoverer of a cancer cure. Yet, you are the guest of honor. Why? (Whittier College)

Choosing an Essay Topic

Sometimes, the college application will specify the essay topic. More often, a general topic is suggested, or the topic is left entirely up to you. Use a lot of care when selecting an essay topic. While no legitimate topic is wrong, your choice shows your preferences, your values, how you think, your creativity, your sense of humor, and your depth of knowledge.

Choosing an essay topic that does all these things is not easy. It takes time and forethought. Unfortunately, most applicants fall into the so-called "90-percent trap"—the 90 percent of applicants who write nearly identical essays. Sure, the essay topics are slightly different, but the writing style, tone, and general subject matter of each essay are similar. These essay-writers draw the same cliched moral lessons out of whatever they choose to write about, whether it's winning the big game, dealing with the death of a relative, or traveling to a foreign country.

So, you must choose an essay topic that shows what your personality is like, something you really want to write about and that the admissions officer hasn't read a million times before—not an easy task. The important thing is to take your time picking a topic, and really think it through. Don't go with the first thing that comes to mind; in fact, that's the one topic that you should never write about it, because it's bound to land you in the "90-percent trap." Don't be afraid to discard an essay topic if the essay isn't working. Keep searching until you come up with a topic that will produce an essay that really shows who you are.

Coming Up with Topic Ideas

The first step when given an open-ended essay question or a question with a very general, broad topic is to brainstorm what you will write about. Plan to spend at least a week just coming up with possible essay topics.

Bright Idea
Keep your personal profile close at hand to help come up with ideas when brainstorming.

At this point in the process, anything goes. Write down whatever pops into your head. Any idea may lead you to the foundation of your brilliant essay.

To get started coming up with essay topics, try answering the following questions:

- What are your special talents or skills?
- What personality traits do you value most in yourself?
- What is unique about you? What makes you different from everybody else?
- What accomplishments are you most proud of?
- What are your hobbies?
- What are your favorite things to do outside of class?
- What have you done during the last few summer vacations?
- Where have you traveled? What were some specific things that happened on the trips?
- What was the best day of your life? What was the worst?
- What was the most memorable experience you had with your family? With your friends? In class?
- What was the most embarrassing experience you've ever had?
- What events in your life caused you to change?
- What are some difficult decisions that you've had to make or some dilemmas that you've faced?
- What do people often say about you? Do you agree with them?
- What are your favorite books, plays, movies, sports, and literary characters?
- What fiction have you been reading? What magazines? Any nonfiction, comic books, or poetry?
- Who have been the most influential or interesting people you have known? What historical figures have inspired you?
- What are your dreams and goals for the future? What do you want to accomplish in your life?

If these questions lead to other questions that you can answer or if other topic ideas come to mind during the brainstorming session, go ahead and write them down. Every idea is worth considering during this free-for-all session. You'll work on narrowing the field of potential ideas later.

Narrowing the List

After you've brainstormed, give yourself some time to think about the ideas that you came up with. Perhaps one of your ideas will fire up your imagination and get you thinking about specific events to write about. Perhaps one item on your list leads to other ideas. It's always a good idea to let the creative juices stew for a couple of days and see whether your brainstorming session automatically leads you to the best topic to write about.

If you have trouble focusing on one particular idea, read over your list again. At this point, think about which topics you could write the most interesting essays about and which ones will produce a dull or hackneyed essay. Cross off any topics that don't seem original, aren't important to you, or don't reflect your personality.

Not everyone has had great triumphs or tragedies in their life; in fact, very few of us have. Don't make the mistake of thinking that you have to write about some earth-shaking event. Often a poignant, detailed essay about an ordinary event can be more powerful and more illuminating of the personality behind the writer.

Read over the ideas that are left on your list once again. Consider which one might lead to the most original, most interesting essay. Which topic are you most passionate about? Here are some issues to think about when considering your focused list of topic ideas:

- Is the topic something that you think a lot of other applicants might write about, like a trip, sports, or your parents? If it is, do you have a unique approach to the topic so your essay will stand out from similar essays?

- Will this topic interest the admissions officer? Will it grab the reader's attention? You might want to discuss your list of remaining essay topics with a parent, teacher, or advisor to see what topics they find particularly interesting or unusual.

- Does the topic excite you? Does it show some insight into the real you? Will you be able to write passionately about it?

- Does the topic highlight strong qualities of your character or important things that you have accomplished?

- Can the reader identify with the essay? Writing about feelings and dilemmas that the admissions officer can relate to will result in a more memorable essay.

- Can you provide specific examples or interesting anecdotes to support your topic? An essay that tells a story, with concrete details, will result in a more interesting essay.

- Can you adequately explore the topic within the limits of the essay given on the application? If the application form specifies that the essay should be no more than 500 words long, you need a topic that you can thoroughly write about in that small amount of space.

At this point, you may have as many as five to ten ideas still remaining on your list. Prioritize these ideas, ranking the ones that you're most passionate about at the top of the list. Don't throw away your list even after you settle on a final topic. You may need ideas for other college and scholarship application essays. Or once you get started writing about a promising idea,

Watch Out!
Don't crib your essay from a book that showcases successful college application essays. You won't fool the admissions officer—they have a lot of experience reading essays, and their warning bells go off when they come across an essay that doesn't seem to match what they know about the author.

it may just fizzle. The only real way to know whether a particular idea can become a great essay is to try to write it.

Use the first draft of your essay to explore your chosen topic, to find out whether the topic interests you and whether you can sustain your passion about the topic throughout the entire essay. Don't worry about whether the essay is perfect at this point; instead, concentrate on getting your thoughts and ideas on paper. This is the "do or die" time for an essay topic. If something just isn't working, don't waste any more time on it. Instead, pick another topic and see where it takes you.

What You Shouldn't Write About

You should avoid certain essay topics. Some of them are so common that the admissions committee has read thousands of essays on the exact same theme. Some are so dull (or are fascinating only to you) that the admissions officer will forget about what you wrote five minutes after reading your essay. With some topics, you'll come off seeming arrogant or like a smart aleck. And with some, you run the risk of offending the admissions officer, which will definitely hurt your chances for admission.

Avoid the following essay topics at all costs:

- *The importance of a college education:* This is probably the number-one most common essay. It will be very difficult to be original and creative with this tired old topic.

- *How you felt when you won the big game:* Here's another topic that way too many applicants write on. Similar topics to avoid include how serving on student government taught you leadership, how traveling abroad taught you independence, or how joining a sports team taught you the importance of working together. Admissions officers have read these essays thousands of times before.

- *"Big" issues, like the meaning of life, world peace, or race relations:* A college application essay is too short to adequately cover a broad issue, and an essay on one of these themes will very likely lack in specifics. If you do choose a big topic, pick something that you are actively involved in and have a passion for; for instance, if you participate in the environmentalist movement, write about a specific experience connected with that involvement. The key is to make the essay topic a personal one, not one that's far removed from you.

- *The death of your grandmother or your dog:* It's very difficult to write an essay on these topics that's not full of cliches. College application essays should also focus on positive subjects, rather than negative ones.

- *Teen angst:* Yeah, we all went through it, but that doesn't make it interesting to anyone except other teens. This is another subject that admissions committees have seen a thousand times. Again, go for the upbeat topic rather than the downer.

- *How much you love yourself:* Or variations on the theme, such as how smart you are or how talented you are. You'll come off sounding arrogant, and you'll probably turn off the reader.

- *How great you did on the SAT:* Do not use the essay to focus attention on other parts of your application. Don't reiterate your extracurricular activities, emphasize the awards you have won, or repeat your grades. The admissions officer already knows all this. The essay is intended to provide *additional* information about you.

- *An explanation of why your SAT score stinks:* Why accentuate your shortcomings? You'll probably sound like you're avoiding taking responsibility for your bad score or any other shoddy spot on your academic or extracurricular record. Instead, try to show your best side—focus on your achievements, not your failures.

- *Your girlfriend or boyfriend:* The admissions officer just doesn't care about your sweetheart and how you feel about him or her.

- *Sex, religion, politics, and controversial social issues:* These are considered taboo subjects at the dinner table for a reason. You don't want to risk offending or turning off the reader.

You may wonder whether you should write a humorous essay. If you can get away with it, humor is an effective tool and will definitely be a plus for your application. If you can make an admissions officer laugh out loud, he or she *will* remember you. But keep in mind that many people think they are funnier than they actually are. Admissions officers hate essays that try to be funny but fail or that employ immature or silly humor. Several objective opinions are necessary to evaluate whether a humorous essay is effective; have your parents and teachers read the essay, not just your friends.

Rather than trying to write something funny, it's a much better idea to simply tell an interesting story. If you are a natural wit and the story is naturally funny, the inherent humor will come through without much extra effort on your part. And that will make for a much better essay.

Another common question is whether to take a risk with your essay. As with all gambles, both the potential downsides and benefits are big. A daring essay topic or unusual writing style may capture the admissions officer's attention and help you stand out when it comes time to make that final decision. Or it may turn the reader off entirely. You have no way of knowing which.

Generally, it's better to take a risk than to turn in a boring essay. One thing that a risky essay will do is get you noticed. Also, admissions officers tend to be open-minded and won't dismiss an essay out of hand just because it's not conservative enough (although you may want to rethink this approach if you are applying to a very conservative school).

At most schools, each essay is read two or more times. So, if you do turn off one reader, you may win the next one's heart. It's better for your essay

Watch Out!
While it would be interesting to write about something that the admissions officer may not k now much about, such as your ham radio hobby, make sure that you can adequately explain the subject within the confines of the essay. Don't rely on the admissions officer having special knowledge about the subject of your essay.

to stir up strong emotions in the reader, whether those emotions are positive or negative, than to not elicit any reaction at all.

Above all, keep in mind that the essay is supposed to express who you are. If you don't take risks in real life, then you probably shouldn't take risks in your essay. It will come off sounding false to the reader. But if you are a natural risk-taker, let that part of your personality shine through in your essay.

I don't advise taking too big a risk, however. Don't write your essay in iambic pentameter, for instance, or submit cartoons in lieu of an essay (unless the application form says you can). The primary purpose of the essay is to judge your writing skills, and these approaches won't allow the admissions committee to do that.

Bright Idea
Type your essay, unless told otherwise in the application form. Handwritten essays are very difficult to read.

Focusing Your Essay

Admissions officers read thousands of essays. You'll find it easier to grab the admissions officer's attention if you write about particulars. Narrow your focus to one very specific topic. Travelogues, autobiographies, or broad issues are often too general and will hurt you. Instead of writing about your entire trip to Europe, for instance, focus on one memorable meal or the time that you get lost in Rome. Instead of writing about your family, narrow the topic to one holiday tradition or special event that makes your point.

The most important part of your essay is the introduction. The opening is where you have to catch the admissions officer's attention and hook him or her into carefully reading the rest of the essay (instead of just skimming it and throwing it back on the pile). The introduction should pique the reader's curiosity by posing questions and presenting dilemmas. It should be catchy and creative. Spend a lot of time crafting the opening paragraph of your essay.

Here are some ideas for creating a compelling introduction:

- Start with a surprise or a mystery, something that startles the reader and makes him or her want to read past the first sentence.

- Raise an intriguing question or dilemma, something that the reader will want to learn the answer to.

- Use memorable, specific descriptions to paint a scene or introduce a mood. Appealing to the five senses is an effective way of making descriptions come alive.

- Forget long-winded introductions—launch into the story right away. Beginning with dialogue is an effective way to jump right into the story, especially if your essay describes an event that happened to you.

Your introduction should be fairly brief. Don't get too carried away with your creativity. You'll lose the reader's interest if you don't segue into the main body of the essay soon.

Never use the opener to tell the reader what you plan to write about in the essay. Don't make your opening sentence, "I want to tell you about my summer vacation" or "I am going to write about the most important moment of my life." Just jump in and begin the story.

When you finish writing the first draft of your essay, go back and reread the introduction. If it's dull, takes too long to get to the point where the story actually starts, or simply repeats what you say later in the essay, cut the first paragraph. Often, your essay is more powerful without it.

The rest of the essay should revolve around the common theme, the topic that you settled on. It should tell a story and progress logically from one idea to the next, coming to a natural ending that ties everything together.

While the ending should come to a conclusion that is naturally drawn from the rest of the essay, it shouldn't simply summarize the main points given in the essay. The best closings present a single important thought or strong image that lingers with the reader. A good way to create an effective closing is to refer back to the opening, especially if you introduced a clever or unusual thought in the first paragraph.

I can't teach you how to write effectively in one chapter. The best way to learn is to read lots of other essays—both successful college application essays and essays by professional writers—and study what makes those essays effective. Recommended essay collections are listed in Appendix C, "Recommended Reading."

Essay-Writing Dos and Don'ts (Mostly Don'ts)

The most important "do" when it comes to writing college application essays is this: Do rewrite and revise. The first draft is never the best draft. You will probably have to rewrite the essay several times to perfect it. That's why it's such a good idea to get started on your application essays early, so you'll have plenty of time to rewrite, revise, and receive feedback from objective readers.

After you complete a draft, it's always a good idea to let it sit for a day or so. When you come back to the essay, you'll approach it with a fresh eye.

When you rewrite the essay, look for ways to add more detail, cut repetition and awkward phrasing, show instead of tell, and connect ideas in a smooth flow. Delete everything that doesn't relate to your main argument or theme. If any particular word, sentence, or paragraph bothers you, try rewriting it in two new ways—one should "feel" better to you.

Keep the following tips in mind when writing and rewriting your college application essay:

- *Don't write what you think the admissions officer wants to read.* This will always result in an insincere, vague essay. Writing about who you really are, *your* concerns and thoughts, is a whole lot easier and will reveal more about yourself, which is what the admissions committee actually wants to see, anyway.

Watch Out!
Never repeat the essay question in your opening sentence. Too many essay writers employ this tired opener.

66

What is something that a college applicant can do to significantly hurt his or her chances for admission? *Not proofreading his or her essay—very important!*
—Lori Boatright, Admissions Counselor, Furman University

99

- *Don't write the standard five-paragraph essay with an introduction, three points of support, and a closing that you learned how to write in school.* Everyone writes these essays, and they're boring. In college, you won't write papers like this. Don't do it on your application. Instead, let the topic dictate the structure of the essay, so that the essay flows naturally from one idea to the next. (But just because you aren't writing a standard five-paragraph essay doesn't mean that your essay shouldn't have a clear beginning, middle, and end.)

- *Don't gush.* Don't tell the admissions officer that it's been a lifelong dream to attend this college and that you'll die if you aren't admitted. Avoid words like "best" and "worst," as in "winning the spelling bee was the best experience of my life" or "losing the big game was the worst thing to ever happen to me." Make every word honest and sincere.

- *Don't use stock phrases.* While you should build in transitions from one point to another, don't use phrases like "as a result," "secondly," or "in addition." Don't start your last paragraph with a phrase like "in conclusion" or "in summary." Avoid cliches.

- *Don't make spelling or grammatical errors.* Admissions officers read essays with a red pen in hand, so don't let silly mistakes be the one thing to catch the reader's attention. Proofread your essay several times, and get someone to proofread after you. Don't rely on a spellchecker or a grammar-checking program.

- *Don't use a thesaurus or Bartlett's quotations.* Peppering your essay with multi-syllabic words or lofty quotes to make it seem more impressive is one of the oldest tricks in the book, and the admissions officer will see right through it. Besides, a hallmark of good writing is using simple, vivid words and being as clear and concise as possible.

- *Don't begin your essay with a quotation.* It's been done before, a million times.

- *Don't use a distant, academic tone.* The college application essay is meant to be fairly informal. Adopt a tone that expresses your personality and helps express what's unique about you.

- *Don't write a scholarly essay or a research paper.* A well researched paper may be perfect for your English class, but it doesn't tell an admissions officer anything about you. Besides, the reader will probably suspect that you recycled an old term paper instead of writing an original essay.

- *Don't be vulgar, tasteless, or tell off-color jokes.* If you offend the admissions officer, he or she won't support you for admittance to the school.

- *Do use vivid, precise language.* Choose language that shows rather than tells. Use one precise word instead of three vague words. Avoid passive verb constructions at all costs.

- *Do read your essay out loud.* Reading your essay aloud is the best way to determine whether it's written in a natural voice—your voice. It can also help you catch awkward sentences, passive voice, and stilted language.

- *Do have others read the essay.* This is the most important step of all. Your parents, siblings, friends, English teacher, and guidance counselor can give you valuable feedback on your essay, and the more people who read it, the better your essay will be. Don't neglect getting help from others

The college application essay puts your writing skills under scrutiny. Your writing reflects your powers of persuasion, organizational abilities, style, and mastery of standard written English. If you have developed strong writing skills, you already have a serious edge over other applicants. You've just spent 12 years learning how to write—now is the time to put that knowledge to work.

Just the Facts

- The college application essay is your best opportunity to show admissions committees the real you; an original, dynamic, well written essay can easily push an average applicant into the accepted pile.

- College application essay questions tend to be broad and general, but questions usually fall into one of four categories: questions about you; questions about why you want to attend the college; creative questions; and open-ended questions with no specific topic.

- Choosing a specific topic for your essay is the most important step in writing the essay; devote a lot of time to finding a topic that's original, that you can write passionately about, and that expresses your personality.

- Admissions committees use the application essay to scrutinize your writing skills, so you must revise, rewrite, polish, and proofread your essay many times in order to make the best impression.

Bright Idea
Get a good style guide that will help you write your best. I recommend *On Writing Well* by William Zinsser and *The Elements of Style* by Strunk and White.

Maximize Your Test Scores

GET THE SCOOP ON...
The importance of standardized tests for getting into college
▪ The standardized test controversy ▪ How to prepare for
standardized tests ▪ Deciding whether to take a test-prep course ▪
What to do when test day arrives ▪ Proven strategies to use
when taking the tests

PART IV

The Unofficial Story on Standardized Tests

D uring your junior and senior years of high school, you will be taking a lot of standardized tests. All college-bound students take either the Scholastic Assessment Test (SAT) I or the American College Testing (ACT) Assessment. You may also have to take up to three SAT II Subject Tests, depending on the requirements of the schools to which you are applying. Your scores on these tests are supposed to supplement your high school record and other information about you that the admissions officer assesses to determine your qualifications for the college. Test scores also allow the admissions officer to compare you to other students across the country.

The first thing to do is to find out which standardized tests your schools require or recommend. Most colleges and universities—89 percent—accept scores from either the SAT I or the ACT (some prefer one test to the other, though). Some colleges require you to take specific SAT II Subject Tests, while others allow you to choose which ones to take. Many colleges are also interested in your scores on Advanced Placement (AP) exams, but these aren't usually required. And recently, some schools have dropped their reliance on standardized test scores for admissions decisions (you'll learn more about that later in this chapter).

How Important Are Standardized Test Scores to Colleges?

An applicant's standardized test scores show colleges how well the applicant has prepared for college and the applicant's ability to complete first-year college work. How important these scores actually are in making admissions decisions varies from college to college. Some schools rely heavily on them when deciding whom to accept, while others don't even require you to submit them. In most cases, they are a very important part of the admissions package, but test scores alone won't make or break your chances for admission.

Colleges use standardized test scores, particularly the SAT I and ACT, to accomplish three goals:

- *To amplify the picture of your academic abilities:* In combination with your high school grades, standardized test scores help admissions officers measure your academic abilities and achievements. Perhaps you pursued a challenging high school courseload and earned grades that were good but not great. Or maybe your classroom grades were hampered by difficult personal circumstances, such as the loss of a parent or the need to work through high school. In those cases, good standardized test scores can help confirm that you are brighter than your grades alone suggest.

- *To determine the balance of your knowledge and skills:* Colleges want to see a reasonable balance in scores on the different sections of the SAT I or ACT. They also want to see good scores on SAT II Subject Tests in a variety of subject areas. For example, while a 1200 on the SAT I is always a good score, it's much better to score a 600 on each part rather than a 780 on math and a 420 on verbal. Colleges consider the "balanced" student more promising than an "unbalanced" one, such as a math whiz who's lacking in communication skills. (The exception to this rule is if you are applying to a technical institute or an engineering program— those schools weigh your math score more heavily than your scores on the other parts of the test. But you will still need a decent verbal score, according to the school's standards, to succeed.)

- *To judge your standing within the pool of applicants:* Your college application—not only your test scores but all of your credentials—isn't read in a vacuum. The admissions committee measures you against the hundreds or thousands of other students who also applied to that college. Standardized test scores give colleges a consistent way of judging applicants from different regions of the country and different high schools against each other.

It's important to remember that your SAT I or ACT score alone won't make or break your chances of admission. Plenty of students have gotten into even the most selective colleges and universities with less-than-perfect test scores. Colleges take into account *every* aspect of your academic and personal record, and standardized test scores are just one part of that record. Certain parts of your record, especially your courseload, grades, and essay, count for much more than your standardized test scores at many colleges, particularly the more selective schools.

When you look through college guides, you'll often see a standard ACT and SAT I score listed for each school. This number usually refers to the *average* score of accepted applicants, rather than to some cutoff number. Don't worry if your score is lower than that number—you still stand a good chance of getting in, especially if the rest of your record is strong. It's a good idea to ask an admissions officer at the schools where you're applying about how much emphasis that school places on standardized test scores when deciding whom to admit, especially if you feel anxious about your scores or if you're letting your scores prevent you from applying to the schools where you really want to go.

Of course, it won't hurt your chances to get the best score possible. So, don't slack off. It's still important to prepare for each standardized test you take and to do your best on the tests.

But remember that while you can certainly be admitted to the college of your dreams with a less-than-perfect standardized test score, a perfect test score alone will never get you into college. You need the coursework, grades, extracurricular activities, letters of recommendation, and well-written essay to back up that test score, or colleges won't be interested.

The Standardized Test Controversy

The last two decades have seen a significant increase in skepticism regarding the value and authority of standardized tests. Standardized college admissions tests, like the SAT I and ACT, when considered along with high school transcripts and class ranks, are supposed to predict how well students will perform in college. But recent studies have shown that these tests do *not* accurately predict how certain groups of students—notably women, African Americans, Hispanics, and students from low-income families—will perform in college.

Studies also show that the tests do not favor students who can't afford coaching, students from poor urban schools, students who speak English as a second language, and students whose parents did not go to college. Consequently, these groups of students have fewer opportunities to attend the most prestigious colleges and universities and to share in scholarship money.

One academic study compared two admissions strategies, one using just the high school record, and the other using both the high school record and SAT I scores. More than 90 percent of admissions decisions were the same under both strategies. But when SAT I scores were considered, a greater number of otherwise academically qualified minority and low-income applicants were rejected.

A 1993 study by the MIT admissions office showed that female high school students were capable of performing better at MIT than their SAT I Math scores indicated. MIT compared the SAT I and college grades of men and women enrolled in the same majors, and found that in nearly every department, women's grades equaled or exceeded men, but their SAT I Math scores were lower.

The test administrators recommend that colleges and universities consider SAT I and ACT scores along with all the other parts of the application

The SAT or the ACT are *not* the be-all and end-all of college admissions. In the past we have had students come in with below-average scores and graduate in four years with 3.0+ GPAs.
—Todd Leahy, Admissions Counselor, Wofford College

Unofficially...
Colleges focus on your best SAT I scores. A sizeable minority—up to 40 percent—combine your highest Verbal and Math scores if those occurred on different days. Just a few insist on considering only your most recent scores. The admissions office will generally tell you their policies.

Unofficially...
Standardized tests are not infallible. The SAT I, for example, has an error range of 30points. That means that a student who scored 1150 one day could have easily scored 1120 or 1180 on another.

package, especially high school grades and courseload. Despite this recommendation, many colleges still set cutoff scores—often unpublicized—below which no student is considered for admission. Many other schools, particularly the large state universities, admit students on the basis of numerical formulas that incorporate SAT I or ACT scores. There is ample evidence that a large number of colleges and universities overweigh standardized test scores when deciding which applicants to admit.

If the amount of weight placed on standardized test scores by the colleges where you're applying concerns you, ask. In most cases, the admissions officer will honestly tell you how much emphasis the school places on test scores and how much weight the school gives to the high school record, the essay, and other parts of the application package when making admission decisions.

Another problem with the overemphasis on standardized test scores is that it leads some students, particularly minority students, to forego applying to the more competitive colleges because they're afraid that their test scores are too low to make them viable candidates. Bates College, a highly competitive liberal arts school in Maine, found that after it stopped requiring standardized test scores, the percentage of minority students applying to and enrolling in the school doubled.

In addition, standardized test scores are frequently used for purposes for which they have not been validated. Several scholarship programs—the National Merit Scholarship program is the most prominent—use standardized test scores as a cutoff or as the sole determination of who receives scholarship money. The National College Athletic Association (NCAA) sets a fixed SAT I or ACT cutoff score; students whose scores fall below this cutoff cannot participate in NCAA athletic programs, even if they are otherwise academically qualified. And many special academic programs, such as the Johns Hopkins Center for the Advancement of Academically Talented Youth, use standardized tests to select participants.

One result of the shift in perception about standardized testing is that hundreds of colleges and universities are beginning to consciously de-emphasize the importance of standardized test scores when making admissions decisions. For example, the University of Texas system has begun admitting in-state applicants ranked at the top of their classes, regardless of their performance on the SAT I. Also, the University of California at Berkeley has discarded the numerical cutoff that was previously used to remove some applicants from consideration. And the University of North Carolina at Chapel Hill, while still sorting applicants by the numbers, now searches for qualities that might override mediocre test scores, instead of rejecting those students outright.

Another result has been that an increasing number of colleges, like Bates College, have chosen to disregard test scores altogether in making all of their admission decisions. They find that with thoughtful analysis of the other parts of the application package, they can make equally good choices without considering applicants' test scores.

FairTest, a national organization devoted to fair and open testing at all grade levels, maintains a current list of colleges around the country that don't require SAT I and ACT scores for some or all of their undergraduate applicants. As of this writing, FairTest's list includes 284 colleges that don't require test scores or have made submitting test scores optional. Some of these schools are widely known and respected institutions. (Some of the schools on the list still require students to submit test scores, but they don't use the scores to make admissions decisions.)

All of the following colleges and universities don't require applicants to submit either SAT I or ACT scores (although some consider these scores when making admissions decisions if you do choose to submit yours):

- Antioch College (Ohio)
- Athens State University (Alabama)
- Audrey Cohen College (New York)
- Bates College (Maine)
- Bowdoin College (Maine)
- California University of Pennsylvania
- Caszenovia College (New York)
- Charter Oak State College (Connecticut)
- City University of New York—City College
- City University of New York—Medgar Evers College
- City University of New York—York College
- Dickinson College (Pennsylvania)
- Hampshire College (Massachusetts)
- John Wesley College (North Carolina)
- Lake Erie College (Ohio)
- Martin Methodist College (Tennessee)
- Marygrove College (Michigan)
- Michigan Technological University
- Mt. Sierra College (California)
- Muhlenberg College (Pennsylvania)
- National American University (South Dakota)
- Sheldon Jackson College (Alaska)
- Shimer College (Illinois)
- South College (Florida)
- South College (Georgia)
- Southeastern University (Washington, DC)

- St. John's College (Maryland)
- State University of New York at Farmingdale
- Thomas College (Georgia)
- University of Maine at Farmington
- University of Wisconsin at Stevens Point
- Wheaton College (Massachusetts)
- Wright State University (Ohio)

FairTest's more extensive list includes colleges and universities that don't require standardized test scores, or have made standardized testing optional, or don't require test scores for certain groups of students, such as in-state students. To view the complete list, visit FairTest's website at http://www.fairtest.org/, or send a self-addressed, stamped envelope to the following address:

> Tests Optional
> FairTest
> 342 Broadway
> Cambridge, MA 02139

You do have the option of foregoing standardized testing altogether, if you want to apply only to schools on FairTest's list. That said, two observations follow.

- First, the vast majority of American colleges and universities—including nearly all of the country's most prestigious and competitive institutions—still require scores on either the SAT I or ACT from their applicants.

- Second, if you do decide to skip the exam process—either from a conviction about the unfairness of testing, or from a belief that testing will hurt rather than help your chances—you'll have to rely that much more heavily on the other elements of your application package. It will be up to you—with help from your parents, counselors, and teachers—to figure out how your grades, essay, letters of recommendation, and the other elements of your application package can fully convey all the positive qualities that you have to offer.

Schools that eliminate standardized test scores still want the strongest possible students; they have simply chosen to seek those students through other means. The challenge of proving that you are such a student remains with you.

Getting Ready for the Tests

The test-makers may say that studying beforehand won't vastly improve your scores, particularly on the SAT I and ACT. I disagree, and numerous studies back me up on this. Your scores on any standardized test will improve if you prepare. By "prepare," I don't just mean studying the material that is tested.

It's also important to familiarize yourself with the format of each test you will take by learning what types of questions appear on the test, memorizing the directions for each question type, studying sample questions, and taking actual practice tests under timed conditions.

One particularly helpful side effect of test preparation is that it often reduces the fear and anxiety that many high school students feel about college admissions tests. You'll certainly do better on the test if you feel more relaxed and confident going in.

Many students can adequately prepare for standardized tests on their own. This is certainly the most cost-effective method, as you can order study guides and sample tests for a much lower price than you'd pay for a tutor or to attend a test-preparation course. It's also the most flexible solution. You don't have to keep to a classroom schedule, but can study whenever you have the time and at your own pace. If you take a test-prep course, you may have to sacrifice valuable extracurricular activities in order to make time for the extra classes.

A wide range of study materials is available for each standardized test, including books, software, videotapes, audiotapes, and online resources. In this section, you'll learn about the methods and materials that can help you prepare for any standardized test. In the next two chapters, you'll learn test-prep strategies for each specific standardized test that you're likely to take.

Printed Study Materials

Books and other printed study materials to help you prepare for the SAT I, ACT, SAT II, AP, and CLEP exams abound, and of course, some materials are better than others. You'll find a selected list of the best study guides in Appendix C, "Recommended Reading."

I recommend study guides that emphasize test-taking practice and give you actual questions from the tests to study, rather than those that emphasize strategies and tips. This is particularly important when preparing for the math portions of the SAT I and the ACT. Besides, you'll learn all the tips and strategies you need in this book.

The most valuable types of printed study materials are practice exams. The best of these are actual exams that were previously used; only the test-makers themselves, the College Board and ACT, publish these. Previously used exams give you the best idea of the format of the test, the kinds of questions that are asked, and where the most difficult questions are found. You can take the exams under timed conditions to learn how much time to spend on each question and what your weakest areas are, and to predict the scores that you'll receive on the actual tests.

You can order practice exams directly from the College Board (for the SAT I, SAT II, AP exams, and CLEP exams) or from American College Testing (for the ACT)—look in Appendix D, "Important Addresses," for contact information. Also, check your guidance office or school library for practice tests and other free test-preparation materials.

Timesaver
If you have access to the Internet, you can quickly order practice and study materials from the College Board's website at http://www.collegeboard.com/ or American College Testing's website at http://www.act.org/.

Test-Prep Software

Test-prep software can supplement your study and practice program. By comparison with a book, software programs have certain advantages and disadvantages. The relatively vast memory capacity of a CD-ROM means that a large amount of information—thousands of sample questions, for example—can be stored on a tiny disk, which is easier to carry around with you than a fat paperback book. And when you take a practice test on your computer, the computer can instantly and accurately score the test, and can rapidly diagnose your strengths and weaknesses.

Software has its downside, of course. Like any other form of information, a software program is only as good as the people who create it, and just as books vary in quality, so do software packages. Remember that the sample tests created by commercial test-prep companies and individual experts, while often good, lack the authenticity of real exams. Therefore, don't assume that the sense of an exam you get from a CD-ROM is necessarily accurate. Unless the test questions come from the test-makers themselves, it may not be.

A second possible drawback in using software to prepare for these standardized tests is that the tests themselves are not computerized. When you practice on a computer, you're distancing yourself from the actual test-taking experience. It's a bit like training for your driver's test using a joystick and video monitor—useful practice, maybe, but not quite the same as the real thing.

You can practice many test-taking strategies only on pencil-and-paper tests, such as marking up reading passages. When you practice on the computer, you forego the opportunity to sharpen these skills. And you avoid the problem of getting used to the pencil-and-paper answer sheet, which must be filled in accurately and in a specific way in order to be graded correctly.

Moneysaver
Software is more costly than books. As of this writing, you can buy an official guide containing 10 full-length practice SAT I exams for just $17.95. By contrast, the official test-prep software, *One-on-One With the SAT*, is priced at $29.95.

For all of these reasons, I urge you to use printed practice tests for at least part of your test-preparation strategy, so that when you take the real exam, you won't be jarred by the experience of working with an old-fashioned number-two pencil.

Video and Audio Test-Prep Packages

A small number of videotapes and audiotapes are available for students who enjoy those forms of teaching. As with software, the instructional medium is quite different from the medium of the test itself. But if you find it more interesting to learn through the voice of a "live" instructor, you may want to look for video or audio programs to help you study.

Online Resources

At this time, the Internet is not yet a major source of test-preparation materials—that will probably change over the next couple of years. You can register for tests, order score reports, and purchase study materials online, but there isn't enough hard information or practice tests on the Web to make up a true test-prep program.

The College Board, ACT, Princeton Review, and Kaplan all have large, active websites with lots of useful, general information about taking the tests and applying to colleges. In terms of test-preparation materials, you'll find little or nothing on these websites that you can't locate more quickly and easily in a book.

Appendix B, "College Admissions Resource Guide," lists various software, video, audio, and online resources that can help you prepare for standardized tests.

Other Proven Ways to Prepare

College admissions tests, particularly the SAT I and the ACT, are designed to measure students' academic abilities developed over time through schoolwork and other learning experiences. All of the experts agree—the best way to prepare for standardized tests is to take challenging courses in high school and do well on them. This curriculum purposefully teaches the test-taking skills and general knowledge needed to do your best on the tests. Fortunately, you're already doing this, because you know that colleges count a challenging courseload and high grades among the most important qualifications for admission.

The following are some other ways that you can prepare in the long term to score your best on the standardized tests:

- *Develop your math skills.* Take a challenging math course every year. Review basic algebra and geometry fundamentals before the test. If math is your weak point, retake a class or get individual tutoring.

- *Read, read, read!* One of the most important ways to prepare for the exams is to practice reading so you build your reading comprehension skills. Read a newspaper every day, and then summarize each article you read or discuss the content of different articles with your family. This is a great way to build comprehension of what you read while you keep abreast of current events.

- *Build your vocabulary.* Learn to love reading for pleasure. Try to read one novel or nonfiction book outside of assigned homework each month— you will learn new words used in the proper context. If you encounter an unfamiliar word, always look it up in the dictionary. Remember that colleges value well-read applicants.

Should You Take a Test-Prep Course?

There has been a lot of debate about the efficacy of test preparation services, such as the Princeton Review and Kaplan. The services themselves claim to increase your standardized test scores by as much as 140 points. Studies by the College Board show that the average score increase is much more modest, no more than 20 to 50 points. Both sources are biased—the test-prep services because they want you to take their courses, the College Board because it administers most of the tests and sells its own test-prep materials. So, who are you going to believe?

Watch Out!
Your friends don't have special knowledge about the SAT I or any standardized test, so be careful what rumors you listen to, and take them all with a grain of salt. If you prepare for the tests beforehand, then you should have no problems, no matter what horror stories you hear.

As I said in the previous section, you will probably score better if you do prepare, and the longer you prepare, the better the results. If you are self-motivated and disciplined, you can adequately prepare on your own using study guides and practice tests. But if you require a less independent approach or if you need a teacher's instruction, you may want to consider taking a test-prep course.

Research by the College Board (which administers the SAT I, SAT II, and AP exams) has shown the following general trends concerning the efficacy of test-prep courses:

- Short-term preparation courses (about 20 hours) improve scores by an average of 10 points on the verbal section and by an average of 15 points on the math section.

- Longer-term preparation courses (about 40 hours) improve scores by an average of 15 to 20 points on the verbal section and by an average of 20 to 30 points on the math section.

- Beyond the first 20 or 30 hours of coaching, typical score gains are minor.

- Preparation courses that teach math content rather than test-taking tips tend to result in greater score gains.

There are four kinds of test-prep courses, each with its own advantages and disadvantages:

- Individual tutoring
- School-based programs
- Local commercial programs
- National commercial programs

Individual Tutoring

In this kind of test-prep course, you work one-on-one with a tutor. The backgrounds, knowledge, and skill levels of tutors vary widely. Some tutors are recent college graduates who help students prepare for exams they themselves took not long ago. Others are high school teachers who moonlight as test-prep tutors. Very few work as tutors full-time. If you're looking for a good tutor, ask around; your friends, your parents' friends, or one of your teachers may be able to make a good recommendation.

Individual tutoring can be an excellent way to prepare for an exam. Scheduling is more flexible, and when "crunch time" comes and you need intensive work for a week or two before test day, you can more easily arrange for extra hours. The cost depends on your tutor's credentials, but generally speaking, individual tutoring is a cost-effective option—you pay only for the hours you need to spend with the tutor.

For many students, working with an individual teacher is highly motivating. Knowing that you can't hide when you don't know the material—easier to do in a classroom—gives some students the extra push they need to study and practice between tutoring sessions. And an individual tutor can focus on the topics you need help in, rather than having to stick to a pre-set curriculum.

It's up to you to decide whether the tutor has the right background to make a difference in your test scores. Being an experienced high school teacher certainly helps, because the skills involved in explaining complex topics are hard to develop in any way other than spending years in the classroom. You may have trouble finding a qualified tutor in your area, especially one who is equally knowledgeable in all areas of the test that you are preparing for.

School-Based Programs

Many high schools offer test-preparation courses before or after classes, during the lunch hour, or on Saturday mornings. Such programs are often free of charge. If your school offers such a course, strongly consider attending it.

Just as with individual tutoring, the quality of the instruction in a school-based program is quite variable—and all-important. Some teachers are very savvy about the skills needed to score highly on standardized tests—those are the teachers you want. Unfortunately, a school-based course may not give you a lot of choice when it comes to who teaches the class.

You have an advantage here, however, in that the teachers are generally part of the school's regular faculty. That means you probably know them or can find a classmate who has taken a course with them. Ask around. If the teacher gets high marks, that's a big plus. Another way to gauge the quality of the teaching is to find out how long the current teacher has been working in the test-prep area. If you can arrange a conversation with the teacher to ask about what will be taught and how, you may pick up a clue or two.

A school-based program may be a good choice for you if you feel you'll benefit from the convenience of classes held in your own school, and if the idea of working with teachers you already know appeals to you. On the other hand, if you're fed up with the same old faces and places by the end of the regular school day, this "advantage" may really be a disadvantage.

Local Commercial Courses

Commercial courses are run as for-profit businesses. A commercial course differs from individual tutoring in that it involves group study, a fixed class schedule, and a pre-arranged curriculum that usually covers all areas of the exam.

Local courses are staffed by area residents and aren't part of some nationwide program. In fact, local commercial courses are often run by individual tutors who want to expand their businesses.

Local test-prep courses offer some definite advantages. The same small group of teachers who owns and operates the business usually also teaches the classes. These are generally people with high school teaching experience. This means that you usually know who your teacher will be in advance, and you can ask friends, family, and teachers at your school how good the

Bright Idea
If you want to focus on a particular area of the exam, look for a tutor with special expertise in that area. For example, if algebra is your weakness, a skilled high school math teacher may be the best tutor for you.

Bright Idea
If you can't take a test-prep course, why not form a SAT I or ACT study group with other students at your school? All of you can purchase the same test-prep materials and work through them together. As a group, you can help each other stay on-task and understand difficult concepts.

test-prep teacher is. The classes are generally small—5–15 students. Individual tutoring is often available to supplement the classroom work for an additional fee.

Consider a local commercial course if your community has one with a good reputation. Before signing up, check with your local Better Business Bureau as to whether any complaints have been filed about the test-prep business in recent years. Also, try to find out what materials are used in the course, and get a look at them before you sign up. Any textbooks should be up-to-date. Model exams should preferably be drawn from the archives of real exams and published by the test-makers.

If you don't need the individual attention that a tutor can offer, and if you want a program that covers all of the topics and skill areas on the exam, then a local course may be a good choice for you.

National Commercial Courses

These programs bear much the same relationship to the local commercial courses as McDonald's bears to your neighborhood hamburger place. The nationwide courses are big businesses operating in a standardized fashion throughout the country, offering a product that's generally consistent and reliable in quality. You may not get the individual attention that a local tutor or teacher offers, but there are advantages that, for many students, outweigh any negatives.

Two major national test-prep schools offer SAT I and ACT courses. The larger and older is Kaplan Educational Centers. Newer and somewhat smaller, though also widely available, is Princeton Review.

A large staff of writers and editors develops the books, lesson plans, and study guides that Kaplan teachers use, and they constantly monitor changes in the exam and update the materials frequently. In addition to classroom lesson plans, Kaplan creates many other materials:

- Diagnostic tests, which generally use actual test questions to measure students' strengths and weaknesses.

- Homework materials, including sample tests and study guides.

- Instructional materials on CD-ROM and video.

Princeton Review is quite competitive with Kaplan in terms of the number, kinds, and quality of their course materials. One difference between the two schools is the sharper "attitude" that Princeton Review brings to the test-prep process. Princeton Review takes a somewhat cynical tone in its teacher and written materials, while Kaplan is slightly more subdued and conventional. (The difference is much less marked than it used to be, however.)

A typical test-prep course includes 12 class sessions, each three to four hours long. Several sessions are devoted to full-length practice tests. Students also have many opportunities for additional study and practice: office hours when students can visit are scheduled; workshops are offered

Watch Out!
Avoid a test-prep course that sounds like it will mainly be practice test sessions; you can do that on your own.

on specific test topics; and libraries of videotaped classes and workshops, as well as computerized exams for self-testing purposes, are available.

National courses are costly, ranging between $700 and $900 at Kaplan and Princeton Review. For most of us, these prices represent a significant investment.

When you invest in a national commercial course, you're paying a lot to support a significant infrastructure—not just the teacher in your classroom, but a staff of writers, editors, video production specialists, and more. This may be a worthwhile expenditure if you can take full advantage of what you're paying for. Thus, a national commercial course is most valuable for the student who attends every class, works diligently through the hundreds of pages of home-study materials, takes advantage of the teacher's office hours and special workshop sessions, and visits the school center for additional study and practice sessions (and who can afford the cost of the course in the first place).

If you've decided that a significant improvement in your test-taking skills is important to you because of a particular college you hope to attend, and if the financial cost of a national commercial course is affordable for your family, then by all means consider signing up for such a course. But before you do, ask yourself these questions: Do I have the time and the self-discipline to make use of all or most of the classes and materials available? Am I willing to eliminate some other activities from my schedule over a period of several months in order to make the most of what the commercial course has to offer? Am I sufficiently committed to the goal of attending a particular competitive college to make this kind of sacrifice worthwhile? If your honest answers are "yes," then investigate the national test-prep programs. If not, weigh the other alternatives.

Choosing a Test-Prep Course

See Table 9.1 for a breakdown on the different kinds of test-prep courses to help determine which one might be right for you.

When Test Day Arrives

The big day is here. Even the actions you take the night before and the morning of the test can improve your score. Follow these tips to make sure that you're running in optimum condition:

- Forget cramming the night before. Last-minute study probably won't make a difference in what you know, but it can make you more anxious and tired. Get a good night's sleep instead.

- Before you go to bed, put out everything that you'll want to take with you to the test center, including your official admission ticket, a photo ID, three number-two pencils with erasers, a calculator, a watch (without an alarm), and a high-energy snack.

- Set your alarm. If possible, have a backup system (like Mom or Dad) to wake you if the alarm fails.

Watch Out!
Be careful how much time you devote to test preparation. If you spend so much time preparing that your grades and extracurricular activities suffer, you'll only end up hurting your chances for admission to selective colleges.

Unofficially...
Let's put things in perspective. Standardized tests do not measure your intelligence, how well you learn, or how well you will do in your life. They just (arguably) predict your success during your first year at college—that's all.

TABLE 9.1: PROS AND CONS OF THE DIFFERENT KINDS OF TEST-PREP COURSES

Individual Tutoring

Pro	Con
Flexible scheduling	Variable teaching quality
Instruction tailored to your needs	Unlikely to be equally effective in all test areas
Can be highly motivating	Few or no special instructional materials

School-Based Program

Pro	Con
Little or no cost	Variable teaching quality
Convenient location	No change of scenery
A teacher you know	Quality of instructional materials may vary

Local Program

Pro	Con
Local and so usually convenient	Variable teaching quality
Pre-set curriculum covering the entire exam	Guarantee and payment policies need to be examined
Generally small classes taught by a locally known teacher	Quality of instructional materials may vary

National Program

Pro	Con
Wide availability throughout the country	High cost
Consistent, uniform program frequently updated by a knowledgeable staff	Instruction may be impersonal
Voluminous study and practice materials available	Extensive materials may seem overwhelming

WHICH PROGRAM SHOULD YOU TAKE?

Individual Tutoring	School-Based Program	Local Program	National Program
If you need the motivation of working one-on-one with a teacher; if you need help only with one or two specialized areas of the exam.	If the program at your school is well taught by experienced teachers; if you like the convenience of a class close to home.	If your community has one that comes well recommended; if you need a program covering the entire range of topics on the exam.	If you have the time, energy, and motivation to take advantage of the wide array of study and practice materials available; if cost is not an issue.

- Eat a good breakfast so you won't get hungry during the test. Bring a snack with you, like a granola bar or a piece of fruit.

- Dress in layers. You don't know whether the test room will be frigid or if the heat will be blasting. Wear clothes you can add or remove so that you'll be comfortable during the test no matter what.

- Know how to get to the test center, and plan to arrive well before the start of the test. Leave plenty of time to travel, in case you run into traffic problems.

- Before the test starts, make certain that your accommodations are comfortable. You should have a comfortable chair, an adequate writing surface, plenty of light, and a quiet space. If you're left-handed, you should have a left-handed desk. You should be able to easily see and hear the proctor. If any of these conditions are lacking, ask for help.

Test-Taking Strategies That Work Every Time

When you're actually taking the SAT I, SAT II, ACT, or an AP or CLEP exam, you can do several easy things to improve your score:

- Bring a calculator, if it's allowed. Research shows that students who use calculators score slightly better on the math portion of the tests, because they don't miss any questions due to computational errors.

- Memorize test directions beforehand. Remember—for every five minutes you spend reading the directions, you'll have five fewer minutes available to answer questions.

- Instead of immediately beginning to answer questions when told to do so, take 30 seconds or so to overview each section. Check the format, contents, and length of the section, looking for questions that you can easily answer and those that you want to leave until last. Get a good idea from the start how much time you can safely spend on each question.

- Complete the easy questions first, since they earn just as many points as the hard questions. You don't have to work through the questions in order (just be extra-careful that you fill in the answer grid correctly if you skip around).

- Make educated guesses on multiple-choice questions. Eliminate any answers that you know are wrong and then guess from the remaining choices.

- Fill in the answer grids carefully. Check often—at least once every five questions—that you're marking the answer grid correctly.

- Use your test booklet to make notes, cross off answers that you know are wrong, work out math problems, and mark skipped questions in case you have time to come back to them later. Any notes that you make in your test booklet won't be scored.

Watch Out!
If you requested special accommodations for the test, try to arrive extra early. You may need to find a different room or building, and the test administrators may have to do some last-minute scrambling to get all the details in place.

- Don't worry about answering every question. You don't have to get every question right to get a good score.

- Don't spend too much time on one question. Each question, easy and hard, is worth the same amount of points. If you get stuck on a question, just mark it in the test booklet and move on—you can come back later if time allows. If you really have no idea what the answer to a question is, generally it's better to skip the question than to try a random guess.

- Pace yourself. Keep track of the time remaining and budget how much time you'll devote to each question.

- If you have time, review your answers. When you review questions slowly, you may find a better answer. It's a popular misconception that your first instinct is the best answer; if during your review, you find a better answer, don't hesitate to change it.

- If you only have five minutes left and still have questions remaining, overview the remaining questions, decide which ones look easiest and quickest, and answer them promptly, making educated guesses if necessary.

- Try to stay relaxed. Don't let test-day anxiety hurt your confidence. Keep things in perspective—your test scores won't make or break your chances for college. At worst, you can always retake the test.

Just the Facts

- Don't stress too much over your test scores; while they are an important part of the application package, your scores alone will *not* keep you from going to college.

- Long-term preparation for standardized tests can significantly improve your scores; the best forms of test preparation are taking challenging courses, improving your reading and math skills, and taking lots of practice tests under timed conditions.

- Test-prep courses and tutoring can be costly and often aren't necessary if a student is motivated and disciplined enough to prepare on his or her own; however, if you require individualized attention in one test area or if you need the motivation that a teacher can provide, look into taking a test-prep course.

- Don't try to cram for standardized tests—it won't help you. Instead, get a good night's sleep and go into the test feeling relaxed and confident.

- While taking the test, remember to make educated guesses, fill in answer grids correctly, pace yourself, and don't spend too much time on any one question—following all of these strategies can help you get a better score.

Bright Idea
If you find that you mismarked your answer sheet, raise your hand and get the proctor's attention. Explain the problem and ask for a few minutes after the test with your answer sheet only to make corrections. This request will probably be granted.

GET THE SCOOP ON...
Determining which test to take ▪ Figuring out when to take the
test ▪ Learning about the preliminary tests ▪ Strategies for tackling
the SAT I ▪ Strategies for tackling the ACT ▪ Where to find free study
aids and practice tests

Doing Your Best on the SAT I or ACT

It's almost impossible to avoid it. If you're planning to apply to college, you pretty much have to take one of the standardized college admissions tests—the SAT I or the ACT. Just thinking about these tests raises anxiety levels in the average high school student. You've probably already heard all the horror stories about how difficult the tests are and how crucial the scores are to getting into the top schools.

Too many students let themselves get way too worked up about these tests. As I explained in the last chapter, colleges don't weigh standardized test scores as heavily as you might imagine. And even if they do, the SAT I or ACT is not a one-shot deal—you can always take the test again if you're unhappy with your scores.

One of the best ways to alleviate test anxiety is to become familiar with the test before you take it. Learn what the questions are like, what you will be tested on, and what your score is based on before test day. Arm yourself with proven strategies that increase your confidence and help you score higher. This chapter will help you with all of that. You'll also get valuable advice about which test to take, when to take it, and where to find free test-prep materials.

Which Test Should You Take?

The SAT I is the most widely taken of the two college entrance exams; it is most often given in the Northeast, along the east coast, and in the West. In the Southeast, Midwest, and Rocky Mountain region, more students take the ACT. As a rule, colleges and universities prefer to see scores that most of the high school students in their region take. Therefore, the Ivy League schools prefer to see SAT I scores, and schools in the Midwest prefer ACT scores.

The majority of colleges and universities will accept a score from either test. At a few schools, you're required to submit scores from one particular test (every school lists such requirements in its application materials). You may not even know where you will apply in your junior year when you first take the tests, so it can be difficult deciding which one to take.

One way to decide is to try to figure out which test you'll perform better on. Both tests cover the basic skills and knowledge that you should have acquired throughout secondary school. Both tests assess a student's chances of succeeding during his or her first year in college. But beyond that, the tests are very different. Depending on your particular strengths and weaknesses, you may score significantly better on one test than the other.

In general, the SAT I focuses more on test-taking strategies, while the ACT focuses more on factual knowledge and specific skills. To put it another way, the SAT I tends to reward mental cleverness and quickness. The ACT tends to reward students who have mastered the basic information in their high school English, math, and science courses.

The following are the main differences between the two tests:

- *Number of questions:* There are about 140 questions on the SAT I and 215 questions on the ACT, but both tests last three hours. That means you have less time to spend on each question on the ACT.

- *Scoring:* On the SAT I, you get two subscores—Math and Verbal—and one overall combined score. On the ACT, you get a separate score for each of the four sections, plus a comprehensive score; you also receive subscores in each section (except Science Reasoning). Therefore, ACT scores tell colleges more about your specific academic strengths and weaknesses.

- *Number of answer choices:* For most of the questions on the SAT I, you have five choices to select from. For most of the questions on the ACT, you have only four answer choices. If you guess randomly on the SAT I, you should get 20 percent of the questions correct; if you guess randomly on the ACT, you should get 25 percent correct.

- *Guessing penalty:* The SAT I deducts a fraction of a point on most sections for incorrect answers. This is supposed to offset the number of questions that you would get right if you guessed randomly at the answers. The ACT does not deduct points for incorrect answers, so you can guess without penalty.

- *Math:* While both tests cover the full range of high school math, the SAT I has two types of questions not found on the ACT: quantitative comparisons that ask you to decide whether one quantity is greater than another; and a set of problems that you must solve and write your answers in the grid instead of picking from multiple choices. On the other hand, the Math section on the ACT includes trigonometry questions (only a handful), which you won't find on the SAT I.

- *Verbal:* Both tests rely highly on reading passages and multiple-choice questions to test verbal skills. The ACT poses questions about punctuation, grammar, and rhetoric (or writing skill), while the SAT I does not. The SAT I focuses more on critical reading skills, with longer reading passages. Also, the SAT I heavily tests vocabulary; the ACT doesn't test it at all.

- *Science:* The SAT I doesn't test science skills at all. The ACT has an entire section devoted to testing whether you understand scientific theory and experimentation procedures.

Here's another thing to think about. Many colleges require up to three SAT II Subject Tests in addition to the SAT I. If you take the ACT, several schools—including Bryn Mawr, Boston College, and Duke—waive the SAT II requirements, saving you hours of testing and preparation time. Testing policies vary from school to school, so don't assume that you'll get out of taking all SAT II Subject Tests just because you take the ACT. Check the specific requirements of each school where you're applying.

If you're still having trouble deciding which test to take, try completing a practice SAT I and a practice ACT to see which one you're likely to perform better on. If you felt more comfortable with the question types, format, or time limits of one test over the other, then that's the one you should take.

Of course, you can always take both tests, if they are both given in your area and the registration fees aren't too exorbitant for your family. In fact, many students do just that. Submitting scores from both tests gives the colleges one more piece of information with which to assess you and can often help your chances of admission if you end up scoring significantly higher on one test than the other.

If you've already taken one test, and you're considering taking the other, you may wonder what score you should expect to get on the second test based on how you did on the first. Table 10.1 compares composite ACT scores with corresponding combined SAT I scores.

Bright Idea
If you don't score well on the SAT I, you may find that the ACT provides a different, sometimes better reflection of your overall academic performance because the ACT tests four major subject areas instead of two. In that case, you may want to take both tests.

TABLE 10.1: COMPARING ACT AND SAT I SCORES

ACT Composite Score	SAT I Combined Score
11	500–510
12	520–580
13	590–650
14	660–700
15	710–750
16	760–800
17	810–850
18	860–890
19	900–930
20	940–970
21	980–1010
22	1020–1050
23	1060–1080
24	1090–1120
25	1130–1160
26	1170–1200
27	1210–1230
28	1240–1270
29	1280–1310
30	1320–1350
31	1360–1400
32	1410–1450
33	1460–1500
34	1510–1550
35	1560–1590
36	1600

Deciding When to Take the Test

It's a good idea to take the SAT I or ACT for the first time as a junior in high school, during the spring semester. You should be well-prepared for the test by this time, and taking it early ensures that your scores are ready when you start applying to colleges. Your test scores may help you decide to take an additional class or two as a senior, and you have time to retake the entire test in the fall of your senior year (plus a test-prep course, if you need one) if your scores need improvement.

Unless you score perfectly the first time, it's always a good idea to take the test twice. Most students find that their test scores rise the second time they take the test. If you prepare in a focused and disciplined way before your second exam, you have the opportunity to achieve a significant score increase. (Turn to Chapter 12, "After the Tests," for more information about deciding whether to retake a standardized test.)

If you take the SAT I or ACT as a junior, you have a lot of flexibility in deciding when to test, because the tests are given so many times in the year. But if you decide to retest as a senior, your options quickly narrow, especially when you factor in college application deadlines.

Check the application deadlines for the colleges where you're applying. Determine which college sets the earliest deadline, and count back eight weeks from that date—this is the *latest* date you should take the test. This allows a little extra time for your score report to be sent to the college.

Suppose that, working backwards from your earliest college deadline, you determine that the latest date to take the SAT I or ACT is in December of your senior year. If you can, take the exam one or two test administrations earlier, in October or November. That way, you have the choice of taking the exam one more time if you still don't get the scores you want. And there's another benefit—you'll get the test over with, and you won't have to worry about it when you're busy completing your applications and polishing your essays.

Registering for the SAT I

The SAT I is usually administered seven times a year: in early October; early November; early December; late January; late March or early April; early May; and early June. You should find plenty of SAT I bulletins and registration forms in your guidance office. You can also request registration materials directly from the College Board, which administers the test:

College Board SAT Program
P.O. Box 6200
Princeton, NJ 08541-6200
(609) 771-7600

You'll need to register well in advance of your chosen test date. Regular registration deadlines are about four weeks prior to the exam. You can register late for an extra fee (currently $15), but this only gives you a few more days. So, don't put off registration.

Watch Out!
If you're applying under an early decision or early action plan, the October test date may be too late to retake the SAT I or ACT. Consider taking the test during the summer if you plan to apply early.

When you register by mail, you'll fill in a fairly lengthy computerized form, which requires you to blacken in ovals using a number-two pencil. Take your time filling out the form; it's easy to make mistakes. Be especially careful when looking up and transferring the code numbers for the test center where you want to take the exam and the code numbers for the colleges that you want to receive your test scores.

If you find that all the test centers are 75 miles from your home, you don't need to make a time-consuming trek. The College Board can arrange a special test location for you. You'll have to enter a special code as your first-choice test center and enclose a letter explaining the problem.

If you have access to the Internet, you can also register for the SAT I online at http://www.collegeboard.org/. You'll need a credit card to pay the registration fee.

Once you register, you can use the phone to do things like register for subsequent tests, request a change in test center, or add colleges to your score report list. The number to call is 1-800-SAT-SCORE (TTY is 1-609-882-4118). Expect to pay a fee for each new service you request.

Taking the SAT I isn't cheap. Currently, the minimum fee to register is $23.50. And if you sign up for the Question-and-Answer Service or the Student Answer Service, request a few additional college score reports beyond the four you get for "free," and throw in one or two other services, the cost can easily climb to $70 or more.

If your family finances make SAT I fees a problem, visit your high school counselor and ask for information about getting the fees waived. Be sure to check in with your counselor at least a week before the registration deadline, so there is plenty of time to get the necessary paperwork completed. Also talk to your guidance counselor if you are learning disabled, if you require special accommodations because of a physical disability, or if you need to take the test on Sunday due to religious reasons—special arrangements can be made for you.

Bright Idea
The Question-and-Answer Service or Student Answer Service enables you to get detailed information about how you did on the SAT I, which can be very useful for preparation if you retake the exam. There is a fee ($5 to $10), but it's well worth it.

Registering for the ACT

The ACT is usually given six times a year, in late September, late October, early December, early February, early April, and early June. Note that the September test date is available only in a limited number of states: Arizona; California; Florida; Georgia; Illinois; Indiana; Maryland; Nevada; North Carolina; Pennsylvania; South Carolina; Texas; and Washington.

You can pick up registration materials in your high school guidance office. If you have Internet access, you can also register for the ACT online at http://www.act.org/aap/REGIST/elecreg.html. You will need a MasterCard or Visa to pay for the registration fee if you register online.

The basic registration fee for the ACT is $21, which includes sending score reports to four colleges. If you can't afford the basic registration fee, you may be eligible for a fee waiver. You can request a fee waiver only through your high school guidance office, so see your guidance counselor for more information.

Registration deadlines usually come four to five weeks before the test date, so you have to start thinking about registration early. You can register late for a fee of $15; the late registration deadline usually falls two to three weeks before the test.

If you miss the registration deadline for the ACT, you can try to test as a standby. Just bring your registration folder and fee payment with you to the test center on the day that you want to try to take the test. Standbys are admitted on a first-come, first-served based, and only if space, testing materials, and testing staff are available after all the registered students have been admitted. This option also costs more than if you had registered ahead of time ($51).

If you require special testing accommodations—if you have a physical or learning disability, if you are homebound or confined to a hospital, or if your religious beliefs prohibit Saturday testing—you can request them. The booklet, *Registering for the ACT Assessment,* provides instructions on how to request special accommodations. Your guidance counselor can also help.

To get answers to your questions about registration, contact American College Testing directly:

> ACT Registration
> P.O. Box 414
> Iowa City, IA 52243-0414
> (319) 337-1270

Taking a Preliminary Test

An excellent way to practice for the SAT I or ACT is to take a preliminary test during your sophomore or junior year. The preliminary test shows you what the actual test is like, lets you assess your skills and see where you need improvement, and forecasts your scores on the main test. SAT I test-takers take the Preliminary SAT/National Merit Scholarship Qualifying Test (PSAT/NMSQT) during the fall of their junior year, while ACT test-takers take the PLAN during the fall of their sophomore year. (You can also take the PSAT during your sophomore year, if you want additional practice.) Virtually all of the test-taking strategies that you'll learn in this chapter apply to the preliminary tests as well.

Judging by your scores on the PSAT or PLAN, you can determine how much preparation you need for the "big" test. Because you take the preliminary test so early, you should have plenty of time to complete a test-prep course or several test-prep study guides before SAT I or ACT time rolls around. Preliminary test scores are *not* reported to college, so you can take the test as early or as many times as you like without fear that your scores will affect your chances for admission.

The PSAT/NMSQT has one important added benefit. A good score on the test may also qualify you for the National Merit Scholarship program (for more information about the National Merit Scholarship program, turn to Chapter 15, "Searching for Scholarships"). It also has a half-hour Writing Skills section, which helps you prepare for the SAT II Subject Test in Writing, which many colleges require.

For more information about the PSAT/NMSQT, contact:

PSAT/NMSQT Office
P.O. Box 6720
Princeton, NJ 08541-6720
Phone: (609) 771-7070
TTY: (609) 882-4118
psat@collegeboard.org

Preliminary tests are administered by your high school—you register through your guidance office. The PSAT is given on two dates in October, while the PLAN is given on several dates from September through December. (If you're homeschooled, contact the principal or guidance counselor at a local high school to arrange to take the preliminary test well in advance of the fall test dates, preferably during the previous June.)

Finding Your Way Around the SAT I

The SAT I lasts three hours and is divided into seven sections:

- Three Verbal sections, two of them 30 minutes long and one 15 minutes long

- Three Math sections, two of them 30 minutes long and one 15 minutes long

- One additional 30-minute section containing either Verbal or Math questions, called the "equating section"

The equating section contains questions that won't count toward your final test score. This section is included partly to ensure that the test is fair; it uses a statistical process intended to equalize scores across two or more editions of the exam. The other purpose of the equating section is to test newly written questions before they are given to students "for real."

Don't count on being able to recognize the equating section when you take the test—it looks just like all of the other sections, and it can appear anywhere in the test. Do your best on all the sections, and don't worry about which one is the section that won't count.

You need to know three things about the format of the SAT I:

- *The sections may appear in any order.* Your SAT I booklet could start with either a Verbal section or a Math section, and the equating section can appear anywhere in the sequence. Verbal and Math sections usually alternate, but they needn't always. Most often, the two 15-minute sections come last.

- *Several forms of the test are given at any time.* The test-makers refer to the different editions of the SAT I as "forms." Each form has a different batch of questions (called "items"). On any given test day, several forms are used, not only across the country but even within the same test room. The person sitting next to you may be working on a completely different exam. (Among other benefits to test-makers, this discourages cheating!) So, don't be alarmed if you notice that your neighbor is working on a Verbal section while you're working on a Math section—it's no mistake.

▪ *The test-makers may change the test format if they wish.* Don't assume that your SAT I exam will precisely follow the format outlined here or even in the official guides provided by the test-makers. Although variations are rare, they do happen. And from time to time, the test-makers experiment with new formats and new types of questions.

Strategies for Answering Verbal Questions

There are three types of Verbal questions:

▪ Analogies

▪ Sentence Completions

▪ Critical Reading

Each Verbal section contains a mixture of each type of Verbal question. The questions aren't divided equally. For example, one Verbal section may have six analogy questions out of 30 total questions, while another Verbal section may have 14 analogy questions out of 35 total questions.

Analogies

Analogies test your vocabulary and your understanding of how words relate to each other. These questions are designed to test general vocabulary words that a well-rounded high school student should already know. They don't test specialized knowledge or classroom learning. Still, it pays to build your vocabulary before the test, both by studying word lists and by reading a lot.

Each analogy question presents a pair of words that are related in some way; these are called *stem words*. The stem words are followed by five answer choices, each consisting of another word pair. Your task is to choose the word pair that is related in the same way as the stem words are. Here's an example:

CRUMB : BREAD ::

(A) ounce : unit

(B) splinter: wood

(C) water : bucket

(D) twine : rope

(E) cream : butter

Establish the relationship between the stem words before you look at the answer choices. The best way to do this is to make up a short sentence that uses the two stem words meaningfully, defining the logical relationship

Bright Idea
Reset your watch to noon as each new section begins, so you can tell at a glance how many minutes remain to complete that section.

Watch Out!
The most common trap on analogies is picking an answer because the words it contains are similar to the stem words— both the stem words and the answer pair have to do with cooking, for instance. Ignore surface similarities and look deeper to find the most similar logical relationship.

between the two words. Then, try plugging each of the answer pairs into the sentence. Only one should work!

For example, in the question given above, you might make up the following sentence: "A <u>crumb</u> is a very small piece of <u>bread</u>." Then, plug in all of the answer choices. Only answer choice B makes sense when used in the same sentence: "A <u>splinter</u> is a very small piece of <u>wood</u>." Therefore, B is the correct answer.

Here's one way to improve your SAT I Verbal score—study the roots of words. Often, you can use word roots to figure out the meanings of words you don't know. For example, if you know that "chronos" means "time," then you know that the words chronograph, chronology, synchronize, and anachronistic are all related to the concept of time. If you happen to know what "graph," "ology," "syn," and "ana" mean, then you can figure out the meanings of all those words even if you've never seen them before.

Your SAT I test will probably have a total of 19 analogy questions, out of 78 total Verbal questions. Thus, analogies count as 24 percent of your overall Verbal score. To score well, you should answer analogy questions at a rate of better than one per minute.

Sentence Completions

Sentence completion questions test your understanding of sentence structure. They also further test your vocabulary. Each question consists of a sentence with one or two blanks, plus five answer choices. You have to select the answer choice that best completes the sentence. The best answer completes the meaning of the sentence *without* adding any new ideas.

Here's an example of a sentence completion question:

Medieval kingdoms did not become constitutional republics overnight; on the contrary, the change was _____.

(A) unpopular

(B) unexpected

(C) advantageous

(D) sufficient

(E) gradual

Each sentence in a sentence completion question contains two ideas, which are connected in some way. Understanding how the ideas in the sentence are connected will help you solve sentence completions.

In the example given, the sentence has two distinct parts, divided by the semicolon. Ask yourself how the two parts are connected. Both parts of the sentence talk about "the change." The first part tells us something about what the change was *not*, namely that it didn't happen overnight. The second part tells us something about what the change *was*.

Therefore, both parts of the sentence talk about the same topic—the historical change—but they approach the topic differently. The first half expresses the idea negatively, and the second half expresses it positively. Once you see this, you can guess the meaning of the missing word. The change was *not* an overnight change, so look for a word that means the opposite of overnight. The only answer that fits the bill is answer choice E, "gradual."

Don't even look at the answer choices until after you've read the sentence and established the connection or connections—some sentences have more than one. First, try to guess the missing word or what the missing word means. Then, scan the answers, looking for the one that means the same as your guess. Since all of the answer choices will make sense in the sentence, this method keeps you focused on choosing the one *best* answer.

Your SAT I exam will probably have a total of 19 sentence completions, out of 78 total Verbal questions. Like analogies, sentence completions count for 24 percent of your total Verbal score. To score well, try to answer sentence completions at the rate of one per minute.

Critical Reading

On critical reading questions, you must demonstrate that you can comprehend the content of written material, both fiction and nonfiction. Critical reading questions account for more than half of the Verbal questions on the SAT I, and they count for 49 percent of your overall Verbal score.

You are given a passage of 400 to 850 words to read, followed by a series of multiple-choice questions. The questions ask about the main ideas, details, inferences, arguments, and tones of the passages. Virtually every critical reading set also includes one or more questions about the vocabulary used in the passage.

Spend about one minute per question on any group of reading passages. For example, when you tackle a set of two passages with a total of 15 questions, plan to spend 15 minutes on the entire set. Expect to spend about half of that time reading, and the other half answering the questions.

Critical reading on the SAT I poses a unique time-management problem. Unlike the other question types, critical reading requires you to spend a large chunk of time doing something *before* you look at the questions— namely, reading the passage itself. Under the circumstances, with time pressure a real concern for most students, it's easy to get impatient. The temptation to rush through the passage in your haste to start filling in answers may be very great.

Don't do it! Unless you invest some time in getting to know the reading passage, your chances of answering most of the questions right are pretty slim. I recommend the three-stage reading method, a proven technique long taught and used by skilled readers as the best way of getting the most possible information out of a piece of writing. If you practice the three-stage method, you'll soon find that you're gathering more information out of what you read even more quickly than before.

Here are the three steps:

Timesaver
Sentence completion questions are often long, complex, and confusing. Don't worry about understanding the topic of the sentence. Concentrate on looking for key words and phrases that tell you what kind of connection is being made in the sentence—that's the quickest way to get to the answer.

Bright Idea
All SAT I questions count the same number of points. Reading comprehension questions are often the most difficult and time-consuming questions. So, leave them until last in any Verbal section, because you will probably complete more questions overall.

1. *Preview:* Either skim the entire passage, or read only the first and last sentences of each paragraph in the passage. This gives you some idea of what the passage is about and how it is organized before you actually read it. If you know generally what the passage is about before reading it, you'll understand it better. Spend about 30 seconds on this step.

2. *Read:* Go ahead and read the passage through.

3. *Review:* Scan the passage one more time, reminding yourself of the main ideas, most important details, and overall structure. Like previewing, this should be a fast process—spend no more than 30 seconds to review an average passage.

Keep in mind that the SAT I is not about speed-reading. If you can read at an average rate of 250 words per minute, as most high school students do, you'll have plenty of time to read the passages on the exam using this method. If you're unsure of your current reading speed, test yourself with a sample passage and a watch. Count the words and divide by the number of minutes spent reading to determine your reading rate.

Strategies for Answering Math Questions

Half of the SAT I tests the math skills you learned in your high school math classes, ranging from basic arithmetic through geometry and Algebra II. There are three scored Math sections:

- Regular Math
- Quantitative Comparisons
- Grid-ins

Regular Math

The Regular Math section tests your ability to complete standard math problems. You will find problems in arithmetic, algebra, and geometry on this section, all with five multiple-choice answers. You'll be given a varied mixture of problem types, including word problems, problems that involve reading and interpreting graphs and charts, geometry problems with and without diagrams, and a few straightforward arithmetic and algebra problems.

Your SAT I exam will probably have a total of 35 multiple-choice math problems, out of 60 total math questions. They count as 58 percent of your overall math score.

Plan to answer multiple-choice math problems at a rate of almost one per minute. The test-makers give you slightly more time than this, so if you finish one question each minute, you'll have a little extra time to check your work.

Read each question carefully and make sure you know what is being asked and what form the answer should take. If you read hastily, you may answer one particular question when, in fact, the test-makers are asking a different one.

Timesaver
Read with your pencil in your hand. Mark main ideas as you find them by underlining or circling them. To review, simply reread the phrases you marked.

Timesaver
For math problems with complicated formulas and several variables, it can actually be faster to plug in the multiple-choice options for each variable than to use formulas to figure out what the variables are.

Don't get bogged down in lengthy or complex calculations. Most SAT I math questions are deliberately designed to make complicated calculations unnecessary. The test-makers are more interested in seeing whether you understand the basic structure of the problem than whether you can correctly complete a series of computations. If you find yourself starting a complicated set of calculations, stop—you're probably overlooking a simple shortcut.

It is not always necessary to work with exact numbers in solving the math problems on the SAT I. Sometimes the fastest and even the most accurate way to an answer is to round off the numbers and "guesstimate." Glance at the answers. If they are all close together, you need to find a fairly precise answer. But if they are far apart, you can work with approximate numbers and still come up with a result that's close enough to lead you to the right answer.

You are allowed—and even encouraged—to use a calculator when taking the SAT I. But if you're smart, you'll be very selective in using the calculator. Most students should touch the calculator on only one question out of four, or less. Here's why:

- Math questions on the SAT I are specifically designed *not* to require a calculator. The exam focuses on mathematical reasoning, not on your ability to perform computations.

- It's easy to hit the wrong key, hit the right key twice instead of once, or make other mistakes when using a calculator, especially when you are hurriedly working with big numbers.

- You may be lulled into a sense of false security because you rely on the accuracy of the machine. Therefore, you may overlook a math mistake that you'd otherwise spot.

- If you *do* suspect a math error when using your calculator, it's impossible to retrace your steps, since you have no notes to check.

A calculator can be a useful tool, especially if you suddenly blank out on what 8×7 is (it happens to the best of us). But don't rely on it too heavily. If you find yourself working the calculator on all or even most of the questions, you're overdoing it. Put it aside, and grab it only when really necessary.

Most importantly, start work on each question *without* the calculator in hand. The key is to decide what the question is asking, what information you have, and how to get from here to there. Only after you've figured these things out should you start calculating.

Quantitative Comparisons

This section tests your ability to examine sets of numbers and determine relationships between them. Questions always follow the same format: Two quantities are presented, one in Column A and the other in Column B. You have to select the quantity that is greater (either A or B), choose C if the two

Bright Idea
When in doubt on a math question, try something. The problem will often suggest a procedure you've used in math class—use it even if you can't see how it leads to the answer you want. Quite often, tinkering with the numbers quickly leads you to the solution.

Timesaver
Basic geometry facts and formulas are given in the Reference Information at the start of each Math section. If you go blank, this makes a handy survival tool. But every time you refer to it costs precious seconds. You should know this information backwards and forwards, so that looking it up during the test is rarely necessary.

quantities are equal, or choose D if you don't have enough information to decide.

Here's what a typical quantitative comparison question looks like:

<u>**Column A**</u>   <u>**Column B**</u>

a is 30% of b

b is 40% of c

| Percent that
a is of c | 11 |

The question starts with two lines of information that is centered between Column A and Column B. This information isn't part of either column but instead is provided to help you interpret the values given in the columns. You're to assume that this information is true and that it applies to whatever quantities appear in the columns underneath. The quantities that you're supposed to compare are enclosed in the boxes.

You need to answer quantitative comparisons at the rate of one per minute. To do well on this section, compare without calculating. These aren't conventional math problems; you aren't required to find the *exact* value of any quantity. Think quickly about the quantities, looking for a fast way to decide which is bigger. In most cases, you can do that with approximate values or with no definite values at all.

You must make the two columns look alike to compare them. In the example given, column B contains a simple integer. So, your plan should be to turn Column A into a simple integer as well. To do that, you'll have to use your math skills. Since the shared information tells you that a is 30 percent of b and b is 40 percent of c, you can tell that a must be 30 percent of 40 percent of c:

$$30\% \times 40\% = 12\%$$

Now, you have a quantity for column A—12—that can easily be compared to Column B. Column A is greater, so the correct answer is A.

When in doubt about how to get started comparing the two columns, try something! It may not be obvious what the test-makers want you to do with either quantity. If so, start messing around with the quantities, using whatever mathematical techniques strike you as natural or logical. Chances are good that some method you've employed dozens of times in math class will yield the results that the test-makers are looking for.

Your exam will probably have a total of 15 quantitative comparisons, out of 60 total math questions. They count as 25 percent of your overall math score.

Grid-Ins

In this section, you're being tested on your ability to figure out your own answers to math problems, without the crutch of multiple choices. This

Watch Out!
For many quantitative comparisons, it's impossible to determine the precise value of one or both quantities. This may tempt you to opt for answer D, "the relationship cannot be determined." Not necessarily! Even imprecise or vague quantities can sometimes be compared.

section includes the same kinds of problems as the Regular Math section, but you have to fill in your answers on a special grid. Thus, you can use the same strategies that you used to answer the multiple-choice math problems to answer grid-ins. Just don't guesstimate—you need to come up with a precise answer for these questions.

If you use the special answer grid incorrectly, you will needlessly lose points. The best way to prepare for this section is to practice until you're comfortable with the procedure. Keep in mind that there is often more than one correct way to fill in a grid. Sometimes, there is an entire range of correct answers.

Here are some tips to help you fill in the special grid correctly:

- Mark no more than one oval in any column.

- If your answer requires fewer than four spaces, you can start and end in any space on the grid. For example, if the correct answer is the single digit 6, you can put it in any one of the four spaces available—all would be counted as correct by the scoring machine. The other spaces should be left blank.

- Although it's not required, write your answers in the boxes at the top of the columns. This will help you fill in the ovals accurately.

- Some problems may have more than one correct answer. In such cases, grid only one answer.

- No question has a negative answer. Other answers that are impossible to grid are those that must contain symbols, like x or π, and numbers with more than four digits. If you come up with an answer like this, your calculations are wrong. Go back and rework the problem. (But remember that fractions like $1/100$, which would require five spaces to grid, can be expressed as decimals (.01) and so can be gridded).

- Mixed numbers like $2^1/_2$ must be gridded either as a decimal (2.5) or as a fraction ($5/_2$), or they won't be scored correctly. (Use the division sign to enter fractions.)

- If you obtain a decimal answer, enter the most accurate value the grid will accommodate. For example, if you obtain an answer like .6666..., record the result as .667. Less accurate values like .66 or .67 are not acceptable. (Don't grid in zeroes before a decimal point.)

Your SAT I exam will probably have a total of 10 grid-ins. You need to answer grid-ins at the rate of about one-and-a-half minutes per question. Grid-ins count as roughly 17 percent of your overall math score.

A General Guessing Strategy

It is not a good idea to wildly or randomly guess at answers on the SAT I. (And if you're running out of time, it's definitely not a good idea to darken the remaining bubbles on your answer grid and hope you get some of them right.) That's because the SAT I penalizes you for each incorrect answer. If

Watch Out!
If you mis-grid an answer on the Grid-Ins section, you'll lose the point, even if you did the math correctly.

Bright Idea
Be especially aggressive in guessing on this section of the SAT I. Unlike the other question types, grid-ins are scored with no guessing penalty. Therefore, you can't possibly lose points for any answer you give—and it's always possible to guess right and gain a point or two.

you just make a random guess, you're much more likely to get the question wrong than right, and to lose points.

Here's how incorrect answers are scored on the SAT I:

- For each incorrect answer on the Grid-Ins section, you lose nothing.

- For each incorrect answer on the Quantitative Comparisons section, you lose one-third of a point.

- For each incorrect answer on every other section, you lose one-quarter of a point.

That doesn't mean that you should never guess. The penalty is designed to compensate for *random* guessing. But *educated* guessing is a proven way to boost your score on the SAT I.

With educated guessing, you first eliminate one or more of the answer choices as definitely wrong—go ahead and cross those answers out in your test booklet. Then, you guess from the remaining answers. The odds of choosing the right answer go way up if you employ this strategy.

The truth is, you should rarely have to randomly guess. You almost always have at least some information that you can use to improve your odds of guessing correctly. On a math problem, for example, you might figure out the answer must be less than 20, so any answer choice greater than 20 has to be incorrect. Or on a verbal question, you might sense that the answer should sound more negative than positive, thus eliminating a couple of answer choices. Any time you have even a clue as to what the right answer is—or is not—it pays to guess.

This doesn't mean that if you're running out of time, you should just fill in all A's on the remaining questions. Skipping a question on the SAT I won't count against you, but making an incorrect guess will. If you have no idea as to the correct answer, or if you're running out of time and still have questions left, it's better to leave those questions blank.

You Don't Need to Answer Every Question to Get a Good Score

There are many differences between a standardized test like the SAT I and the classroom tests that you're used to taking. Here's a crucial one. To do well on a classroom test, you need to answer 80 to 90 percent of the questions correctly, or more. Not on the SAT I. You can earn a high score by answering two-thirds to three-quarters of the questions correctly.

Think about that for a minute. On a classroom test, if you get 66 to 75 percent of the questions right, you'll earn a grade of D or (at best) C. On the SAT I, the same percentage right yields a grade that's the equivalent of a B+!

This fact about the SAT I has several important implications for you:

- *You don't have to answer every question.* In truth, most students omit some questions on each test section. And that's perfectly okay. Even if you leave two or three questions blank on each section, you can still score

Watch Out!
On the SAT I, the easiest questions come near the front of a set (except on the Critical Reading section). If the answer to a question near the end of a set seems way too obvious, go back and reread the question carefully—it may be a trick question.

well into the 1400s, provided you perform well on the questions you do answer.

- *Getting a handful of questions wrong is not fatal.* If you run into a series of tough questions—five questions based on a reading passage that you find very hard to understand, for example—don't despair. You can still earn a high overall score, as long as you don't let the few "killer questions" get you down.

- *Almost everyone gets some questions wrong.* It's a deliberate feature of the SAT I. Everyone can't score 1400 or more. The test-makers' job is to create a test that yields a broad range of scores. This proves that they are differentiating among students, which is what they are paid to do. To accomplish this, they write questions that vary greatly in difficulty. So, when you take the SAT I, expect each section to include a few questions you find very, very difficult. Answer them as best you can and move on. Almost no one gets every question right.

- *Every question is worth the same amount.* Some of the questions will be very hard. You may find that it takes you two or three minutes to solve some of the math problems—an eternity on the SAT I. Others will be shockingly easy; the answer may jump out at you as soon as you see the question. The easy questions are worth just as much as the hard ones. The test-makers only look at how many questions you answer right; they couldn't care less which ones they are. That's why it's so important to complete the easy questions first, and then go back and work on the hard ones (if you have time)—you'll answer more questions and improve your score.

These general rules apply to almost every standardized test, not just the SAT I. So, what are you stressing about?

Finding Your Way Around the ACT

The ACT Assessment consists of four tests in English, reading comprehension, mathematics, and science reasoning. The test lasts almost three hours and is composed of 215 multiple-choice questions.

Strategies for Answering English Questions

The English section is divided into five passages, each with 15 questions. It tests your knowledge of the conventions of standard written English—punctuation, grammar, usage, and sentence structure—and your rhetorical skills—writing strategy, organization, and style. It does *not* test spelling or vocabulary.

Three scores are reported for the English test:

- A total test score based on all 75 questions

- A subscore in Usage/Mechanics based on 40 questions

- A subscore in Rhetorical Skills based on 35 questions

Generally, most students score better on the English section than on the other parts of the ACT. That's why the test-makers decided to make the English section harder. The English section is 45 minutes long. There are 75 questions. So, you get about 30 seconds to answer each question, less time per question than on any other section of the test. You'll have to move fast.

Almost all of the English questions follow the same format. A word, phrase, or sentence in a passage is underlined. You have four options: to leave the underlined portion alone by choosing NO CHANGE (which is always the first answer choice); or to replace the underlined portion with one of three alternatives.

You can save time by skimming the passage first, before tackling the questions. You may find that you don't have to go back and reread to answer some questions.

Timesaver
The directions for the English section are long and complicated. You'll save a significant amount of time if you memorize the directions beforehand, so you don't have to waste time reading and understanding them when you take the test.

When eliminating answers, look for choices with grammatical, punctuation, stylistic, and logical problems. A single question can test several different kinds of writing errors. Choose only the answer that makes the sentence or passage make sense and is correct grammatically.

Some of the questions—about 10 percent—don't follow this standard format. Instead, you are asked a question and given four possible responses. These questions usually appear at the end of a passage and ask about the meaning, purpose, or tone of a paragraph or of the passage as a whole. They may also ask you to determine the proper order of words, sentences, or paragraphs that have been scrambled in the passage. Most of the responses to this type of English question are either "yes" or "no," plus an explanation of why that is true. Pay careful attention to the reasoning—that's what will determine the correct answer.

Strategies for Answering Reading Questions

The Reading section of the ACT has 40 questions and lasts 35 minutes. This section contains four passages of about 1000 words each, each followed by 10 questions. Each passage falls into a different category: social studies; natural sciences; humanities; and prose fiction. They are written at the same difficulty level as college freshman textbooks. When you count the time needed to read through the passages, you have approximately 30 seconds to answer each question.

There are three categories of Reading questions:

- *Questions about specific details:* These questions refer to information explicitly stated in the passage.

- *Questions about inference:* These questions require you to use reasoning to determine meanings implied in the passage.

- *Questions about the big picture:* These questions require you to draw conclusions, comparisons, and generalizations based on the passage as a whole.

As with the critical reading section of the SAT I, you'll do better on the ACT Reading test if you follow this three-step approach to each passage:

1. *Preview:* Either skim the entire passage, or read only the first and last sentences of each paragraph in the passage. This gives you some idea of what the passage is about and how it is organized before you actually read it. If you know generally what the passage is about before reading it, you'll understand it better. Spend about 30 seconds on this step.

2. *Read:* Go ahead and read the passage through.

3. *Review:* Scan the passage one more time, reminding yourself of its main ideas, most important details, and overall structure. Like previewing, this should be a fast process—spend no more than 30 seconds to review an average passage.

Read with a pencil in your hand. While you're reading, mark up the passage in your test booklet, looking for key ideas and important supporting details. When you review, go back and scan the parts that you marked.

Three scores are reported for the Reading test:

- A total score based on all 40 questions

- A subscore in Social Studies/Science reading skills based on the 20 questions in the social studies and natural sciences sections of the test

- A subscore in Arts/Literature reading skills based on the 20 questions in the prose fiction and humanities sections of the test

Unofficially...
Reading questions on the ACT do *not* test the rote recall of facts that aren't given in the passage, isolated vocabulary words, or rules of formal logic.

Strategies for Answering Math Questions

The Math section of the ACT lasts one hour and contains 60 questions, which works out to answering one question per minute. Some questions will take you very little time to answer, while others will require much more time. Try to answer the easiest questions first, and leave the hard ones until later. You'll be able to answer more questions in the time allotted.

All of the Math questions are multiple-choice, with five possible answers (unlike the other sections, which have only four possible choices). Questions cover pre-algebra, elementary algebra, intermediate algebra, coordinate geometry, plane geometry, and some trigonometry. They aren't ordered by difficulty, but questions that test the most basic math skills tend to come earlier in the section, while those that test more advanced math skills fall closer to the end.

You will be expected to know basic formulas and have basic computational skills to answer the questions on the Math section. Knowledge of complex formulas and extensive computation are not required, however. The exam tests your ability to solve practical math problems using reasoning, not your ability to perform complicated computations. If you find yourself bogged down in extensive computations, stop and reread the problem— you are probably approaching it from the wrong angle or making it too difficult.

Timesaver
About a third of the Math questions on the ACT show a diagram. For almost half of these questions, you can get a reasonable answer by simply looking at the diagram.

You are allowed to use a calculator on the ACT, but you don't have to. All of the questions on the Math section can be solved without a calculator, and for many problems you won't even want to use one. Doing scratchwork can clarify your thoughts, and you'll have notes to refer to if you have time to review your answers.

It is handy to have a calculator, in case you blank out on a simple computation like 9×6 (it can happen). If you decide to bring a calculator, choose one that you use regularly and that you're already familiar with. (Make sure your calculator is one that's permitted by ACT.)

The Math section produces four reported scores:

- A total test score based on all 60 questions
- A subscore in Pre-Algebra/Elementary Algebra based on 24 questions
- A subscore in Intermediate Algebra/Coordinate Geometry based on 18 questions
- A subscore in Plane Geometry/Trigonometry based on 18 questions

Review the following math topics before test time:

- *Pre-algebra:* decimals; fractions; integers; square roots; exponents; scientific notation; factors; ratio; proportion; percentages; linear equations in one variable; absolute value and ordering numbers by value; simple probability; data collection, representation, and interpretation; simple descriptive statistics

- *Elementary algebra:* evaluation of algebraic expressions through substitution; using variables to express functional relationships; understanding algebraic operations; solution of quadratic equations by factoring

- *Intermediate algebra:* the quadratic formula; rational and radical expressions; absolute value equations and inequalities; sequences and patterns; systems of equations; quadratic inequalities; functions; modeling; matrices; roots of polynomials; complex numbers

- *Coordinate geometry:* graphing and the relations between equations and graphs, including points, lines, polynomials, circles, and other curves; graphing inequalities; slope; parallel and perpendicular lines; distance; midpoints; conics

- *Plane geometry:* properties and relations of plane figures, including angles and relations among perpendicular and parallel lines; properties of circles, triangles, rectangles, parallelograms, and trapezoids; transformations; the concept of proof and proof techniques; volume; applications of geometry to three dimensions

- *Trigonometry:* trigonometric relations in right triangles; values and properties of trigonometric functions; graphing trigonometric functions; modeling using trigonometric functions; use of trigonometric identities; solving trigonometric equations

Strategies for Answering Science Reasoning Questions

The Science Reasoning portion of the ACT lasts 35 minutes and has 40 questions. The questions measure the reasoning skills required in the natural sciences: interpretation; analysis; evaluation; and problem-solving. The Science Reasoning section does *not* test scientific facts or principles. All it requires is a basic knowledge of scientific processes and procedures, and a little common sense.

This section consists of seven sets of scientific information, each followed by five to seven questions. As with the Reading section, you have an average of 30 seconds to answer each question, once you take into account how much time you need to spend reading the passages. It's a good idea to read through the passages before moving on to the questions, but don't worry about the specific details of the passages during your first read-through.

Typically, three of the passages present scientific data. For these passages, you need to read data from graphs or tables. The easier questions simply ask you to report the data. Harder questions ask you to draw inferences or note patterns in the data. When reading data, be on the lookout for three characteristic patterns:

- Extremes, or maximums and minimums

- Critical points, or points of change

- Direct or inverse variation, or proportionality

Another three passages discuss research summaries of several related scientific experiments. They require you to understand the way scientific experiments are designed, what they prove, and how to interpret the results.

The final passage usually presents opposing views or theories on the same scientific issue. In this type of question, you must either apply a principle logically or identify ways of defending or attacking a principle. Don't try to figure out which viewpoint is the "right" one; instead, just focus on understanding the different viewpoints. Also, don't worry if you don't completely grasp one of the arguments. Many of the questions hinge on just one of the positions.

Only one score is reported for this test section—a total score based on all 40 questions.

A General Guessing Strategy

Unlike on the SAT I, there is no penalty for incorrect answers on the ACT. Therefore, it is to your advantage to answer as many questions as you can, even if you have to guess to do so.

The best kind of guessing is educated guessing. That's when you eliminate one or more of the incorrect answer choices and then guess from the remaining choices. Your odds of selecting the right answer shoot way up if

Watch Out!
You will not be able to use a calculator on the Scientific Reasoning portion of the test.

Timesaver
If time is a problem, focus on questions that require analyzing data from a single table or graph.

Unofficially...
Some of the Science Reasoning passages are very difficult to understand, but generally these passages have the easiest questions.

Bright Idea
If you guess on a question that you think you can figure out given more time, mark the question in the question booklet or write its number on your scratch paper. If you have time after you've completed all the questions, go back and give the marked questions more thought.

you make an educated guess. If you have any clue about what the answer should or should not be, go ahead and guess—it can only help you.

Even if you have no idea at all of what the correct answer is, a guess still gives you a chance of getting the question right. Not answering at all ensures that the question will be counted wrong. If you're about to run out of time, mark all the remaining blanks with the same letter. According to the law of averages, you should get some portion of those questions right.

Finding Free Study Materials and Sample Tests

Practicing beforehand by taking actual SAT I or ACT tests under timed conditions is a proven way to prepare for the tests. But you may not have the funds available to take a costly test-prep course or even to purchase study guides and sample tests. Don't worry—you can still find study materials, for free!

You can get a free copy of *Taking the SAT I: Reasoning Test* from your guidance counselor's office. This booklet provides test-taking tips, hints to help you get ready, and a complete test to practice with. If you have access to the Internet, Princeton Review publishes a practice test on its website at http://tester.review.com/ (you'll have to register to take the sample test, but it's free).

ACT provides a free sample test for practice in the booklet, *Preparing for the ACT Assessment,* that comes in the registration package. If you have access to the Internet, you will also find a complete sample test on the ACT website at http://www.act.org/aap/STRAT/4SampleTests.html.

Finally, check with your guidance office or school library for other SAT I or ACT study materials they may have to loan out. If you're a junior and just starting to take the tests, ask your senior friends if they have any old study guides they don't need anymore. (And share the wealth by passing them on when you're done with them.)

If you need more help, College PowerPrep offers free SAT I and ACT preparation courses on the Internet. Each week, you'll get a new learning module, as well as free software and strategies to use taking the tests. Sounds like a bargain to me! To find out more, go to http://www.powerprep.com/.

Another good website to help you review is College Base at http://library.advanced.org/17038/, where you'll find problems and answers for various concepts on the SAT I and ACT. These problems are designed to give you a good idea of what skills are tested and the basic concepts that are covered by the tests.

There are lots of other ways to prepare besides purchasing a study guide that says "SAT" or "ACT" on the cover, and they won't cost you a dime.

Here's what you can do if you're taking the SAT I:

- Review math fundamentals.

- Read, read, read; practice looking for key ideas in what you read.

- Beef up your vocabulary; get a parent to create word lists or flash cards, and study new words every day.

Here are some suggestions for how to study if you're taking the ACT:

- Review math fundamentals; concentrate on the topics outlined earlier in this chapter.

- Review grammar and punctuation rules.

- Review the fundamentals of scientific experimentation and data interpretation.

Just the Facts

- Understand the differences between the SAT I and the ACT, and plan to take the test that better demonstrates your academic strengths; many students take both tests to ensure that colleges see their best scores.

- The best time to take the SAT I or ACT first is during the spring semester of your junior year; then, you have time to work on your weak areas and retake the test before college applications come due.

- Taking a preliminary test, like the PSAT/NMSQT or the PLAN, is ideal preparation for the "big" test.

- The SAT I consists of Verbal and Math questions; become familiar with the different question types and the content covered to do your best on the test.

- The ACT consists of four sections—English, reading, math, and scientific reasoning—so it's important to become familiar with the different question types and the materials covered to get the best score.

- You don't have to spend a lot of money to prepare for the SAT I or ACT; free study materials are available from the test-makers, your guidance office, or school library, and on the Internet.

Bright Idea
Organize a study group to help review basic math topics covered on the exam or to practice vocabulary words. Ask your math or English teacher to lead one or two study sessions and go over fundamentals with your group.

GET THE SCOOP ON...
Taking more standardized tests beyond the SAT I or ACT ▪ The SAT II
Subject Tests—which ones you should take, how to prepare for
them, and test-taking strategies ▪ The AP exams—which ones you
should take, how to prepare for them, and test-taking strategies ▪
The CLEP exams—what they can do for you and how to prepare for
them ▪ Getting more information about all of these testing programs

Taking SAT II, AP, and CLEP Exams

Chapter 11

Just when you've gotten past the SAT I or ACT and you start to relax, you find that you have to take even more tests. SAT II, AP, CLEP—the alphabet soup of standardized testing—can be overwhelming. The key is to get organized early and make a plan. Find out what tests the kinds of colleges where you want to apply require, and what extra achievements those colleges like to see in applicants. Determine what your academic strengths and interests are, and plan to take tests that show those talents to your best advantage. Know your limits—don't take too many tests or overreach and take tests that you aren't ready for. And most importantly, don't get so overwhelmed with standardized testing that you forget to enjoy your time as a high school junior and senior.

This chapter will help you make sense of all the tests beyond the "big one." You'll discover which tests you should be taking and how to prepare for them. But before that, you'll find out *why* you should take these tests at all.

Why You Should Take More Tests

Tests, tests, tests—I'm sure you're sick of them by now. The last thing you probably want to do is take more standardized tests.

But you should take more, as many as you can comfortably prepare for and score well on. Beyond the SAT I, consider taking a selection of SAT II Subject Tests, AP exams, and CLEP exams. Admissions committees love to see good scores on all of these exams, and scoring well gives you four big advantages when applying to and going to college:

- Taking several standardized tests shows admissions committees that you're willing to challenge yourself academically by tackling a number of difficult courses and doing well in them; this is the number-one quality that most admissions committees look for in their applicants.

- High standardized test scores show admissions committees your level of achievement in specific subjects. For instance, if you want to major in physics, several high scores on science and math standardized tests demonstrate to colleges that you'll be an asset to their physics programs.

- The more standardized test scores you submit, the better the admissions committee can compare you to similar students around the country. This is especially important for homeschooled students and students who attend nontraditional high schools, but anything that makes you stand out from the crowd can work to your advantage, no matter who you are.

- High scores on any of these tests could earn you college credit or exempt you from required freshman courses, so when you get to college, you don't have to waste time repeating classes in subjects you already know—you can take something fun instead!

Once you get the SAT I or ACT over with, you have a lot of options. You can choose the kinds of tests to take and the specific subjects to take them in. So, you can show off what you do best and stack the deck to maximize your test scores.

There are three kinds of achievement and placement tests that colleges consider:

- *SAT II Subject Tests:* These one-hour exams test your knowledge on specific core subjects that you study in high school. Of all the advanced tests, they are the easiest—you don't have to take any special courses or study for a year to do well. Many college applicants take at least one and as many as three, four, or five of these tests.

- *Advanced Placement (AP) exams:* These tests are designed to come at the end of a year-long, intensive AP course, which is supposed to duplicate college-level work. AP courses are a great addition to your transcript— colleges love them—and a high score could easily exempt you from required freshman-level college courses. The AP program isn't for everyone, though; it requires a lot of extra work and discipline, as well as a high level of achievement in the high school courses you've already taken.

- *College-Level Examination Program (CLEP):* This program enables you to demonstrate your knowledge in college freshman- and sophomore-level courses and thus earn credits for those courses. It's intended for the most advanced students—those who have studied rigorously or completed coursework beyond the level of their high school classes. The rewards are great, though; if you do well, you can start college as a sophomore, enabling you to earn your degree faster or to have time to take a double major or pursue a special academic program.

In this chapter, you'll learn more about each testing program. You'll discover what tests are available and which ones are best for you to take. You'll also learn how best to prepare for each kind of test. These testing programs

Unofficially...
For some students, just the thought of taking a standardized test can inspire feelings of dread. You don't have to put yourself through it. Many colleges don't require SAT II Subject Tests. If the schools where you're applying do require SAT IIs, completing a test-prep course and taking several practice tests should ease your anxiety. You can also select the Score Choice option when registering, which means that your scores won't be released to the colleges until you see them first.

give you the opportunity to show colleges what you can really do, so don't pass them up!

Understanding SAT II Subject Tests

The only standardized tests beyond the ACT or SAT I that colleges usually require are one to three (usually three) SAT II Subject Tests. Unlike the SAT I, the SAT IIs test your knowledge in specific courses that you complete during high school.

Some schools specify exactly which SAT II Subject Tests they want you to take; others leave the choice up to you. Find out which Subject Tests are required or recommended by the colleges where you're applying as soon as possible. That should give you plenty of time to register and prepare for all of the Subject Tests that you need.

Like the SAT I, the SAT II Subject Tests are scored on an 800-point scale. Each exam lasts one hour. There are over 20 SAT II Subject Tests in five broad subject areas. The following sections provide a brief rundown of the material covered by each test, the test format, and how best to prepare.

English SAT II Subject Tests

There are two SAT II Subject Tests in the English category: literature and writing.

Literature Subject Test

- *What it tests:* How well you read literature.

- *Test format:* Sixty questions based on six to eight reading selections.

- *Materials covered:* English and American literature and other literature written in English in prose, poetry, and drama forms, dating from the Renaissance through to the 20th century.

- *The skills you'll need:* High levels of reading comprehension and verbal ability; the ability to interpret poetry and prose from different periods and cultures; and a good working knowledge of basic literary terminology.

- *How to prepare:* Read English and American literature from a variety of historical periods and literary genres.

Writing Subject Test

- *What it tests:* How well you express ideas in writing and whether you can recognize errors in written passages.

- *Test format:* Sixty multiple-choice questions and a 20-minute essay on an assigned topic (the essay doesn't require specialized knowledge in any particular subject).

- *Materials covered:* Common writing problems like being consistent, expressing ideas logically, expressing yourself clearly and precisely, and following the conventions of standard written English.

Bright Idea
Even if your colleges don't require any SAT II Subject Tests, the admissions officers will still look at your scores, so it can only help your chances to take one or more Subject Tests and do well on them.

Unofficially...
The Literature SAT II Subject Test does not require specific knowledge of any particular literary period, author, or work.

Timesaver
When preparing for
the Writing Subject
Test, it helps to look
at sample questions
and other students'
essays. You'll find
both on the College
Board website plus a
lot more information
about the test at
http://www.
collegeboard.org/
sat/html/students/
wst001.html.

- *The skills you'll need:* The ability to clearly and effectively express your thoughts on a topic, using appropriate organization, sentence structure, word choices, and punctuation; and the ability to identify sentence errors and improve written passages.

- *How to prepare:* Take the test after having studied and practiced writing for several years. Read sample essays and write practice essays.

History SAT II Subject Tests

There are two SAT II Subject Tests in the history category: American History and Social Studies; and World History.

American History and Social Studies Subject Test

- *What it tests:* Your knowledge of material commonly taught in high school American history and social studies courses.

- *Test format:* Ninety to ninety-five multiple-choice questions.

- *Materials covered:* American political, economic, social, intellectual, and cultural history and foreign policy from the pre-Columbian period through to the present.

- *The skills you'll need:* A familiarity with American history; the ability to recall basic historical facts; and the ability to analyze and interpret historical materials.

- *How to prepare:* Take a one-year course in American history (taking other social studies courses and reading materials outside of class can also be helpful).

World History Subject Test

- *What it tests:* Your understanding of key developments in global history and the major cultures of the world; your ability to use basic historical analysis techniques, such as weighing, interpreting, and applying historical evidence.

- *Test format:* Ninety-five multiple-choice questions covering all historical fields.

- *Materials covered:* Political, diplomatic, intellectual, cultural, social, and economic history of all areas of the world from prehistoric times to the present.

- *The skills you'll need:* A familiarity with historical terminology, cause-and-effect relationships, geography, and the other data necessary to understand major historical developments; a grasp of the essential concepts of historical analysis; and the ability to use historical knowledge to interpret data in maps, graphs, charts, and cartoons.

- *How to prepare:* Take a variety of history courses, including a world history course that focuses on world cultures or area studies.

Foreign Language SAT II Subject Tests

There are six SAT II Subject Tests in the foreign languages category that are reading only: French; German; modern Hebrew; Italian; Latin; and Spanish. There are seven SAT II Subject Tests in this category that include a listening component: Chinese; French; German; Japanese; Korean; Spanish; and English Language Proficiency. The Foreign Language with Listening tests are only given in November; you have to bring an acceptable cassette player with earphones to the test.

Reading-Only Foreign Language Subject Tests

- *What they test:* Your reading ability in the language.

- *Test format:* Eighty to eighty-five multiple-choice questions in two formats: vocabulary and grammar questions in sentences or longer paragraphs; and reading comprehension questions based on passages from fiction, nonfiction, newspaper and magazine articles, and everyday materials.

- *Materials covered:* Vocabulary and grammar in context, and reading comprehension.

- *The skills you'll need:* A wide-ranging knowledge of the language.

- *How to prepare:* Take three or four years of the language in high school, complete two or more years of intensive study, or gradually develop competence in the language over a long period (through travel or a bilingual household, for instance).

Foreign Language Subject Tests With Listening

- *What they test:* Your understanding of the language in spoken and written forms, and ability to use the language in a culturally appropriate way.

- *Test format:* Eighty to ninety multiple-choices questions in the following formats: listening comprehension questions based on short spoken dialogues and narratives about everyday topics; vocabulary and usage questions requiring the correct completion of sentences and paragraphs; and reading comprehension questions based on passages from fiction, nonfiction, newspaper and magazine articles, and everyday materials.

- *Materials covered:* Listening comprehension, vocabulary, grammar, correct usage, and reading comprehension in the language.

- *The skills you'll need:* A wide knowledge of the spoken and written language and of the culture of the language.

- *How to prepare:* Take three or four years of the language in high school, complete two or more years of intensive study, or gradually develop competence in the language over a long period (through travel or a bilingual household, for instance).

Latin Subject Test

- *What it tests:* Your reading ability in Latin.

- *Test format:* Seventy to seventy-five multiple-choice questions.

- *Materials covered:* Selection of appropriate grammatical forms of Latin words; identifying Latin words from which English words are derived; translation of Latin into English; completion of Latin sentences; selection of alternate ways of expressing thoughts in Latin; and comprehension of prose and poetry written in Latin.

- *The skills you'll need:* A wide-ranging knowledge of Latin.

- *How to prepare:* Take two to four years of Latin in high school, or gradually develop a competence in sight-reading Latin over a period of years.

English Language Proficiency Subject Test

- *What it tests:* Your understanding of spoken and written standard American English and how well you function in a classroom where English is spoken.

- *Test format:* Eighty-four multiple-choice questions concentrating on the practical and academic use of English, including two listening sections and one reading comprehension section.

- *Materials covered:* Listening and reading comprehension of standard American English.

- *The skills you'll need:* A wide-ranging knowledge of standard American English.

- *How to prepare:* This test is intended for students who attend US high schools whose best language is not English and who have completed two to four years of an English as a Second Language program; students who studied at an international school where courses are taught in English can also take it.

Math SAT II Subject Tests

There are two SAT II Subject Tests in the math category: Mathematics Level IC and Mathematics Level IIC.

Both Subject Tests require a scientific or graphing calculator. You can get by without one, but you'll be at a disadvantage. Use a calculator that you're already familiar with, and make sure it is in good working condition before the test. Bring a backup calculator or extra batteries to the test with you. Only some of the questions require the calculator, and using a calculator to answer some questions may hurt you, so think through how to solve each problem before picking up the calculator.

Mathematics Level IC Subject Test

- *What it tests:* Your understanding of the material taught in three years of college-preparatory mathematics courses.

- *Test format:* Fifty multiple-choice questions; a scientific calculator is required for approximately 40 percent of these questions.

- *Materials covered:* Algebra, geometry, trigonometry, data interpretation, functions, statistics and probability, and miscellaneous math topics; ability to use a computer and determine when the use of a calculator is required.

- *The skills you'll need:* A familiarity with a scientific or graphing calculator and knowledge of when to use it; and knowledge of several of the following topics: algebra; plane Euclidean, three-dimensional, and coordinate geometry; basic trigonometry; algebraic functions; elementary statistics; data interpretation; and miscellaneous topics like logic, elementary number theory, and arithmetic and geometric sequences.

- *How to prepare:* Take at least three years of math courses—two years of algebra and one year of geometry. Practice using a scientific or graphing calculator in your math classes.

Mathematics Level IIC Subject Test

- *What it tests:* Your understanding of the material taught in three-plus years of college-preparatory mathematics courses.

- *Test format:* Fifty multiple-choice questions; a scientific calculator is required or useful for approximately 60 percent of these questions.

- *Materials covered:* Algebra, geometry, trigonometry, functions, statistics and probability, and miscellaneous math topics; the ability to use a calculator and to know when the use of a calculator is required.

- *The skills you'll need:* Familiarity with a scientific or graphing calculator and knowledge of when to use it; and knowledge of several of the following topics: algebra; three-dimensional and coordinate geometry; trigonometry; functions; statistics, including probability, permutations, and combinations; and miscellaneous topics like logic and proof, elementary number theory, sequences, and limits.

- *How to prepare:* Take four or more years of college preparatory mathematics: two years of algebra; one year of geometry; and one year of pre-calculus or trigonometry. Routinely practice using a scientific or graphing calculator in class.

Science SAT II Subject Tests

There are three SAT II Subject Tests in the science category: Biology E/M (Ecological/Molecular); Chemistry; and Physics.

Biology E/M Subject Test

- *What it tests:* Your understanding of general biology, with special emphasis on either ecology or molecular biology.

- *Test format:* A common core of 60 multiple-choice questions, plus 20 ecological or molecular questions.

Unofficially...
You aren't expected to have studied every topic covered by the Math Level IC or Level IIC Subject Test to score well.

- *Materials covered:* Cellular biology, classical genetics, organismal biology, and diversity, plus either ecology and evolution or molecular biology and evolution.

- *The skills you'll need:* The ability to recall and understand the major concepts of biology; the ability to apply the principles of biology to solve specific problems; the ability to organize and interpret the results of observation and experimentation; the ability to draw conclusions or make inferences from experimental data, including data presented in graphic and tabular form; a knowledge of simple algebraic concepts, including ratios and direct and inverse proportions, and the ability to apply these concepts to solving word problems; and a familiarity with the metric system.

- *How to prepare:* Take a one-year course in biology, either a general survey course or a course with emphasis in ecology or molecular biology. Take a one-year course or more in algebra. Obtain experience in the laboratory.

The Biology Subject Test is a little different than the other SAT II Subject Tests. You decide on test day which version of the test to take—the ecological test (Biology-E) or the molecular biology (Biology-M) test—by gridding the code for your chosen test on the answer sheet. Only questions pertaining to the test code that you grid are scored. Choose the area for which you feel you are best prepared. You can take both versions of the test if you like, but not on the same day.

Chemistry Subject Test

- *What it tests:* Your understanding of chemistry.

- *Test format:* Eighty-five multiple-choice questions; one section of questions that ask you to determine which statement is true or false, and if the first statement is true, whether the second statement is a correct explanation of the first; and a periodic table for reference.

- *Materials covered:* Structure of matter, states of matter, reaction types, stoichiometry, equilibrium and reaction rates, thermodynamics, descriptive chemistry, and laboratory work.

- *The skills you'll need:* An understanding of the major concepts of chemistry; the ability to apply the principles of chemistry to solve specific problems; the ability to organize and interpret the results of observation and experimentation; the ability to draw conclusions or make inferences from experimental data, including data in graphic and tabular form; laboratory experience; the ability to handle simple algebraic relationships and apply them to solving word problems; a familiarity with the concepts of ratio, direct and inverse proportions, scientific notation, and exponential functions; and a familiarity with the metric system.

Bright Idea
Because high school science courses differ from school to school, most students find questions on topics they aren't familiar with on the science Subject Tests. You may want to review the parts of your textbook that aren't covered in class or read outside texts as part of your test-preparation efforts.

- *How to prepare:* Take a one-year course in chemistry at the college-preparatory level. Take one year or more in algebra. Obtain laboratory experience.

Physics Subject Test

- *What it tests:* Your understanding of physics at the college-preparatory level.

- *Test format:* Seventy-five multiple-choice questions.

- *Materials covered:* Mechanics; electricity and magnetism; waves; heat, kinetic theory, and thermodynamics; modern physics; history of physics; and measurement, math, and laboratory skills.

- *The skills you'll need:* The ability to recall and understand the major concepts of physics; the ability to apply physical principles to solve specific problems; a knowledge of simple algebra, trigonometry, and graphical relationships, including ratio and proportion, and how to apply these concepts to solving physics problems; and a familiarity with the metric system.

- *How to prepare:* Take a one-year college-preparatory course in physics. Take courses in algebra and trigonometry. Obtain laboratory experience.

Deciding Which SAT II Subject Tests to Take

Most selective colleges require three SAT II Subject Tests. You can pretty much count on the Writing Subject Test being required. In addition, the college may specify one of the math tests.

Often, you get to choose one or two Subject Tests. Make your choice based on your academic strengths, to show your talents to their best advantage. If you've taken several years of a foreign language, take the appropriate language test. If you plan to study science in college, make one of your Subject Tests a science test.

Most of the SAT II Subject Tests are given six times a year, on the same days as the SAT I, except for the March/April test date, when no Subject Tests are given. (And no, you can't take the SAT I and SAT II on the same day.) The World History test is given only in December and June, and the Foreign Language with Listening tests are only given in November. The dates of the Foreign Language Reading Only exams vary considerably: the French and Spanish tests are typically given five times a year, the Latin exam twice a year, and the rest once a year, so you have to take care not to miss the limited test dates for those Subject Tests.

Register for the SAT II by picking up a copy of the SAT Program Registration Bulletin in your school's guidance office, or by contacting the College Board directly for a copy. You can take up to three Subject Tests in one day. You can also change your mind on test day and select another Subject Test offered that day instead of the one you registered for. The only

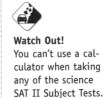

Watch Out!
You can't use a calculator when taking any of the science SAT II Subject Tests.

exception to this rule is the Foreign Language with Listening tests—you must pre-register for those.

Don't take more than two SAT IIs in one sitting if you can avoid it, because the subjects covered by the test are so different and the tests can be difficult. You'll probably find it easier to study for fewer tests at a time as well.

Keep in mind that it can take up to six weeks for your scores to reach the schools where you're applying. Make certain to register to take all the required SAT II Subject Tests well before the application deadlines, so that the colleges will receive your scores in time.

You might want to take advantage of the SAT II Score Choice service, particularly if you're worried about how you performed on one of the tests. This service puts your scores on the SAT II Subject Tests on hold, not to be released to colleges until you decide to release them. It gives you control over which Subject Test scores colleges see. You must pay a fee of $6.50 for each score report you send out, though; you won't get the four-colleges-for-free deal. (Seniors testing in October or November shouldn't use this service—colleges won't receive your scores on time.)

Preparing for the SAT II Subject Tests

Because the SAT IIs test your knowledge in specific subject areas, preparing for them is a little different than preparing for the SAT I. Take most Subject Tests—math, sciences, literature, history—as soon as you complete the course, so the material is still fresh in your mind. You'll do better on the other Subject Tests, such as writing and foreign languages, after several years of study—take these near the end of your junior year or in the fall of your senior year.

Also take practice tests to familiarize yourself with the test format, the types of questions, and the directions. You can obtain free copies of sample tests from your guidance office. While you're there, pick up a copy of *Taking the SAT II: Subject Tests,* a free booklet that includes sample questions and test directions for each test. If you want more practice, order *Real SAT II: Subject Tests* for $17.95 from the College Board to get 20, full-length practice tests in 18 different subjects—it even comes with free listening test cassettes. Visit the website at http://www.collegeboard.org/ or call (800) 323-7155 to order the book.

College Board offers an online service called EssayPrep that helps you prepare for the SAT II Writing Subject Test. It works like this. You purchase an access code and write an essay on one of the topics provided (preferably under timed conditions, just like on the real test). Then, you submit your essay to the service over the Internet. Within five days, you'll receive an evaluation of your essay by the same people who score the actual exams. You also get to look at other student essays on the same subject, so you can figure out what other students did to make their essays especially good. The fees are low ($10 to $25, depending on how many essays you write for evaluation) so

Timesaver
Remember the basic strategies for taking the SAT I—they apply to the SAT II, as well. Memorize directions before-hand. Do the easier questions first; they come at the beginning of each set. Make educated guesses when you can, and skip questions if you have no idea of the answer.

if you have Internet access, this is a good way to practice. Go to http://cbweb6.collegeboard.org/writewellCB/html/essintro.html.

Understanding AP Exams

Many high schools offer Advanced Placement (AP) courses in several subjects. These demanding classes give you the chance to try college-level work in high school, and colleges look favorably on any AP courses that show up on your transcript because they prove that you're willing to challenge yourself academically and that you're more prepared to meet the demands of college courses.

Generally, you'll get the opportunity to take AP courses during your junior and senior years in high school. Pick and choose wisely which courses you take. Don't overload yourself with AP courses and sabotage your entire grade point average for the year—depending on your academic skills, two or three is plenty, four is borderline. Opt first for AP classes in your strongest subjects and in the subjects that you intend to pursue in college.

AP courses are not easy, so it's important to know your limitations. AP classes move much faster than your regular high school courses, and they cover a lot of material. You'll probably have to read and write much more than in your other classes, and you'll have to do more problem-solving and data analysis. Think carefully before you sign up for an AP course. Ask yourself if you can do the extra work required and keep up with the fast pace. If you can, taking the course definitely benefits you.

Most high schools with AP programs have an AP coordinator. Bring your questions about whether to take a particular AP course to this person. The AP coordinator can also help you with questions about the exams.

At the end of the AP course—in mid-May—you'll take a standardized AP exam, which lasts about three hours. You have until mid-June to decide which colleges to report your AP scores to (a fee is charged for each report). AP scores are released in early July.

Colleges don't require AP exams for admission, like they do with SAT II Subject Tests, but they treat AP scores seriously. AP tests are graded on a scale of one to five. A score of four or five on AP exams taken at the end of your junior year can definitely improve your chances for admission.

In addition, a good AP exam score can enable you to earn college credit or place out of lower-level required courses while at college. You may think that you don't need to take AP exams at the end of your senior year, when you've already been accepted to college—what difference can it make? Well, if scoring a four or five on an AP exam enables you to bypass required freshman courses at the college, it can make a big difference—you can get a head start on your major or have more time to take fun and interesting courses while in college. If you take enough AP exams and do well, you can even start college as a sophomore.

Unofficially...
Is it better to take an AP course and get a B or to take the regular class and get an A? Most admissions officers say they prefer to see the AP course with the B.

Moneysaver
At $75 a pop, AP exams are costly. But they can actually save you money, if you use AP scores to place out of required college courses. A course credit at a state university can be worth more than $250, and at a private college, you can save $2,700 or more.

If you've completed an AP course, go ahead and take the exam, even if you don't think you'll do well. You don't have to determine which colleges, if any, see your score until after you get first peek. So, if you get a low score, you can keep it to yourself, but if you get a high score, you can still reap all the benefits.

You don't necessarily have to take the AP course if you want to take the corresponding exam, although the course is certainly the best preparation for the exam. But you may not have a choice if your high school doesn't offer the AP course you want or if you are a homeschooled student. With enough time and discipline, you can prepare on your own and do well. The key is in-depth study over a long period of time in the subject covered by the AP exam.

Unofficially...
Two-thirds of all students who take AP exams receive a score of at least three, which most colleges regard as an indicator of an ability to do successful work at the college.

To get started, get a copy of the Course Description for the AP exam that you want to take. The Course Description outlines the course content that you need to study in detail and lists the skills that you must demonstrate at the end of the course. It also provides a description of the exam and sample multiple-choice and free-response questions from past exams for practice. You can order Course Descriptions separately for each course from the College Board for $12, or get a complete set for $100.

Types of AP Courses and Exams

You certainly have a lot of choice when it comes to which AP courses and exams to take (although your choices may be limited by what your high school offers). The following is an overview of all the AP courses, to help you plan your AP strategy:

- *Art History:* The course covers the major forms of artistic expression from a variety of cultures. Take it if you've done well in other humanities courses, like history and literature, and in the studio arts.

- *Biology:* The course is equivalent to a college introductory biology course. Take it after successfully completing your high school biology and chemistry courses.

- *Calculus AB and BC:* Both courses represent college-level mathematics courses. Calculus BC covers more topics and is designed to qualify students for placement and credit one course beyond that granted for Calculus AB. Before taking either course, you should have four years of high school math under your belt, and you should thoroughly know algebra, geometry, trigonometry, analytic geometry, and elementary functions.

- *Chemistry:* The course is equivalent to a college introductory chemistry course. Take it after completing your high school chemistry course and high school mathematics courses through Algebra II. It's also a good idea to have already taken high school physics before taking AP Chemistry.

- *Comparative and United States Government and Politics:* The US Government course gives students an analytical perspective on government and politics in the US, while Comparative Government gives students a basic understanding of diverse political structures and practices around the world. Students may take both exams at the same time for a single fee.

- *Computer Science:* This is a new course, first offered in 1998–99, which teaches C++ programming as well as the basics of computer science. Take it if you have computer programming experience, if you want to study computer science in college, or if you just want to acquire more experience with computers (which can never hurt).

- *English:* Get used to reading—you'll be doing a lot of it. If you've performed strongly in English and other humanities courses in the past, and if you're a good writer, this is a good course to take.

- *English Language and Composition:* This course helps students become skilled readers and writers. It's equivalent to the first-year college writing course and thus concentrates on writing styles used for college papers and essays.

- *English Literature:* While writing is a heavy component, this course concentrates on careful reading and critical analysis of literature. Again, this course is a good choice for students who have performed strongly in their English classes in the past.

- *Environmental Science:* This course was first offered in the 1997–98 school year. It focuses on the science behind environmental problems and issues. Prospective students should have successfully completed one year of life science and one year of physical science.

- *European History:* This course teaches the major events, trends, and themes in European history. It stresses analysis of historical evidence and expressing historical understanding through writing. Students should have a strong background in history and the other humanities, and they should be good writers.

- *French Language:* Students who enroll should already have a good command of grammar and vocabulary, as well as competence in listening, reading, writing, and speaking. Generally, you should take the course as a third- or fourth-year foreign language student after already having successfully completed substantial coursework in the language.

- *French Literature:* This course on the study of literary texts in French is designed for students with advanced French-speaking skills. You will need a proficiency in French language skills, at least three years of French, and a strong background in the analysis of literature.

- *German Language:* Generally, students take this advanced language course as a senior, after already having studied German for several years.

- *Human Geography:* This course will be offered for the first time in the 2000–01 school year. In it, students study the patterns and processes

Bright Idea
As on the SAT, points are deducted from AP exams for incorrect answers to compensate for random guessing. If you have no idea what an answer is, don't guess. But if you can eliminate one or more possibilities, go ahead and guess—your chances of getting the right answer are much higher.

that have shaped human understanding, use, and alteration of the Earth's surface. The also learn about the methods and tools that geographers use.

- *International English Language:* This course is given to foreign students who are studying English in preparation for study in the US. Potential students should already have a good command of English grammar and vocabulary and should be in the final stages of their pre-university training.

- *Latin:* There are two courses, Vergil and Latin Literature; students may take one or both exams in any given year. Students should already have completed extensive Latin coursework before taking the AP course.

- *Macroeconomics and Microeconomics:* Together, these courses give students a thorough understanding of the principles of economics. They are good courses to take if you intend to pursue a study of economics or related topics in college.

- *Music Theory:* This course introduces students to music theory and procedures. You should already be able to read and write musical notation. You should also be able to perform in voice or on a musical instrument.

- *Physics:* There are two AP courses, Physics B and Physics C; Physics C covers fewer topics, but they are examined in greater depth and with more analysis and mathematical sophistication. It's recommended that you take the high school physics course before tackling AP Physics, although some students have been able to handle AP Physics as an intensive first-year course; concurrent or previous study in calculus is also highly recommended.

- *Psychology:* Designed to parallel a college introductory course in psychology, this course introduces students to the study of all the major subfields within psychology and the methods psychologists use. Take it if you have a strong background in science and social science, and if you intend to pursue psychology in college.

- *Spanish Language and Spanish Literature:* These courses are similar to the French Language and French Literature courses (see previous entries).

- *Statistics:* Students with a strong proficiency in mathematics are encouraged to take this course, along with AP Calculus and AP Computer Science. The course also benefits students planning to take an AP science course the same year, as well as students who plan to study engineering, psychology, sociology, health science, or business in college. The only prerequisite for AP Statistics is successful completion of Algebra II.

- *Studio Art:* This course is the only AP class that doesn't have a corresponding exam; instead, students submit portfolios for evaluation at the end of the year. This course is intended for serious art students only.

Take it if you have previous training in art and you're highly interested in pursuing the study of art in college.

- *US History:* Most students who have a strong proficiency in the humanities and an interest in history take AP US History during their junior year, instead of the required American history high school-level course.

Tackling the Free-Response Section

Many AP exams have a free-response section. This section does not include multiple choice answers. Instead, you must write essays on several topics. Naturally enough, this section causes the most anxiety in students taking the exam. You may not be used to writing essays under timed conditions (but you'll have to do it in college all the time, so this is good practice for you).

Here are some tips for improving the essays that you write for the free-response section of the AP exams that you take:

- If you have a choice of essay topics, select the questions that you are best prepared to answer. Try to avoid answering questions that invite easy generalizations. Instead, look for questions for which you can build answers filled with concrete, specific, supporting details.

- Before you start writing, carefully read the question and identify the elements that must be addressed in the response. Free-response questions often have several parts, and your essay should address each part. While reading the question, consider what facts and ideas you learned during the year that you can incorporate into your response.

- Don't start writing right away! First, determine what your thesis statement is and make a brief outline of how you want the essay to progress. The essay should have a clear focus, a logical progression of ideas, and appropriate details that support the main idea. (Organizational notes won't be scored.)

- If you're unfamiliar with the subject matter of the question, don't panic. Take the time to make some notes. You've probably heard something about the subject before—give yourself a little time to remember what it is. Always write something; you may earn points for partial credit, but you won't get anything if you leave the question blank.

- State your thesis and supporting points clearly. Position your supporting evidence so that it is obviously tied into your thesis and directed to the question.

- If you use specific terms, define them. If you refer to specific works of literature or historical periods, summarize them briefly. Let the reader know that you know what you're talking about.

- Don't pad your essay, use grandiose words, or compose long, convoluted sentences in an effort to make your essay look more substantial than it really is. In many cases, the scorer is judging your writing ability as well as your knowledge of the subject that you're writing about. Don't

Unofficially...
The Advanced Placement program has another advantage, one that's not so apparent. It eases the transition to college by giving students experience with completing college-level work and moving at the pace of a college course while they're still in high school.

Bright Idea
On essay questions with several parts, organize your essay so that it addresses each part of the question in the same order as they appear in the question itself. You'll come up with a better orga-nized essay.

Watch Out!
Pay close attention to the directions of the free-response sections. You may have to answer only one out of three questions in Section I and all of the questions in Section II—you don't want to get the directions wrong or mix up the sections, which would hurt your score.

Bright Idea
You may need to include diagrams in an essay on a sci-ence exam. If so, you'll maximize your score by labeling diagrams correctly, inserting them in the appropriate place in the essay, and referring to them within the body of the essay.

waste time providing background information on a topic if it's not nec-essary to thoroughly answer the question. Limit your essay to what you know about the subject, even if it seems too short.

- Pay close attention to the little details, and proofread your essay after writing. Incorrect spelling or very poor grammar does count against you. It is okay to cross out words and sentences, insert a new part, or move a part from one place to another, but make sure that you clearly and legibly mark any changes you make.

- Stay aware of the time. Don't spend so much time planning that you're still writing when time runs out. You definitely won't have time to write a rough draft and then revise your answer.

For practice, you may want to try answering free-response questions from previous AP exams. You can order copies of past AP exams and free-response questions directly from the College Board (see the address at the end of this chapter). If you have Internet access, visit the online store at http://www.collegeboard.org/shopping/ for extra-easy ordering of past exams. You'll also find sample multiple-choice and free-response questions from each AP exam under the course descriptions at http://www.collegeboard.org/ap/students/subjects.html.

If the free-response section still worries you, the College Board offers an EssayPrep service for the free-response sections of the biology, English lan-guage, English literature, and US history AP exams. It's similar to the EssayPrep service for the Writing SAT II Subject Test—you submit sample essays on actual exam topics and receive an evaluation within five days by the same people who grade the actual test. Depending on how many essays you want to have evaluated, the service costs between $15 and $36—not bad for the valuable feedback you get. You have to have Internet access to use the service, though. To find out more, go to http://cbweb6.collegeboard.org/writewellCB/html/essintro.html.

Strategies for Math and Science AP Exams

Even math and science AP exams have a free-response section. This section may call for an essay or a diagram, or it may ask you to work a complicated problem with several steps (or all of the above). Because real people score the free-response section of the math and science APs, rather than a com-puter, you can employ several strategies to help better your score.

Follow these tips when answering free-response questions on math and science APs:

- Before beginning to answer the free-response questions, read through them all. Decide which ones you are most prepared to answer, and solve those questions first.

- Many free-response questions are divided into several parts, with each part calling for a different response. Credit for each part is awarded independently, so try to solve each part of the question. Even if you don't receive any credit for Part A, you may still get full credit for Part B or C.

- Organize your work. Show all of the steps you took to reach your solution. You want the person reading the exam to be able to easily follow your reasoning.

- Show all of your work. You will receive partial credit for a partial solution. You may also receive credit for correct thinking, even if you get the answer wrong, if the person scoring the exam can see evidence of the process you went through to solve the question on paper.

- You don't have to simplify all numerical expressions or carry out all of the calculations. You will usually receive most or even full credit in any event.

- Pay attention to units, and keep track of them as you do calculations. You can lose points if the units are wrong or missing from the answer.

Preparing for Foreign Language APs

All modern language AP exams test four major skills: reading; writing; speaking; and listening. Practice is the key to success. Take every opportunity, both in class and out, to improve your language skills.

Here are some ideas for how you can practice outside of class:

- Tune in to foreign TV and radio programs.

- Attend undubbed foreign films.

- Listen to audiotapes and watch videotapes recorded in the language.

- Speak in the language as much as possible; practice with a friend.

- Read a variety of materials in the language: fiction, essays, poems, plays, cartoons, advertisements, and newspapers.

- Visit your high school's language laboratory regularly for extra practice.

Understanding CLEP Exams

I'm sure that before you picked up this book, you were already familiar with SAT II Subject Tests and AP exams. Almost everyone on the college track takes at least one of these exams, and usually a lot more. But you may never have heard of CLEP exams or even been aware that such an extensive college credit program existed.

CLEP stands for College-Level Examination Program, and it enables you to earn college credits before you even leave high school. CLEP is the most widely accepted credit-by-examination program in the country. More than 2,800 colleges and universities participate in the program.

Taking a CLEP exam, and scoring well, enables you to place out of required or entry-level college courses, so you can spend more time at college taking upper-level and specialized classes. CLEP exams measure how much you have learned in a subject, regardless of where that learning

Watch Out!
On math and science AP exams, don't just write down a bunch of equations hoping that the correct one is there so you'll get partial credit. You may actually lose points for giving extraneous or incorrect information.

Bright Idea
If you are taking a foreign language AP exam, you'll need to be familiar with operating the recording equipment and recording your answers to questions. Ask your teacher or AP Coordinator to provide at least one test run with the recording equipment before test day.

occurred—in or out of the classroom. If you've completed independent study or advanced coursework through homeschooling, taken community college courses, or participated in a specialized internship, you may be a candidate for the CLEP program.

Deciding Whether to Take a CLEP Exam

Before deciding whether to take a CLEP exam, find out if the college you plan to attend awards course credit based on the exam and what an acceptable exam score is. Although it's best to take the exam while the material is fresh in your mind, it's also a good idea to wait until you're certain which college you will attend. That way, you won't waste the time if your college doesn't participate in the CLEP program.

Call the admissions office at the college and ask the following questions—the answers should help you make up your mind:

- Do you give credit for CLEP exams? If so, which exams do you give credit for?

- How much credit is given?

- For which requirements or courses is the credit given?

- What is the minimum score required to receive credit?

Types of CLEP Exams

There are 34 CLEP exams in two broad categories: General and Subject. You can take as many CLEP exams as you'd like. Most colleges specify a maximum number of credits that you can earn through testing, though.

The General exams cover material taught in required courses during the first two years of college. A satisfactory score on each General exam usually earns three to six semester hours of credit. All of the exams, except for English Composition, consist entirely of multiple-choice questions. They last 90 minutes.

The General exams cover the following broad subject areas:

- *College Mathematics:* The exam deals with material taught in college math courses taken by students majoring in fields that don't require advanced mathematics. It tests knowledge of arithmetic, algebra, geometry, data interpretation, understanding of logic and sets, the real number system, functions, probability, and statistics.

- *English Composition:* The exam covers different kinds of writing and the principles and conventions of standard written English; an essay is required.

- *Humanities:* The exam covers material taught in fine arts and introductory literature survey courses. It includes questions on painting, sculpture, music, film, dance, architecture, drama, poetry, fiction, and nonfiction.

- *Natural Sciences:* The exam covers the material taught in introductory college biology and physical science courses for non-science majors. It covers topics like the classification of organisms, evolution, genetics, organisms, cells, ecology, atomic and nuclear structure, chemical elements, thermodynamics, classical mechanics, electricity, astronomy, and geology.

- *Social Sciences and History:* The exam covers material taught in introductory social science and history college courses, including political science, economics, sociology, psychology, geography, anthropology, US history, Western civilizations, and world history.

The General exams are designed to test knowledge of college-level courses, not high school courses. Take one of these exams only if you've completed a significant amount of college-level work—if you've taken several community college courses in one of the General subject areas, for instance, or if you've completed college-level work through distance learning or homeschooling.

The Subject CLEP exams cover materials taught in equivalent college-level courses. You may do well on one of these exams if you've taken the equivalent course at a local community college or if you've completed a specialized internship. Typically, colleges grant the same course credit to students who earn a successful score on the CLEP exam as they do to students who successfully complete the course.

Each exam lasts 90 minutes and is composed of multiple-choice questions; the four composition and literature exams also have an optional 90-minute essay section that some colleges require to earn the credit.

You can take CLEP exams in the following specific subjects:

- American Government
- American Literature
- Analyzing and Interpreting Literature
- Calculus with Elementary Functions
- College Algebra
- College Algebra-Trigonometry
- College-level French Language
- College-level German Language
- College-level Spanish Language
- English Literature
- Freshman College Composition
- General Biology
- General Chemistry
- History of the United States I: Early Colonizations to 1877
- History of the United States II: 1865 to the Present
- Human Growth and Development
- Information Systems and Computer Applications

Bright Idea
When preparing for CLEP exams, visit your local college bookstore and determine which textbooks and other materials the courses covered by the exam use. Those materials make the best study aids.

- Introduction to Educational Psychology
- Introductory Business Law
- Introductory Psychology
- Introductory Sociology
- Principles of Accounting
- Principles of Macroeconomics
- Principles of Management
- Principles of Marketing
- Principles of Microeconomics
- Trigonometry
- Western Civilization I: Ancient Near East to 1648
- Western Civilization II: 1648 to the Present

Registering for a CLEP Exam

Nearly 1400 colleges and universities across the country administer CLEP exams. There are two types of CLEP test centers. Open test centers admit anyone who registers; they administer CLEP exams each month of the year. Limited test centers restrict testing to students who have been admitted to or are enrolled in the college where the test center is located. Contact the test center where you plan to take the CLEP to confirm which kind it is.

You must contact the college directly to determine the appropriate registration procedure and to order a registration form. You then send the completed registration form to the test center at that college, along with a check for the registration fee of $44 plus the test center administration fee, usually $10. Contact the CLEP program directly to get a list of test centers and obtain more detailed registration information.

Getting More Information

Educational Testing Services and the College Board administer all of the testing programs described in this chapter. If you have any questions about the tests or want to request any of the free informational materials, contact the College Board directly at one of the following addresses.

Questions about SAT II Subject Tests:

> College Board SAT II Program
> P.O. Box 6200
> Princeton, NJ 08541-6200
> (609) 771-7600
> satII@collegeboard.org

Timesaver
Interested in whether your college gives credit for CLEP exams or where the nearest test center is? Consult the College Board's searchable database at http://www.collegeboard.org/clep/students/html/student.html—click on Colleges Granting Credit/Test Centers.

Questions about AP exams:

AP Services
P.O. Box 6671
Princeton, NJ 08541-6671
Telephone: (609) 771-7300
TTY: (609) 882-4118
apexams@ets.org

Questions about CLEP exams:

CLEP
P.O. Box 6601
Princeton, NJ 08541-6601
Telephone: (609) 771-7865
clep@ets.org

Just the Facts

- Taking standardized tests beyond the SAT I or ACT, and doing well on them, can improve your chances for admission and exempt you from required courses once you get to college.

- Most college-bound students take one to three SAT II Subject Tests; it's best to take the writing and foreign language tests after several years of study and to take all the other tests immediately after completing a course in the subject.

- The AP program gives students the chance to complete college-level work while still in high school; taking a few AP courses and doing well on the exams definitely boosts your chances for admission to the more selective colleges.

- The CLEP program helps students earn college credits for the academic work they do outside the classroom; this program is ideal for home-schooled students and for students who have completed a great deal of independent study or who have taken community college courses.

- If you have any questions about these testing programs, don't hesitate to contact the appropriate division of the College Board, the organization that administers all of these tests.

GET THE SCOOP ON...

Understanding your test score reports ▪ When to cancel your test scores ▪ Determining whether to retake a test ▪ How to dispute scores that you think are incorrect ▪ What to do if you're accused of cheating on a standardized test

After the Tests

Chapter 12

Despite the use of computers to score standardized tests, it has always taken a while for students to receive their score reports in the mail. The score report for the SAT I, for example, is supposed to arrive within three weeks, but students say that four to five weeks is more common, and even longer delays aren't unusual. The wait can be nerve-wracking.

While you're waiting for your test scores to come back, don't agonize over how you did or assume that the way you feel about the test is an indication of your real performance. Students who think they did poorly often get surprisingly high scores.

Here's why. When you took the exam, you spent more time puzzling over the hardest questions—the ones you may have gotten wrong—than over the easy ones, which you whizzed through. So, when you think about the test later, your main memory is of struggling to figure out the toughest problems. That selective recall isn't necessarily an accurate gauge of how you did overall.

Even after you receive your scores, though, your work may not be done. It's time now to analyze your scores and what they mean, which may be a little more complicated than you realized. And you may have some important decisions to make—especially about whether to try taking the exam again. In this chapter, you'll discover what you need to know to win this phase of the standardized testing game.

Understanding Your Score Report

The score that you receive on a standardized test is not merely the sum total of questions you answered correctly, or a percentage based on a 100-point scale. That would be too simple.

Instead, the test-makers add up all of the correct answers (and subtract points for incorrect answers on the SAT I, SAT II Subject Tests, and AP exams). This produces what is called a "raw score." Then, they plug that raw

Watch Out!
If you haven't received your scores by six weeks after the test date, contact ETS or ACT. Also, call your colleges and ask whether they received your score report. If they haven't, there may be problems at ETS or ACT. Unfortunately, you can't do much about it but sit tight.

score into a complicated scoring formula to produce the final score, your scaled score. On the SAT II, your scaled score may be 1100, while on the ACT it may be 25. How's that for confusing?

To make matters worse, after taking a standardized test, you receive a score report—a piece of paper that can be harder to decipher than your physics textbook. This score report contains your scaled score on each part of the exam (for the SAT I and ACT), your total combined (SAT I) or composite (ACT) score, and a lot more information about how you did on the test.

It's well worth the time figuring out what everything on the score report means. This information can help you compare your score against the scores of other students, find mistakes, or determine what you need to study if you decide to retake the test. This section describes the score reports of each of the major standardized tests.

The SAT I Score Report

The SAT I score report offers a lot of valuable information about how you performed on the test. But even savvy test-takers don't always find it clear. Here's a point-by-point description and explanation of what your score report tells you:

- *Your Verbal and Mathematical scores:* These are your three-digit scaled scores. Each score ranges between 200 (low) and 800 (perfect). Average or mean scores vary from year to year and even from test to test, but both Verbal and Math scores have averages close to 500. The front of your score report tells you how your Verbal and Math scores compare.

- *Your score ranges:* These are windows approximately 60 points deep—30 points on either side of your scaled score—which ETS provides because of the imprecision of SAT I scores. If you scored 590 on the Math section of the SAT I, that doesn't mean that your "true" math ability equals *exactly* 590 (whatever that would mean). Your score is just ETS's best estimate as to how good you are at math, based on one morning's performance on one batch of questions. To reflect this imprecision, your score report includes a score range of about 560 to 620, indicating statistically that it is ETS's opinion that your "true" math ability *probably* falls somewhere in that range.

- *Your percentile scores:* You'll also receive two sets of percentile scores, both Math and Verbal. One set compares your performance to that of a large group of high school seniors from around the country who have said that they plan to go on to college; the other set compares you to students only from your home state. The percentile score indicates what percentage of these students scored *lower* than you on the test. So, if you have a percentile score of 70, it means that 70 percent of students did less well than you. Obviously, the higher your percentile scores, the better.

■ *Information to help you decide whether to retake the test:* One section of your score report provides information to help you decide whether to retake the SAT I, based on your performance this time. This section shows the percentage of students with the same Verbal or Math scores who scored higher, lower, and the same when they retook the test, as well as the average number of points gained or lost. While this section gives you a general idea of whether your score will improve when you retake it, you should base your decision on many other factors as well. You'll find help with deciding later on in this chapter.

■ *Your scores by question type:* If you are at all dissatisfied with your overall scores, this section of the score report may be vitally important to you. It shows how you did on each question type. The two test areas are handled a little differently. The Verbal area is broken down by question format—critical reasoning, analogies, and sentence completions. The Math area is broken down into two general subject areas: arithmetic and algebraic reasoning, and geometric reasoning. For each question type, you'll see how many questions you got right, how many you got wrong, how many you omitted, your raw score, and your percentile score.

■ *Your scores on other SAT tests:* Your score report also lists your scores on any SAT I or SAT II Subject Tests you took in the past—up to six of each. It's handy to have all of these numbers in one place.

■ *ID information:* This section repeats the personal information that you entered on the registration form. It also lists your registration and test center numbers, which can be useful if you need to register for another test, order more score reports, or dispute your scores.

■ *College profile data:* You'll also receive a printout with some information about the colleges and scholarship programs to which you had your test scores sent. It includes some blindingly obvious facts that you surely already know—whether the school is a college or university, for instance—as well as some useful facts that you probably already uncovered elsewhere, such as the range of SAT I scores earned by most of the school's entering freshmen. If you filled out the Student Descriptive Questionnaire when you registered for the SAT I, this portion of the score report compares your responses with the characteristics of the colleges where you chose to send scores.

So, what's a good SAT I score? Well, that depends on a lot of things. It depends on what colleges you're applying to and their set standards for admission. It depends on how many students you are competing against for admission and how high their scores are. It depends on your other credentials. And it depends on how heavily the schools where you're applying weigh the SAT I in making admissions decisions.

Generally speaking, students who score a 650 or greater on the Verbal section and a 650 or greater on Math are definitely capable of doing the

Timesaver
The table under Scores by Question Type can be a useful guide if you decide to retake the SAT I— it will help you locate the test areas where you need the most extra work and where you have the best chances of improving your scores next time.

Unofficially...
Your current SAT scores are maintained in an active file for one year after your high school graduation. After that, your scores are kept on microfiche indefinitely. You can write the College Board for a copy of your score report at any time, even years after you take the tests.

work at any college in the country. Scoring a 1300 doesn't automatically mean that every school will accept you, but it certainly puts you in the running for even the most selective schools.

And don't despair if you get less than a 1300—not many people do. You still have an excellent shot at getting into a very good college, especially if the rest of your application package is impressive.

Check Table 12.1 to help determine what SAT I scores different colleges are looking for. This table lists colleges at a variety of selectivity levels and the range of average SAT I scores (approximate values) of students who are admitted to those schools. Because these scores are averages, many accepted applicants scored above or below these ranges, so treat the listed scores as general guidelines only, not as rigid cutoffs.

TABLE 12.1: AVERAGE RANGES OF SAT I SCORES OF ENROLLED STUDENTS AT DIFFERENT COLLEGES AND UNIVERSITIES

Selectivity	Average SAT I Scores of Enrolled Students	Schools
Highly selective	1400–1600	California Institute of Technology
		Massachusetts Institute of Technology
	1300–1500	Brown University
		Dartmouth College
		Duke University
	1200–1400	Georgetown University
		University of Virginia
		Washington University
Very selective	1150–1350	Furman University
		Kalamazoo College
		University of Michigan at Ann Arbor
	1100–1300	Lehigh University
		State University of New York at Binghamton
		Syracuse University
	1050–1250	James Madison University
		Texas A&M University at College Station
		University of Miami
Moderately selective	1000–1200	Hollins University
		University of Massachusetts at Amherst
		Warren Wilson College

Selectivity	Average SAT I Scores of Enrolled Students	Schools
	950–1150	Georgia State University
		Purdue University
		Simpson College (California)
	900–1100	Coker College
		Pace University
		Western Washington University
Somewhat selective	850–1050	Ball State University
		California State University at Long Beach
		Green Mountain College
		Kent State University
		San Diego State University
Not very selective	800–1000	Huron University
		North Carolina A&T State University
	700–900	Sul Ross State University
		Virginia State University

Unofficially...
Only about 20 of the 1,000,000 students who take the SAT I each year receive a perfect score.

SAT II Subject Tests Score Reports

The score reports for SAT II Subject Tests that you take look very similar to the score report for the SAT I. The main difference is that you receive just one score for each test, whereas the SAT I provides separate scores for the Math and Verbal sections, and a combined score for the entire test. But the other parts of the score report are similar; you'll see a score range for your score and percentiles comparing you other students who also took the test, for instance.

The score report for the Writing Subject Test includes a special section that outlines the number of questions you answered right, wrong, and omitted for each question type, just like on the SAT I. You'll also see your raw score for the test and an estimated percentile score for college-bound seniors based on the specific edition of the Writing Subject Test that you took.

You won't see a percentile for your writing sample, however. Instead, you'll receive a writing subscore (graded on a scale of 20 to 80) that tells you how well you did on the essay part of the test. You'll also receive a subscore for the multiple-choice section of the test, which reflects your ability to recognize errors in usage and sentence structure and to express ideas clearly.

The score reports for the Foreign Language with Listening Subject Tests also have subscores: one for the reading portion of the test, and one for the

Bright Idea
If you need to send a writing sample to colleges where you're applying, you can request an official copy of the essay you wrote for the Writing Subject Test from the College Board (for an additional fee). Colleges receive the writing sample six weeks after you make the request.

Timesaver
ETS offers a score-by-phone service to alleviate the waiting game, so you can get your SAT scores about two weeks after you take the test. (There's an extra charge for this service.) Call 1-800-SAT-SCORE after 8:00 a.m. EST at least 13 days after your test date.

listening portion. An additional usage subscore is reported on the Chinese, Japanese, and Korean tests. As on the Writing Subject Test, these subscores are given on a 20 to 80 point scale.

Like the SAT I, the SAT II Subject Tests are scored on a 200 to 800 point scale (except for the English Language Proficiency Test, which is scored on a scale of 901 to 999). The average score varies from year to year and depends on the Subject Test that you take. Table 12.2 provides a rundown of the average scores for each SAT II Subject Test, based on the scores of high school students who took the tests during the 1998–99 school year.

There's no established benchmark for a good score on the SAT II Subject Tests; whatever the college of your choice demands is the score you should shoot for. A score of 600 or more on any of the SAT II Subject Tests is considered a good, solid score by most colleges.

The ACT Score Report

When you take the ACT, you actually receive 12 different scores. The most important one is the composite score—your overall score for the entire test—which equals the average of your scores on each of the four sections, the subject scores. In addition, you receive seven subscores for the English, reading, and math sections.

While ACT composite scores range from 1 (very bad) to 36 (perfect), nearly half of all test-takers fall within a narrow range of 17 (poor) to 23 (above-average). The national average falls around 20; to attain that score, you need to answer only slightly more than half of the questions correctly.

Like SAT scores, ACT scores are not precise. All standardized tests involve some measurement errors. To compensate for this, the test-makers came up with a standard error of measurement that estimates the amount of error in test scores. On the ACT, the standard error of measurement is about two points for each subject score and subscore, and about one point for each composite score.

Therefore, you should think of your ACT scores as a range, rather than as a precise number. To show this, the score report gives the ranks of your scores as dashed lines that roughly indicate the amount of measurement error involved. The ranks show the percentage of high school juniors and seniors who recently took the ACT and who scored at or below each of your scores.

Use these ranks to understand which of the four broad subject areas tested on the ACT are your strongest areas and which are your weaknesses. A high rank in English, for instance, indicates that you're well suited to study related subjects in college. A low rank in any subject tells you that you should concentrate on study in that area if you decide to retake the ACT.

When you registered for the ACT, you reported your high school grades in up to 30 specific courses. The average of those grades on a four-point scale is shown below your ACT scores on the score report that the colleges receive. This is supposed to encourage colleges to weigh your high school grades along with your test scores when considering you for admission. The

TABLE 12.2: AVERAGE SCORES ON SAT II SUBJECT TESTS

Subject Test	Average Score
American History	588
Biology	600
Chemistry	606
Chinese with Listening	749
English Language Proficiency Test	961
French	600
French with Listening	599
German	607
German with Listening	574
Italian	648
Japanese with Listening	651
Latin	597
Literature	591
Math Level IC	574
Math Level IIC	649
Modern Hebrew	586
Physics	639
Spanish with Listening	603
World History	569
Writing	569

Unofficially...
Colleges don't usu-
ally consider ACT
subject scores and
subscores when
deciding whether to
admit you; the com-
posite score is the
important one.
Colleges may use the
subject scores and
subscores to award
advanced placement,
to determine if you
qualify for specific
scholarships, or to
help you select a
major or first-year
courses.

college score report may also include predictions about your performance in specific majors and courses.

As with the SAT I and II, a good ACT score depends on where you're applying to college, those schools' standards for admission, what other students in the applicant pool scored, and how heavily the schools weigh standardized test scores when making admissions decisions.

To help determine what ACT scores different colleges are looking for, look at Table 12.3. This table lists colleges at a variety of selectivity levels and the range of average ACT scores (approximate values) of students who are admitted to those schools. Because these scores are averages, use them as guidelines only, not rigid cutoffs; keep in mind that a certain number of students accepted to the schools scored above the averages, and a certain number scored *below*.

AP Grade Reports

The process of scoring and reporting your grades on AP exams is quite a bit different than that for other standardized tests. The major difference is that AP exams are graded on a simple five-point scale. Your score tells colleges how qualified you are to receive college credit or advanced placement in the subject in which you took the AP exam.

Here's how the grades break down:

AP Exam Grade	What It Means
5	Extremely well qualified
4	Well qualified
3	Qualified
2	Possibly qualified
1	No recommendation

Timesaver
If you can't wait for
your AP grades, you
can call the auto-
mated grade-
reporting service at
1-888-308-0013 any
time on or after
July 1. You have to
pay a fee to use this
service.

Most colleges consider a grade of 3 or higher a sufficient score to award advanced placement or college credit for the subject in which you took the exam. More selective colleges may only consider a grade of 4 or 5 to be sufficient.

AP Grade Reports are released to the colleges you designate, your high school, and you by mid-July after you take the exam. Each AP Grade Report lists the grades on all of the AP exams that you've ever taken, both that year and in previous years (unless you requested that some grades be withheld).

Deciding Whether to Cancel Your Scores

Occasionally, a student knows on the day of the test that he or she has truly bombed. Most often, the problem is physical; people do get ill, sometimes unexpectedly, and the stress of a standardized test can worsen the early symptoms of a flu bug or stomach virus. Once in a great while, the student simply freezes up and is psychologically or emotionally unable to finish the

TABLE 12.3: AVERAGE RANGES OF ACT SCORES FOR ENROLLED STUDENTS AT DIFFERENT COLLEGES AND UNIVERSITIES

Selectivity	Average ACT Scores of Enrolled Students	Schools
Highly selective	29–36	Harvard University
		Massachusetts Institute of Technology
		Rice University
	27–32	Amherst College
		Northwestern University
		Stanford University
Very selective	26–30	Oberlin College
		University of Richmond
		Vanderbilt University
	24–28	Creighton University
		Pepperdine University
		University of Texas at Austin
	22–26	Florida State University
		University of California at Davis
		University of Minnesota at Twin Cities
Moderately selective	20–24	Hofstra University
		Montana State University
		Spelman College
	18–23	Eastern Washington University
		George Mason University
		University of New Orleans
Somewhat selective	17–21	Georgia College and State University
		Roosevelt University
		Sam Houston State University
Not very selective	15–19	Chicago State University
		Lincoln University (Missouri)
	14–18	Alabama State University
		Paine College

test. And sometimes an ill-prepared student realizes in despair that he or she really should have studied and practiced before sitting down on test day.

If any of these calamities befalls you, you have the option of canceling your scores. ETS or ACT will wipe clean your score slate for a particular date at your request. Your test won't be graded, and neither you nor any college will know how well (or poorly) you did.

Keep the following caveats in mind if you are considering canceling your test scores:

- You must request score cancellation almost immediately. You can ask the test proctor for a cancellation form and fill it out on the spot, or you can cancel by notifying ETS or ACT via mail or fax (by the Wednesday following your exam for the SAT I and SAT II). For AP exams, you must send in cancellation requests by June 15 after taking the exam.

- The request to cancel your test scores is irrevocable. Once you cancel your scores, they can never be reinstated. And you can't cancel just one portion of the test—just the Verbal or the Math on the SAT I, for instance. The entire test must be wiped out.

- If you took more than one test that day—if you took two or three SAT II Subject Tests, for instance—you must cancel the scores of *all* the tests. You can't just cancel the score of one test and let the others stand. The only exception to this rule is if you take a Math or Foreign Language with Listening Subject Test and your calculator or cassette player malfunctions; in that case, you can cancel the score for only the affected test.

- No score will be reported to anyone, but your college score reports after subsequent test days will note that you did take the exam previously and chose to cancel your scores. Most colleges don't care about this, but who knows? It could raise a question in the mind of an admissions officer if your application is borderline.

- You won't receive any refund of your testing fee.

Obviously, canceling your scores is a fairly serious step. Probably most significantly, if you cancel the scores for a test that colleges require—the SAT I, ACT, or SAT II Subject Test in Writing, for instance—it puts you in the position where you must retake the exam a few months later, by which time college application deadlines may be looming. The sense of pressure you feel on this subsequent test date may be even greater than before. Therefore, you should cancel your scores only if you really must—illness being the most likely culprit.

If you want to cancel the score of an SAT I or SAT II Subject Test, contact the following address:

SAT Score Cancellation
225 Phillips Blvd
Ewing, NJ 08618
Fax: (609) 771-7681

If you want to cancel ACT exam scores, contact the following address:

ACT Records
P.O. Box 451
Iowa City, IA 52243-0451

On AP exams, you also have the option of withholding grades, which works a little differently than score cancellation and isn't quite so final. A signature is required to withhold any AP exam grade, so you must write to the AP program by June 15 after you take the test to make the request. In your letter, include your full name and home address, the years that you took AP exams, the name, city, and state of the college you will attend, and the names of the exams for which you want a grade withheld.

You have to pay a $5 fee for each grade you withhold from one college. The grades aren't reported to colleges, but they are still sent to you and your high school. You can release the hold at any time, but you must notify the AP program in writing to do so.

Even so, think long and hard before withholding AP exam grades from colleges. A low exam grade is unlikely to hurt you, especially if you took the exam as a senior, since admissions decisions were already made long ago. Also, colleges recognize that applicants with any AP experience are better prepared to meet the demands of college courses, so submitting all evidence of your college-level work is generally to your advantage. Remember that you probably won't get the chance to retake the exam, and even a score of 2 or 3 can earn some credit at many colleges.

To cancel or withhold AP exam grades, contact the following:

AP Services
PO Box 6671
Princeton, NJ 08541-6671
Fax: (609) 530-0482

Unofficially...
If you take the ACT more than once, ACT maintains a separate record for each test date. Colleges receive only the score reports from the test dates that you designate. This ensures that you maintain control over which test scores colleges see.

Deciding Whether to Retest

Should you retake the SAT I, the ACT, or an SAT II Subject Test if you're not satisfied with your scores? In many cases, the answer is yes. Here are the important factors to consider when making up your mind:

- *How do the scores you've already received match the credentials wanted by the colleges of your choice?* You should have in mind target test scores based on the admission requirements of the schools you want to attend, as well as other credentials that you bring to the table, such as your high school grades. If the test scores that you've already earned fall outside the range in which most freshmen at your top college choices score—or if they are at the lower end of that range—you should strongly consider retaking the test.

- *Do you see discrepancies between your test scores and your grades?* If you notice that your scores fall well below what should be expected of a student with your grade point average, consider retaking the test. The first time you took the exam, you may have had an "off" day or you may have suffered from test anxiety that adversely affected your score. The scores on your retest will probably more accurately reflect your actual level of academic performance.

- *How often have you taken the test?* If you've taken the SAT I or ACT twice or more previously—and especially if you prepared beforehand—you may have already tapped most of your potential for improvement. But if you've tested just once or never before—especially if your preparation in the past was superficial—there's every reason to believe that your score can go up, perhaps significantly.

- *Can you identify test areas with potential for improvement?* You're an especially strong candidate to retake the exam if your score report reveals specific areas of weakness. For example, if you performed well on all of the Verbal areas of the SAT I except analogies, where you got most of the items wrong, a targeted practice program focusing on analogies can boost your overall score significantly. Similarly, if a particular math area gave you trouble the first time around, work with a review book, teacher, or tutor to master that topic, and the chances are good that your Math score will rise on test number two.

- *Do you have time to invest in preparing for another test?* Look realistically at your plans for school and other activities. Before you schedule another exam, make sure that you can block out several hours during the weeks before the test for study and practice. If you take the second test cold, without any real preparation or warm-up, you may wind up spinning your wheels, earning scores no higher than your first scores.

Help with Retaking the SAT I

Thanks to truth-in-testing laws, ETS now offers (for a fee, of course) two services that let you examine the SAT I test you took more closely. These services are invaluable for the student who is considering retaking the exam.

The more extensive of the two programs is the Question-and-Answer Service. It's available for most test administrations, depending on the date when you take the exam (check the current SAT I bulletin for specifics). If you apply for this service, you'll receive a copy of the actual test questions from the SAT I you took, an answer key, scoring instructions, and a printout of the answers you gave. (Equating sections aren't included.) You can request this service at the time you register or up to five months after taking the exam. It's a good investment.

For some test administrations, ETS is not legally required to release the questions publicly. Therefore, ETS keeps them secret so they can be used again on future tests, thereby saving the work and expense of writing a fresh exam. For these tests, the Question-and-Answer Service isn't available.

Instead, ETS offers the Student Answer Service. They won't give you a copy of the test questions, but you will receive a printout of your item-by-item performance and an indication as to the general subject area of each question. It's much less valuable than the Question-and-Answer Service, but if it's all you can get, request it.

Help with Retaking the ACT

ACT offers a similar service, the Test Information Release service. You can request this service up to three months after you take the ACT by sending in a copy of the Test Information Release Order Form, found in the *Using Your ACT Assessment Results* booklet included with your score report.

There are two levels of the service. For $10, you can order the List Release service, which includes a list of your answers, a copy of the test questions used to determine your scores, a list of the correct answers, and a table to convert raw scores to composite scores. For $20, you can order the Answer Document Release service, which includes all of the above plus a copy of your answer sheet.

These services are available for only a limited number of test dates, generally the December, April, and June test dates. You can't order copies of your questions and answers if your take the ACT on any other date.

Obviously, studying the questions that you missed can point you in the right direction if you decide to retake the ACT and you need to figure out what subject areas require the most study. Checking your answers is also a good first step if you suspect that your test scores were incorrectly calculated or if you have a dispute with a particular test question.

Disputing Your Score

On rare occasions, a student becomes convinced that one or more of his or her test scores is inaccurate. You have two options if this happens to you. You can request hand scoring to check the accuracy of your scores, or you can officially challenge a test question or procedure that you feel kept you from getting the best score.

Requesting Hand Scoring

Sometimes, a student finds a discrepancy between the answer choices he or she is supposed to have made and the choices he or she remembers making. It's rare, but it happens. The machine that read your answer grid could have malfunctioned, for example.

If you strongly believe that your scores are inaccurate, your best option is to request hand scoring of your answer sheet. You can do this up to five months after taking the exam, using the order form you received with your score report. (As you probably guessed, there's a fee for this service.)

You'll get a new score report within six weeks. If any discrepancies are found, the hand-scored version prevails (even if the new score is lower).

Watch Out!
Don't forget to review every test area, at least briefly, before you retest. Although you may need to focus the bulk of your study on algebra (for example), it's important to keep your verbal skills sharp, too. You don't want to gain points on one section while losing them on the others.

Unofficially...
ACT research shows that of the students who took the ACT more than once, 55 percent increased their composite score, 22 percent had no change, and 23 percent decreased their composite score. On average, students' composite scores increased by .8 points from first to second testing.

ETS or ACT will send a notification letter containing the new scores to all of your colleges, and the test-makers will refund your hand-scoring fee. Check the informational booklet included with your score report to find out how to request hand-scoring of your exam.

Challenging a Test Question or Procedure

A more complicated problem arises if you become convinced that you were harmed by an inaccurate, flawed test question or by some unfair procedure on the day of the test—a mistake by the proctor, incorrect timing, a disruptive environment, or a misprinted test booklet, for instance. You can appeal such problems, but be prepared for a fairly lengthy process.

If you feel burned by a test procedure or question, write down all of the details that you can remember as soon as possible after the exam. Then, send a registered letter to the appropriate test-makers.

You must send the letter by the Wednesday following the test date if your complaint is about the SAT I or SAT II. Send complaints by overnight mail or fax to:

> SAT Assessment Division
> 225 Phillips Blvd
> Ewing, NJ 08618
> Fax: (609) 771-7710

For the ACT, you can send in a complaint up to one year after the test date (enclose a copy of your score report with your complaint). Send complaints and notifications of errors in your scores to:

> ACT Records
> P.O. Box 451
> Iowa City, IA 52243-0451

In your complaint, include your name, address, birth date, gender, Social Security number, and test registration number, and mention the name of the test you took, the test date, and the name and address of the test center you used. In your letter, explain what happened and why you think it was unfair. If you're disputing a test question, describe the question as you remember it, include the question number and section number, and explain your concern.

The test administrators will investigate your complaint and respond. In most cases, they will defend their test procedure or question (and often they are right to do so). If you aren't satisfied, you can request several further levels of appeal, culminating in a formal review by an independent panel. It's up to you to decide how significant your complaint is, how strongly you feel about it, and how much time and effort you want to invest in this process.

ETS and ACT are obviously not perfect. In the years since truth-in-testing laws made challenges to test questions a genuine option, they have been forced to admit errors in over a dozen test questions, increasing the scores

Timesaver
Ordering the Question-and-Answer Service (SAT I) or Test Information Release service (ACT) is a quick and easy way to check your answers if you think that your exam was incorrectly scored.

Unofficially...
In the past, test-question challenges have been much more effective in regard to math questions than to verbal ones—not because the verbal questions are "better," but because it's far easier to demonstrate actual errors on math questions.

of hundreds of thousands of students. So, don't hesitate to challenge the test-makers if you're convinced it's appropriate. The only way powerful institutions like ETS and ACT can be kept responsive to human concerns is if individuals hold them accountable for their actions, right and wrong.

If You're Accused of Cheating

If you fall under suspicion of cheating, you're in for an unpleasant experience, whether or not you are guilty. Although the test administrations make an effort at due process, the adjudication of such cases is basically an internal process controlled by the test-makers.

This doesn't mean that you are helpless or that you should meekly accept a "guilty" verdict if you really are innocent. Here's some advice as to what to do if you find yourself accused of misconduct on any standardized test:

- Insist on understanding the accusation and the process. Make sure that the test-makers inform you as to exactly what misconduct is supposed to have occurred, so that you can marshal evidence in your defense.

- Enlist the help and advice of your parents and a guidance counselor, teacher, or other trusted advisor. This is an important problem that can seriously affect your college prospects, and the bureaucracy you will face can be intimidating. Don't try to handle it alone.

- Communicate with ETS or ACT clearly and in writing. Use registered mail and keep copies of all your correspondence with the test-makers. Make sure that you "admit" nothing that is not completely true.

- As soon as you can, make detailed notes of everything you remember about your test-preparation and test-taking experience. In particular, if you remember anything odd that happened on the day of the exam, jot it down. A mistake by a proctor, for example, may innocently explain some discrepancy that the test-makers think is suspicious. Be as complete and accurate as possible. The sooner you make these notes, the clearer and more convincing your memory of events is likely to be.

- Provide the test-makers with any facts that could help clear you. If you know why the test-makers suspect you of wrongdoing, you may be able to resolve the dispute. For example, if you're suspected of cheating because you left the test room several times during the exam, you may want to ask your doctor to provide a letter confirming that you were suffering from a stomach complaint on the day of the test (if that was the case).

- Consider enlisting legal help. In America, of course, final recourse in disputes between groups and individuals is to the law. Most wrangles with test administrators don't require the help of a lawyer, but you may want to consider this option if you've been unjustly accused, if the test-makers refuse to resolve the dispute quickly and fairly, and if the cost is not a major problem for you and your family.

- If the dispute is not resolved within a reasonable amount of time—four to six weeks—insist on your right to retake the exam as soon as possible, at no charge to you. The test administrators are supposed to provide this service to give an innocent test-taker the chance to demonstrate his or her abilities without penalty and free from any cloud of suspicion.

Sometimes, the test administrators investigate a student solely because of a dramatic score increase. If you're in this category, be prepared to explain (and document, if possible) how you prepared for the second test. Describe your use of coaching, tutoring, books, software, and any other test-prep tools, and estimate the number of hours you devoted to study before the exam. A convincing account of your significant test-prep efforts can go a long way toward showing that your score increase was produced not by trickery but by good old-fashioned hard work.

Just the Facts

- The score reports that you receive for the standardized tests you take can be confusing, but they contain a lot of important information that you can use to compare yourself to other high school students and to determine what areas need more study if you retake the exam.

- Canceling your scores is permanent; take this step only if you're absolutely certain that you performed poorly—if you became ill during the test, for instance.

- Many students will see an improvement in their test scores when they take the test for the second time, especially if they spent a lot of time beforehand focusing on specific test areas that needed improvement; however, taking a test more than two or three times is not likely to result in an improvement in scores.

- If you feel that your scores were calculated incorrectly, that a test procedure was unfair, or that a test question was incorrect, go ahead and dispute the problem; it may result in your receiving a higher (and more accurate) score.

- Occasionally, students are accused of cheating on a standardized test; if this happens to you, and you're innocent, fight it—your college career may be at stake.

The Ins and Outs of Financial Aid

PART V

How Financial Aid Works

Applying for financial aid can generate a lot of stress and worry for parents. Many parents experience their first mini heart attacks when they take a good look at the cost of going to college and compare that to their yearly incomes. At the same time, they're faced with the cumbersome financial aid process, with its seemingly endless, complex forms.

Don't panic! The whole point behind financial aid is to make college affordable for all families, and most families qualify for some form of aid. Besides, the financial aid application process isn't as complicated as it seems at first glance. In this section of the book, you'll learn everything that you need to know to survive the financial aid application process.

What College Really Costs

College students are more than just seekers of knowledge—they are also consumers in the academic marketplace. And all good shoppers know the value of comparison-shopping. Comparing the costs of different colleges, while a complex task, pays off.

The cost of attendance—the total amount that it costs a student to attend a particular college—includes all of the following:

- tuition and required fees
- books and supplies
- room and board
- transportation and personal expenses
- miscellaneous expenses, such as student loan fees, childcare, costs related to a disability, or the cost of a study-abroad program

Table 13.1 shows a breakdown of average costs at four-year private and public schools for the 1998–99 school year, according to the College Board.

225

When estimating how much it will cost for you to go to college, keep in mind that tuition prices rise much faster than inflation from year to year.

AVERAGE COSTS FOR ONE YEAR OF UNDERGRADUATE COLLEGE FOR THE 1998–99 SCHOOL YEAR

Type of Student	Tuition and Fees	Books and Supplies	Room and Board	Personal Expenses and Transportation	Total
Four-Year Public Schools					
Resident	$3243	$662	$4530	$2023	$10,458
Commuter	$3243	$662	$2098	$2502	$8505
Out-of-state	$8417	$662	$4530	$2023	$15,632
Four-Year Private Schools					
Resident	$14,508	$667	$5765	$1593	$22,533
Commuter	$14,508	$667	$2101	$2094	$19,370

As you can see from the table, the most basic dividing line between higher education institutions in terms of cost is public versus private. Private schools simply tend to be pricier. But before you cross all private schools off your list of colleges, consider this: Public schools are far from cheap, and out-of-state tuition at many of the most respected public universities rivals that of the average private school.

Many students don't even consider the more expensive private schools because the high cost of tuition scares them off. One of the cardinal rules of financial aid is that you should never choose a school based on the tuition quoted in the college brochure. Because of the way financial aid works, your bill will most likely end up the same whether you go to Princeton or State.

In fact, higher-priced private colleges like the Ivy League schools are more likely to offer need-based aid than lower-priced or public schools. Princeton University began this trend when it vowed not to require a student loan when the family's income was under $40,000 per year (close to the national median). And all of Harvard University's scholarship aid is based on financial need.

Another important consideration is the school's endowment. Rich schools—those with hefty endowments—have more money to give in aid than the poorer schools. Many of these schools can afford to meet at least a large portion of the financial need of all students. At some, the average need-based grant ranges from $10,000 to $15,000.

Rich schools also have greater flexibility when it comes to awarding financial aid. Since it's their money, they're not tied to the rules and restrictions that govern public funds from federal and state government.

Generally, heavily endowed schools are better able to consider an individual student's special circumstances when making up financial aid packages. The college's own literature should list the school's endowment.

But depending on your family's financial circumstances, private school tuition may not be affordable to you and you may not receive enough aid to make up the difference. In that case, you may be concerned that a degree from a public university, which you can afford, won't be worth as much as one from a private school, which is well out of your price range. It's true that a degree from Yale or Harvard does carry a certain cachet. But many public universities are holding their own. In fact, in the *U.S.News* 1999 college rankings, 15 out of the top 50 schools were public institutions, including the University of California at Berkeley, the University of Michigan at Ann Arbor, the University of Virginia, and my own alma mater, the University of North Carolina at Chapel Hill.

Tuition and Fees

So what exactly does the tuition and fees "sticker price" cover? Tuition is the charge for the education that you're getting—the reason that you're going to college in the first place (I hope). It covers professors' salaries, classroom and laboratory equipment, classroom maintenance, utility costs, and the like. Fees pay for other services provided by the college, such as libraries, computer labs, student activities, and the health center.

Books and Supplies

The cost of books and supplies doesn't fluctuate as much from school to school as tuition and fees, but it can add hundreds of dollars each semester to the bill and must be counted in. These costs, particularly for textbooks, vary depending on the field of study, so it's important to find out typical figures from the academic department or from students within the major.

For instance, courses in the computer and engineering fields often require much more expensive books than English, history, or foreign language courses. In addition, majors that require you to take a lot of laboratory courses, such as chemistry and biology majors, can end up adding a significant amount to the total bill in the form of lab fees. Also, consider that some courses require more supplies than others; for example, you'll probably spend quite a bit on canvases, brushes, and paint for an entry-level art class, even if you're not an art major. The cost of books, fees, and supplies should never prevent you from entering a desired major; you should definitely plan for the extra expense in advance.

Room and Board

Room and board can make up a huge chunk of college costs. These costs can be simply measured if you plan to live in a dormitory—it's part of the total bill. According to the Department of Education, slightly more than one-quarter of all full-time college students live on campus.

Moneysaver
College costs can vary considerably across the country. The average tuition and fees for private schools in the Southwest ($10,701) is much lower than for private schools in New England ($19,211). So, shop for schools nationwide to find the best bargains.

Unofficially...
Tuition has long had a habit of rising faster than the rate of inflation. Tuition and fees for the 1998–99 school year rose approximately 4–5 percent over the previous year, while inflation only rose approximately 2 percent. Students also paid 3–5 percent more for room and board.

Don't think that bypassing the dorm simply clears the room and board cost from the college budget. Off-campus living expenses could run even higher, with huge variations from school to school. The difference between paying for an apartment in Athens, Georgia, and in Cambridge, Massachusetts, is enough to skew comparisons of schools that might otherwise appear to be similarly priced. Sharing an off-campus apartment with one, two, three, or even a whole gaggle of roommates can help you save a ton of money on room and board, however.

Even if you commute from home to school, you won't save as much money as you might think. You must count in costs such as public transportation fares or money for gas, parking, and upkeep of a car. And don't count on cutting the budget by eating home-cooked meals. Irregular class hours will force you to buy at least one meal a day on or near campus.

Speaking of eating, most colleges offer several meal plan options that you can tailor to your particular living situation. If you live on campus, you can purchase a meal plan that enables you to eat most of your meals in the cafeteria (which will probably help you save money on pizza and take-out meals). But if you get an apartment off campus, you can purchase a smaller meal plan, so you can eat some meals in the cafeteria while attending classes and studying, and cook the rest at home, which often costs less. (You'll find more information about cutting costs while at school in Chapter 18, "Surviving Freshman Year.")

Transportation and Personal Expenses

Transportation is a frequently overlooked budget category that can easily add thousands of dollars to the bundle of college costs. Students who live off campus have to take into account the costs of gas, car maintenance, and parking fees or the costs of public transportation. And many schools don't permit freshmen to keep cars on campus, so if you own a car and live in the dorm, you have to figure in the costs of garaging it off campus.

Attending a college far from home can significantly elevate transportation costs. Travel expenses include airfare, train tickets, or bus tickets for as many trips home as you think you'll make during the school year—and once homesickness sets in, you may find yourself going home more often than you thought you would. For financial aid purposes, colleges often budget students for two round trips home each year at the lowest-possible cost.

Personal expenses usually add up to more than most parents expect. Although students have historically lived on the cheap, the Gap generation is more prone to fancy accessories than its grubbier parents. Even the Seattle grunge look could be expensive if you shopped at fancy department stores for those fashionably worn-out lumberjack shirts. And don't forget to add in miscellaneous costs, such as laundry, toiletries, medical insurance and health care, stereo equipment—and the list goes on. Often, this is the easiest area to economize on, but one trip to the mall can blow your personal expenses budget for the next month. (Turn to Chapter 18 for some practical help on putting together a college budget.)

Miscellaneous Expenses

The amount you'll spend in this category highly depends on your personal circumstances. For example, if you have a child, take into account the costs of childcare, insurance, and room and board for your child. If you have a physical or learning disability, you need to figure in the costs of special equipment, transportation, or tutoring services. Other special circumstances include unusually high supply costs, as for an art student, and health insurance for students no longer covered by their parents' health plans.

You're not expected to pay for all of these expenses on your own, if you can't afford them. Because these expenses are considered part of the total cost of going to college, financial aid awards can help pay for them. If you have unusual expenses, discuss them with the financial aid officer at the school you're planning to attend. They may substantially affect how much financial aid you qualify for and increase your overall award.

Basic Types of Financial Aid

Financial aid comes in three basic flavors:

- *Grants and scholarships* don't need to be repaid or maintained by a job. Grants are usually based on financial need alone, while scholarships are given to students who have met some criteria, such as academic or athletic merit, regardless of whether the student needs the money to help pay for college.

- *Loans* are the most widely available sources of financial aid. You must repay them someday, but the interest rates for student loans are often lower than for commercial loans, and payments are deferred until after the student has completed college.

- *Work-study* lets students work 10–15 hours per week to gain money to help pay for school.

You and the financial aid officer at the college of your choice will negotiate a financial aid package that will probably contain a combination of all three of these varieties of aid.

Your aid will come from a number of sources, from the most massive federal programs down to institutional funds unique to your school. Aid might come from the state, private foundations, the college, or even an employer. Aid from a federal government program or a state agency is known as public aid; sources like employers, donors, and foundations are known as private aid. The financial aid officers at the schools where you're applying can tell you specifically what financial aid programs—federal, state, and institutional—the school offers. (You'll learn more about the different sources of financial aid throughout the next few chapters.)

Bright Idea
Most colleges publish a "consumer brochure" that sets out the typical expenses of attending that school. That brochure is a helpful starting point for coming up with a college budget. If your school doesn't include such a brochure with the information packet, ask the admissions office if they can provide one.

Timesaver
Do you have more questions about financial aid? If you have access to the Internet, check out the newsgroup soc.college.financial-aid. Several financial aid officers and consultants monitor this newsgroup and are happy to offer up advice.

How Much Aid Will You Get?

Determining how much financial aid you qualify for can seem like a mysterious, behind-the-scenes process that has very little relation to reality. Although it's impossible to determine how much financial aid you'll receive without actually applying for aid, you can make a reasonable guess once you have an idea of how financial need is determined and what circumstances qualify a student to receive aid.

Applying for financial aid begins with your application at the federal level; other aid providers, like your school, look to the information you provide to the federal government to determine how much aid to award you. The basics of applying for federal aid are the same, regardless of which colleges you're applying to.

Are You Eligible?

You must meet some basic eligibility requirements to qualify for federal financial aid. First, you must be what the government calls a "regular student," which means you are enrolled in an institution of higher learning to get a degree or certificate.

You must be enrolled at least half time to receive aid from the federal programs. The term "half-time" means the following:

- At schools measuring progress by credit hours and academic terms (semesters, trimesters, or quarters), half-time enrollment is at least six semester hours or quarter hours per term.

- At schools measuring progress by credit hours but not using academic terms, half-time enrollment is at least 12 semester hours or 18 quarter hours per year.

- At schools measuring progress by clock hours, half-time enrollment is at least 12 hours per week.

Individual schools may choose to set higher minimums than these.

Eligibility also depends on citizenship: You must be an American citizen or an eligible non-citizen. If you aren't a citizen, you must be a US national or a US permanent resident with an Alien Registration Receipt Card (I-151, I-551, or I-551C). If you have an Arrival-Departure Record (I-94) from the INS showing a designation of refugee, asylum granted, indefinite parole, humanitarian parole, or Cuban-Haitian entrant status pending, you are also eligible. (Students with an F-1 or F-2 student visa are not eligible for federal aid.) Finally, you must have a valid Social Security number.

If you're male and 18 years old, you must sign a "statement of registration status," which states that you have registered for the draft. If you don't register, you can't get aid. (If you say you registered but you really didn't, there could be repercussions; the Department of Education has begun to turn the list of liars over to the Justice Department.)

To boil it all down, if you're a US citizen who plans to attend college full-time and earn a degree, you are eligible for federal financial aid.

Determining Dependent or Independent Student Status

Few financial aid questions are as important—or as frequently misunderstood—as whether you are considered a dependent or independent student. If you're considered a dependent student, your parents must report their income and assets along with yours. If you're classified as an independent student, you report only your own income and assets (along with your spouse's, if you're married). As a dependent student, you have the advantage of working together as a family to finance your education. But independent students qualify for more aid and can borrow more under federal student loan programs.

Many college applicants mistakenly believe that they can be classified as independent students if their parents don't claim them as dependents on their tax returns. This has no effect on whether you are classified as a dependent or independent student. The *only* way you can be classified as an independent student is if you can answer "yes" to one or more of the following questions:

- Are you 24 years old or older?

- Are you married?

- Are you enrolling in a graduate or professional educational program, such as law school or medical school?

- Do you have legal dependents other than a spouse? (If you and your dependent children live with your parents who provide more than half the support, you probably won't be classified as independent.)

- Are both of your parents dead, or are you a ward of the court? (Orphans are considered independent only if they don't have an adoptive parent or legal guardian.)

- Are you a veteran? (Former National Guardsmen, Reservists, or former members of the Armed Forces who received a dishonorable discharge are not automatically eligible for independent classification.)

If you don't automatically qualify as an independent student, but you feel that special circumstances dictate that you should be given independent status, the school's financial aid officer has the power to reclassify you. Although the financial aid officer has every reason to look to your parents to shoulder the burden of the costs of your college education, the switch to independent status occurs from time to time. But this is very rare and happens only under the most unusual circumstances, and only when it has been proven by the proper documentation.

Calculating Your Financial Need

As you enter the world of financial aid for college, you quickly become familiar with the term "needs assessment." Most agencies that award financial aid perform needs assessments to determine eligibility for that aid. Although each agency may have its own specific and unique qualifiers, in

Watch Out!
If your parents refuse to provide financial assistance, or if they won't complete the application, that does *not* qualify as special circumstances under which you may be classified as an independent student. Talking to a financial aid officer may change your parents' minds, or the officer may be able to locate temporary emergency funds for you.

general, the difference between what the college costs (including room and board, books, and other supplies) and what your financial circumstances indicate you can afford to pay determines the amount of your financial need, or your eligibility for financial aid.

Here's how financial need is calculated:

Total cost of attending the college of your choice	College Cost
Minus the Expected Family Contribution (EFC)	− EFC
Minus aid from other sources (such as private scholarships or employers)	− Other Aid
Equals your financial need	= Need

Your EFC is the total amount that the federal government estimates that you, as a family, can contribute toward college costs. This number is determined by analyzing your overall financial circumstances. Family income is the major factor in determining your EFC, *not* the balances of your savings accounts or the worth of trust funds and other assets.

Your EFC figure will most likely vary from school to school, depending on which formula the college uses to determine financial need. Some schools use the federal formula established by Congress, called the Federal Methodology, while others go by what's known as the Institutional Methodology. Typically, the Institutional Methodology results in a higher EFC. So, it's important to know what each school expects. Ask the school's financial aid officer before you apply.

In very basic and general terms, the EFC is made up of these parts for dependent students:

- Contribution from parental income
- Contribution from parental assets
- Contribution from student income
- Contribution from student assets

Assets can include cash, savings accounts, checking accounts, real estate, a business or farm, and investments. Schools that use the Institutional Methodology to calculate need also count the equity of the family home as an asset. Retirement funds and pensions are not considered assets by any methodology.

Family expenses, such as taxes, support of dependents, and the college costs of an older child or parent, are taken into account when calculating the EFC. Some schools also allow deductions for unusual family expenses, such as paying for a nursing home, expenses related to a disability, and tuition at a private school for a younger child.

It's practically impossible to estimate your EFC in your head. To use a free, Web-based calculator to help you figure out your EFC and your estimated

Unofficially...
When families earn $15,000 or less, the needs assessment excludes any consideration of assets.

amount of need, go to http://www.finaid.org/calculators/finaidestimate. phtml.

Although your EFC may seem to be an unattainable amount, you can finance it if you carefully plot out a strategy that combines different economic sources, including loans, savings, a part-time job for the student, and current income. It's never too late to start saving for college, although the sooner you start, the better. A financial or investment advisor is probably the best resource to help you achieve your goals.

Maximizing Your Financial Need

There are several proven, legal, and ethical strategies that you can employ to make yourself eligible for more financial aid:

- Save money in the parents' names, not the child's. A much larger percentage of the child's savings is counted toward the EFC.

- Spend the student's assets and income on college and other necessary expenses (like a car) before spending the parents'.

- Pay off consumer debt first, such as credit card balances and car loans. Education loans generally have much lower interest rates than consumer loans.

- Accelerate necessary expenses, such as buying a new car or computer, to reduce available cash before applying for financial aid, particularly if you've been saving money toward that expense.

- Minimize capital gains in the year before applying for financial aid.

- Maximize retirement fund contributions in the year before applying for financial aid (retirement funds are not considered when calculating the EFC).

- If grandparents or other relatives want to give the student money to help pay for college, ask them to wait until the student graduates and then use the money to help repay loans.

- Parents should go back to school to further their education at the same time as their children are attending college (just so long as the parent is genuinely enrolled in a higher education course).

- Make an appointment with the college's financial aid officer to review unusual family circumstances that may qualify you for more aid.

What If You Don't Qualify?

Even families who earn too much to qualify for need-based financial aid can find money for college. Turn first to liquid assets, such as savings accounts. Families who have been saving for college for a long time are in the best position. Many state financial aid agencies and private banks even offer special tuition savings plans with interest rates designed to keep up with the rising cost of tuition. But even saving for just a year or two can make a dent in the EFC.

Watch Out!
Even if your financial need figure is high, you can't count on receiving that entire amount in financial aid awards. Colleges have limited amounts of aid available. Many schools have instituted a policy of meeting only part of the need of everyone who qualifies for financial aid.

Moneysaver
It's never too late to start saving for college. Begin by breaking your EFC into annual, monthly, or weekly saving goals. And make sure that you're getting as high a rate of return on your savings as possible. A good financial advisor can help you achieve your goals.

Many families are afraid that if they save for college, then they won't qualify for financial aid. This is true, to an extent. But the formulas for estimating the EFC rely much more heavily on family income than on assets, such as savings. So, if you did save for college, you do have to contribute a little more than a family with a similar income that did not save. But you also already have the money to finance your EFC—the family who didn't save does not. So, you can avoid graduating from college with a huge debt burden, unlike the family who didn't save.

Another way to help pay for college is to obtain a summer job or a part-time job during the college years. The student employment office at your school can help you locate a school-year job, either on campus or with a local business. High school students should save all or part of their earnings from summer jobs and part-time jobs to help defray the costs of college.

Don't overlook loans. Even if you don't qualify for financial aid, you can still borrow through the federal student loan programs to cover part of your EFC. Although the loan is unsubsidized—meaning that you're responsible for paying for all of the interest, which begins to accrue right away—the interest rate is generally lower than what you'd get for a commercial loan. Most lenders permit students to delay paying the interest until after graduation. Parents can also borrow through the federal loan program or obtain a private education or home equity loan to help meet costs. (You'll find out more about obtaining student loans in upcoming chapters.)

Another important source of college money (and by far the most desirable) is merit scholarships, which aren't awarded based on need. The majority of students overlook a gold mine of private scholarships because they don't know where to start searching or when to ask (but you'll get a leg up on them when you get to Chapter 15, "Searching for Scholarships"). Start looking for merit scholarships as early in the financial aid application process as possible. The two largest sources are the school you're attending and private groups, although some states also offer non-need-based aid.

Finally, you may be able to cut the costs of attending college in various ways that might not have occurred to you initially. Turn to Chapter 16, "Looking Elsewhere for Aid," for more information.

Why You Should Apply for Financial Aid

Watch Out!
Don't withdraw money from a retirement fund to pay for college—it's not worth the penalties you'll have to pay and the depletion in retirement savings. If necessary, take out a loan using your retirement fund as collateral instead.

I cannot stress this enough—don't skip applying for financial aid just because you think you won't qualify. Many families forego applying for aid because they think the family income is too high or that they have too much in savings. *Everyone* who plans to go to college should apply for financial aid—no exceptions. You never know when special circumstances might qualify you for aid, such as having an older sibling in college.

The following are the most common worries and concerns that parents have about applying for financial aid and why you shouldn't let these concerns stop you from submitting a financial aid application:

- *The application form requests too much personal information.* With pages and pages of forms to fill out, the financial aid process may seem intrusive and intimidating. In addition, you may feel reluctant to share private financial information when you don't know who'll be reading it. Once you get started, you'll soon find that the forms aren't as complicated as they seem at first, and that the information requested is no more than what the IRS wants to know every year.

- *Financial aid is charity; I should be able to pay for my kids' education myself.* Just because you need financial aid doesn't mean that your income isn't up to snuff or that you've failed to take responsibility for your children—it's the rare family that can afford the high cost of college these days. The premise of financial aid is that students should be responsible for paying for their own education, but they don't yet have the means; therefore, the government provides aid as an *investment.* A college degree usually means that the student will get a higher-paying job, contribute more to society, and pay more taxes over the course of his or her lifetime.

- *I don't want to take on a huge debt burden.* It's true that most families have to borrow to pay for college. But an education loan is not like borrowing to pay for a vacation or credit card debt. It's a wise investment that will produce a good return—a professional career for your child. Also, education loans often carry lower interest rates and fewer penalties than consumer loans.

- *Financial aid is so confusing; there's too much to learn, and I'm bound to make mistakes.* The financial aid application process can be intimidating. Don't be afraid to seek out help and advice from the high school guidance office, your state's financial aid agency, and reliable Internet resources (you'll find a selection of the latter in Appendix B, "College Admissions Resource Guide"). The absolute best resources are the financial aid offices at the colleges where you're applying; the financial aid officers there are usually happy to explain the requirements for their schools and work with you when you go through the application process. During the campus visit, set up an appointment with a financial aid officer—you'll probably find afterward that you feel much more relaxed about applying for aid.

You may feel intimidated about talking to the financial aid officer because you don't know what questions to ask. The following are some issues that you should bring up when you meet with the financial aid officer:

- Ask about the school's loan default rate—the percentage of students who attended the school, took out federal student loans, and later defaulted on paying those loans. If the school has a high default rate, it may no longer be eligible to participate in certain federal aid programs, and thus can't offer that money to you.

- Find out what financial assistance is available through the school, including all federal, state, institutional, and private aid programs, and how to apply for those programs. You'll learn the names of individual programs in the next few chapters—make a note of them, so you know which ones to ask about.

- Find out what the school's financial aid policies are. Does the school calculate need using the Federal Methodology or the Institutional Methodology? Does the school have a need-blind admissions policy, or are admissions decisions based partly on ability to pay? Does the school guarantee to meet all or part of each student's financial need? Is financial aid awarded on a first-come, first-served basis? Is there a per-student limit on aid or a standard "unmet need" figure for each student? Does the student have to demonstrate a minimum level of need before even qualifying for financial aid?

- If you are awarded financial aid, ask how and when you'll receive it. Do financial aid awards go directly to the school to pay for tuition and fees? Will you receive any leftover aid, and must you use that money to pay for specific bills, such as room and board? Will the school revoke your aid if you don't make satisfactory academic progress, and what is the school's standard for that progress?

- Find out whether the school has any special aid or scholarship programs that may apply to you. If you plan to major in a certain field, departmental scholarships may be available. If you're a female or minority student, the school may have grant programs in place that you qualify for.

- Ask about the school's refund policy. If you enroll but never start classes, you should get all or most of your money back. Even if you start classes but leave before finishing out the semester, you may be entitled to a partial refund. If you received federal aid, though, some or all of the refund is returned directly to the aid programs.

Watch Out!
Even if you don't finish your first semester in college, you'll have to repay any student loans that you received, less the amount of the school refund returned to the lender.

A Financial Aid Timetable

So, how do you get started? For most students, the high school guidance office is the first place to go. Virtually all of the information on application procedures and requirements, as well as local scholarship opportunities, arrives at the guidance office first. Also attend any financial aid nights sponsored by your high school. As you begin to search for colleges and narrow down your selections, you should certainly request financial aid information from the schools where you're seriously considering applying (this material is generally included as part of the standard information packet by the admissions office).

The Free Application for Federal Student Aid (FAFSA) is the standard form for applying for aid from the federal government, and it's also the primary application form used by most colleges and universities. Some schools also require an application called the College Scholarship Service (CSS) Financial Aid PROFILE or their own supplemental financial aid application. In addition, you may have to submit a state financial aid form, depending on where you live. Ask the financial aid officer at each college where you're applying which forms are required.

Table 13.2 is a calendar that outlines the most important dates in the financial aid application process. This timetable will help you plan everything that you need to accomplish. Be stringent about meeting these deadlines—try to be early when possible. You'll find out why later in the chapter.

Timesaver
Always save a copy of your application and worksheets as a backup, whether filing electronically or submitting a paper form. The school may need to see these copies later, or you may need to refer to them if you find errors in your aid package.

TABLE 13.2: CALENDAR OF IMPORTANT FINANCIAL AID DATES

When	What to Do
Junior Year of High School	
During the year	Take the PSAT/NMSQT in October; your score may qualify you for a National Merit Scholarship.
	During campus visits, meet with a financial aid officer at each college.
	Obtain financial aid information and applications from the schools where you want to apply. Ask about the deadlines for each form.
	Start researching scholarship programs that you may qualify for.
Senior Year of High School	
Fall	You should already have the application forms for all the schools where you're applying.
	Register for the CSS/Financial Aid PROFILE if any of your schools require it.
	Begin filling out all required financial aid applications, including the FAFSA.
	Continue researching for scholarships. Apply for scholarships with early deadlines.
January	Complete and file the FAFSA as soon as possible after January 1.
	Complete and submit any other required financial aid forms—the CSS/Financial Aid PROFILE, the state form, or the school's form—as soon as possible (you can file these forms before January 1, if you have all of the necessary information).

TABLE 13.2: CALENDAR OF IMPORTANT FINANCIAL AID DATES (CONT.)

When	What to Do
February–March	Review the Student Aid Report (SAR)—the form you get back from the federal processing agency—and correct any errors.
	Double-check that the colleges received all of your financial aid information well before the final deadlines (which usually fall during this period).
	Spend the rest of the winter applying for private scholarships.
April	College acceptances and financial aid packages start coming in. Study financial aid awards carefully—they may help you make up your mind about where to go to college. Contact a financial aid officer at the school if you have any further questions or concerns.
May	Send your nonrefundable deposit to the college you decided to attend.
	Decline aid awards from all schools where you decided not to go.
	Create a college budget and begin applying for additional private student loans, if necessary.
During college	
January	You must apply for financial aid all over again. You'll need to do this every year. But you can save time by submitting a Renewal FAFSA, which means that you have to list only the financial information that changed during the previous year.

How to Apply for Financial Aid

While the financial aid application process may seem dauntingly complex, when you break it down into its separate steps, there's really not that much to it. You'll spend much of your time filling out the requisite financial aid forms and then waiting to see what you get. In this section, you'll learn exactly what happens in this process. So, as you get started, you'll know exactly what to expect, which should help you feel more in control.

The Three Commandments of Applying for Financial Aid

Before getting down to the nuts and bolts of applying for financial aid, keep in mind the following three unbreakable rules of applying for financial aid:

1. Be prompt!

2. Be accurate!

3. Be organized!

Be Prompt

Be stringent about meeting each financial aid application deadline required by the schools where you're applying. Since many financial aid programs are distributed from a fund of limited size, wasting time can waste money. Start applying for federal aid right after January 1—as soon after you receive your W-2 forms as possible. (No, you can't apply before the first day of the year.)

The final deadline set by the federal government for submitting the FAFSA is June 30, but you'll only hurt yourself by putting off applying until the last minute. For one thing—and I can't stress this enough—colleges require that you file financial aid applications much earlier than the June 30 deadline. Some schools want your applications as early as February 15! The amount of money available for financial aid is limited for many programs; this money runs out fast, and when it's gone, it's gone. State aid agencies also set their own deadlines, which usually fall a lot sooner than June 30, too. If you miss any of these deadlines, your financial aid package could be cut by as much as 50 percent.

It's a common misconception that you must wait to apply for financial aid until after a college has accepted you. Schools often don't send out admission letters until late spring—and by that time, a lot of the available money has already been allocated. Just remember this one simple rule: The earlier you apply, the more money you're likely to get.

So let me say it one more time: *File your financial aid application early.* The best time to file? January 1, the first day that you can turn in the application.

Be Accurate

Complete all of the blanks accurately and legibly on every financial aid application form required by the colleges to which you're applying. Read the instructions fully. Any mistakes can cause the overworked aid agencies to send your form back to you to be redone. You'll not only have to do more work, but you'll delay the processing of your financial aid application—and that delay could keep you from receiving as much aid as you could have gotten had you done it right the first time.

Never leave any spaces blank on any financial aid form; where a question doesn't apply, simply write in N/A or 0 and move on. Some agencies return forms that have blanks, and the paper runaround can cause you to miss important deadlines. This is especially important on the FAFSA, which has almost 100 blanks—as many as one in seven forms are returned due to mistakes. Safeguards built into the electronic version of the form, streamlined instructions, and reducing the number of questions have reduced this error rate, however.

If you have trouble making sense of the FAFSA, you can call the Federal Student Aid Information Center for help:

- General questions: 1 (800) 4-FED-AID

- Questions about submitting the FAFSA electronically: 1 (800) 801-0576

Bright Idea
Fill out your IRS forms at the same time that you apply for financial aid. Having completed tax forms on hand will make completing the financial aid forms easier. If you have to wait on a tax return, report estimated income based on the previous year's return; just don't overestimate your income!

- Questions about the status of your application: 1 (319) 337-5665
- TDD number for the hearing-impaired: 1 (800) 730-8913

Be Organized

If there were ever a reason to get organized, this is it. You have to keep track of all of your applications to different colleges and the various financial aid forms required by those colleges. Make copies of every form that you send out, and keep a schedule of deadlines and what you have to do to follow up. You've already started a file for each school that you applied to—keep financial aid information in these files, as well. The checklist in Chapter 7, "Creating an Exceptional Application Package," provides a handy way to track the financial aid forms that each college requires, when they're due, and when you sent them out.

Many financial aid guides go so far as to recommend sending all aid correspondence via certified mail so that you'll have a record of the items being received. The College Board, on the other hand, says that registered mail is a bother and slows the application process. If you apply well in advance, though, spending the money is worth the added security.

It's a very good idea to clean up your own records before you get started. Organize all of your financial records in one place, and keep them handy so that you can consult them easily. Gather up your tax records, including your W-2s or, if you don't have those yet, your tax returns from the previous year.

Moneysaver
By getting organized from the start, you'll find it easier to fill out your forms again next year—and remember, you have to apply for financial aid every year.

The Financial Aid Forms

The forms that you must fill out to apply for financial aid vary from state to state and from school to school. Your school will let you know which forms you must complete and will provide them to you. While not easy, none of these forms is impossible to fill out on your own.

In most cases, you will have to submit the U.S. Department of Education's Free Application for Federal Student Aid (FAFSA). Submitting this form puts you in the running for all of the federal financial aid programs, and many schools and states use the FAFSA as the application form for their aid programs, as well.

Your school's financial aid application instructions will give you the information you need about applying for other forms of aid—several states, for instance, require that you fill out still more forms to apply for their own aid programs. The state forms tend to be shorter and easier to complete than the FAFSA. You may not have to fill out the FAFSA at all if you already have to complete one of the state forms. Checking a box on the forms tells the state to send your financial information along to a federal processing center.

It's also a good idea for students applying for private or institutional funds to check with their target schools to see whether the school requires supplemental forms or whether the student must follow additional procedures to apply for the aid. Some of the more selective private schools may require the College Scholarship Service's CSS/Financial Aid PROFILE form in addition to the FAFSA, for instance. The school's own application and the state applications might have separate deadlines that you need to consider.

Once you've applied, the processing agency will take between four and six weeks to turn your application around. You may be asked to confirm information or to correct the forms and then return them. The reprocessing will add another two or three weeks to your wait.

Getting the FAFSA

You can apply for financial aid many ways, but it all starts with the FAFSA. You have several options for obtaining a copy of the FAFSA and submitting it to a federal aid processing center:

- You can apply electronically through your high school.

- You can apply electronically through the Department of Education's website at http://www.fafsa.ed.gov/. According to the Department of Education, this is the fastest way to apply.

- You can use the FAFSA Express software; it runs on computers that use the Windows operating system and have a modem. You can find computers with the FAFSA Express program at many high schools, public libraries, and Educational Opportunity Centers. Or you can order the software on diskette by calling 1 (800) 801-0576, or download a copy yourself from the Department of Education's website by going to http://www.ed.gov/offices/OPE/Students/apply/fexpress.html.

- You can forego technology altogether and get the version of the form that comes on old-fashioned paper. Ask at your high school guidance office, college financial aid office, or contact:

  Federal Student Aid Information Center
  P.O. Box 84
  Washington, D.C. 20044-0084
  1-800-4-FEDAID

Filling Out the FAFSA

Be as accurate and as neat as you can when completing the FAFSA. Use a number 2 pencil. Don't jot notes in the margin that may interfere with processing the form. Round all amounts to the nearest dollar. And don't attach any explanatory documents, like tax returns—they'll just wind up in the shredder.

The following are the sometimes-confusing questions asked on the FAFSA and tips for answering these questions (line numbers refer to the 1999–2000 FAFSA and may differ slightly in later versions):

- *Your name (lines 1–3):* Your name must match exactly the name on your Social Security card. Use the same name consistently on every aid and college application that you submit.

Watch Out!
Don't send the form by fax or overnight express; using anything but the regular postal service or the in-place electronic filing procedures only slows down processing of your application.

Timesaver
If you fill out the paper FAFSA, use the preprinted return envelope that comes with the form to make certain that you return it to the correct address.

Watch Out!
You must get married on a date *before* you file the financial aid application, or you'll still be considered a dependent student for that year. Your independent ranking won't become effective until the following year.

- *Your permanent mailing address (lines 4–7):* List your legal, home residence; don't use the address at your college.

- *Your Social Security number (line 8):* This is probably the most important question—your Social Security number identifies you throughout the financial aid application process. Putting down the wrong number or omitting the question will result in costly delays.

- *Are you a US citizen? (lines 14–15):* If you aren't a citizen, include your alien registration number; this number is cross-checked with the Immigration and Naturalization Service and confirms that applicants who aren't US citizens are legal residents and thus eligible for aid.

- *Marital status (lines 16–17):* Use these lines to report the student's marital status, not the parents' status.

- *Enrollment status (lines 18–22):* If you plan to attend college full-time, mark that option for each semester during the upcoming year when you'll be at college. If you're not sure whether you'll be attending during a particular session, mark "full-time" anyway.

- *Your grade level (line 31):* Report how far along you are toward completing your degree in terms of a year's worth of credits, not the number of years you've attended college; high school seniors should enter 1 for "first year/never attended college."

- *High school diploma/GED (line 32):* If you're a high school senior and you plan to graduate at the end of the year, answer "yes."

- *In addition to grants, what other types of financial aid are you interested in? (lines 34–35):* Mark "yes" for each option, so you'll be considered for all available kinds of aid.

- *Student's financial information (lines 38–52):* All of these questions pertain to the student, not the parents. If the student is married, include the spouse's financial information in this section also. If any question doesn't apply to you, enter 0 (zero) in the blank.

- *Student status (lines 53–58):* If you can answer "yes" to any of these questions, then you are eligible for independent student status, and your parents don't have to complete Step Four.

- *Parents' financial information (lines 61–82):* If the student is a dependent (if the student answered "no" to all of the questions in lines 53–58), both parents must fill out this section completely. If the parents are divorced, only the parent who the student lived with most or who provided the greater amount of support during the past year needs to complete this section. If that parent has remarried, the stepparent's financial information is also required.

- *Number of college students in household (line 78):* The greater the number of family members in college, the higher the need for aid; to qualify, the family member must carry at least six credit hours per term and be pursuing a degree or certificate.

- *What colleges do you plan to attend? (lines 83–93):* You can request that up to six schools receive your Student Aid Report. You have to list the schools' Title IV School Codes; obtain these codes from the school's financial aid office or get a list at your high school guidance office, local public library, or on the Web at http://www.ed.gov/offices/OSFAP/Students/apply/search.html.

- *Date and signature (lines 96–99):* Any parent or preparer who supplied information must also sign, or the form will be returned. If you are married, your spouse must sign the form as well. If you submit an electronic copy of the FAFSA, you must print, sign, and send a separate signature page.

- *Unusual circumstances:* Fill out the FAFSA completely; make an appointment with your financial aid officer to discuss the unusual circumstances.

The CSS/Financial Aid PROFILE

The CSS/Financial Aid PROFILE is a financial aid form administered by the College Board and required by many private colleges and universities. The schools use the CSS/Financial Aid PROFILE to determine applicants' eligibility for private aid, such as grants, loans, and scholarships funded by the schools themselves.

You can register for the CSS/Financial Aid PROFILE at high school guidance counselor offices, college financial aid offices, and online at http://www.collegeboard.org/finaid/fastud/html/proform.html. You will receive a paper application in the mail approximately one week after you register. You can also complete an online version of the form at http://profileonline.cbreston.org/.

The CSS/Financial Aid PROFILE is similar to the FAFSA, but there are a few important differences:

- You can submit the CSS/Financial Aid PROFILE in the fall (the earlier, the better).

- You have to pay a $5 fee to register for the CSS/Financial Aid PROFILE, plus an additional $15 for each school or scholarship program where you need to submit the form (filing the FAFSA is free).

- You have to answer questions specific to the school or scholarship program that you're applying to.

- You have to provide more detailed financial information, such as whether your family owns a home.

The CSS/Financial PROFILE uses the Institutional Methodology, while the FAFSA uses the Federal Methodology. Thus, the CSS/Financial Aid PROFILE takes into account more factors when calculating the EFC, such as the equity of the family home. The Institutional Methodology also assumes a minimum student contribution of between $900 and $1200 per year.

Timesaver
You don't have to fill out a separate FAFSA for each college that you're considering. The FAFSA allows you to list all the schools where you're applying, so that they all will receive a copy of your Student Aid Report.

All of this means that your EFC is typically higher and the amount of financial aid you qualify for is typically lower at schools that use the Institutional Methodology. But on the bright side, schools that use the Institutional Methodology typically grant their financial aid officers more leeway in negotiating financial aid packages based on a student's specific financial circumstances.

Should You Hire a Financial Aid Consultant?

Moneysaver
If you just need a little help with the financial aid forms, you shouldn't have to pay for the services of a financial aid consultant. Many colleges run free workshops and otherwise offer help on completing the forms.

Most students still get most of their financial aid advice from high school guidance counselors or college financial aid officers. While this is often a good route to take, sometimes such officials are overworked or can't keep up with changes in the financial aid scene on top of their other duties. Thus families often can't get the high-quality, individual attention they desire from the usual free channels. At the same time, many families look for help in filling out financial aid forms and in managing the complex applications process—the same way families hire experts to help file their tax forms.

That's why many families have turned to independent financial consultants, many of whom are former guidance counselors and financial planners. But some of these firms walk a fine line between what is acceptable, what is unethical—and what is illegal.

Independent financial aid-finding services might help find more money, but it might come at the expense of your conscience. While a college financial aid officer is likely to describe the world as it is, a paid financial planner is more likely to describe that world as it could be, going so far as to offer suggestions of ways for parents to hide income from disclosure requirements on financial aid forms. Advisors might recommend shifting assets into retirement accounts, annuities, or universal life insurance policies or to grandparents, non-custodial parents, or other relatives—none of which needs to be listed on financial aid applications.

Although this is not illegal, some college financial aid officers claim the practices are unethical at the least and that they take aid money away from truly needy students. So, think twice before following any strategies that try to circumvent the system. A good rule of thumb to follow is this: If you would feel uncomfortable telling a college financial aid officer about a strategy that you're using, then don't use it.

The penalty for lying on federal financial aid forms can be as high as ten years in jail; you can read that part right by the signature line. At the very least, falsifying financial aid records is treated as a crime requiring probation, community service, a fine, and a felony charge on your record. The Departments of Education and Justice are starting to crack down on parents who lie on their applications, and so far they've recovered $3.4 million (which the offending parents had to pay back). Remember that even though the financial aid planner is advising you to lie, you're the one who's taking the risk.

Many schools have a verification process in place, in which a certain percentage (at least one-third) of students must provide full documentation of every piece of information listed on their financial aid forms. College financial aid officers are very scrupulous about checking up on parents' separation or divorce status, or whether a parent is actually enrolled in a higher education course. As a rule, officers scrutinize the forms prepared by financial aid consultants much more carefully than the other forms that pass over their desks, and if the officer thinks that you lied on your form, he or she can request even more documentation or disallow your claim. Paid consultants are required to sign the FAFSA, even if they don't fill it out on your behalf. (Be wary of any consultant who refuses to sign the FAFSA.)

Beyond the familiarity with fancy footwork, many experts question whether these financial aid entrepreneurs provide much of a service. Orlow Austin, financial aid director for the University of Illinois at Urbana-Champaign, performed an informal check on such services. Austin asked students who were already receiving aid from his office to file with financial aid-finding services. He found that once the services had gotten their fees of $40 or more, they rarely uncovered more sources of financial aid than the students had already procured through the school's own financial aid office. Austin also points out that while many of these services offer a money-back guarantee, students rarely take the trouble to ask for a refund—largely because the aid process is so complex that students don't know when they haven't been well served, and they also tend to blame themselves for not working hard enough to pursue financial aid avenues.

Finally, many of these self-proclaimed financial "experts" know a lot less about financial aid than they let on. They could be stockbrokers or financial wizards who have sniffed out an opportunity in education costs, but many of them haven't done the necessary homework needed to serve the individual student. For example, some consultants advise parents to remove their child as a claimed exemption from their previous year's tax return, with the idea of qualifying the child as an independent student; however, as was discussed earlier in the chapter, financial independence alone isn't enough to gain independent status, so parents who follow this advice only wind up paying more taxes. And like stockbrokers, many financial aid consultants are just pushing the hot instrument of the moment—a tuition aid plan that has recently burst on the scene that will earn them a healthy commission if they can force it on you. The one-size-fits-all approach rarely works when it comes to searching for aid opportunities.

If you do decide to speak with a financial advisor, protect yourself. Anyone can call himself or herself an investment advisor, so it's important to find someone with special expertise—not someone whose experience is limited to filling out his or her own children's financial aid forms. A Certified Financial Planners (CFP) has at least three years of experience and has taken at least a two-year course in financial planning and a six-part

Bright Idea
It pays to establish
a strong relationship
with the financial
aid officer at your
college. That person
is most likely to
have special knowl-
edge about what is
available at your
school. He or she
may also recommend
a trustworthy finan-
cial aid consultant if
you really feel that
you need one.

certification exam. College finances make up a part of that training and testing.

The Institute of Certified Financial Planners can refer you to a CFP in your area who specializes in college planning. Contact the Institute at:

> Institute of Certified Financial Planners
> 3801 East Florida Avenue, Suite 708
> Denver, CO 80210
> 1 (800) 322-4237
> E-mail: icfp@icfp.org
> http://www.icfp.org/

Just the Facts

- The cost of going to college isn't limited to the tuition; it also includes "hidden" costs such as room and board, transportation, books, supplies, lab fees, and personal expenses.

- Financial aid comes from many different sources—from the federal government to the college itself—and includes need-based grants, merit-based scholarships, loans, and work-study.

- When you apply for financial aid, the government or school uses a formula to calculate how much you are expected to contribute to the cost of college, based on family income and assets. The difference between this amount and the total cost of attending the college is your financial need, or the total amount of aid you can qualify for.

- Some families don't apply for financial aid because they think they won't qualify or because of other concerns, but this is a mistake. Anyone who is going to college should apply for financial aid—you never know what you might get.

- Financial aid application deadlines come early at many schools, and aid money is quickly depleted, so it's to your advantage to file financial aid applications as early as you can—long before you know which college you will attend.

- To apply for federal aid and for aid in most states and at most schools, you need to file only the FAFSA, the Department of Education's financial aid form (applying is free). Some schools or states may require additional forms, such as the CSS/Financial Aid PROFILE, so it's crucial to check the requirements for your schools.

- Although you may be tempted to hire a financial aid advisor to sort out the complicated financial aid application process, be wary of advisors who aren't experts in financial aid or who advise you to cross the ethical line. Unless your financial circumstances are complicated, you should be able to complete the forms on your own, with the help of college financial aid officers.

GET THE SCOOP ON...
What happens after you apply for financial aid ▪ What the federal
government kicks in ▪ What your state government kicks in ▪
What your school kicks in ▪ Understanding federal student loans ▪
How to negotiate for more aid

Understanding Your Financial Aid Award

Congratulations—you've filed all the financial aid application forms. Now comes the hard part. I know what you're saying: "Filling in all those forms, making sure there are no mistakes, getting them in on time—that was the easy part?" Unfortunately, yes. Because now financial aid awards start to come in, and you have to decipher them.

Unfortunately, it's not as simple as choosing the college that gave you the most money. You have to figure out what kind of aid you have received, where the money is coming from, what kind of debt burden you'll incur, and how much the aid reduces the cost of attending each school. If you're unhappy with your aid award or think you deserve more money, you have to decide whether to try negotiating your financial aid package with the school.

This chapter will help demystify the confusing world of financial aid awards. You'll learn exactly what kinds of financial aid programs contribute to your award and who funds each program. You'll also discover how to compare award packages from different colleges and the best way to negotiate for more aid.

What Happens After You Apply for Financial Aid

Your application for federal aid through the FAFSA or the other forms is used to generate a Student Aid Report (SAR), which arrives about four weeks after submitting the FAFSA. The SAR is also sent to the schools that you listed on the FAFSA. If four weeks pass and you don't receive the SAR, check on the status of your application with the Federal Student Aid Information Center by calling (319) 337-5665; if you applied with the Web-based FAFSA, check your application through the website at http://www.fafsa.ed.gov/ instead.

Timesaver
If you apply using
the Web-based FAFSA
or FAFSA Express,
you'll receive your
SAR approximately
one week after your
completed applica-
tion, including a
signature form, is
submitted.

The SAR puts your data into a financial aid Cuisinart and figures out whether you qualify for federal student aid. It generates a Student Aid Index number, which lets you know whether you qualify for a Pell Grant, and an Estimated Family Contribution (EFC) number, which determines whether you qualify for other federal financial aid programs.

If an asterisk appears next to the EFC figure, that means that your application was selected for verification, which is like an IRS audit. You may have to verify everything from income to household size to taxes paid, using documented evidence. You may have a long one-on-one with your financial aid officer and have to fill out a verification worksheet. At least one-third of financial aid applicants are selected for verification, in order to cut down on the cheating. If you don't comply, you can kiss your aid goodbye.

If you qualify for financial aid, your SAR arrives in three parts:

- Part 1, the Information Summary, tells you how to check the SAR for errors.

- Part 2, the Information Review Form, is used to correct any errors in the SAR.

- Part 3, the Pell Grant Payment Document, is used by your school to decide how much money to give you.

The first thing you should do is check the SAR for errors. If the SAR is correct and you don't need to make changes, you can receive financial aid based on that information. If you do need to correct errors, fill out Part 2 as directed and return it to the address listed. While necessary, this step does delay processing of your financial aid award. You can also use Part 2 to release your SAR to additional colleges.

Didn't get the Pell Grant? Don't worry—very few applicants do. But now you have something very important—your EFC number. Send that information to the financial aid officer at each school where you applied. The financial aid officer then uses the EFC to figure out whether you qualify for other types of financial aid.

Once the schools have all the information they need, they put together an aid package that will probably include a combination of grants (precious few), loans (too many), and work-study employment. You'll receive an award letter that notifies you of what your aid package contains. This document gives you an idea of the probable cost of attending that school, how your financial need was determined, what your need turned out to be, and the composition of the aid package.

Though you don't want to accept an offer before you've had time to think it through, you need to move quickly. Schools set response deadlines: If you don't respond to your aid letter within that time, you could miss out on the funds that have been offered to you.

If you haven't decided which school to attend, you should probably accept the aid package from each school that offers one. Accepting the aid package does not obligate you to attend the school, but it's the only way to keep your options open. This isn't to say that you should keep a number of colleges on a string—choose your college as quickly as possible so that the schools you don't choose can distribute the financial aid money they were going to give you to other students. (Be sure to notify the schools that you're not going to attend that you're declining their offers.)

But before you leap to accept that award, evaluate your offers with a cold eye. Don't let big numbers fool you; pay special attention to how much of the offer is made up of grants and how much is made up of loans. Are all the costs of attending the school listed in the aid package, or will the costs of books, personal expenses, and travel add on to that amount? Which schools tossed in special awards for academic or athletic merit? If scholarships are offered, are they renewable or are they one-shot wonders that will leave you high and dry next year?

Break out your calculator and compare the loan interest rates offered by different institutions, and check out whether the payback requirements for those loans are especially onerous. And as for work-study offers, keep in mind the study load before you, and ask yourself whether you'll be able to juggle work and school right off the bat.

Use the following worksheet to evaluate the financial aid awards you receive and to compare each college's aid package. You'll find all of this information in your award letter; if you can't find a piece of information, call the school's financial aid office and ask for it.

After you decide which college to attend, follow all of the instructions in the award letter exactly. You may have to send more information to the financial aid office or select a lender. You may also have to complete even more forms that were sent along with the letter and return them, along with any other required materials, to the school.

Finally, don't become so focused on money that you forget about the other important qualities of a college. No amount of financial aid will buy happiness at a school that isn't right for you. If you have to pay a little more to go to the right college, then it's worth it. (The next two chapters will give you advice on what to do if you're still coming up short, even after the financial aid award.)

Federal Sources of Financial Aid

The federal government is by far the largest source of financial aid, providing nearly 70 percent of the aid awarded each year, mostly through low-interest, federally guaranteed loans. In 1997–98, the federal government, through the Department of Education, made available more than $42 billion dollars in student aid. So, it pays to know something about the major federal programs, since they are your first source of aid.

Unofficially...
It's not all or nothing. You may accept part of the award and reserve the right to appeal any objectionable parts. But if you decide not to accept some part of the aid offer, the school may not be able to restore that aid later if you change your mind.

Watch Out!
Some schools offer a sweet deal to entice talented freshmen, but then dramatically change the deal in later years—by reducing grants and increasing loans, for instance. Be suspicious of deals that seem too good to be true, and always ask whether grants are renewable.

	College 1	College 2	College 3	College 4
Name of College				
Award Deadline Date				
Cost of Attendance (listed in the award letter)				
Other costs not listed				
Total Cost				
Grants and Scholarships				
Pell Grant				
SEOG				
State				
College				
Other				
Other				
Other				
Work-Study				
Total				
Loans				
Perkins				
Stafford				
Other				
Other				
Total				
Cost to Attend				
Total Cost of Attendance				
Minus Total Financial Aid Award				
Equals Net Cost to Attend				

Federal aid falls under the following broad programs:

- Pell Grants
- Campus-based programs
- Federal student loan programs

You don't have to apply for each of these programs separately. The only thing you have to do to be considered for all of the federal aid programs is file the FAFSA.

This section describes the grant and work-study programs sponsored by the federal government. Since the ins and outs of federal student loans are so complex, and since more students qualify for a federal student loan than for any of the other federal aid programs, this category of aid is covered separately later in this chapter.

Pell Grants

Before I even describe Pell Grants and how tough it is to get money out of this need-based federal program, I can't stress this point enough: *Even if you think you couldn't possibly be eligible for a Pell Grant, you should apply.* Many other aid programs require that you first apply for a Pell Grant. If you bypass this step, you'll pass up a large amount of possible aid, including the federal student loan program.

So, if you're serious about getting financial aid, apply for a Pell Grant every year that you attend college. How do you apply for a Pell Grant? You guessed it—by filing the FAFSA.

Pell Grants are, as the name implies, grants—you don't need to repay them. Though the funding for Pell Grants comes from the federal government, your school gives you the money—or, in some cases, merely credits your tuition account. Pell Grants are disbursed at least once per term.

The Pell Grant award changes from year to year, depending on how much funding Congress allocates to the program. For the 1998–99 school year, the maximum award was $3000. The budget for Pell Grants isn't limited—there is no cap on the number of Pell Grants that can be handed out in a given year. Washington budgets according to its expectations and hopes for the best. If program budgets get tight, however, the Secretary of Education can shave the maximum award somewhat.

The amount of the grant you may receive is not standardized. Different schools, with their varying tuition, disburse different amounts. In 1997–98, individual grants ranged from $400 to $2700, with the average grant falling around $1700. Pell Grants typically go to students from low-income families; in 1997–98, the average yearly family income of dependent students who received Pell Grants was $19,260.

Eligibility for Pell Grants is determined by the standard Federal Methodology formula that was passed into law by Congress and is used to calculate your EFC. If that figure falls below a certain threshold, you'll be eligible for a Pell Grant. The Student Aid Report (SAR) tells you if you qualify for a Pell Grant.

If you receive a Pell Grant, you can use it for five years of undergraduate study, or for six years if you pursue a course of study that normally requires more than four years to complete. Factors that exempt students from the five- and six-year limits include the death of a relative, personal illness or injury to the student, or the need to take remedial courses. Your school might have other rules for extending Pell Grant support.

Campus-Based Programs

"Campus-based" simply means that financial aid officers at each school administer the programs. Your financial need, how much aid you get from other sources, and the availability of funds at your school determine how much aid you receive from a campus-based program.

Unlike Pell Grants or federal student loans, the campus-based programs aren't entitlement programs. The government gives each school a set amount of cash. When the money is gone, it is really gone—no more campus-based aid can be given out until the next year's allotment comes through.

Not every eligible student receives aid from these programs. The schools set their own deadlines, so ask at your school's financial aid office and apply as early as possible to catch some of the money before it runs out.

Three of the federal programs are campus-based (although not all schools participate in all three programs):

- Federal Supplemental Educational Opportunity Grants (FSEOG)
- Federal Work-Study (FWS)
- Federal Perkins loans

Federal Supplemental Educational Opportunity Grants

These grants are awarded to undergraduates based on financial need— "exceptional financial need" is the way the government brochures put it. Pell Grant recipients with the lowest EFCs are the first in line for one of these grants. Depending on your need, when you apply, and the funding level at your school, you may receive between $100 and $4000 a year (the average grant in 1997–98 was $700).

Federal Work-Study

This is basically a part-time job. Most undergraduates are paid by the hour and often at minimum wage (graduate students may receive a salary). Jobs are awarded based on need, the size of FWS funds at your school, and the size of your aid package. The average yearly amount earned through the FWS program during the 1996–97 academic year was $1194, with half of the recipients typically coming from families with an annual income of less than $30,000.

The range of work-study jobs is limited only by the imagination of your school's financial aid office, and many financial aid officers have surprisingly broad imaginations. Thus, your school might have arranged myriad jobs on campus, from cleaning out the baboon cages to helping run the projectors for college movies. The program also encourages off-campus community service work and work related to your field of study, so it can help you get your foot in the door by giving you work experience in your chosen field.

Federal Perkins Loans

These are low-interest loans for students with "exceptional" financial need. They're also an exceptionally good deal at just five percent interest, and you don't have to start repaying until nine months after you graduate. The school acts as the lender, but the loan is made up of government funds. Undergraduates can borrow $3000 a year, up to a total of $15,000. Over half of the loan funds go to families with a yearly income of $30,000 or less.

State Sources of Financial Aid

It's a continuing trend among the states to increase their support for higher education, and all 50 states offer grant aid. In 1996–97, the states awarded nearly six percent of all the available financial aid; the majority of that aid was need-based. State contributions to the State Student Incentive Grant (SSIG) program and other need-based grant programs accounted for $3.2 billion, while state-sponsored loans gave out $300 million. And these numbers will probably continue to rise.

Each state is different, however, and some states spend far more than others. Five states—California, Illinois, New Jersey, New York, and Pennsylvania—award about 60 percent of the national total, $1.5 billion altogether in undergraduate need-based aid.

But don't pack up and head for the Big Apple yet. While there are plenty of ways to look at how much money states spend on their college students, it's hard to come by numbers that make sense. Less populous states argue that just citing raw dollar amounts spent overall is misleading, because they end up spending more per capita on their small number of students. Some also complain that the full extent of their aid doesn't show up in standard measures; for instance, several states argue that their public colleges and universities are so inexpensive that students don't need much financial aid—so that the states are penalized in the rankings for having a strong economic climate and helping students out with low tuition.

Each state has one agency that oversees most of the student aid distributed by the state and administers the state's financial aid programs. Your state's financial aid agency is the best source for up-to-date and comprehensive information about the aid programs offered by your state. You'll find contact information of all the state aid agencies in Appendix D, "Important Addresses."

Moneysaver
Federal Perkins loan payments can be deferred in case of unemployment, and they can be reduced or even canceled if you pursue certain much-needed professions, including teaching in designated low-income schools, working in certain family service agencies, or joining Head Start, VISTA, the Peace Corps, or other public-service agencies.

Watch Out!
Generally, state-sponsored financial aid programs are available only to state residents and can be used only at in-state colleges and universities. Other restrictions may apply; for example, some programs may only be used at the state's public colleges and universities.

Need-Based Financial Aid from the States

Most states give away plenty of money to moderate- and low-income students who can demonstrate financial need. These programs run the gamut from a modest grant to a complete free ride. For the latter, however, you often have to enroll early—before you enter high school in many cases. You also have to maintain a certain grade point average, perform well in college preparation courses, and you may even have to pledge to stay off drugs! But you can't beat the rewards, and these programs go a long way toward giving some students a shot at a college education who might not otherwise have been able to go.

The largest need-based state grant programs include the following:

- Cal Grant (California)
- Educational Opportunity Fund (New Jersey)
- Guaranteed Access Grant (Maryland)
- Monetary Award Program (Illinois)
- Tuition Assistance Program (New York)

In addition, many states offer low-interest loans similar to the federal student loan program (which you'll read about later in this chapter). The state's aid agency should have all the information you need on student loan and grant programs for state residents.

Unofficially...
Although need-based aid accounts for over 90 percent of state-grant dollars awarded to undergraduates (according to the National Association of State Scholarship and Grant Programs), non-need-based programs are growing. Of the non-need pool, the biggest chunk of cash goes into academic scholarships. So, study up! It pays.

Non-Need-Based Financial Aid from the States

The range of state aid is dizzyingly broad, and effectively demonstrates the political process at work. Along with the standard varieties of need-based aid, states are now moving heavily into non-need-based aid programs, such as awards for academic achievement.

Non-need-based aid usually falls in one of three categories:

- *Tuition equalization programs,* which reduce the difference in tuition costs between public and private schools in the state
- *Scholarship programs or merit awards,* which reward academic achievement and are largely aimed at charming academic talent into staying in-state
- *Categorical aid programs,* which encourage students to enter particular fields of study like math and science, or which help special constituencies like minorities or dependents of veterans and police officers

As with all state programs, some give a lot more money than others. In the 1993–94 school year, for example, most of the growth in non-need-based programs can be attributed to Florida and Georgia, which bumped up spending by more than $26 million. But your state having a new program doesn't automatically mean that money will shower upon you. The spurt in no-need monies is still puny compared to the massive amounts that go to undergraduates based on financial need. Again, check with your state's aid agency (listed in Appendix D) to find out what programs are available and how you can apply for them.

The best benefit a state offers is the protection it gives its own citizens in the form of in-state tuition at its public institutions. Resident status is also a requirement for eligibility for most state-funded aid programs, as is attending an in-state college or university. If you plan to go to a public school out of state, some students find it worthwhile to take the time beforehand to establish residency in the state of choice—often by moving there early and getting a job.

But since establishing residency takes up to two years in some states, many students feel they just don't have the time. Also, many dependent students can't easily establish residency in another state unless their entire family moves with them.

State-Administered Federal Aid Programs

The states administer several federally funded aid programs. This makes the crazy quilt of state aid programs more consistent, giving you some program names to look out for when going over state aid information, such as the following:

- *State Student Incentive Grant (SSIG) program:* This program has played a significant role in encouraging every state to develop and administer its own need-based grant program. While the states administer the program and decide individually whether the grants apply to full- or half-time students, the federal government partially funds the program. The annual maximum is $2500, and the minimum is $100.

- *Robert C. Byrd Honors Scholarship program:* This program is designed to promote academic excellence. It recognizes 13 students from each Congressional district for outstanding academic achievement, providing $1500 for the first year of higher education study.

- *Paul Douglas Teacher Scholarship Program:* This merit-based program is intended to encourage students who graduate in the top-ten percent of their classes to become teachers. The states may give each student a grant or they may assume part of the student's education loans; the student must then teach in a designated teacher-shortage area. Because this program relies on funding from Congress, it isn't offered every year.

Tuition Savings Plans

The hottest trend lately in state-administered aid is the tuition savings plan. Although these plans go by different names in different states, they're all pretty much the same when you get down to the fundamentals. The goal of the plans is to enable parents to easily save for college over a long period of time, usually starting when the child is still in grade school (or younger). When you put your money in one of these plans, it's guaranteed to rise in value at the same rate as college tuition.

Here's how the typical plan works: Your parents start an account and put away an amount each year that represents a percentage of the tuition price

Unofficially...
Attracted to an academic program offered in another state but don't want to give up aid from your own state? Many states have established agreements that allow you to take advantage of your home state's aid while studying elsewhere, especially if the program you're pursuing isn't readily available at in-state schools.

Watch Out!
If you are a home-schooled student, you must pass a test to qualify for federal student aid. The test is supposed to determine your ability to benefit from a college education. Call 1 (800) 4-FED-AID for more information. Many states also require that you take the GED to qualify for state aid.

(often there's a minimum annual deposit); all the money goes into a pooled fund; and state and federal taxes on the earnings are deferred until you make withdrawals to pay for your college bills. Many times, the state doesn't require you to pay taxes at all.

These plans are aimed at middle- and upper-income families, although some states have made provisions that make them more attractive to low-income families. Generally, you should get into a tuition savings plan early—before entering high school—and some states set a maximum age level for when you can get started.

Prepaid tuition and college savings plans offer several advantages:

- You save quite a lot in deferred federal and state taxes, which are levied on the student, *not* the parents, when the plan's earnings are used to pay for college.

- These plans are simple to use; parents don't have to know a lot about investing or manage their own investments.

- Minimum payments tend to be lower than those required by most mutual funds, so these plans are often more affordable.

- These plans offer a better return of investment than certificates of deposit or savings accounts, but carry a lower risk than stocks and bonds.

- Many plans enable you to lock in all or part of the current tuition price—a good way to preserve buying power, since tuition typically increases at twice the rate of inflation.

- These plans can help parents keep on track with their savings; for example, you can set up an automatic monthly deduction from your checking account.

On the other hand, these plans limit you to a particular set of schools—usually public, in-state colleges and universities—and the value of the plan is significantly reduced if you elect not to attend one of the state-sanctioned schools. If you move out-of-state after joining a plan, you usually can still attend a participating school, but the family must often make up the difference between in-state and out-of-state tuition. Depending on your family's circumstances, you may be better off putting college savings in mutual funds or other investments that outpace inflation.

Currently, 36 states offer prepaid tuition programs. (You can find a listing of these states and their agency contacts in "State Contacts for information about Prepaid Tuition Programs" in Appendix D.) Almost all of the remaining states are considering a prepaid tuition plan or are in the process of developing one.

Aid from Your School

Next to the federal and state governments, colleges and universities are the largest contributors to the financial aid pot. America's colleges have about

Watch Out!
Unlike parents' other assets, of which six percent are counted toward the EFC, effectively 100 percent of the assets in a prepaid tuition plan are counted. It doesn't make sense to shift a large sum to a savings plan in the student's senior year to keep it from being counted toward the EFC—this tactic will probably end up *reducing* the amount of aid you qualify for.

$5 billion in their own funds to help students. This aid comes in the form of traditional financial aid like need-based grants, loans, and work-study, as well as merit-based scholarships—which all goes into your financial aid package along with the federal and state aid that you receive.

The last few years have also been building years for college and university endowments, with hundreds of millions of dollars flowing into schools as diverse as Harvard University to the University of Washington (thanks, Bill Gates!). Some, but certainly not all, of this endowment money has gone into scholarship funds. Other college funds might find their way to students in the form of tuition discounts for prepayment, aid in receiving loans, and other innovative programs. Most schools also keep funds on hand for short-term emergency loans for students.

As a practical matter, this means that it behooves you as an academic consumer to keep in mind the school's bottom line while trying to make your college choice. It may seem an obvious point, but a school with a bountiful endowment like billionaire Harvard is in a better position to offer you financial aid than a less wealthy institution. And a school that is truly strapped financially could burden you with tuition increases once you enter—or even fold. It happens.

With that chilling thought behind you, take a look at each broad category of student aid from the colleges.

Grants and Scholarships

Just as the states have provided increasing amounts of money for scholarship programs to attract academic stars, the individual schools have been hustling to gain the prestige of enrolling academically talented students. If you earn a certain grade point average or score higher than a certain level on the SAT I or ACT, many schools will offer you enticements to attend. Some schools also provide special lures for valedictorians or students who have achieved other academic honors. Your school's financial aid office will tell you about any school-funded scholarships that you might qualify for.

Not every school promotes academic scholarships; the nation's most prestigious institutions attract a consistently high level of scholar, so many don't really need to offer academic scholarships as such. Financial aid from these schools is almost universally need-based. Academic scholarships are most important to schools on the make—those institutions that are trying to build an academically strong student body but don't have the academic traditions of the Ivy League schools as a draw.

Financial need is a factor in most academic scholarships. Most schools offer a no-need minimum of a small amount—often less than $300. Beyond that, demonstrated need can up the annual award into the thousands. Still, it's worth asking your school whether it gives out any special no-need academic scholarships and whether you qualify.

Sometimes, individual departments within the school also offer scholarships, such as the engineering or journalism department. If you already

Moneysaver
Yes, you can get something for nothing—some colleges don't charge any tuition at all, including Berea College, College of the Ozarks, Cooper Union, Webb Institute, and the service academies. Of course, the competition to get into these schools is fierce.

know what your major will be, check with the department directly to find out if any scholarships are available.

Colleges are also the major sources of athletic scholarships. If you're an athlete of any kind and looking for more money to help pay for college, turn to Chapter 15, "Searching for Scholarships," for additional information.

Loans

Many colleges now offer long-term or short-term emergency loans out of their own funds. Ask at your school's financial aid office to find out if it has such a program.

Many of these school-funded loans help students who don't otherwise qualify for need-based aid and offer lower interest rates than education loans from commercial banks. Fairleigh Dickinson University uses some of its foundation money to subsidize interest on parent loans to keep interest rates low. Other schools, like Lafayette College in Pennsylvania, pay the interest on student loans while the student is attending college, taking the pressure off students and their families during the college years (you must pay the school back within 12 years of graduation).

Tuition Payment Plans

More and more colleges and universities are looking for ways to take the sting out of paying college tuition bills. For many of them, this means offering plans that make it possible to get around paying for college all in one formidable annual chunk. There are as many tuition payment plans as there are colleges, and plans at different schools that sound similar may have significant differences.

Washington University in St. Louis, a trailblazer in providing innovative payment programs, was one of the first to offer a Tuition Stabilization Plan in 1979. This program freezes the cost of tuition for students who pay tuition up-front; the school offers a loan program to make the huge payment possible.

Another school with a number of payment plans is the University of Pennsylvania. Its Penn Plan offers a veritable smorgasbord of payment options that allow students to freeze their tuition by making hefty payments up-front or simply to pay tuition on a monthly basis instead of once a year. The school even offers a revolving line of credit (credit card-style) for non-tuition expenses.

Colleges are also getting smarter about giving students and their families more ways to pay for college. Many schools now allow students to pay tuition through regular electronic fund transfers from bank accounts or through credit cards. But look out for the interest rate on those credit cards! Some of the rates charged by banks on their cards would make a loan shark blush.

Watch Out!
To participate in an installment plan, you may have to pay a fee. Some schools may charge interest at a fixed rate or on the remaining balance owed to the school. Others require you to start paying well before the semester starts. Ask about the costs of payment plans before signing up.

Paying on the Installment Plan

Realizing that most people can't just write a $5000 check for tuition each semester, more schools are allowing families to pay tuition on the installment plan, or using their own endowments to make tuition loans that the families repay in installments. These plans soften the blow by letting you spread out the semester's tuition into more manageable monthly installments.

A wide selection of schools, ranging from the University of Michigan to Muskingum College, provide such plans, often with lower interest rates than those you would get on commercial loans. The installments might run monthly or as little as two payments per semester; they can sometimes be stretched out over several years. Check with your school for more details.

Many private companies are willing to make a little money by acting as go-betweens for you and your school. These companies make the lump payment to the college for you; you then work out a repayment schedule with the company, paying a small fee (between $40 and $75) that includes insurance on the life of the parent for the balance of the debt. Often, the school must enroll in the plan before the student can use it (check with your college's financial aid office). The following are some of the more widely used college-financing companies:

- Academic Management Services: 1 (800) 635-0120
- EduServe Technologies: 1 (800) 445-4236 (ask about the Tuition Installment Plan)
- FACTS Tuition Management System: 1 (800) 624-7092 or http://www.factsmgt.com/
- KNIGHT College Resource Group: 1 (800) 225-6783
- USA Group: 1 (800) 348-4607 or http://www.usagroup.com/ (ask about America's Tuition Plan)

Putting the Money Up Front

Schools like having money in the bank, and the sooner they get it the better. They can earn interest on it, invest it, and otherwise have fun with it. That's why they are willing to make attractive offers in return for getting money quickly that you would eventually pay them anyway.

A number of schools offer discounts on tuition (up to 10 percent) for students who prepay their entire semester's worth or year's worth in a single chunk. Other schools give students a bonus for paying in advance. Bonuses may be a set dollar amount, such as $100, or a percentage of the amount of the deposit, such as two percent. Again, check with your school to see whether it offers such programs.

Innovative Come-Ons

Many of the smaller, private schools have tried to find eye-catching ways to cut the cost of attendance. Some of the methods are almost hucksterish in

Moneysaver
By taking advantage of installment plans, you may not have to borrow as much as you thought to meet the cash-flow problems of paying tuition bills.

Watch Out!
Prepayment bonus and discount plans can carry strict restrictions. For example, they may be limited to students who don't receive financial aid from any other source. You'll probably qualify for a higher discount if you pay a year in advance (rather than a semester).

nature, but if you already like the school, why not take advantage? The following is a list of a few come-ons that have been offered here and there; see if your school uses any of them:

- *Guaranteed tuition:* Some schools, such as Baylor University and Santa Clara University, guarantee that tuition costs won't increase during the four years that the student attends the school; a deposit or the entire tuition in full is sometimes required to take advantage of these plans.

- *Buy four, get one free:* Some schools guarantee that if you don't earn your degree in the traditional four years—due to needed courses not being offered every semester, for instance—the fifth year is free. Clark University has an innovative accelerated degree program that lets you earn both a Bachelor's and a Master's degree in five years, with the fifth year being free.

- *Remissions for work:* Many schools provide free room and board in exchange for working a certain number of hours per week for the school; resident advisors and other dorm workers often receive this deal.

- *Profiting by leadership:* Some schools offer a tuition break for taking a leadership role in student organizations, such as at the newspaper or in student government.

- *Rewarding academic achievements:* Many colleges offer special awards to the top enrolled students; others may convert some of your student loans to grants if you maintain a high GPA.

- *Matching scholarships:* Some schools match church scholarships, state regents awards, Dollars for Scholars awards, or other outside scholarships that you get.

- *A legacy:* Tuition breaks for children of alumni are common.

- *Volume, volume, volume:* Many schools now offer discounts for bringing other family members along—not just siblings, but also Mom, Dad, or Grandma. Lake Erie College in Ohio even accepts twins for the price of one—a higher-education two-for-one.

- *Bring a buddy:* Several schools give you a tuition discount for convincing a friend to attend.

- *Try before you buy:* Some schools let prospective students try their first credits at a discount or take the first semester at a very low fee, or they may offer free courses to high school juniors and seniors or run a free summer program. These courses count as real courses, and earn transferable college credits.

- *Off-hour rates:* Colleges may set lower credit hour charges for any courses that you take during off-hours—evenings, weekends, and summers.

- *Lotteries:* A few schools (or their student organizations) sponsor tuition lotteries. If your number comes up, your year is free. This applies only to students who already attend the school, of course.

- *"Adopt-a-student" programs:* In these programs, the school gets local businesses to contribute. The companies participate to give something back to the community and to raise their public relations profile—but many of them get something more out of the deal. Sometimes, these programs require the recipient to work at the company after graduation. This could be a back-door way for enterprising students to get the job they want and to make extra money while attending college. Check with the financial aid office or student employment office for details.

- *Tuition matching:* Some private schools now match tuition with public schools to stay competitive; for instance, Bard College charges students in the top-ten percent of their high school graduating class the same tuition as they would pay at a public school in their home state.

- *Differential pricing:* Schools offer discounts for any number of odd reasons. Some give students a price break on less desirable housing—that could mean anything from teensy rooms to no air conditioning. Others charge less for some majors than for others. Options like these give you a little more control over how much your college education will cost. The school's financial aid office can tell you if any of these benefits apply to you; also check with the campus housing and food service offices to see whether any discounts are offered.

- *Moral obligation scholarships:* These awards are a gift from the school to you—granted with a moral (but not a legal) obligation to pay the money back after graduation. Along with their feel-good charm, these programs pack a potent tax benefit: Since the payback is technically construed to be a gift to the school, the student gets a tax deduction.

Colleges are constantly thinking up new, headline-grabbing alternatives; keep an eye on the media for programs that pop up unexpectedly.

The Lowdown on Loans

Federally guaranteed student loans are the Department of Education's major avenue for disbursing federal financial aid. The federal government provides low-interest loans to both students and parents. The best loans—those with the lowest total interest and the easiest repayment terms—go directly to students to help them meet their financial need. Slightly more expensive loans, with more immediate repayment terms, are also available for students and parents to help pay for the EFC; these loans are very good options for any family having trouble paying for college.

Private student loans are an entirely different category; for more information on these, turn to Chapter 16, "Looking Elsewhere for Aid."

Loans for Students

There are two main kinds of low-interest loans for students: the Federal Direct Student Loan (Direct Loan) Program; and the Federal Family Education Loan (FFEL) Program. Collectively, they're called Stafford loans.

Unofficially...
Some schools' come-ons aren't so big, but are still tempting. If you live in the dorm the first two years at the University of Alabama, the last two years are rent-free. And at Webster University, students who study abroad at one of the college's European campuses fly round-trip for free.

Timesaver
If your school participates in the Direct Loan program, the FAFSA form doubles as your loan application, saving you some paperwork. If your school participates in the FFEL program, your school's financial aid officer or state guaranty agency can help you connect with a lender.

Direct loans come directly from the federal government and are administered by federally run Direct Loan Servicing Centers. FFEL loans involve private lenders like banks, credit unions, and savings and loans; your state's loan guaranty agency or a private agency chosen by the state administers these loans. Aside from that difference, the two loan programs are pretty much the same; which program you get your money from depends on which program your school participates in. Like the Pell Grant program, an unlimited number of students can receive Stafford loans.

If financial need remains after subtracting your EFC, your Pell Grant eligibility, and your financial aid from other sources, you can borrow a subsidized Stafford loan to cover all or part of the remaining need. These are the best of the Stafford loans to get. With a subsidized loan, the government pays the interest while you're in school and for six months after you graduate. So, you have time to start working before you have to start making loan payments, and the overall amount that you have to repay is lower.

If you don't have need remaining, you can still borrow a Stafford loan for your EFC or the annual Stafford loan borrowing limit, whichever is less. But this is an unsubsidized loan; you must pay *all* of the interest. If you qualify for an unsubsidized loan, your interest charges begin from the time you first get the loan until you pay it in full. You may opt to postpone repayment until you graduate, but interest will accrue during the entire time that you're in school.

You can mix and match subsidized and unsubsidized money, so long as both loans come from the same program—either the FFEL or the Direct Loan program. Depending on your need, Stafford loans can add up to a total of $23,000 for a dependent undergraduate student or $46,000 for an independent undergraduate student, with no more than $23,000 of that amount in subsidized loans.

Dependent undergraduate students can borrow in the following increments:

- Up to $2625 per year for first-year students enrolled in a program of study that lasts at least a full academic year
- Up to $3500 for students who have completed their first year of study and the remainder of the program lasts at least a full academic year
- Up to $5500 a year for students who have completed two years of study and the remainder of the program lasts at least a full academic year

The numbers add up a little differently for independent undergraduates or dependent students of parents who don't qualify for a PLUS loan:

- Up to $6625 for first-year students enrolled in a program of study that lasts at least a full academic year (only $2625 of this amount may be in subsidized loans)
- Up to $7500 for students who have completed their first year of study and the remainder of the program lasts at least a full academic year (only $3500 of this amount may be in subsidized loans)

▪ Up to $10,500 a year for students who have completed two years of study and the remainder of the program lasts at least a full academic year (only $5500 of this amount may be in subsidized loans)

Note that these maximum borrowing limits apply even if you borrow a combination of subsidized and unsubsidized loans. Since you can never borrow more than the cost of attending your college minus the amount of aid that you've received, your individual borrowing limit could easily fall beneath these maximum amounts.

The interest rate on Stafford loans varies from year to year, but it has consistently remained below market value—and, in fact, it's a better deal than can be found anywhere this side of the five-percent Perkins loan. The maximum interest rate is 8.25 percent, and the rate is often lower while you attend college.

Stafford loans cost some money up front. An "origination fee" of four percent plus an insurance fee of up to one percent, both of which are deducted directly from your loan disbursements in installments, are administered. The state guaranty agency might also take its cut—up to three percent—also taken out proportionately from each disbursement as an insurance premium. You could also be charged late fees and collection costs if you don't keep up with your payments.

Loan disbursements are made through your school in at least two installments per academic year. Loan money must first be applied to school charges—tuition, required fees, and room and board. If anything is left over, you can use it for other college expenses, such as books and supplies, or your school may hold the funds until later in the term.

You have to start paying back Stafford loans six months after you graduate, leave school, or drop below half-time student status. (You can start repaying unsubsidized loans earlier than that, if you want to reduce the total amount of interest that you'll pay.) You usually have five years to repay the debt, though some lenders allow as many as 10 years—perhaps as many as 12 to 30 years under the Direct Loan program. The amount of your payments (down to a minimum of $50 per month) and the length of the repayment period usually depend on how much you borrowed and whom you borrowed it from.

Your loan may be forgiven if the school closes before you graduate or if your school falsely certifies the loan. You'll still have to repay the loan if you don't complete your degree, if you switch schools or majors, or if you don't get a job after graduating. The loan cannot be canceled for these reasons.

The government will come after you vigorously if you default on any federal student loan. They may notify credit bureaus of your default, thus scarring your credit rating. They may also ask your employer to deduct money from your paycheck, hold your tax refunds against the amount that you owe, and even sue you. If you find yourself unable to make loan payments, a range of options is open to you, including deferring payments, setting up alternative payment plans, and consolidating student loans at lower interest

Moneysaver
Repayment on Stafford loans can be deferred, postponed, or even reduced, depending on your circumstances. You can defer repaying your loans while you continue your studies, if you encounter economic hardship, or if you can't find full-time employment for up to three years after graduating.

rates. Your lender or Direct Loan Servicing Center will go over these options with you and help you come up with a way to pay.

Loans for Parents

Like Stafford loans, PLUS loans provide additional funds for educational expenses—but these are not need-based. PLUS loans go to parents. As with Stafford loans, these low-interest loans can either come directly from the federal government through the Direct Loan program or from a lender through the FFEL program. The government guarantees all PLUS loans, though.

PLUS loans carry no set annual or maximum borrowing limit. The yearly borrowing limit on PLUS loans equals the cost of attending the college *minus* any financial aid you get; so if it costs $6000 per year to attend college and the student has received $4000 in other financial aid, that student's parents can borrow up to $2000. Therefore, you can get a PLUS loan to make up the EFC *and* any financial need remaining after the college makes up your financial aid award.

PLUS loan interest rates are variable, although they can't rise higher than nine percent. For the 1997–98 fiscal year, the interest rate was set at 8.98 percent. Parents who receive PLUS loans also have to pay guarantee and insurance premium fees, as for the Stafford loans that go to students.

The school receives the loan disbursements at least twice during the academic year. Loan money goes first to paying for required school charges, such as tuition, fees, and room and board. Any remaining money goes to the parents, who can then apply it against any college-related expenses.

Any parent whose child enrolls in college at least half time and who is a dependent student can apply for a PLUS loan. Parents don't need to demonstrate financial need to qualify, but they do have to pass a credit check. If you're turned down because of bad credit, you can still receive a loan if a relative or friend who can pass the credit check agrees to endorse the loan. You may also be able to demonstrate extenuating circumstances to make up for failing the credit check. Finally, parents must meet citizenship requirements and not be in default on any student loans themselves to qualify.

You usually must begin repaying interest on a PLUS loan within 60 days after first getting the money, with no grace period. You have up to 10 years to repay the loan. A graduated repayment plan, which starts out with low payments that gradually increase over the repayment period, may also be available.

Deferments are possible in times of economic hardship or unemployment, but only on the loan principal; interest continues to pile up during the deferment period. Also, some lenders permit parents to make interest-only payments while the student is enrolled in college. There are very few avenues for cancellation or reduction of a PLUS loan. They include death (but not disability) of the student, or if the school closes its doors before the student can complete the program of study.

Negotiating for More Aid

You want to attend a particular school, but the award letter was a major disappointment. Is there anything you can do to change the school's mind?

As you've already learned, financial aid officers have a degree of latitude within which to change their estimates of a student's financial need, especially in cases of hardship. If you're dissatisfied with your aid award, you can put together a case for more aid and present it to the financial aid officer. The sooner you do this, the better: As the first day of the fall semester approaches, the aid officer's discretionary power dries up with his or her funds. Also, schools that dispense mostly federal and state funds, which are strictly controlled, have less latitude in changing aid awards than schools that primarily distribute their own money.

The financial aid officer has the power to adjust some part of the financial aid package in a process known as *Professional Judgment.* Professional Judgment refers to the financial aid officer's power, delegated by the federal government, to adjust a student's EFC, the total cost of attending the college, or the dependency status of the student. But no financial aid officer will adjust an aid award without just cause.

A radical change in your life or in your family's financial circumstances will change the way the financial aid officer sees you and your plea for aid. So, be sure to bring any special circumstances to the attention of your financial aid officer as soon as possible, especially if the changes occurred since you filed the FAFSA.

If one of your parents dies, for instance, contact the school's financial aid office, since the loss in family income certainly should be reflected in your aid package. If one of your parents becomes unemployed or retires, if your parents get divorced, or if someone in your family incurs high medical costs, these circumstances can also change your status. Losing benefits like child support or Social Security, or a loss due to a natural disaster or fire, can sway a financial aid officer. Anything that makes you substantially poorer increases your chances to receive aid.

By the same token, anything that makes the family richer will in many cases increase the EFC and lower your chances for receiving aid in upcoming college years. For example, capital gains, winning the lottery, cashing out a retirement account, or netting a significant raise may decrease your eligibility for financial aid. If you can control it—if you can keep from realizing a capital gain, for instance—put the windfall off until after graduation.

You may also be able to negotiate for more aid if you're the kind of student that the school really wants, especially if you're academically overqualified for the school. If you're an academic genius, an athletic superstar, or a musical prodigy—of if you have some other quality that schools find exceptionally valuable—then you may have a lot of colleges courting you.

One way to woo you is to offer substantial financial aid awards, made up mostly of grants rather than loans. If you really want to attend one particular school but you didn't receive enough financial aid from that school, you

Timesaver
If you think you deserve more merit-based aid, rather than need-based aid, you need to talk to an admissions officer rather than a financial aid officer. Admissions officers are generally more willing to negotiate merit aid, especially if someone else decided not to attend the school, thus opening up some scholarship money.

can always ask the financial aid officer if the school can do better. The worst that the aid officer can say is "no."

Try for a face-to-face meeting with the financial aid officer, so long as the travel expenses aren't prohibitive or the school isn't too big to provide that kind of personal service. If you can't travel to the school, make an appointment to discuss the aid package over the phone. Fax any new relevant information to the financial aid office, so that the aid officer can review the materials before you meet. The aid officer will need to see documentation of any unusual financial circumstances that your family has encountered or proof of unusual expenses that you may have, such as childcare costs or expenses associated with a disability.

During the meeting, don't just demand that an aid officer match or beat offers from other schools. You're not shopping for a car, and this kind of negotiation tactic is likely to backfire. Instead, explain that other colleges have asked you to contribute less, but that you really want to attend this particular school. You may want to show the financial aid officer the offers that you've received from other schools for informational purposes—but don't be pushy.

The best tactic is to politely present yourself in the best possible light to the financial aid officer—make the school want you. Push your abilities and accomplishments and the reasons that you and the school make a good match. Explain exactly why you think that the amount that the school has asked you to contribute presents an undue burden, and be ready to justify your reasons with documented evidence. Finally, listen carefully to the financial aid officer's reasoning for giving you the aid award that you got— the aid officer may not have taken into account certain factors that could make a big difference.

You'll do best if you remember the old adage: It's nice to be nice. Financial aid officers suffer a lot of abuse. You don't want to add to the stress in your aid officer's life. Present your case politely, and ask for help from the aid officer in understanding your aid package, so that you establish a cooperative relationship (and an atmosphere in which the aid officer actually wants to help you find more aid!).

Just the Facts

- Compare aid awards from different schools carefully; don't just look at which school gave you the most money but also at the kind of aid you received, whether the aid will be renewed all four years, what your debt burden will be, and how effectively the aid award reduces the total cost of attending that school.

- The federal government is the largest source of financial aid, with a variety of grant, work-study, and low-interest loan programs designed to help out college students who have exceptional financial need.

- The states contribute quite a bit of money to financial aid coffers; state aid programs range from traditional grants and loans to a variety of non-need-based scholarships, innovative college incentive programs, and prepaid tuition plans.

- The next-largest contributor of financial aid dollars are the schools themselves, who kick in grants, academic and athletic scholarships, and temporary loans; prepaid tuition plans, installment plans, and other innovative come-ons can also make it easier to pay the tuition bill.

- The bulk of your financial aid award will probably come from the federal student loan program, which many students qualify for; students can borrow subsidized loans to meet financial need, and they can borrow unsubsidized loans to help pay the EFC.

- If you think that your aid award wasn't good enough, or if you believe that unusual financial circumstances warrant more aid, your best recourse is to sit down and discuss the situation with the financial aid officer at your school—but remember, politeness pays!

GET THE SCOOP ON...
How scholarships may not really help you pay for college • How to get the largest scholarship awards • The National Merit Scholarship program • Getting athletic scholarships • Finding scholarships for particular fields of study • Searching for scholarships based on ethnicity, gender, and religion • More places to look for scholarship money • Scholarship search services • Avoiding scholarship scams

Searching for Scholarships

Scholarships are a very attractive form of financial aid. First of all, you don't have to pay them back. Also, you don't usually have to demonstrate financial need to win a scholarship, which makes them a viable alternative for middle-class students who don't qualify for much financial aid.

Scholarships generally reward a special talent, such as academic, athletic, or artistic prowess. They also may be awarded based on what field you want to study, your ethnicity, your gender, your religion, where your parents work, where you live, or the clubs you joined during high school. Since scholarships are so specialized, somewhere out there must be a scholarship with your name on it.

But unfortunately, scholarships make up a relatively small part of the financial aid picture, much smaller than many people believe. In reality, private aid is only a small part of the total amount awarded each year—less than five percent. And many scholarships carry daunting eligibility requirements—the old "red-haired Methodist from Georgia" problem. Most students don't win a private scholarship, and of those who do, the average award is less than $3000. With the time that you must spend searching out scholarships that you qualify for, filling out applications, and writing essays, the rewards may not seem worth it.

Nonetheless, hundreds of millions of dollars are available in private scholarships—not an amount to take lightly. The scholarship programs listed in this chapter just scratch the surface of what's out there, so don't neglect searching on your own using the search services listed in this chapter and the printed guides listed in Appendix C, "Recommended Reading." Just remember to go after the big money from federal, state, and school sources first and early, and then concentrate your efforts on picking up private scholarships.

The Skinny on Scholarships

When people talk about money for college, they usually aren't talking about the federal, state, and college aid programs that really do make up the bulk of financial aid awards. No, they're talking about scholarships. Winning a scholarship is exciting, even if it's only for $100. It means that you're a winner, that someone out there recognizes that you have talent and wants to reward that talent.

But you should know that scholarships are not usually the answer to your problems paying for college. You must report every scholarship dollar that you earn to the financial aid office at your school. And guess what they do with that information? They factor it into your overall aid award, thus reducing the financial aid amount that the school was going to give you. Your EFC remains exactly the same.

So, scholarships are not free money over and above the financial aid that you've already received. They won't make a dent in what you're expected to pay for college. That's why it's so important to concentrate your efforts on getting aid through the federal, state, and college channels first. You're much more likely to receive more money from these sources than from the private scholarship programs.

On top of that, searching and applying for scholarships requires an enormous amount of work. You'll spend hours in front of the computer and poring through scholarship guides, looking for programs that you qualify for. You'll then have to spend even more time learning about each program, filling out lengthy application forms, writing essays, gathering letters of recommendation, and making sure that your application is absolutely perfect. Successful scholarship winners report that they spent 10–14 hours on every application they submitted. And since awards tend to be low, you must submit dozens of applications to win a significant amount of money.

So, why should you pursue scholarships at all? Well, depending on who you are, there are some good reasons:

- If the bulk of your financial aid comes in the form of loans, winning scholarships can reduce your debt burden. When financial aid officers add your scholarship money to your aid package, the first thing they should subtract is aid from loans. (If they take away grant aid instead, you need to schedule an appointment to discuss the situation with your financial aid officer.)

- Your school may give you very little aid or no aid at all, regardless of how much you qualify for. In those cases, scholarships can help defray what you'll pay out of your own pocket for college. Since many scholarship awards are based on factors other than financial need, students who qualify for very little financial aid are eligible for a wide variety of scholarships.

- Winning scholarships is impressive. Later, you can list your scholarship awards on resumes, graduate school applications, and grant applications.

How to Maximize Scholarship Awards

The first thing to remember when applying for scholarships is to limit your applications to only the awards that you are truly eligible to win. Many students think that if they take a scattershot approach and apply for every and any scholarship they find, they're bound to win something. Not so. If you don't meet the scholarship's often-rigid eligibility requirements, your application goes straight into the trash—literally. Why waste your time?

Everything that you've already learned about applying to get into college comes back into play when applying for scholarships:

- *Be organized:* Keep a file on all the scholarships you apply for. Build a scholarship spreadsheet with the name of the award, sponsoring organization, when you requested the application, when you received it, amount of award, deadline, requirements, and so on.

- *Be prompt:* Get your applications in early. Sometimes, scholarship programs stop accepting applications well before the published deadline, so being early really might get you the worm in this case.

- *Be accurate:* Follow instructions exactly and answer questions honestly.

- *Be complete:* Fill out every application blank and submit all of the supporting materials asked for. Keep your personal profile close-to-hand to make completing endless applications easier.

- *Be neat:* Produce professional-looking, typed application forms, and proofread your applications for errors before submitting them. The one thing that disqualifies most applicants, besides not meeting the scholarship qualifications, is a messy application or one that's filled with spelling errors.

You'll probably have to write even more letters of recommendation for your scholarship applications.

Fortunately, scholarship application essays, while generally shorter than college application essays, often cover the same topics. Therefore, you can simply rewrite an essay that you already wrote for one of your college application forms.

Sometimes, a scholarship application asks for a very focused essay. In those cases, you'll find yourself faced with the task of writing yet another essay from scratch. You should be an old hand at essay-writing by now. Also, you're not expected to spend weeks crafting essays for scholarship applications, as you are for college applications. So, relax and concentrate on writing an original, honest essay that conveys something meaningful about you

Bright Idea
If you find out about a scholarship that you want to apply for, contact the sponsoring group directly for an application. Always send a self-addressed stamped envelope with your inquiry, or you may not receive a response.

Watch Out!
Many scholarship deadlines come early in the year, often before second semester starts. It pays to start seeking scholarships early—as early as your junior year of high school, if possible.

Unofficially...
The following schools attract the most National Merit Scholars, over 100 a year: Brigham Young; Harvard; Iowa State; MIT; Northwestern; Princeton; Rice; Stanford; Texas A&M; University of California at Berkeley; University of Florida; University of Oklahoma; University of Southern California; University of Texas at Austin; and Yale.

and makes the award committee really want to give you that scholarship. And keep a copy of every new essay you write—you never know when you may be able to recycle all or part of it, especially if you apply for numerous scholarships.

Keep to conservative topics when writing scholarship application essays. And choose a topic that is squarely in line with the mission of the group sponsoring the scholarship. Read the published judging criteria and scholarship information carefully, and try to determine the "ideal" applicant for that scholarship, which you can then try to emulate. If you don't know much about that group, do some research before sitting down to write your essay.

The National Merit Scholarship Program

Just about everybody who intends to go on to college ends up taking the PSAT/NMSQT in their junior year of high school. It helps you prepare for the SAT I—and, more importantly, it puts you into competition for financial awards that can put a good deal of money in your pocket. But the competition is stiff. A mere 15,000 of the millions of students who take the PSAT/NMSQT each year are eligible to compete for National Merit Scholarship awards.

Some schools, like Texas A&M University, work extra hard to recruit National Merit finalists and scholars because of the prestige that winning the award brings to the institution. So although the actual amount of money received by finalists is usually not that great, it can get you offers of more attractive financial aid packages as schools vie for you.

There are three types of National Merit Scholarship awards:

- *$2000 National Merit Scholarship:* The National Merit Scholarship Corporation awards about 2000 of these one-time-only awards each year. Financial need is not considered.

- *College-sponsored National Merit Scholarships:* Fewer than 250 colleges offer about 3300 scholarships to National Merit finalists each year, paying for them out of their own funds. The scholarships range from an annual $250 non-need grant to a maximum of $2000 annually. Beyond that $250 minimum, the award must make up half of the student's calculated financial need. To be eligible for a school's National Merit Scholarship, you often have to list that school as your *first* choice with the National Merit Scholarship Corporation.

- *Corporate-sponsored National Merit Scholarships:* Like the school-sponsored awards, the roughly 2500 corporate-sponsored scholarships are renewable for all four years of college. And like the school-sponsored awards, they range from a minimum of $250 to $2000 per year (although some do run higher). While some of these programs apply to students with no direct tie to the corporation, very, very few of these awards go to students whose parents don't work for the sponsoring corporation.

For the most up-to-date information available on the National Merit Scholarship program, contact the organization directly:

National Merit Scholarship Corporation
1560 Sherman Avenue, Suite 200
Evanston, IL 60201-4897
(708) 866-5100

Getting Athletic Scholarships

Don't laugh. Even if you're not going to win the Heisman Trophy, there could be athletic scholarships for you out there. (If you are going to win the Heisman Trophy, you're not going to worry about paying for college, anyway.) Although your skills might not have gotten you far at Big State U, some of the smaller schools you're considering may be happy to have you—and willing to supply a little money to entice you.

And not just in football, basketball, or baseball. Many schools offer scholarships in sports you might never have thought of, including archery, badminton, bowling, crew, fencing, gymnastics, lacrosse, sailing, skiing, synchronized swimming, and volleyball.

If you hope to net an athletic scholarship, you need to talk not just with your high school guidance counselor but also with your coach. Together you can figure out which schools' athletic programs might want you. Numerous college guides break down athletic scholarships by sport to make your search easier (check Appendix C for a selected list of scholarship guides).

Don't expect schools to come recruiting you, especially if you aren't an all-star or your sport isn't one of the big ticket-sellers. Let your target schools know that you're an athlete and that you would like to continue playing your sport at college. Send the coaches at the most likely schools a letter detailing your athletic achievement and pointing out that you would need financial aid. Be ready to provide the coaches who respond to your letter with more information, letters of recommendation, newspaper articles about you, and perhaps a tape showing you in action. Start this process early—in your sophomore or junior year, if possible.

The type of athletic scholarship money that the college can give and the athletes who are eligible to receive that money depend on which athletic association, if any, the school is affiliated with. The majority of colleges and universities are affiliated with either the National College Athletic Association (NCAA) or the National Association of Intercollegiate Athletics (NAIA).

NCAA Division Schools

More than 900 schools belong to the NCAA, which oversees intercollegiate athletics, including recruitment and financial aid. NCAA member schools belong to one of three divisions, with Division I schools competing at the

Timesaver
Definitely check the "yes" box beside Student Search Service or ACT Student Profile when you take standardized tests. This sends information about you to scholarship programs. Some programs, like National Merit, won't even consider you unless you check this box.

Unofficially...
If you're home-schooled, you can still be a college athlete. In 1996, the NCAA developed guidelines to allow homeschooled athletes to compete in Division I and II programs. Students must receive an SAT I score of 1110 and provide proof that they have completed 13 courses that meet the NCAA's core requirements.

Bright Idea
Create an athletic resume that lists your stats, personal data, names of coaches, any camps or summer programs you've attended, and any honors you've won to send to coaches at colleges where you want to apply.

major-college level. The differences between the divisions generally concern the number of sports that the school must sponsor and the amount of athletic-related student aid that the school awards.

Division I and II schools may award athletic scholarships up to the full amount of tuition and fees, room and board, and cost of books. Division III schools may award financial aid up to the cost of attendance, but this aid must fulfill financial need; these schools cannot award merit-based athletic scholarships.

In each division, four-year scholarships are not guaranteed. Your award is good for one year and may be renewed each year for a maximum of five years. In addition, you must meet the NCAA's academic eligibility requirements before you can receive any athletic-related financial aid.

If you have further questions about the regulations governing eligibility for athletic scholarships at NCAA schools, or if you'd like a directory of member schools, contact the NCAA directly:

NCAA
P.O. Box 6222
Indianapolis, IN 46206-6222
(317) 917-6222
http://www.ncaa.org/

NAIA Member Schools

More than 300 schools belong to the NAIA. Member schools may award financial aid to student athletes only up to the costs of tuition, room and board, and mandatory fees, books, and supplies. Again, the student athlete must meet academic eligibility requirements specified by the NAIA.

For more information on these requirements and for a directory of member schools, contact the NAIA directly:

NAIA
6120 S Yale Avenue, Suite 1450
Tulsa, OK 74136
(918) 494-8828
http://www.naia.org/

Other Athletic Associations

Some of the schools you apply to may belong to one of the smaller athletic associations, which impose their own requirements for athletic awards and eligibility.

If your school is one of the 26 members of the National Christian College Athletic Association (NCCAA), contact the following address for more information:

NCCAA
P.O. Box 1312
Marion, In 46952
(765) 674-8401

Email: nccaa@bright.net

http://www.bright.net/~nccaa/

If your school is one of the 24 members of the National Small College Athletic Association (NSCAA), contact the following address for more information:

NSCAA

113 East Bow Street

Franklin, NH 03235

(603) 934-4152

http://users.lr.net/~dmagee/

College money aimed specifically at women often takes the form of athletic scholarships; for an up-to-date listing of such awards, write for general information to:

Women's Sports Foundation

Eisenhower Park

East Meadow, NY 11554

1 (800) 227-3988

E-mail: wosport@aol.com

http://www.lifetimetv.com/WoSport/index.html

Scholarships for Needed Professions

One type of scholarship program with a lot of money to give attempts to woo students into specific professions where more talented people are needed, such as teaching or the health professions. To get more students into these areas, government and private organizations hold out the promise of cash.

Teaching

The Paul Douglas Teacher Scholarship program is the federal government's most lucrative program to attract bright students into the field of teaching, administered by the states. Awards go to students who rank in the top 10 percent of their graduating class (or who have GED scores recognized by the state to match that ranking). Washington, D.C., allows the states to award each recipient up to $5000 each year.

Sound great? It is. But look out for the catch—each year that the student receives the scholarship has to be repaid with two years of teaching. If the student doesn't fulfill this requirement, the student must repay the money, with interest. Check with your state's financial aid agency for specific eligibility criteria, which varies from state to state.

When contacting the state agency about the Douglas scholarships, ask about other teaching programs that the state may offer—many states heavily promote teaching in exchange for service in state after you graduate, generally in underserved areas. Private foundations also offer teaching scholarships.

Moneysaver
Federal law requires that each school must offer athletic scholarships equally to both men and women. That means that a considerable amount of athletic scholarship money is available for female athletes.

Watch Out!
Congress doesn't always allocate money to the Paul Douglas Scholarship Fund, which means it may not be offered in the year you start college. Lately, it's been off more than on.

Health Professions

On the federal level, several well funded programs exist to draw students into what the Department of Health and Human Services calls "shortage areas" in the health professions. Most of these are directed toward graduate study—fields like medicine, osteopathy, dentistry, veterinary medicine, optometry, podiatry, pharmacy, chiropractic, and public health. Rest assured that when you finish your pre-med program, several federal programs are available to help students who can demonstrate financial need.

Programs that benefit undergraduates and are sponsored by the Department of Health and Human Services are listed in Chapter 16, "Looking Elsewhere for Aid." Remember, too, that the military provides many scholarship opportunities within the health professions for students who join ROTC or who enlist in the Armed Forces. (For more information about money for education available from the military, again see Chapter 16.) Generally, your school's financial aid office carries up-to-date information on these programs as well.

States are also large contributors to funds that entice students into the health professions. Nursing scholarships are by far the most plentiful, but many states offer programs aimed at future doctors, dentists, and even veterinarians. Check with your state's financial aid office to learn about these programs.

For information on private programs in the health professions, check with your college financial aid office and with the advising office within your academic department.

Scholarships from Professional Organizations

If you've made your career choice—even if it's not an understaffed field—you might qualify for aid from the professional associations that serve the field. An industry group exists for every trade and profession, from dental hygienists to hotel management to wine experts. Of course, most of this money gravitates toward schools that have well regarded programs in the field, such as journalism at Northwestern University or meat science at Sul Ross State University. Still, many professional groups offer "portable" scholarships that aren't tied to a particular school.

For more information, turn to *Gale's Encyclopedia of Associations*. This reference is one of the most valuable resources for your scholarship search—you'll use it again and again to locate organizations that sponsor scholarship programs that you might qualify for. But it's very expensive—your local library should have a recent copy. Write to all the organizations you find that have anything at all to do with your field of study and inquire about scholarship opportunities.

Scholarships for Diverse Groups

Student aid for minorities falls into broad areas that have contributions from all sources—federal, state, the schools themselves, and private groups.

I won't list every program offered at the state, college, and local level—there are just too many. Write to your home state's aid agency for more detailed information about minority scholarships available in your state. And of course, check in with your high school guidance counselor and your college financial aid officer. Finally, consult scholarship guides and search services for programs aimed at your particular minority group, ethnic group, or religious affiliation.

Money for Minorities

To find money, minority students should look primarily to the states, colleges, and private organizations. Several states have funded programs to enhance the opportunities of minority students, from the Cal Grant B program to the Florida Seminole-Miccosukee Indian Scholarship Program. Contact your home state's financial aid agency for information.

The federal government has developed a number of programs to aid Native Americans who want to go to college. The Bureau of Indian Affairs (BIA) Higher Education Program provides need-based scholarships and loans to Native American tribal members who have at least one-fourth degree Native blood. Awards typically range from $500 to $4000 per year. Your school's financial aid office should have information on the different programs, or you can get applications from your home agency, tribe, or area office of Indian Education. Or write:

> Bureau of Indian Affairs
> Office of Indian Education Programs
> 1849 C Street, NW
> Washington, D.C. 20240-0001
> (202) 208-3711
> http://www.doi.gov/bureau-indian-affairs.html

Colleges are trying to fulfill their federal commitment to affirmative action programs by working harder to recruit and retain qualified minority students. Even in these times of political attacks and reassessment of affirmative action guidelines, many schools still recruit vigorously, and many have minority affairs officers on campus who, in conjunction with the financial aid office, can help you find your way to academic funding.

Private organizations also do what they can to add to the numbers of minority students in higher education. A well known source of money for African-American college students is the United Negro College Fund (UNCF), which favors students attending its member colleges and universities. For more information on UNCF-sponsored scholarship programs and for a list of schools that participate in the UNCF, contact:

> United Negro College Fund
> 8260 Willow Oaks Corporate Drive
> Fairfax, VA 22031
> 1 (800) 331-2244
> http://www.uncf.org/programs/programs.htm

Watch Out!
To qualify for most scholarships for Native Americans, including those offered by the BIA, you must be an enrolled member of a federally recognized tribe. A Certificate of Indian Blood is generally accepted as proof of membership.

The Congressional Hispanic Caucus Institute has developed one of the most comprehensive collections of financial aid information and scholarships specific to Hispanic students. There is no charge for this service, and bilingual assistance is available. All you have to do is call 1 (800) EXCEL-DC.

Another good source of information is the Hispanic Scholarship Fund, the largest Hispanic scholarship-granting organization in the country, which administers its own awards and provides a lot of valuable information on other scholarship and financial aid sources for Hispanic students. For more information, contact:

> Hispanic Scholarship Fund
> One Sansome Street, Suite 1000
> San Francisco, CA 94104
> 1 (877) HSF-INFO
> http://www.hsf.net/scholarship/

While many scholarships for minorities come from religious organizations and civic groups, professional associations supply many more. The best-known program aids African-American, Hispanic, and Native American students interested in engineering careers; the program is funded through the colleges, and you apply through your school's financial aid office. For a list of schools that participate in the program, contact:

> NACME, Inc.
> The Empire State Building
> 350 Fifth Avenue, Suite 2212
> New York, NY 10118-2299
> (212) 279-2626
> http://www.nacme.org/sch.html

Moneysaver
To find out if your chosen profession has a minority scholarship program, first look up the group in a reference work like *Gale's Encyclopedia of Associations*. Contact the group and ask whether minority scholarships exist.

There's even a free scholarship search service on the Web just for minority students, provided by the Minority On-Line Information Service (MOLIS). Simply choose your race or heritage from the menus, and the service hunts down scholarships that you might qualify for. To access the service, go to: http://www.fie.com/molis/scholar.htm.

Money for Women

The money for women in higher education comes almost exclusively from the colleges and private sources. One good source of information about such programs—besides your school's financial aid office, of course—is the American Association of University Women. This group also sponsors many scholarships and grants. For more information, write:

> AAUW Educational Foundation
> Department 60
> 2201 N. Dodge Street
> Iowa City, IA 52243-4030
> (319) 337-1716 ext. 60
> http://www.aauw.org/3000/felgrawa.html

Another motherlode of scholarship and loan money for women is through professional organizations, such as the Business and Professional Women's Foundation. Write to the following address for more information (include a self-addressed, stamped envelope):

Scholarships
Business and Professional Women's Foundation
2012 Massachusetts Avenue, NW
Washington, D.C. 20036
(202) 293-1200
http://www.bpwusa.org/foundation/foundation.html

Another professional association with a lot of scholarship money to offer female students is the Society of Women Engineers. If you think you might want to study engineering or a related field, don't neglect this opportunity. Write for more information to:

Society of Women Engineers Headquarters
120 Wall Street, 11th Floor
New York, NY 10005-3902
(212) 509-9577
Email: hq@swe.org
http://www.swe.org/SWE/StudentServices/Scholarship/
brochure.htm

Money for Disabled Students

The U.S. Department of Education operates a Clearinghouse on Disability Information, which provides help and information to disabled students on all aspects of going to college, including getting financial aid. For more information, contact:

Clearinghouse on Disability Information
U.S. Department of Education
330 C Street SW, Room 3132
Washington, D.C. 20202-2524
(202) 205-8241 (TTY also)

Another good resource for information about financial aid and services available to disabled colleges students is the Office of Disability Support Services at your school. Your state financial aid agency may also support scholarship programs for the disabled; many states have programs in place for the blind and their dependents, for example.

Money for Gays and Lesbians

Some private and college-funded scholarship programs are geared toward gay, lesbian, bisexual, and transsexual students. The Fund for Lesbian and Gay Scholarships offers money to students who can demonstrate financial need and who are involved in the community. Write to:

Moneysaver
Don't forget to list expenses related to your disability when applying for financial aid. Your aid officer will consider these expenses when determining your need. Expenses can include special equipment and services, necessary transportation, and medical expenses not covered by insurance.

Whitman-Brooks
The Scholarship Fund
P.O. Box 48320
Los Angeles, CA 90048-0320
(213) 650-5752

The Uncommon Legacy Foundation also offers $1000 scholarships to 100 lesbian students each year. Get more information by contacting:

Scholarship Committee
An Uncommon Legacy Foundation, Inc.
150 West 26th Street, Suite 602
New York, NY 10001
(212) 366-6507
http://www.uncommonlegacy.org/

Money from Religious Organizations

Churches and religious organizations have a lot of money to give to their members. Groups like the Aid Association for Lutherans, the National Baptist Convention, and the Hillel Foundation host contests and offer scholarships, grants, and loans. Find these groups through your church, your campus Bible Chair, or in *Gale's Encyclopedia of Associations*. If you accept a scholarship sponsored by a religious organization, you might run into a number of restrictions, including a requirement of religious study or of attending a church-sponsored school—don't apply for any scholarship if you don't want to carry out the obligations that come along with the money.

Money from Ethnic Societies

Sure, you're proud to be an Armenian. But did you know that your Armenian ancestry could qualify you for scholarships? The Armenian Relief Society has many available. So does the Armenian General Benevolent Union, which offers both scholarships and loans.

Are you a woman of Greek descent? Perhaps you have a relative in the Daughters of Penelope. If so, you might qualify for one of that organization's awards, such as the Helen Karagianis Memorial Award or the Pota Sarastis Memorial Award.

Obviously, I've only scratched the surface of available ethnic funds. Many national groups in the US sponsor programs to help each new generation better itself through higher education. If you or your parents aren't members of such organizations, you can find their names and addresses in *Gale's Encyclopedia of Associations*, available in your library. Send a request for information on college aid, along with a self-addressed, stamped envelope.

Other Sources of Scholarships

Many private organizations and foundations provide scholarships, although the amounts awarded are usually small. But if you have the time to search

Timesaver
There are many other sources of aid money for gay and lesbian students. Good places to start include the Gay, Lesbian, and Straight Education Network ((212) 727-0135 or http://www.glsen.org/) and the gay and lesbian association at your school (if there is one).

for and apply to the scholarship programs that you qualify for, you may come up with an extra few hundred (or few thousand) dollars to put toward your tuition bill. And as I'm sure you've discovered while researching the costs of college, every little bit helps. This section will point you toward some important sources of private scholarship funds.

National Scholarship Programs

Some scholarship awards carry a fair amount of prestige with them, along with a substantial amount of money. Competition for these programs is fierce, and they generally go to only the top students. But if you qualify and win, it could pay for your entire college education. Winning the award also adds an impressive line to your college applications, graduate school applications, and resume.

The following are the most well known and substantial of these national scholarship programs:

- *The Coca-Cola Scholars Foundation* awards 150 scholarships to high school seniors each year—100 get $4000, and the other 50 get a whopping $20,000. (Children of Coca-Cola employees cannot apply). For more information, call 1 (800) 306-COKE or visit the website at http://www.thecoca-colacompany.com/scholars/index.html.

- *National Alliance for Excellence Honored Scholars Program* awards 50 renewable scholarships each year, with awards ranging from $1000 to $5000. There is an academic and an artistic competition. For more information, write National Alliance for Excellence, 20 Thomas Ave., Shrewsbury, NJ 07702, call (732) 747-0028, or go to http://www.excellence.org/welcome/default.html.

- *The Presidential Scholars Program* rewards 120 high scorers on standardized tests and 21 students with achievements in the arts with a free trip to Washington; the Dodge Foundation then gives each recipient $1000. You also get to meet the President. You don't apply for this one, though—the program chooses you. (If you want to enter the artistic side of the competition, call 1 (800) 970-ARTS for an application.)

Your Own Experiences and Interests

Think back to your childhood—or to more recent high school experience. If you did volunteer work, you may qualify for scholarships from a charitable organization. If you held down a part-time or summer job, you could get a scholarship from the company where you worked, particularly if it's a major corporation. Scholarships are available for former fast food workers, newspaper carriers, and even golf caddies.

As for your participation in high school activities, you might have made yourself eligible for scholarships if you became a member of the National Honor Society, Boy Scouts, Girl Scouts, 4-H Club, Future Farmers of America, Future Homemakers of America, Distributive Education Clubs of

Watch Out!
Some foundations have rather odd restrictions. The Ernestine Matthews Trust Scholarship, for example, offers around $750 per year—but recipients must sign a statement that they will neither smoke nor use alcoholic beverages while receiving the scholarship.

Moneysaver
The Western Golf Association maintains an Evans Scholars House at 14 universities, where 225 lucky former caddies live for free. The sponsoring organization also covers tuition. Caddies who served for more than two years and show financial need may apply to: Scholarship Committee, Western Golf Association/Evans Scholar Foundation, Golf, IL 60029.

America, or Big Brothers/Big Sisters of America. Check with your high school counselor for other club-sponsored awards that get overlooked.

Consider what your hobbies are and what you do in your free time. There are clubs and organizations to match almost any interest, and many of them have scholarship money to give away. For instance, if you love riding horses, the Harness Horse Youth Foundation has scholarship money to give. If you're a gardening nut, look for awards from the National Junior Horticultural Association. And if bowling is your thing, you could win a scholarship from the Young American Bowling Alliance. Sometimes, you have to join the group first, but the rewards are worth it. Even if you don't win a scholarship, you'll meet people who share your interests and gather another extracurricular activity for your college applications.

Finally, if you have a special talent—particularly an artistic talent—you could qualify for a wide range of scholarship programs. Scholarship money is available for painters, cartoonists, photographers, sculptors, dancers, musicians, singers, actors, and creative writers. These programs tend to be more competitive than other scholarship programs, but if you have the talent, the rewards can be great—in terms of the amount of money you can win and the boost that netting such awards can give you to your future career.

Major programs for arts scholarships include the following (be sure to search for other scholarships aimed at students with your particular talent, as well):

- *Arts Recognition and Talent Search:* Awards go to students who are talented in dance, music, theater, jazz, voice, visual arts, photography, and creative writing. For more information, call 1 (800) 970-ARTS or go to http://www.nfaa.org/arts.html.

- *National Alliance for Excellence Honored Scholars Program:* Awards go to students who demonstrate excellence in any of the performing or visual arts. For more information, write the National Alliance for Excellence, 20 Thomas Ave., Shrewsbury, NJ 07702, call (732) 747-0028, or go to http://www.excellence.org/welcome/default.html.

- *National Federation of Music Clubs Scholarships and Awards:* This group sponsors a large number of competitions and awards in all areas of music. For more detailed information, request the SC3 Competitions and Awards Chart by sending 40 cents, a SASE, and two stamps for postage to National Federation of Music Clubs, 1336 N. Delaware St., Indianapolis, IN 46202.

- *Scholastic Art and Writing Awards:* Awards go to junior high and high school students who are talented in the visual arts and creative writing. For more information, call (212) 343-6893 or go to the website at http://www.scholastic.com/artandwriting/.

Timesaver
Order the free booklet, *Directory of Scholarships and Loan Funds,* which lists aid programs open to Scouts and former Scouts. Send a self-addressed, stamped envelope to: Learning for Life, Boy Scouts of America, 1325 Walnut Hill Lane, Irving, TX 75015.

If your talents run more to math and science, plenty of awards are out there for you. The most prestigious programs, with the biggest awards, include the following:

■ *The Science Talent Search:* Formerly sponsored by Westinghouse—but now Intel has taken over sponsorship duties—this program distributes about $330,000 among 40 winners, with the top prize being a $50,000 scholarship. For more information, call (202) 785-2255 or visit the website at http://www.sciserv.org/stshome.htm.

■ *Siemens Westinghouse Science and Technology Competition:* This is the other big science competition, with a top prize of $120,000. To learn more, see your guidance officer or science teacher, or go to the website at http://www.siemens-foundation.org/index.htm.

Besides these prestigious awards, smaller awards are also available for students who have talent in computer art, computer science, engineering, math, and physics. You'll probably find the most complete information about these programs in your high school guidance office, or ask one of your science teachers.

Taking Advantage of Your Parents' Associates

You can take advantage of your parents when searching for money for college—and I don't mean by picking their pockets. Your parents have probably joined many organizations throughout their lifetimes, organizations that have money to give to children of members. These organizations range from employers and professional organizations to social groups like fraternities, sororities, and civic groups. Sit down with your parents and figure out where to inquire about scholarship opportunities. This section has some suggestions to get you started.

Employers

Your parents' employers are the first places to look for scholarship money, especially if either of your parents works for a major company with large foundations. Since awards are limited to the children of employees, competition may be low. Have your parents inquire about company-sponsored scholarships at the human resources office.

The Military

The Armed Forces have a lot of scholarship money for dependents of active duty, reserve, and retired military personnel and for the children of veterans. If one of your parents currently serves in the military or has in the past, do not overlook this lucrative source of funds. (If you have served in the military yourself, you'll learn more about the financial aid that you could qualify for in Chapter 16.)

To get started, send off for the pamphlet *Federal Benefits for Veterans and Dependents* by sending $3.25 for shipping and handling to:

U.S. Department of Veterans Affairs
Office of Publications
810 Vermont Avenue, NW
Washington, D.C. 20420
1 (800) 827-1000
http://www.va.gov/education/

Unions

Despite the tough times that America's unions are going through, many still offer funds for the education of their members' children. Both the national organization and the local chapters offer scholarship programs. You can get some information from the secretary of your union local; to get the fullest amount of information, write for the comprehensive AFL-CIO guide, *AFL-CIO Guide to Union Sponsored Scholarships, Awards and Student Financial Aid*, which is free to members:

AFL-CIO
Publications and Materials Office
815 16th Street NW, Room 209
Washington, D.C. 20006
(202) 637-5000

Other Organizations

Do your parents belong to any organizations? Whether it's a local civic group, a national professional association, or a specialty group, such as an ethnic group, scholarship money may be available to you. Even your parents' fraternity or sorority in college may have awards to hand out. Find out what organizations your parents belong to and write to those groups, inquiring about scholarship opportunities.

Money from Local Sources

You'll probably have the greatest success finding scholarship money if you start in your hometown. That's because a lot of these scholarship programs are underpublicized, particularly in the major guides and databases, so competition won't be as heavy. If you get lucky, you may be the only one applying during a given year. Also, eligibility requirements—particularly academic requirements—are often lower than for the regional or national programs. While the awards may be small—typically under $1000—if you win enough scholarships, they'll quickly start to add up.

Your city government, county government, or even your school district might have scholarship money or other special programs. Although many of these awards amount to only a few hundred dollars, some offer funds in the thousands.

Don't forget to check into scholarship programs from local organizations, which are available as a multitude of awards. The American Legion is one of the biggest givers. Many of the awards go to the children of veterans, but not all of them. For the most up-to-date listing of the Legion's programs and contests, send $3 to get a copy of the booklet *Need a Lift?* (This pamphlet is also a good source of scholarships for children of veterans.) Write to:

National Emblem Sales
P.O. Box 1050
Indianapolis, IN 46206
Credit card orders only: 1 (888) 453-4466

Other community organizations that award scholarships include the Veterans of Foreign Wars (VFW), the Daughters of the American Revolution (DAR), the Descendants of Signers of the Declaration of Independence, Rotary Clubs, Lions Clubs, Kiwanis, and Jaycees. Inquire at your local chapter.

Finding local scholarships involves some investigative work on your part, since relatively few of these programs make their way into the big scholarship databases. But you can find them—your high school guidance office should have some information. The Chamber of Commerce and public library might have leads, too. Also, keep an eye out for scholarship announcements in the community affairs section of your local newspaper.

Contests

Many of the organizations listed in this section sponsor contests in essay writing and oratory. That's just the tip of the iceberg, with scholarship competitions ranging from science competitions to beauty pageants. And you don't have to be a valedictorian to win a scholarship contest; many of them target students with particular interests, such as foreign languages, science, the arts, leadership, or public speaking.

Each summer, the National Association of Secondary School Principals puts its stamp of approval on a long roster of these programs in its Advisory List of National Contests and Activities. For a copy of this list, send a request for publication #210-9295 and $8.00 plus $3.00 for shipping and handling to:

NASSA
Attention: Sales Office
P.O. Box 3250
Reston, VA 22195-3250

Or read the list online for free at http://nassp.org/publications/contest_activities/index.html.

Taking Advantage of Scholarship Search Services

If you have access to the Internet, you've got an invaluable resource for finding scholarships—electronic scholarship searches. A number of websites

Bright Idea
More and more states are trying to aid bright students with merit scholarships. Some of these programs are based on financial need, but a growing number are not. Write your state aid agency for more detailed information.

Watch Out!
Entering a lot of contests can be time-consuming. Don't get lost on a rabbit trail—go after the big game first by applying for traditional aid and private scholarships that you qualify for. Then, if you have a little extra time, give some of the contests a try.

now offer to quickly hook students up with scholarship money, and many of them are making good on that offer. The best scholarship search services are free! (Even if you don't have Internet access, you may be able to electronically search for scholarships in your guidance office, public library, or community center.)

Table 15.1 lists the best of these scholarship searches. Since so many scholarship programs are out there, you should find the time to complete a search with as many of these services as you can. You never know what you might turn up. Besides, all of these searches are free and won't take you very long to complete.

If you don't have access to a computer, you can still look for scholarships in one of the many books published each year. These books tend to be expensive, so check for them in your school library or guidance office. Turn to Appendix C for a list of good scholarship guides.

Beware of Scholarship Search Services That Charge a Fee

Finally, a word of warning: Many scholarship search services are excellent resources, but others are scams that take your money and either do nothing or print out information that's readily available for free. The biggest tip-off that a scholarship search service is fraudulent is money—if somebody wants a lot of it in order to conduct a search for you, you're most likely dealing with the wrong folks. The bills can quickly outstrip the value of scholarships discovered. In fact, fewer than one percent of users of fee-based scholarship search services actually win an award.

Often, a fee-based scholarship search service won't find anything that you wouldn't have come across on your own with some smart searching. With all of the resources at your disposal—including the free databases on the Internet and the large number of scholarship guides published every year—why should you have to pay someone to find scholarships for you?

Unofficially...
There really are scholarships for left-handed students; Juniata College in Huntingdon, Pennsylvania, has had one since 1978.

Avoiding Scholarship Scams

Because there are so many scholarship programs, and so many students competing for those dollars, scholarship scams have become a booming business. These scams typically imitate legitimate scholarship programs sponsored by government agencies, charitable foundations, and education lenders. They often employ official but meaningless names with words like "national," "federal," "foundation," and "administration" to fool you. But these programs don't give you free money; rather, they try to take money from you.

Don't get taken by one of these scams. Approach every scholarship program with caution, particularly programs you've never heard of before. The following signs are tip-offs that a scholarship program may in fact be a scam:

- The program contacts you first, instead of the other way around.
- The program charges a fee to submit an application or to get information about the award.

TABLE 15.1: FREE SCHOLARSHIP SEARCHES ON THE WEB

Scholarship Search	Web Address	Number of Scholarships Listed
CASHE	http://scholarships.salliemae.com/	unknown
College Board	http://www.collegeboard.org/fundfinder/html/ssrchtop.html	1,000,000
CollegeNET	http://www.collegenet.com/mach25/	600,000
CollegeQuest	http://www.collegequest.com/	800,000
FastAid	http://www.fastaid.com/	unknown
FastWEB	http://www.fastweb.com/	400,000
FreSch!	http://www.freschinfo.com/	130,000
GoScholarshipSearch	http://www.gocollege.com/goscholarshipsearch/index.html	500,000
Scholarship Resource Network	http://www.srnexpress.com/	150,000
U.S.News Scholarship Search	http://www.usnews.com/usnews/edu/dollars/scholar/search.htm	unknown

- The program charges a "disbursement" or "redemption" fee or it charges taxes before it will release scholarship money.
- The program asks you to disclose a bank account or credit card number in order to hold the scholarship.
- The program claims that everyone is eligible for the scholarship.
- The program claims that you're guaranteed to win a scholarship.
- You receive notification of an award by phone, rather than by mail.
- The program can't prove that it has actually awarded scholarships in the past.
- Contact information is sketchy; the phone number may be absent, and the mailing address may be a post office box or a residential address.
- The hype factor is high.
- You must act quickly to be considered for an award.
- Application materials look unprofessional or are full of errors.
- The scholarship sounds too good to be true.

As with scholarship search services, if you're asked to pay a fee, even if it's a low amount, be suspicious. Claims that fees are required to cover administrative or processing costs, or to ensure that only serious candidates apply, are probably false. You should never have to pay to get a scholarship.

Just the Facts

- Private scholarships may not really help you pay for college, because your financial aid officer usually replaces aid that your school already awarded you with any outside scholarships that you win.
- You can maximize your scholarship winnings by applying only for scholarships for which you are truly eligible, tailoring your applications to the mission of the sponsoring application, and turning in a neat, error-free application well ahead of the final deadline.
- The National Merit Scholarship program is a prestigious award, with money available from colleges, companies, and the program itself; you qualify by scoring well on the PSAT.
- Athletic scholarships are not as difficult to come by as you might think, particularly for female athletes and athletes in the less "popular" sports; the key is to inquire early and to understand the eligibility requirements.
- Many scholarship programs, especially from state and federal government, are designed to entice students into needed professions, such as teaching and the health professions.
- Many scholarship programs give money to members of minority groups, religious groups, and ethnic groups; private foundations, civic

Unofficially...
A myth has long floated around that billions of dollars' worth of scholarship money goes unclaimed each year. In reality, most college financial aid offices say that they rarely have un-awarded scholarships, and the ones that aren't given out usually are highly restrictive or have strict deadlines.

and religious organizations, and professional associations typically sponsor these scholarships.

- You can look for scholarships in many places; your best bet is to start locally with your parents' employers and associations, your own clubs and interests, and groups in your community.

- The Internet has made it easier than ever to search for scholarships that match your qualifications; several search services are available on the Web, allowing you to search through millions of scholarships at no charge to you.

- The number of scholarship scams has increased in recent years; to avoid getting swindled, be wary of any scholarship program that requires a fee in order to apply or claim your award.

Looking Elsewhere for Aid

Chapter 16

If you've looked into traditional financial aid sources and still have trouble coming up with the money to pay for college, don't give up. Many options are still open to you. Many of them require a sacrifice on your part—you may have to spend a large part of your college years working instead of having fun, take a couple of years off to serve in the military, or graduate with a hefty loan to pay back—but getting your bachelor's degree is worth it. And several of these solutions have hidden benefits, such as giving you a leg up in the competitive job market.

This chapter describes several alternatives—or supplements—to traditional financial aid that can make it possible for you to go to college. I urge you to explore all of these options before giving up on college altogether. If money is still tight when you get to school, Chapter 18, "Surviving Freshman Year," has suggestions for creating a budget, sticking to it, and saving money while you go to school.

Working Your Way Through College

Yes, you could get a part-time job at as a pizza delivery driver or in the student store. But at best, these 10-hour-a-week, minimum-wage jobs will only defray personal expenses; they probably won't make much of a dent in the actual tuition bill. There are smarter ways to work through college. (A part-time job, particularly one on campus, is a very good way to pick up some pocket money to help take care of the extras, though.)

If you already know what you want to do for a living, you've got a big boost when searching for financial aid. For one thing, you can search out private scholarships tailored to your particular interests, and if your field of study is narrow, your chances of winning money vastly improve. You can also take advantage of state and federal programs that entice students into needed professions, such as the health professions, teaching, or the sciences. Finally, your future employer may pay for much of your tuition or seek out aid from professional associations.

Moneysaver
A number of schools have found ways to compress the four-year college experience into three years, saving 25 percent of education costs. You'll probably have to go to summer school, but tuition costs for summer courses are often less than for courses you take during the regular school year.

Unofficially...
The federal government has consolidated its various work/school programs into a single Student Educational Employment Program (SEEP), administered by the Office of Personnel Management. To learn about employment opportunities, contact your college's career planning and placement office, or get in touch with the federal agency employment office where you want to work.

Cooperative Education

Many employers help put students through college through the burgeoning field of cooperative education. Unlike internships, which tend to be non-paying jobs that students work into their schedules as best they can, cooperative education programs can pay the bills and are an integral part of the school's degree program and your career plans.

In co-op education, you combine your time in the classroom with practical experience on the job. Some 50,000 employers hire on the co-op plan, including the largest provider of co-op jobs, the federal government, which hires nearly 18,000 students each year. You get to try out your chosen profession—kick the tires, drive it around the block—to see whether it's really what you would like to do.

If it is what you would like to do, you have another advantage: Often the firm you worked for hires you after graduation. Fully 40 percent of cooperative education students continue working for their co-op employer after graduation. Another 40 percent find work in fields directly related to their co-op assignments, while about 15 percent enroll in law or other professional schools. Add up those percentages, and its pretty easy to see that "co-oping" leads to jobs. There's something for everyone: You, the student, get a job, and the employer gets a highly motivated workforce.

Not only does cooperative education provide professional skills and a leg up in the employment game, but it also puts money into your pocket during school—roughly $1.3 billion a year in co-op wages nationwide. Co-op participants earn, on average, between $2500 and $8000 each year. Depending on the money that you earn, a co-op job can cover a great deal of your college costs. And since co-op graduates tend to have higher starting salaries than non-co-op grads, you can pay off college loans earlier.

Cooperative education programs are best pursued at technical and engineering schools like Georgia Tech—which places hundreds of students into positions in a five-year degree program—but all kinds of institutions offer cooperative education programs. Almost 1000 community colleges, four-year colleges, and universities boast such programs, including some schools where virtually all of the students participate in cooperative education programs, such as Kettering University, Drexel University, and Northeastern University.

Co-oping takes time. Whether you alternate semesters of work and study or work part-time while attending school, the programs usually require at least five years for you to get your degree. Still, 200,000 students each year seem to feel the time is worth spending.

Get more data on specific co-op education programs by contacting:

National Commission for Cooperative Education
360 Huntington Avenue, 384CP
Boston, MA 02115-5096
(617) 373-3770
http://www.co-op.edu/

Employer Tuition Plans

This is the great unclaimed area of financial aid that you're always hearing about, with billions of dollars available to millions of employees. Unfortunately, a catch-22 is involved: Many companies won't hire you for a good position until you have your college degree. But if you're willing to attend college part-time and start in a lowly position, you'll find many companies that will pay for your education.

The company wants to make sure it gets its money's worth, so employer tuition plans generally come with a hitch or two. The most important hitch: You have to make the grade. In "reimbursement" plans, you have to put up the tuition money at first; you get the money back only when you have successfully completed the course—in some programs, that means with a grade of B or better. In other programs, the company pays up front, but you'll still have to repay the company if you drop out or flunk. Also, you might have to commit to stay with the company for a certain number of years after you graduate. Still, an understanding boss can help you to frame your educational needs in such a way that they fit in nicely with the company objectives.

Another stickler in this area is the IRS, which ruled that the courses you were taking had to be job-related to qualify as a benefit. If you take any course that isn't directly related to your work but your employer still pays for it, you have to declare the cost of the course as taxable income. Of course, your entry-level job is probably so narrow that few of the courses required for a degree could qualify as job-related. If you're lucky enough to have a more broadly defined job, such as in management, you might be able to justify taking courses like English lit and anthropology.

But don't despair entirely. Under the Tax-Reform Act of 1986, you can deduct up to $5250 worth of employer-paid tuition, even if the courses you take don't directly relate to your job. Although that won't cover tuition costs at most private institutions, it could easily pay for tuition at an in-state public college or university.

Starting a Side Business

Instead of relying on your college for a moderate-to-low-paying work-study job, why not strike out on your own? If you have an entrepreneurial flair, you might find that a little investment of time and effort can provide you with a comfortable living while you go to school—and after. For example, Michael Dell began selling computers while he was in college; now his company sells millions of dollars' worth of IBM-compatible computers each year under the Dell Computer logo.

On a smaller scale, you might find plenty of opportunity among your fellow students. Students know students; once you've identified an item that you need, you can buy it in bulk and offer it to others who share your needs. This explains the proliferation of student-run services that offer discounts on everything from computer disks to lecture notes. One enterprising group of students even offered speedy delivery of birth control devices.

Moneysaver
Guides to employers who offer tuition programs are commercially available, but they tend to be expensive; look for them in the public library, or get them through your school library or guidance counselor.

Offering services can often make a lucrative side business, as well. Students who own a computer can make extra money typing term papers, formatting graphs, or creating computer art. Tutoring is another form of self-employment. And if you have a particular hobby or skill, such as DJ talent, auto repair, or astrology, you might be able to turn it into a money-making service.

And you might even be able to make your career interest pay. If your school doesn't have an established cooperative education program, you might be able to work something out on your own. are you an aspiring journalist? Write freelance articles. If your interest is politics, why not see whether part-time positions are open in a nearby politician's office? You'll line your pocket and pick up real-life experience at the same time.

Letting the Military Pay

How you feel about the military in general will determine whether you skip this section. The simple point is this: Unless you have conscientious objections to serving in the Armed Forces, the military could be the best way to finance your college education. The military offers a number of ways to help students pay for college, although none of today's programs match the generosity of the GI Bill that educated the post-World War II generation. In return for the years of military service, you receive everything from a cheaper education to one that costs no money at all.

Service Academies

Service academies like the Military Academy at West Point offer a high-quality, tuition-free college education. Each branch of the service has its own academy with its own character and traditions. These academically rigorous institutions are excellent, especially for the technical fields, and you can't beat the price. They're also much more difficult to get into than most other colleges and universities, including the Ivy League schools. When you graduate, you'll receive a Bachelor's degree and a commission in the military.

For more information on applying, contact the service academies directly; they're listed in Table 16.1.

ROTC Programs

If you'd rather not attend a service academy—or can't get in—chances are that your school has a Reserve Officers Training Corps (ROTC) program on campus, which can also help you pay for college. Full scholarships are available that almost completely pay for tuition, fees, and books.

Ad hoc ROTC scholarships are announced all the time to attract students into areas the military feels a need to beef up—usually in the technical fields or health professions. Other scholarships are specifically geared toward aiding minority students. Even without ROTC scholarships, students

TABLE 16.1: CONTACT INFORMATION FOR THE SERVICE ACADEMIES

Service Academy	Address	Phone Number	E-mail Address	Website
U.S. Air Force Academy	USAF Academy Admissions USAF Academy, CO 80920	(719) 333-1110	webmail.rr@usafa.af.mil	http://www.usafa.af.mil/
U.S. Coast Guard Academy	Director of Admissions 29 Mohegan Ave. New London, CT 06230-8102	(860) 444-8500	admissions@cga.uscg.mil	http://www.cga.edu/
U.S. Merchant Marine Academy	300 Steamboat Rd. Kings Point, NY 11024	(516) 773-5000	admissions@usmma.edu	http://www.usmma.edu/
U.S. Military Academy	606 Thayer Rd. West Point, NY 10996	(914) 938-4041	admission@www.usma.edu	http://www.usma.edu/
U.S. Naval Academy	Candidate Guidance Office 117 Decatur Rd. Annapolis, MD 21402-5018	(410) 293-4361	Use the form at http://www.usna.edu/ Admissions/reqinfo.htm	http://www.nadn. navy.mil/

in the ROTC earn $100 each month in their junior and senior years (but they receive nothing as freshmen and sophomores).

Contact information for the various ROTC programs is listed in the following table.

TABLE 16.2: CONTACT INFORMATION FOR ROTC PROGRAMS

Armed Forces Branch	Phone Number	Web Site
Army	1 (800) USA-ROTC	http://www.armyrotc.com/
Navy	1 (800) USA-NAVY	http://www.navyjobs.com/college/html/sub_money.html
Air Force	1 (800) 522-0033 ext. 2091	http://www.airforce.com/welcome/welcome.html
Marine Corps	1 (800) MARINES	http://www.marines.com/

Joining Up

After serving active duty in a branch of the Armed Forces, you stand a good chance of going back to school and having all or part of your tuition picked up by Uncle Sam. The new Montgomery GI Bill is an education benefits program offered by each of the Armed Forces (including full-time National Guard duty). It matches the soldier's contribution to a college fund; after emerging from the Armed Forces, a student-to-be can amass a war chest of more than $19,000.

Timesaver
If you join the Armed Forces first, you will probably earn college credits for your military training, which will reduce the number of classes that you'll have to take to get your degree.

The Armed Forces offer many other higher education programs as an incentive to get you to sign up. For example, the Army and Navy both have college fund programs that can give you up to $50,000 toward tuition when combined with the Montgomery GI Bill (the Marines has a similar program that can give you up to $30,000 when combined with the GI Bill). For more information on these programs and on the Montgomery GI Bill, contact your local military recruiter.

Taking Advantage of Federal Programs

The Department of Education and the Armed Forces aren't alone in providing financial aid; the federal government has several other ways of helping students get through school. Scholarships, loans, job training, and money to pay back existing loans are available from a variety of federal programs. Many of them are directed toward influencing career choices—producing more medical professionals, for instance.

Department of Health and Human Services Programs

Next to the Department of Education and the Armed Forces, the Department of Health and Human Services is probably the biggest contributor of dollars toward higher education. If you intend to make one of the health professions your career, you should look into these federal programs.

The following are a few of the most prominent programs sponsored by the Department of Health and Human Services; if you want more information about any of these programs, call (301) 443-4776:

- **The Nursing Student Loan Program** applies to students at certain nursing schools. Students must demonstrate financial need. The student can then receive up to $2500 each year at a fixed low-interest rate. For more information, ask your nursing school's financial aid officer.

- **Financial Assistance for Disadvantaged Health Professions Students** provides up to $10,000 per year to full-time students in medicine, osteopathic medicine, and dentistry in exchange for service after graduation. Not only must students prove exceptional financial need, but they must also come from a disadvantaged background. Again, ask your school's financial aid officer about this program.

- **The National Health Service Corps** provides a number of scholarships, fellowships, and student loan repayment programs for students pursuing a degree in the health professions who work in underserved communities after graduating. For more information on this program, ask your school's financial aid officer or visit the website at http://www. bphc.hrsa.dhhs.gov/nhsc/.

- Undergraduates pursuing degrees in pharmacy can qualify for two programs that are otherwise restricted to graduate students: the **Health Profession Student Loan** (HPSL) and the **Health Education Student Loan** (HEAL). Your departmental financial aid advisor should help you find information on these programs.

Public Service

In 1993, the Clinton administration introduced a program of volunteerism—the AmeriCorps program—that gives participants a good chunk of money for college—$4725—in exchange for performing public service for 10 to 12 months. In addition, participants receive a small living allowance and health insurance while working, and they may qualify for forbearance on any federal student loans that they hold.

The AmeriCorps program is like a domestic Peace Corps, and its 40,000 members perform whatever services are needed in the community where they're assigned, in the areas of education, public safety, human needs like health and housing, and the environment. Your assignment may range from tutoring to trail building to fundraising.

For more information about joining AmeriCorps, contact:

Corporation for National and Community Service
1201 New York Avenue, NW
Washington, D.C. 20525
1 (800) 94-ACORPS
E-mail: acorps@infosystec.com
http://www.cns.gov/americorps/joining/index.html

Bright Idea
As campus-based programs, the school administers these programs and funds them in a lump sum from the government. Campus-based programs can run out of money, so check your school's deadline and apply early in order to snag some of the funding.

Moneysaver
The Department of Labor administers the Job Training Partnership Act, a tuition aid program for the economically disadvantaged and others facing employment barriers. To request more information, write to the Office of Employment and Training Programs, Room N4469, U.S. Department of Labor, 200 Constitution Ave. NW, Washington, DC 20210.

Tax Breaks That Help Pay for College

The 1997 Taxpayer Relief Act introduced many tax benefits to help parents and students pay for higher education, and similar deals may be coming down the pike. These tax cuts effectively made the first two years of college affordable for anyone, regardless of income. Once the changes are fully phased in, over 12.9 million students are expected to benefit from them.

Keep in mind that these tax laws are brand new, and it could take several years to clarify the restrictions and eligibility requirements. A knowledgeable, up-to-date tax advisor is your best asset for figuring out these complicated laws and for keeping abreast of changes in the next few years.

One of the most important cost-cutting programs instituted by the 1997 Taxpayer Relief Act is the HOPE Scholarship tax credit. The idea behind this program is that any student should have the chance to have at least two years of education beyond high school, and so the HOPE Scholarship tax credit effectively pays two years' tuition at the average community college or vocational school. While geared more toward these two-year schools' significantly lower tuition rates, the HOPE Scholarship can make a big dent in the cost of the first two years at a four-year college.

Here's how it works: A 100-percent tax credit applies to the first $1000 of required tuition and fees (after deducting grants, scholarships, and other tax-free aid), and a 50-percent tax credit applies to the second $1000—essentially paying for up to $1500 of tuition per year. You can't apply this credit to non-required fees, books, room and board, or other expenses associated with going to college. And the credit is available for only the first two years of higher education, whether that be at a community college, vocational school, or four-year school. To qualify, the student must be enrolled on at least a half-time basis in a degree or certificate program.

Starting in the junior year, the Lifetime Learning Credit, another provision of the Taxpayer Relief Act, comes into play. The Lifetime Learning Credit gives you a tax credit of 20 percent on the first $5000 of tuition (subtracting tax-free aid first), so you could earn a maximum credit of $1000. In 2002, you'll be able to claim a 20-percent tax credit on the first $10,000 of tuition—good news if you or your child will start college in the year 2000 or later.

There's no limit to the number of school years when you can take the Lifetime Learning credit. Juniors and seniors in college, as well as graduate students and adults returning to school, are all eligible. Also, there are no restrictions on how many members of the family can receive a HOPE Scholarship credit or Lifetime Learning credit. (The same person can't claim a HOPE Scholarship credit and a Lifetime Learning credit in the same year, however.)

But take note of one important distinction between these two tax credits: The HOPE Scholarship credit applies separately to each student, while the Lifetime Learning credit applies to the total amount of tuition paid. It doesn't matter how many students are in the household—each one receives the same HOPE Scholarship tax credit during their first two years of higher education. By contrast, the Lifetime Learning credit applies only to the first $10,000 total tuition you pay in a year, irrespective of how many family members attend college or what the tuition bill is for each of them. A couple with one child attending a $15,000-a-year school would receive the same Lifetime Learning credit as a couple with three children each attending a $10,000-a-year school (assuming that both couples qualify).

The following are some other important restrictions on claiming a HOPE Scholarship or Lifetime Learning tax credit that you should know about:

- You can't claim the credits for any educational expense for which you have already claimed a tax deduction.

- Neither credit can be claimed in the same year you receive a distribution from an Education IRA.

- Married couples must file jointly to claim the credit.

- If the parents are divorced, and one parent claims the child as a dependent while the other parent pays the educational expenses, neither parent is eligible for the credits.

- The credits can be applied to required tuition and fees only.

Finally, the HOPE Scholarship and Lifetime Learning programs are designed to meet the needs of middle-class and low-income families. This tax credit is phased out for joint filers reporting between $80,000 and $100,000 of adjusted gross income and for single filers reporting between $40,000 and $50,000 of adjusted gross income. Once your income rises over $100,000 (for a married couple) or over $50,000 (for a single filer), you're no longer eligible for the tax credit.

The standard methodologies for determining your EFC will certainly take the added resources provided by these tax credits into account when determining your family's need. The new tax laws haven't been in place long enough to judge their long-term effects on how schools award aid, though. It's certainly possible that schools will simply substitute the tax credit dollars for their own financial aid dollars, absorbing a significant amount of the tax benefit for themselves. It's also possible that the tax breaks will give public universities the incentive to raise tuition—effectively transferring federal funds to the overstressed state budgets. The reactions of colleges will probably differ significantly from school to school and from state to state, so once again, it's important for you to find out how your school calculates need.

If you want more information about these tax breaks, consult your tax advisor or go straight to the source—the IRS. IRS Publication 970, *Tax Benefits for Higher Education*, describes the HOPE Scholarship and Lifetime Learning Credit benefits, as well as other tax benefits for parents and students paying for higher education. You can order the publication at no

Moneysaver
The 1997 Taxpayer Relief Act also makes it easier to pay for higher education using IRA money, excludes a portion of employer-provided education benefits from taxable income, and reduces the tax burden of repaying student loans. It pays to hire a tax-wise accountant so you can take advantage of all the tax breaks available to you.

charge by calling the IRS at 1 (800) TAX-FORM or by visiting the IRS website at http://www.irs.ustreas.gov/.

Getting a Private Loan

Many college students have to take out an education loan to help pay for their education. The typical undergraduate finishes college owing $16,500 in student loans—not a pleasant prospect. Most of us don't like owing money, especially when we're just starting out in life and uncertain of our future career prospects.

Perhaps the scariest result of the growth in borrowing to pay for higher education is that this trend could squeeze many people out of the world of financial aid—and thus college. A recent report sponsored by Congress and the College Board warned that the growing debt burden might represent a threat for society at large, perhaps burdening the current generation beyond its ability to pay. The report further speculated that borrowing was a tougher concept for the poor than for the middle class, and that these groups would have more trouble repaying their loans than better-off students.

This trend toward borrowing most threatens the poor, especially minorities. Some prospective students, uncertain of their ability to find a job lucrative enough to allow repaying a loan, might simply avoid loans, and college, altogether. Thus, borrowing could account at least in part for the fact that African-American and Hispanic students don't attend college in numbers commensurate with their percentages in the population as a whole.

Borrowing is still a smart way to make big-ticket expenses like an education more manageable. While long-term saving and financial planning is still the best way to reduce the burden of college costs, taking out a student loan doesn't automatically mean taking on a lifelong burden. Borrowing to pay for college is a necessary evil—more necessary now than ever. That's why so many colleges, states, and private institutions are presenting innovative loan programs of their own.

Timesaver
The College Board's website has several free calculators that can help you make borrowing decisions. Use these calculators to determine how much debt you can afford to take on and to calculate loan repayments. Go to: http://www. collegeboard.org/ finaid/fastud/html/ fincalc/fcintro.html.

You've already learned about the loan programs offered to students who still have financial need, such as Federal Perkins loans and subsidized Stafford loans. Obviously, these will be your first choices when shopping around for education loans, because they offer the lowest interest rates and the best repayment terms. If you don't have any financial need remaining as determined in your financial aid package, but you still need help paying the bills, you can get an education loan from a private lender—you'll just pay more in interest for it.

The Advantages of Federal Loans

If you don't qualify for a subsidized Stafford loan, first try to get an unsubsidized Stafford Loan (return to Chapter 14, "Understanding Your Financial Aid Award," to review details about the Stafford loan program).

These loans have the following advantages over those that you can obtain from a private lender:

- The federal government guarantees them.
- They have a lower interest rate.
- They have a grace period after graduation.
- There are no credit criteria for qualifying.
- They can be consolidated under the Loan Consolidation program.
- Forbearance and deferment options are available.

As you already know, the federal government sponsors low-interest loans for parents under the Stafford loan program in the form of PLUS loans (return to Chapter 14 to review the terms of PLUS loans). PLUS loans also have many advantages:

- The federal government guarantees them.
- Parents of all income levels can apply.
- They generally carry the lowest interest rates.
- They can be consolidated under the Loan Consolidation program.

Kinds of Private Education Loans

Many families have no choice but to take out a private loan to help meet the costs of college. Private loans help cover the gap between what college actually costs and the limited borrowing amounts allowed by the Stafford loan program. They are also a good alternative for families who don't qualify for federal financial aid. Finally, some private loans offer advantages over PLUS loans for parents; for instance, many private education loans allow parents to defer repayment until after their child graduates from college, while repayment on PLUS loans starts almost immediately.

Parents have a lot of options when it comes to borrowing to pay for their kids' college education—many more than their kids do. Parents can get a home equity loan, a margin loan against investments, a loan against the cash accumulation of a whole life insurance policy, or a personal line of credit from banks and private lenders.

You could also look into a privately sponsored and insured education loan (also called a "supplemental" or "alternative" loan). These supplemental education loans often offer more favorable interest rates and special features than other consumer loans. Eligibility is generally based on your creditworthiness, rather than on your financial need. The terms of these supplemental loan programs can differ greatly from lender to lender, so it's definitely worth your while to shop around for the best deal.

Table 16.3 compares the advantages and disadvantages of supplemental and home equity loans.

Unofficially... Although supplemental education loans are typically lent to parents, creditworthy students may qualify for some programs. A few supplemental loan programs even enable parents and students to borrow jointly. Ask lenders about all the options available to you when shopping around for a loan.

TABLE 16.3: SUPPLEMENTAL EDUCATION LOANS VERSUS HOME EQUITY LOANS

Supplemental Loans		Home Equity Loans	
Advantages	**Disadvantages**	**Advantages**	**Disadvantages**
Generally, no collateral is required.	A clean credit record and acceptable debt-to-income ratio are required to qualify.	Interest is tax-deductible.	The family home is put up for long-term debt at a time when many parents are facing retirement.
Interest rates may be competitive with PLUS loan rates, although this is rare.	Unsecured loans often carry higher interest rates and fees.	Rates and fees are often lower than that of an unsecured loan.	There may be additional fees, such as a title search or appraisal.
You're limited to borrowing only what you can repay, keeping debt manageable.	Borrowing limits may not cover the bills.	Most banks offer them, compared to the few that offer supplemental education loans.	Processing the loan can take up to three months.

Choosing a Lender

Until recently, your lender was invariably a bank, but that's no longer the case. Now, educational organizations, associations, and even the schools all offer private student loans. These non-bank lenders often provide very helpful programs and services free to borrowers, such as professional help with planning how to pay for college and scholarship searches.

Choose a lender carefully, and find one that fits your needs. You're the customer, and you want a lender who will do the best job for you. Your school's financial aid office and your state guaranty agency can help you locate a lender (refer to Appendix D, "Important Addresses," for a list of the state guaranty agencies). Ask each potential lender the following questions:

- *How long will it take to get the loan?* Be sure to tell lenders whether timing is important to you.

- *Do you sell your student loans?* Many lenders sell their loans to secondary markets made up of private and state organizations that specialize in buying student loans, which can confuse the borrower. Try to pick a lender that sells to only one secondary market.

- *Do you use a servicer?* A servicer is a company that processes payments, answers questions, and keeps loan records. If your lender uses one, you'll deal primarily with the servicer, rather than with the lender.

- *Do you capitalize interest payments?* Capitalization enables you to delay making interest payments until you begin repaying your loan, often after graduation. In capitalization, the interest payments are added to the principal of the loan, which increases how much you owe and your monthly payments. A lender may capitalize interest every three months, once a year, or just one time—it's up to the lender. To save big money, try to find a lender who offers one-time capitalization.

- *What types of repayment plans do you offer?* Look for a lender that offers repayment plan options, such as consolidation and graduated repayment.

- *What is your forbearance policy?* Forbearance allows the borrower to postpone repaying the principal of a loan temporarily, but must continue to pay interest charges. Forbearance is usually granted during times of economic hardship or if the student continues his or her education after earning a bachelor's degree. If possible, choose a lender with a flexible policy, in case you run into problems making your payments later on. You never know what may happen.

Another important consideration is how you feel about the lender. Do their representatives seem friendly and helpful, and are they easy to get in touch with? Remember, you'll be dealing with this lender for a very long time—choose one that you feel good about.

The following nationwide lenders all offer private, supplemental loans (many of them also provide subsidized, unsubsidized, and PLUS FFELs, as well):

- *Bank of America:* Beside private education loans, home equity loans, and lines of credit, Bank of America offers the Student Maximizer loan, which supplements federal loans at low interest rates. Contact: 1 (800) 344-8382 or http://www.bankamerica.com/studentunion/.

- *Bank One:* Bank One is one of the largest originators of education loans. Contact: 1 (888) 661-0663 ext. 822 or http://www.educationone.com/.

- *Chase Manhattan:* This bank offers a number of low-interest education loans with a variety of repayment options. Contact: 1 (800) 242-7339 or http://www.chase.com/studentloan/.

- *Educaid (First Union National Bank):* Educaid has loans for all levels of education, including programs for international students, foreign study, and continuing education. Contact: 1 (800) EDUCAID or http://www.educaid.com/.

- *Educap, Inc.:* This nonprofit corporation is the largest provider of private, credit-based education loans. Contact: 1 (800) GO-PLATO or http://www.educap.org/.

- *The Education Resources Institute:* This is the nonprofit provider of the Alternative Loan Program for undergraduates. Contact: 1 (800) 255-8374 or http://www.teri.org/index.htm.

Timesaver
If possible, try to use the same lender for all of your student loans, such as a subsidized and an unsubsidized loan from the FFEL program. Dealing with one company saves you a lot of confusion and time in the long run.

Watch Out!
The advance-fee education loan is a popular scam, which offers a private student loan with unusually low interest, with the requirement that you pay a fee before receiving the loan. But the promised loan never materializes. Real student loans deduct any fees from the disbursement; an upfront fee is never required.

- *GATE Student Loan Program:* This is a nonprofit, private student loan program that works with the schools to offer loans with very attractive terms. Contact: 1 (800) 895-GATE or http://www.gateloan.com/.

- *Key Education Resources:* Several private education loans are available for both students and parents. Contact: 1 (800) KEY-LEND or http://www.keybank.com/educate/.

- *Nellie Mae:* The largest nonprofit provider of education loans, Nellie Mae works with 500 lenders and 1000 schools. Contact: 1 (800) FOR-TUITION or http://www.nelliemae.com/.

- *Norwest:* This lender has several different education loan programs aimed at undergraduates, graduate students, and parents. Contact: 1 (800) 658-3567 or http://www.norwest.com/students/.

- *PNC Bank:* Consistently ranked one of the top-ten education lenders, PNC Bank offers several private loans and innovative discounted student loans. Contact: 1 (800) 762-1001 or http://www.eduloans.pncbank.com/.

- *Wells Fargo:* This well known bank provides a variety of loans for education, including alternative loans, home equity loans, and lines of credit. Contact: 1 (800) 956-4442 or http://wellsfargo.com/per/accounts/student/finaid/.

Managing Student Loans

The loan application process can be intimidating. Follow these hints to better manage your school loans:

- Wait until you receive each school's financial aid package before applying, and evaluate each aid offer carefully; you may decide to go to a school where you'll depend less upon loans.

- Thoroughly explore other sources of aid that don't require repayment, such as private scholarships, before borrowing.

- Borrow only what you need. Tap other assets, such as savings, first.

- Fill out the application completely, and submit it in a timely matter. Respond promptly to all questions regarding your loan application.

- Keep a separate file containing all paperwork pertaining to the loan and a copy of the application. As long as you have the loan, continue to make copies of all related documents, correspondence, and payments to store in this file.

- Take notes during meetings with your loan or financial aid officer.

- Be aware of the loan's disbursement date (when money from the loan is given to the school to pay for tuition and fees).

- Once repayment begins, keep in touch with your lender; notify your lender immediately of any name or address changes.

- Keep up with your payments. Even if you don't receive a monthly bill, you're responsible for making the monthly payment on time.

How Not to Pay for College

College is not the best time to make moneymaking your sole goal. When you're going to college, the last thing you want to do is to spend so much time trying to pay the bills that you can't enjoy the experience—or worse, can't keep up with your studies. There are plenty of bad ways to pay your way through college. In this section, you'll learn about a few of the more common moneymaking schemes to avoid.

Working Yourself Too Hard

The most common mistake when trying to pay for college is simple over-work—taking on two or more jobs to make ends meet. One friend of mine worked his way through law school with no fewer than three part-time jobs. He ended up spending a semester recuperating from hepatitis, and almost had to put off graduating. (Today, he's a successful attorney—still overworked, but getting paid handsomely for it.) Other diseases, such as mononucleosis, commonly spring from exhaustion. Why ruin four great years of your life—not to mention your health—by keeping your nose so close to the grindstone that you can't even enjoy your studies, much less develop a social life?

Burying Yourself in Debt

Consider your future plans carefully before applying for a private student loan. You'll have to earn enough once you graduate to pay off your student loans (and have something left over to live on). If you plan to major in a field that doesn't usually lead to a high-paying job, such as teaching or social work, or if you plan to go on to graduate or professional school, then you don't want to saddle yourself with a lot of debt. But if you plan to major in a lucrative field, such as business or computer science, don't stress too much over the size of your education loans; chances are that you'll get a job after graduating that enables you to easily pay off your loans in a reasonable amount of time.

A general rule of thumb to remember is this: Repayment of undergraduate loans shouldn't exceed eight percent of your estimated gross monthly income after graduation; and repayment of undergraduate and graduate loans combined shouldn't exceed 15 percent. One way to evaluate potential earnings is to consult the U.S. Department of Labor's Occupational Outlook Handbook (http://stats.bls.gov:80/ocohome.htm), which lists typical salaries and educational requirements for different kinds of jobs.

If you don't think that you can handle a large debt burden, look for ways to reduce your reliance on loans. Consider a lower-priced school, such as a state university, where you won't have to borrow so much to pay the tuition. If your second- or third-choice school offered a financial aid package with

Bright Idea
If you have to borrow, the first step is to check that your credit history is accurate and that you haven't exhausted your borrowing capacity. Anything that you can do to clean up your credit record and pay off high-interest debt, like credit cards and car loans, will help.

more grants than loans, it may be worth not attending your top pick just so you can graduate with less debt. Talk to your financial aid officer and explain that you're planning to enter a low-income but much-needed profession to see whether that makes a difference in the makeup of your financial aid package. Finally, look into state loan programs with more manageable interest rates and repayment terms given to students entering needed (but low-paying) professions and to those who plan to continue their studies.

Just the Facts

- There are many smart ways to work your way through college; you could join a cooperative education program, have a current employer help foot the bill, or start your own part-time business.

- The U.S. Armed Forces is a major contributor of education funds, with programs like the free service academies, ROTC scholarships, and offers of college money in exchange for military service.

- The federal government has several other programs that provide money to help for college, including public service programs and grants and loans for students entering needed health professions.

- Many middle-income families are eligible for education tax breaks, like the HOPE Scholarship and Lifetime Learning Credit, which can considerably ease the burden of paying for college.

- Don't discount the possibility of taking out a private education loan; with lower interest rates than many consumer loans plus attractive repayment options, private loans are a viable method for helping any family meet the high costs of college.

- There are certain things that you should *not* do to help pay for college, including working too hard to devote enough time to studying (and enjoy the college experience) or taking on a larger debt burden than you can comfortably handle.

Get Ready for College

PART VI

GET THE SCOOP ON...
Figuring out where to go ▪ Understanding conditional acceptance
and why you got it ▪ How to get off the wait list and into the
college ▪ What to do if a school rejects you ▪ Alternatives to
attending a four-year college

Chapter 17

When the Letters Come In

The time has come. You're hanging out by the mailbox every day and pestering your mail carrier. You and your friends are comparing anxiety stories. Your parents are becoming increasingly happy that you'll be moving out soon.

And then you find yourself sitting at the kitchen table, surrounded by thin and fat envelopes. What now?

Choosing Where to Go

If more than one school accepted you—congratulations! But how do you choose? You may already have settled on a top contender. But if you haven't, here are some suggestions for selecting between many acceptances:

- Refer back to your top-ten list and the notes you made about why you wanted to apply to each college. Determine which of the colleges that accepted you meet the most of your requirements. Draw up a list of pros and cons for each school, and see who comes out on top.

- Revisit the campuses of your top choices. A fresh look can help you decide. Take advantage of any pre-freshman weekends or other events offered by the schools. If you can't get back to campus, return to the website and exchange e-mails with students and professors to ask questions that still concern you.

- Ask the advice of trusted teachers, your guidance counselor, and your parents. They may shed some light on which school is the best match for you.

- Compare financial aid packages. Determine the actual cost of each school by subtracting the amount of aid that you were awarded from the total tuition, room and board, and other costs of attending that school (the worksheet in Chapter 14, "Understanding Your Financial Aid Award," will help you).

Now is a time when parents and students often find themselves disagreeing over college choices. The most common causes of arguments are a college's cost and its distance from home. Take your parents' opinions into account, but remember that the final choice is up to you. If cost really is a serious point of contention, refer back to Part 5 for suggestions on ways to pay—work with your parents to find a way to attend the college of your dreams at a price that they're comfortable paying.

When you decide which school you'd like to attend, send in the nonrefundable deposit before the final deadline. Notify the other schools that accepted you of your decision to go elsewhere, so they can open up positions on their wait lists and reassign your financial aid award.

Once you've selected a school, it's time to select housing. The housing application form usually arrives with the acceptance letter. If you want to live on campus, make certain to return the housing application before the due date. If the school lets you pick your top housing choices, consult your notes from the campus visit and talk to current students to figure out the best places to live.

Conditional Acceptance—What It Means

Conditional acceptance means that you're basically in, but the school requires you to meet some additional requirements before you can be accepted formally. For example, the school may place you on academic probation for the first semester or quarter. You will have to achieve a certain grade point average during that time, or you will be dismissed from the school.

If you receive conditional acceptance, contact a counselor at the school to make certain that you completely understand the terms of the acceptance. Then, decide whether they are terms that you can live with. If you're worried about making the grade, consider going to a school that accepted you without conditions instead.

Getting Off the Wait List

There is a limbo between outright acceptance and outright rejection—that confusing middle ground called the wait list. Wait lists are colleges' insurance policies, a backup of qualified students that admissions officers can pick and choose from in case not enough of the students who were accepted the first time around choose to attend. Being relegated to the wait list at your first-choice college can be very confusing and frustrating, especially when you realize that the long wait to find out where you're going to college is not yet over.

Getting wait-listed doesn't mean that you were rejected, so don't let it discourage you, and don't reject a college simply because it wait-listed you. On the contrary, if you were put on the wait list, you can rest assured that you have all of the qualifications to succeed at that school. You may have landed in the "wait list" category simply because the admissions committee wasn't sure whether there was enough space in the freshman class to admit students at your level, or because the admissions committee was attracted by most of your record but felt that one area was slightly lacking.

But it's important to understand that getting onto the wait list is not an automatic guarantee of acceptance. You just have to wait and see—generally until late May or early June. The number of students accepted from the wait list can change dramatically from year to year. Some years, the school won't even admit anyone from the wait list.

Schools differ as much in their wait-list policies as they do in their admissions policies. Some colleges rank the applicants on their wait list. Others divide applicants into a priority list and a regular list. Other factors can also affect who gets accepted from the wait list. Public schools, for example, must accept a certain percentage of in-state students, so the school may turn to the wait list to increase that number if they turn up short. Schools may also use the wait list to even out the ratio of men to women or to increase the diversity of the freshman class. Therefore, academic merit is often not the deciding factor in deciding which wait-listed students to accept; often, it's the tippers like geography, gender, ethnicity, or a special talent that make a real difference.

You can call or e-mail the admissions office to find out whether it ranks wait-listed students or whether it maintains a priority wait list. If you ask politely, many admissions officers will tell you your rank or if you made it to the priority list, and how many students are ahead of you on the list. To get an idea of how many students are typically accepted from that school's wait list, ask how many wait-listed students were accepted in the last couple of years.

You can sometimes improve your chances of getting accepted off the wait list by apprising the admissions office of your second-semester grades, particularly if you performed exceptionally well. Be sure to tell the admissions officer about any honors you have won, the scores on AP exams or other standardized tests that you took since submitting your application, and any other information that can make a positive difference in your admission. Even sending an e-mail message or letter to let the admissions committee know how interested you are in attending can significantly help your chances (as long as your letter doesn't seem pushy). Selective colleges in particular are much more likely to choose wait-listed students who express a strong interest in attending the school.

The problem is that the schools who did accept you will want a firm commitment from you long before you find out whether you were accepted off the wait list at your top choice. And you have to accompany that commitment with a nonrefundable deposit of $200 or more. It will be too late to go to your second- or third-choice school if you decide to wait and see whether you get accepted off a wait list. So, if you don't get accepted, you're stuck with nowhere to go.

Unofficially...
If you are wait-listed, you may be accepted or rejected on the basis of financial need alone. By this late stage, colleges have already allocated all of their available financial aid dollars, and so they are reluctant to admit a wait-listed student who can't really afford the school.

Go ahead and accept admission at another school that accepted you. If your first choice does eventually accept you, nullify your previous acceptance as soon as possible. You probably won't get your deposit refunded, but at least you won't be left high and dry if you don't get accepted off the wait list.

If You're Rejected

First, don't take it personally. Colleges reject applicants for many reasons, which are sometimes difficult to predict. Besides, the competition is tough. Not every applicant—no matter how qualified—can be admitted.

If you want to know why you were turned down, often your guidance counselor can look at your application and transcript, compare them with the college's requirements, and make an educated guess at the reason. You can also try calling or e-mailing the admissions office to ask someone directly. But because a committee reviews applications at most schools, the admissions office may not be able to tell you the reason you were rejected. It may be something as slight as a B+ in a course in which a competing applicant had an A.

You can appeal your rejection, but many applicants don't succeed. Ask the admissions office for details about the appeal process. Some schools will reconsider the application if you retake the SAT I or ACT and your scores improve, or if your grades increased dramatically during the second semester of your senior year.

If you still have your heart set on attending the school that rejected you, ask the admissions officer about the requirements and process of transferring at the beginning of your sophomore year. It's often easier to get accepted as a transfer student. If you can earn top grades, win some awards, and get involved in clubs at your second-choice college during your freshman year, you have a better chance of being accepted as a transfer student. (And you may just find that you like your second-choice college better, and decide to stay.)

What's most important is making a full commitment to your second- or third-choice college—wherever you decide to go. As I stressed early on in the college search process, all of the colleges that you apply to should be schools where you think you'll be happy. There is no *one* college that's right for you—there are many. No matter where you go to college, if you get excited about starting classes, meeting new people, and getting involved in social activities—instead of dwelling on what might have been—you'll have an easier time adjusting to college life. In fact, you may find that you love the college that you did choose, and after a few months, you may not be able to imagine going anywhere else.

If You Aren't Accepted Anywhere

Don't despair—options are still open to you. Schedule an appointment with your guidance counselor right away to discuss them. You may be able to apply for late admission to colleges where you know you meet all of the requirements. Many schools also have rolling admission polices and thus are still taking applications. Finally, you can choose to attend a community college and transfer to a four-year college as a junior; in fact, many colleges recommend this track for students who aren't completely prepared for college-level work when they graduate from high school.

Applying Elsewhere

Just because it's May doesn't mean that you can't apply to more colleges. Many colleges have rolling admissions policies or continue taking applications up until a few days before the start of the fall semester. If the school has spaces available in its freshman class and you meet or exceed all of the admission standards, you will probably be accepted. The most likely places to apply are public colleges and universities. You will have a much better chance of getting in at this late date if you apply to schools that you are overqualified for and if you limit your applications to in-state schools.

Don't wait! Get your applications in as soon as possible, and apply to several schools. Remember that you won't get in if all the spaces in the freshman class are already filled. But if you apply during May, you may be able to fill the space of someone who was accepted but who decided to go elsewhere.

If you have to apply to additional colleges this late in the game, you probably won't be able to attend a school that is perfectly matched to your goals and interests. Don't worry—you aren't stuck there. You do have the option of transferring to a school that's better-suited to you at the beginning of your sophomore or junior year. If you keep your grades up, you will have a lot of options—many students find that they are accepted as a transfer student to colleges that rejected them the first time around.

Starting at a Community College

If you aren't accepted at any of the four-year colleges where you applied, one of the best alternatives is to start your college career at a two-year community college. If you work hard while you're there, you can easily transfer to a four-year college before your junior year and pick up a prestigious degree. Most four-year schools accept credits from community colleges.

Community colleges have a lot of advantages:

- Most have open admission policies, which means that if you have a high school diploma, you will be admitted. Standardized test scores, such as SAT I or ACT scores, are often not required for admission.

- Many have no application deadlines, so you still have time to apply to a community college, even if you start the process during the summer before you start college.

- They are very inexpensive (and you can get financial aid for community college as well as for four-year colleges). The average community college tuition runs around $1500 per year, so a community college can be

Bright Idea
It may be wise to take a year off. You can spend that time working or traveling abroad; at the same time, you'll solidify your plans for the future, making it easier to choose the right school. Remember, taking some time off doesn't necessarily mean that you won't ever go to college.

Moneysaver
The HOPE Scholarship tax credit was designed with community college students in mind. If your family qualifies, this tax credit can effectively pay all or most of the tuition bill for two years at a community college.

Watch Out!
Admission to a community college may not guarantee admission to a specific academic program within that school, particularly if that program is very popular or selective, such as health-related majors.

a good place to start if you can't find the money to pay for four years at a higher-priced college or if you want to reduce your debt burden due to student loans.

- They are often found close to home, so you can live at home and commute to school, saving yourself money on room and board costs.

- They offer flexible course schedules to accommodate working students and to make commuting easier.

- Most community colleges sponsor student clubs, extracurricular and social activities, and team sports, just like at a four-year college. So, you don't have to entirely give up the college "experience" if you go to a community college.

The low cost of community colleges is particularly advantageous to students who don't yet know what field they want to enter. Two-year schools generally offer a wide array of courses, from automotive technology to zoology. You can dabble in many different areas for a relatively low cost until you find something that you have a passion for. And you never know—that something may be a career for which you couldn't get a degree at a traditional university, such as the culinary arts.

Community colleges are also a good first stop for students who aren't yet ready for the university experience. Perhaps you didn't excel in high school, or you didn't feel that high school adequately prepared you for the academic rigors of a four-year college. At a community college, you can get more attention from instructors in small classes of 30 students or fewer (compare that to the auditorium-style lectures of many freshman and sophomore classes at the larger universities). Community college instructors often have more time outside the classroom to give to their students, because they aren't required to do research or publish, as many university professors are.

The drawback is that transferring credits from a community college to a four-year school can be an iffy process. Before enrolling, check on the transfer agreements that the community college has with four-year schools that you might eventually want to attend. You often have to take specific courses to enter the four-year college as a junior. Plan your academic program with a counselor at your community college to ensure that you are prepared to transfer to a four-year school when the time comes.

Finally, community college is not a good option for everyone. For example, you don't get to live on campus, so you miss out on the experiences of dorm life and some "typical" college activities, like the Saturday afternoon football game or the Friday night fraternity party.

If you decide to go the community college route, the American Association of Community Colleges can help you track down a two-year school that's right for you. Its website even provides a directory of community colleges, organized by state. Contact:

American Association of Community Colleges
One Dupont Circle NW, Suite 410
Washington, D.C. 20036
(202) 728-0200
http://www.aacc.nche.edu/

Moneysaver
Many states offer
grants and other aid
to students who
transfer from a com-
munity college to a
four-year school.
Inquire at your
state's financial aid
agency about these
programs.

Distance Learning

A third of all colleges and universities, including Harvard and Stanford, offer some form of distance learning. Often, the cost is much lower than taking the same class on campus, and you avoid the expenses associated with commuting to school or living in the dorm. It's also much easier to work your class schedule around a full-time job. Finally, the admission standards aren't as high, so distance learning is a good way to get a jump on your college degree while saving yourself some money. After racking up some course credits, you can try applying to colleges again. Or, you can complete your degree without ever setting foot in a classroom.

Distance learning takes several forms:

- *Correspondence courses:* Regents College in New York has the most comprehensive correspondence course offerings, with 26 associate's and bachelor's degrees. You enroll any time and move at your own pace—ideal for students working their way through school. You work with an academic advisor to plan your way. For more information, contact the school directly at Regents College, 7 Columbia Circle, Albany, NY 12203-5159, or go to http://www.regents.edu/.

- *Television:* Some television stations have agreements with colleges to offer courses over the airwaves. For example, Jones Education Company's College Connection lets cable subscribers get course credit that they can later apply toward a degree at participating schools (write College Connection, PO Box 6612, Englewood, CO 80155-6612, call 1 (800) 777-MIND, or visit http://www.e-education.com/collegeconnection/index.html for more information).

- *The Internet:* Virtual universities are the latest trend in distance learning. Over the Internet, you can attend lectures through real-time video, hold class discussions in chat rooms, access course notes on the Web, study in an electronic library, and take exams via e-mail. For example, the fully accredited University of Phoenix has a virtual campus at http://www.uophx.edu/online/. Many states are also considering starting electronic institutions rather than expanding the physical campuses of public universities.

You have to be very careful when choosing a distance-learning program. While some are very good, others offer poorly videotaped, long-winded lectures and little contact with professors, and some programs are outright scams. Beware of programs that promise that you can earn your degree in just a few weeks, for instance. The best way to avoid weak programs is to choose the distance-learning branch of a respected university. Most large universities now offer correspondence courses to compete with community colleges.

Just the Facts

- If more than one college accepted you, you're in a very good position—now it's your turn to decide who to accept and who to reject; base your decision on another campus visit, a comparison of financial aid offers, and weighing the pros and cons of each school that accepted you.

- Sometimes, if a school wants you but has a question about your ability to complete the academic work, it will offer you conditional acceptance, which means that you can attend but must maintain a certain GPA to remain at the school.

- Getting wait-listed at your favorite college can be frustrating; to improve your chances of getting accepted off the wait list, apprise the admissions committee of how your grades have improved over the second semester of your senior year, tell them about any additional honors or awards you've won, and definitely show your enthusiasm for attending that school.

- Rejection is discouraging, but it's not the end of the world; if you were careful to apply only to colleges where you felt you'd be happy, then your second- or third-choice school—which did accept you—can quickly become home.

- If you didn't get in anywhere, don't give up on higher education—you have lots of options, like applying late at a school with rolling admissions, going to a community college, or participating in a distance-learning program.

GET THE SCOOP ON...
What to do before you go ▪ Making it in the dorm ▪ A primer on
choosing college courses ▪ Balancing an academic life and a
social life ▪ Dealing with the common problems of college freshmen
▪ Going to college on a budget

Chapter 18

Surviving Freshman Year

The time has finally come—you're packing up and getting ready to go to college. The first few weeks of college can be a very exciting time, but it can also be overwhelming and even lonely. Adjusting to living in a new place is not easy for anyone, and it becomes even more difficult when you're on your own for the first time in your life. There may even come a time when you feel like giving up and going home.

But hang in there. After you settle in and get used to college life, you'll almost surely find that it's as exciting and fulfilling as you dreamed it would be. The best way to get over the hump is to get involved right from the start—go to all of the freshman orientation programs, join new clubs and teams, and make friends in the dorm.

This chapter will help you get prepared for that first year of college. You'll learn all about the typical problems that college freshmen have— problems with roommates, stress, alcohol, money, and finding time to study—and you'll discover strategies for avoiding those problems. After reading this chapter, you'll have a better idea of what you're in for, and you'll feel less like you're venturing into the great unknown.

One final word—you're not alone. Every freshman at your school is going through the same difficulties adjusting and experiencing the same feelings of homesickness that you are. So, don't be afraid to approach other freshmen—you're all in the same boat. Adjusting to college life will become so much easier once you have someone to talk to and hang out with.

Getting Ready for College

Shopping and packing for the first year away from home can be overwhelming. It will help if you plan what you need to take and try to gather as much of what you need as possible before you leave home. When you first arrive at college, you should be way too busy attending freshman orientation, signing up for classes, and meeting new friends to have to worry about trying to find an alarm clock or some other necessity that you forgot to pack.

While packing, think about where you're going to school. Find out what the weather is like there, in the fall and winter as well as in the summer, and bring the right clothes for all seasons. Whether your college is located in the country or in the city can make a difference in the kinds of clothes and other items you pack. What will you be studying, and does it require a lot of specialized supplies? Finally, where will you live? You'll need more stuff (such as furniture and kitchen supplies) for an off-campus apartment than you do for the dorm.

If you are moving into the dorm (where most freshmen live), it will help if you get in touch with your roommate before the day you're supposed to arrive on campus. The two of you can save some money by splitting the big-ticket items; for instance, one of you can bring the mini-fridge, and the other can bring the microwave. Touching base with your roommate ahead of time will also make you feel more comfortable about your new living situation. Often, the housing office sends you your room assignment early in the summer, along with your roommate's name, telephone number, and home address.

A Packing List

It's not easy to remember every little thing that you have to bring to college with you. I'm sure that everybody forgets something. The following packing list should help cut down on the number of essential little items that slip your mind, though. These are all things that most college freshmen soon find that they can't live without (add your own necessities to the bottom of the list):

☐ Enough clothing to last through the semester (be prepared for all kinds of weather)

☐ Clothes hangers

☐ Backpack or book bag

☐ Raincoat and/or umbrella

☐ Bathrobe

☐ Alarm clock

☐ Pillows

☐ Sheets and pillowcases

☐ Blanket

☐ Comforter

☐ Towels and washcloths

☐ Shower thongs

☐ Shower caddy (for carrying your things between your room and the bathroom)

Watch Out!
Make sure that you take the right clothes for the climate you're going to—not the one you're leaving. Any of you Southerners who are headed up North had better bring all of the following with you: a light coat and a heavy coat, boots, gloves, a hat, heavy clothes, and a scarf. New England natives headed for Miami, leave the heavy sweaters and corduroys at home, and bring shorts, a broad-brimmed hat, and plenty of summer-weight shirts.

Moneysaver
Stores near colleges know that students come to school having forgotten to bring some of the basic necessities. Expect high prices on items like school supplies, toiletries, and dorm furnishings during the first week or so of school at these places. If you buy them at home, you'll probably get them cheaper.

☐ Soap

☐ Shampoo

☐ Conditioner

☐ Hairspray

☐ Mousse or hair gel

☐ Hairbrush or comb

☐ Hair dryer

☐ Deodorant

☐ Toothpaste

☐ Toothbrush

☐ Dental floss

☐ Mouthwash

☐ Nail file

☐ Nail clippers

☐ Razor/shaving cream or electric shaver

☐ Prescription medications

☐ Pain reliever

☐ First-aid kit—bandages, thermometer, and first-aid ointment

☐ Earplugs and night mask (so you can sleep when your roommate wants
   to stay up late)

☐ Sunblock

☐ Laundry detergent

☐ Laundry bag

☐ Roll of quarters

☐ Drying rack (for clothes)

☐ Iron

☐ Ironing board (you can get a small one that sits on a table)

☐ Sewing kit

☐ Shoe polish

☐ Dustcloth

☐ Dust polish

☐ Sponge

☐ All-purpose cleaner

☐ Plate

☐ Bowl

☐ Coffee mug

☐ Glasses

Timesaver
Before packing, go
into your bathroom
and take inventory.
Include on your list
those items that you
use only occasionally
as well as those that
you use every day.

Watch Out!
Dorm regulations
may not allow some
appliances like a hot
plate or microwave;
check with the hous-
ing office first.

- ☐ Basic eating utensils
- ☐ Paper towels
- ☐ Paper napkins
- ☐ Sharp knife
- ☐ Cutting board
- ☐ Bottle/can opener
- ☐ Trash bags
- ☐ Coffee maker
- ☐ Hot plate
- ☐ Mini-fridge
- ☐ Microwave oven
- ☐ Fan (useful even if the dorm has air-conditioning, since you can't control the thermostat)
- ☐ Telephone (if your dorm has phone jacks in the rooms)
- ☐ Answering machine
- ☐ Footlocker to store extra clothing
- ☐ Milk crates or small bookshelf
- ☐ Filing cabinet or cardboard file
- ☐ Area rug
- ☐ Posters and wall decorations
- ☐ Pictures of your friends and family
- ☐ Bulletin board
- ☐ Wall calendar
- ☐ Message board for your dorm room door
- ☐ Desk lamp
- ☐ Light bulbs
- ☐ Extension cords
- ☐ Outlet strip
- ☐ Printer paper
- ☐ Floppy disks
- ☐ File folders
- ☐ Notebooks
- ☐ Index cards
- ☐ Personal organizer
- ☐ Post-It Notes
- ☐ Pens
- ☐ Pencils

- ☐ Highlighters
- ☐ Pencil holder
- ☐ Pencil sharpener
- ☐ Erasers
- ☐ Rubber bands
- ☐ Paper clips
- ☐ Tacks
- ☐ Scientific calculator
- ☐ Ruler
- ☐ Scissors
- ☐ Tape
- ☐ Stapler
- ☐ Staples
- ☐ Hammer
- ☐ Nails
- ☐ Screwdriver
- ☐ Screws
- ☐ Swiss Army knife
- ☐ Stationery
- ☐ Stamps
- ☐ Address book
- ☐ Radio or stereo
- ☐ Headphones
- ☐ Camera and film
- ☐ Flashlight
- ☐ Batteries
- ☐ *Merriam Webster's Collegiate Dictionary*
- ☐ *Roget's Thesaurus*
- ☐ *The Elements of Style* by Strunk and White or *The Chicago Manual of Style*
- ☐ *MLA Handbook for Writers of Research Papers, Theses, and Dissertations*

Buying a Computer for College

Taking a computer to school with you is a very important consideration. Many colleges and universities now require all students to have a computer. Some schools make it easy on you—they provide the computer and add the cost to your tuition and fees. Others simply tell you to bring one with you. If that is your school, find out before you buy a new computer if there are any special requirements, such as the following:

Bright Idea
If you don't want to haul everything with you on your trek to college, pack some of the things you won't need immediately upon arrival into boxes, label them for delivery to your new college address, and mail them off to yourself (or have a family member or friend mail them after your departure). Make sure that you'll have arrived at your college address before the boxes do, though, so they won't lie around unclaimed (and in danger of being stolen) until your arrival.

Unofficially...
College students say that the following are college essentials that no one ever tells you that you'll need: duct tape; cold medicine; tools—hammer, screwdriver, and pliers; flashlight; hot pot; roll of quarters; pre-paid phone card; and electronic organizer.

- Does your computer need to run a particular operating system?

- Will you need a laptop that you can take to classes with you?

- Will you need a modem or a certain kind of network interface card, such as an Ethernet card?

- Will you need a printer?

- Will you need any specific software programs?

- Can you purchase the computer through the school, and if you can, is it cheaper than buying it on your own?

If your school doesn't require a computer, consider bringing one anyway. This isn't a good item to share with your roommate, as you will both probably need to use the computer frequently, and papers often come due at the same time. You'll avoid arguments if you both bring your own.

Consider your needs carefully before investing in a computer. You'll need a good machine that will last all four years, but you shouldn't spend too much, because your computer is bound to be obsolete by the time you graduate. Ask yourself the following questions (and if you don't know the answers, find out from the school):

- *What will you primarily use the computer for?* Most college students need a powerful word processor, but depending on your major, you may require sophisticated multimedia capabilities (art, design, architecture, and computer science majors), complicated computations (math, engineering, and physics majors), or spreadsheet software (business and accounting majors). Be sure to get a computer that has the power to do what you want.

- *Do you want a PC or a Macintosh?* Often, this is a matter of preference; most students can get by with either. If the school typically uses computers of one type, it makes sense to buy a computer of that type. Another consideration is what you'll primarily use the computer for; multimedia and graphic designers prefer the Mac, while Windows is generally a better choice for computer science, science, math, and business majors.

- *Will you use the computer to take notes in class, or will you take it to the library with you?* If so, you'll need a laptop or notebook computer, which, due to their portability, are often more expensive and less powerful than the desktop kind. Also keep in mind that laptops are much more vulnerable to loss and theft; if you get one, insure it.

- *What kind of Internet and networking access is available on campus?* Find out whether you connect your computer to the school network or to the Internet in your dorm room, and if so, the hardware and software you will need.

- *Will you need a printer?* You may not if you can connect your computer through a school network to a printer in one of the computer labs, or if you can put your files on a floppy disk and take it to a central printing center on campus.

Once you've determined what kind of computer system you need, decide how much to spend. These days, you can get a complete computer package for less than $2000, which includes a 17-inch color monitor, a high-speed CD-ROM or DVD ROM drive, a 56K modem, 32MB or more of memory, a high-capacity hard disk, a fast Pentium III or Macintosh G3 processor, basic software—word processor, spreadsheet, and database—pre-loaded, and even an inexpensive ink-jet printer.

Take the time to research your computer purchase. Turn to trusted resources like *Consumer Reports, MacWorld,* and *PC User,* which regularly compare and contrast different brands and models. Also, ask knowledgeable friends, teachers, and co-workers what computers they would recommend.

The Ins and Outs of Dorm Living

Living in the dorm can be lots of fun, but it does have drawbacks. The rooms are typically very small, you have to share a bathroom with several people, and some nights it may get too noisy to sleep or study. Your room may not have air conditioning, and you'll have to spend a lot of quarters on laundry.

But on the other hand, you'll get to know your suitemates and the other residents on your hall very well, there are often organized dorm activities like sports, cookouts, and parties, and it's fun to take a study break in the dorm lounge or TV room. You're also within short walking distance of the classrooms, labs, library, cafeteria, student store, and everywhere else you'll need to go during your day. If you live in the dorm, chances are you won't even need a car (and as a freshman, you probably won't be allowed to have one).

Many colleges and universities offer plenty of choices when it comes to on-campus housing, as you've already seen during the campus visit. Unfortunately, you probably won't get a lot of choice as a freshman—freshmen tend to be bottom on the totem pole when it comes to everything—but explore your opportunities and take advantage of them when your turn comes around.

Living in a dorm will be a lot different than what you're used to. You'll have to get used to living with a lot of different people (including possibly members of the opposite sex), all of whom come from diverse backgrounds and have varying interests. You may find it difficult to study or sleep, or to get used to the lack of privacy and amenities.

If you need help adjusting to dorm life, there are many people around to talk to. The first person to get to know is your Resident Advisor (RA). This person—often an upperclassman—lives on your hall with you and is there to respond to your questions and concerns. If you have problems with your roommate or your neighbors are too noisy, your RA is the one to turn

Moneysaver
The student store at your college may sell computers at a special price for students, and you get technical support and service right on campus. Some schools also offer low-interest loans to students that enable them to buy a computer on credit (many private lenders also have computer loans for students).

Timesaver
Get in touch with an upperclassman (perhaps the sophomore that you stayed with during your campus visit) to ask what dorm life is like, what you'll need, and so on, before you start packing for college.

to. Many dorms also have a faculty overseer—a hall director, residence hall coordinator, or dorm mother—who can help you out with problems, as well.

The biggest adjustment that you'll have to make is living with a roommate, particularly if you've always had your own room. It can be daunting to move in with someone you've never met before, especially if the two of you seem to have little in common. Here are some tips for creating a smooth roommate relationship and for turning a roommate into a friend:

- Get to know each other. Go out for coffee, go to the cafeteria together, or attend one of the freshman orientation activities together.

- Your roommate may come from a different background or part of the country than you. He or she may have different tastes in music, clothes, or friends, or hold different political or religious beliefs. Be tolerant of the differences between you. You don't have to like your roommate, but you do have to live with him or her.

- Share. If you bring a small refrigerator and stereo, let your roommate use them. Many schools tell you who your roommate is before you arrive, so you can call each other and agree beforehand who's bringing what.

- Decide on rules for living together. If you need to study for a big test or work on a paper, schedule some quiet time with your roommate in advance (but remember to return the favor). If you have a lot of early-morning classes and need to get to sleep early, arrange rules about when visitors have to leave. You'll be glad you broached these issues before a problem developed.

- Be honest. If you don't want your roommate borrowing your clothes or having friends over late on school nights, say so when the situation first presents itself. Don't let yourself get into a situation where your roommate habitually does something that you don't like but you're afraid to say anything about it—that type of situation is bound to explode.

- Don't hold a grudge. If you have a problem with your roommate, talk it out. If he or she apologizes or agrees to change the behavior that bothers you, accept it and move on. And if you're in the wrong, apologize yourself.

- Even if you and your roommate don't become the best of friends, be nice to each other. Ask before you borrow something, keep it down when your roommate is studying or sleeping, and help keep the room and any common areas clean.

If you really don't like your roommate, you can talk to your RA or the housing office about switching rooms. But try to stick it out. It may take a little time to iron out the kinks, but if you stay courteous and communicate with each other, you and your roommate should have few problems. Remember that you can always get a new roommate next year.

Moneysaver
Bring a small fridge or rent one for the year, and buy soda from the grocery store instead of out of the machine. You can also store yogurt and milk for in-room breakfasts, or keep pizza and leftovers. Check with the housing office first; some dorms have strict regulations on what appliances you can bring.

How to Choose Classes

Every college and university has a set of core course requirements that every student must take to earn a degree from that school. If, like most college students, you attend a liberal arts college, you will take a selection of courses from each of the academic disciplines—the arts, the humanities, math, sciences, and social sciences—advancing to a certain level in each. While the general subject requirements are specified, the specific courses that you can take in each discipline are, for the most part, left up to you.

Make certain that you know the basic course requirements required to graduate and the courses required for your major, including prerequisites. This knowledge will help you decide which courses to register for and make it easier to plan your courseload for the next four years. When you arrive at college, you will be assigned an academic advisor whose job is to help you plan what courses to take and how to fulfill the requirements of your major. Take advantage of this resource—it could make a difference between earning a degree in four years and taking five or even six years to complete your college education.

At many of the larger universities, required courses fill up early and so may be closed by the time you get to register. You'll have a better shot at getting into the popular courses if you register as early as possible. If your school has a pre-registration system for entering freshmen, go ahead and sign up for classes instead of waiting until you get to school. Often freshmen are last in line to get classes, so don't expect to get into every class that you want. Be willing to take some early-morning or evening classes to get in some of the requirements. Have a few backups in mind when you register in case your first choices are full.

Always remember that college is a time to explore. Don't play it safe—take some classes in subjects you've never studied (or even heard of) before. Don't be afraid to experiment or to expand your knowledge into new areas; take advantage of the smorgasbord of classes offered to you. You may just fall in love with the subject, making it your major and your eventual career.

Keeping Your Grades Up and Having a Social Life

A college life is a busy life. Suddenly, there are a lot of new opportunities, new things to do, and new people to do them with—parties, sports, extracurriculars, staying up till dawn shooting the bull. When do you find time to study while still taking advantage of all the new activities?

It will help if you develop good study skills and habits right from the first day of the first semester. Academics at college are rigorous and require a lot more time and discipline on your part that your high school classes did. Don't ever forget your main goal for going to college: to get an education and earn a degree. Partying has its place, but you don't want to party so hard that your grades drop and you end up flunking out.

Unofficially...
If a particular course is full but you still really want to attend, go to the first class meeting even though you aren't registered for the course. Often, spots open up because some students won't show up. At this point, it's the professor, rather than the registrar, who will get you into the class. Your best shot is to make contact with that prof, and let him or her know how much you want and need that class.

Watch Out!
Try not to schedule classes back-to-back. You'll wear yourself out, and you may not even have time to get from one class to another. Plan your schedule to leave a block of time between each class for studying, reviewing, and eating. As a freshman, though, you may not have a lot of choice.

You must learn three important study skills in order to succeed academically while at college:

- How to manage your time
- How to effectively prepare for class, take notes, and study
- How to organize a good study space

Managing Time Wisely

One of the most difficult things to do during your first year at college is managing your time—getting your studying done while participating in as many college activities as you want. You will probably be busier at college than ever before, and you still won't get to do it all. One of the most important skills you can learn right now is how to say "no"—how to turn down the occasional party or extracurricular activity so that you have time to study and participate in the activities that are really important to you.

The first thing you should do after starting classes and deciding what activities you most want to participate in is to organize your semester schedule, building in adequate time for class preparation, writing papers, and studying for exams. If you develop an effective study routine from the start and stick to it, you won't fall behind in your classes, and you'll find that you do have enough time to get everything done and have a social life, too.

Two of the items on your packing checklist were a wall calendar and a personal organizer. These will be your most valuable time-management tools.

Timesaver
A personal information manager, like Microsoft Outlook, can be a big help in scheduling your semester calendar, reminding you of upcoming due dates and exams, and keeping track of your assignments. Consider investing in such a program, or if one comes pre-installed on your computer, learn how to use it.

On your wall calendar (which should hang right above your study space), mark important dates for the semester, such as the dates of midterms, finals, and other exams, when big papers are due, and the last day to drop classes (you'll find this information on the class syllabus, which the professor hands out on the first day of class). Also, block out prescheduled activities—team practices, club meetings, lab times, and a job or volunteer work. Finally, block out a period of study time each day.

Since you've never actually gone to college before, you may have a hard time estimating how much time to devote to doing homework assignments, writing papers, and studying for exams. In college, you can't procrastinate until the last minute. On average, plan to spend two hours hitting the books for each hour you spend in class—more for the major assignments. You will have to spend a lot more time researching, writing, and rewriting papers in college than you did in high school to earn the same grades. And you will probably spend several days studying for a major exam.

To make sure you get it all done, learn how to set goals for yourself and prioritize your tasks. That's where your personal organizer can help. Each day, make a note of all class meetings, labs, club meetings, practices, and other scheduled appointments for that day. Then, create a list of five to six tasks—both academic and personal—that you want to accomplish that day. Order your list from most important to least important. Concentrate on completing one task at a time, starting with the tasks at the top of your list. That way, if you don't get to something farther down the list, it won't matter so much if you have to carry it over until the next day.

Make the tasks on your list small, specific, and manageable. Say you have to write a 20-page paper for a history class. Don't create a task to write the entire paper all in one sitting. Instead, break it down into small steps, and plan to complete one step each day. You'll have to start working on the paper well before it's due, but you'll end up writing a better paper, and you'll have time to fulfill all your other obligations, as well.

Finally, leave some time free for unplanned social activities. Reward yourself for meeting deadlines by going to a party or going out with friends. But if you haven't accomplished the most important tasks on your daily list, don't be afraid to say "no" if your friends drop by and want you to blow off studying.

Developing Good Study Skills

You will discover a lot of differences between high school and college. One of the major differences is how you prepare for class, complete homework assignments, and study for exams. Another major difference is that you have to take responsibility for getting everything done yourself. You're on your own now—no one is looking over your shoulder to make sure that you do your homework or perform well in class.

Completing College Homework

Homework is not the same in college—it usually isn't collected or checked. Often, the professor won't even tell you what the homework assignment is. You're expected to keep up with assignments yourself.

So, how do you know what assignments are due? On the first day of class, you will receive an all-important piece of paper called a *syllabus*. The syllabus outlines the homework problems, reading assignments, lecture topics, paper due dates, and exam dates for the entire course. Your classmates may throw their syllabi away, or lose them, or turn them into paper airplanes. They may stick them in the back of their textbooks and never look at them again. Don't make this mistake.

Instead, treat your syllabus as if it contained valuable secrets (and it does—the secrets to doing well in the class). When you first get the syllabus, look it over carefully, and read over the major headings and chapters in the textbook. This should give you a good overview of the topics covered in the course and the subject matter to pay extra attention to. Carry the syllabus with you to class, and keep a backup copy in your study area back at your room. Use the information on the syllabus to plan your study schedule, as described in the previous section.

Before each class, check the syllabus to find out what the lecture topic will be and what the reading and problem assignments are for that lecture. Do these assignments *before* class. Even though the professor won't check behind you to make certain that you're doing your homework, that doesn't

Bright Idea
Save the textbooks for every course in your major and related support courses. You will refer to them again and again for tests, research, and refreshing your memory for another class. And when you graduate, you'll have a starter reference library for your field.

mean that you can get away without doing it at all. Keeping yourself on schedule is your job, now that you're in college. You benefit from keeping up with your coursework, and you suffer if you fall behind. It's that simple.

Most college homework assignments consist of reading—endless amounts of reading. But that doesn't mean you can just read the text and be done. You probably won't retain anything that you merely read. You'll better absorb your reading assignments if you learn how to read actively, which means taking notes as you read. Making notes on what you read reinforces the important points and helps them stick in your brain.

While reading the text, make notes of key ideas or highlight them in the book. Keep a stack of index cards handy, so you can create flashcards—the college student's best friend. On the front of the card, write down one important item from the text—a key concept, a major date, a word that needs defining, a formula, whatever you think is important. On the back of the card, write the definition of the concept.

It may seem like a waste of time to make flashcards, but when exam time rolls around, you'll be so glad that you did. Instead of having to skim through a 500-page textbook trying to pick out the important facts and ideas, you'll already have them marked down on your cards. You can quiz yourself off the cards until you know what you need to know. So, while your friends spend all night cramming for an exam, you can prepare in a few hours, get a good night's sleep, and score an A. Trust me on this one.

Taking Class Notes

Many students think the goal of taking notes during class is to write down everything that comes out of the professor's mouth. Some students even tape the entire lecture; imagine having to listen to endless hours of tapes on the night before the final. There is a better way, and you should learn it now.

If you do the reading assignment before class, you'll be in a much better position to take meaningful notes. That's because you'll already know what the textbook covers. If the professor repeats that information, you don't have to waste time writing it down—it's already written down for you, in the textbook.

Instead, you can concentrate on what the professor is actually saying. If the professor introduces new ideas other than what you read in the text, that's what you should take notes on. Also, note down any key ideas that the professor particularly emphasizes. Finally, the lecture may clarify ideas that you didn't fully understand from the reading.

After class is over, take some time to review your lecture notes. Leave plenty of white space in your notebook so that you can make notes on your notes. One thing that you should do is try to outline the lecture, so that you have a better understanding of the key points and supporting details. If the professor outlines the important points of the lecture on a board or overhead projection, you may want to copy the outline in your notes. Also make a list of important keywords, jot down some possible exam questions, and highlight the ideas that your professor stressed the most.

You may feel tempted to skip class from time to time, especially when you realize that in college courses, roll is taken only on the first day of class and that no one is actually making you go. Unless you're genuinely ill, go to class. Each lecture in a college class covers a lot more material than the equivalent amount of time in a high school class; so, if you skip a class, you'll find it much harder to catch up.

You may think that you can just borrow someone's lecture notes, and you'll be set. Think again. Everyone takes notes differently, so a classmate's notes aren't likely to be of much use to you. You'll be better off just going to class and taking your own notes.

If you feel tempted to skip a class, remember what college is costing you. In fact, tack up a list of college costs over your desk—tuition, fees, room and board, books, everything. You're paying all that money for the opportunity to attend class and learn. If you skip a class, you're just throwing away your own money. Think about that for a minute—you're probably ready to go to class now.

Timesaver
Save your notes and papers from all of the classes you take—they may come in handy when you take related classes later.

Preparing for Exams

All semester, you've been a disciplined student. You completed the reading assignments before class. You took notes on key ideas in the textbook and on those given by the professor during lectures. You created flashcards of important facts and concepts. So, when do you get your reward? You guessed it—at exam time.

The final exam, which often counts for at least half of your grade in the class, covers the material that you learned during the entire semester. You can't possibly learn everything you need to know the night before the exam, or even during the week before the exam. But many college students attempt to do just that. They crack open their textbooks for the first time and sit down to read the entire thing in one sitting, while trying to pick out the important points that the exam might cover.

Fortunately, you aren't in that position. You already have a thorough understanding of the material that you need to know, because you've been diligently reading, taking notes, and listening to lectures throughout the semester. When exam time comes, you know what will be covered—the key points underlined in your textbook, written down in your lecture notes, and marked on your flashcards. To prepare, you only have to review this material until you're sure that you know it and understand it. You'll find that you spend less time studying than your ill-prepared classmates, and that you go into the exam feeling more confident and ready to answer any question that the professor might throw at you.

Creating a Study Space

If you create a good study space for yourself, your study efforts will be more effective. A good study space is *not* the couch in front of the TV in the dorm lounge or the back booth at Denny's. Instead, set up an uncluttered, well lit workspace in your room that is dedicated only to studying. Or go to the library—a good alternative if your roommate prefers to play loud music or have friends over during your study time.

Study at the same time and place every day, if possible. This will help you stick to your study routine. Determine when your best study time is. Some people are "morning" people, some are "night owls," and some work best in the early evenings. Take advantage of the times when your brain is working at top efficiency. Reserve your off-peak times for other tasks, like doing the laundry or working out.

Try to ensure that your study time is free of interruptions. Turn down the ringer on the phone, and let the answering machine field any calls. Put a "do not disturb until…" sign on your door. Remember to take frequent breaks; after 30–40 minutes of studying, take five minutes to stretch, walk around, and otherwise give your brain a rest.

Your school may offer study skills workshops, a writing center, tutoring services, and even a note-taking course. Take advantage of these services, particularly if they're free.

It's also a good idea to form a study group with other members of your class. You can help each other understand important concepts and practice with flashcards. But don't let the study group become too social. Plan just one study group meeting a week, and reserve other study times for completing reading and writing assignments on your own.

While your academic life at college is important, it shouldn't become your entire life. College is also about the experience of meeting new people, trying new things, and living on your own for the first time. So, don't hide out in the library or spend all your time studying in your dorm room. Take advantage of the social activities offered during the first week or so of school; they help freshmen get oriented to college life and to meet others in their class. If you're shy, try joining a club or an intramural sports team, or ask some people in your class to discuss a lecture over coffee. What's important is that you get out of your room often and experience everything that college has to offer you.

Common Problems for College Students and How to Deal with Them

Your first year of college is an exciting, energetic time, and I hope that you will look back on it with a lot of fond memories. Unfortunately, freshman year can also be overwhelming, frustrating, stressful, and lonely. Problems can crop up that can affect your academics, your health, everything.

It's important to realize that even though you are on your own, you're not alone. Your college has an extensive support network in place to help you if you encounter problems. You just have to take advantage of all the resources available to you.

In this section, you'll learn about the typical problems that affect college students, particularly freshmen. You'll discover how to avoid these problems and where to go for help if you need it.

Dealing with Stress

Stress is a huge problem for many college students. You've been thrust into an unfamiliar living environment, you're probably homesick, and you no longer have mom, dad, siblings, and old friends to fall back on. At the same time, you must deal with an academic life that's much more rigorous than what you're used to.

If you find yourself under a lot of stress, you need to deal with it, not ignore it or try to compensate in unhealthy ways, such as overeating or turning to drugs or alcohol. Stress is a major problem that can adversely impact your health, as well as your grades.

Here are some proven strategies for avoiding stress and some good ways to deal with feeling stressed out:

- *Give yourself time to get adjusted.* Don't load up on challenging courses or overcommit yourself to extracurricular activities your first semester. Don't worry if you feel homesick or depressed for a while after arriving at school. Give yourself some time to ease into college life.

- *Eat right.* Yes, that's what mom would say, but she has a point. If you take care to not skip breakfast, to eat balanced meals, and to avoid junk food at least most of the time, you'll feel better.

- *Get regular exercise.* There's no better way to work out your stress, and on a college campus, you have a lot of choices of physical activities. You can take a class, join an intramural team, or take advantage of a variety of athletic and recreational facilities within walking distance of your dorm.

- *Get a good night's sleep.* All-night bull sessions are a part of college life, and indulging occasionally won't hurt you. But to keep your stress level down, try to develop a regular routine of when you go to bed and when you get up. Most importantly, don't fall into the habit of staying up all night to cram for a test; you'll feel too tired to perform well, which will only add to your anxiety level.

- *Take a break.* Don't spend all your time studying. If you find yourself getting stressed out, stop what you're doing and go for a walk around campus, get something to eat, or wander down to the dorm lounge.

- *Stay away from drugs and alcohol.* Taking up smoking, drinking, or using illegal drugs is not an effective way to deal with stress. In fact, these "solutions" simply lead to even more and bigger problems. And remember, caffeine is a drug, too—one that a lot of college students overuse.

- *Get help if you need it.* College campuses offer free counseling services to help students deal with stress and other problems—take advantage of them (check at the campus health clinic). If you have problems in your classes, talk to your academic advisor and your professors. Professors get to know the students who regularly come by during office hours; they care more about how those students perform, and will go the extra mile to help them out.

Unofficially...
You can often drop a class even a few weeks into the semester. Take advantage of this option if you find that you overloaded yourself.

The Freshman 15

A big problem for many new college students is what's known as the "fresh-man 15"—those 15 pounds that you put on freshman year because you pig out on too much junk food and don't get enough exercise. We all tend to overdo it our first time out, when Mom isn't around to tell us to eat our vegetables. But remember, it's a whole lot easier to keep from gaining the weight in the first place than to try to shed those extra pounds when the spring break trip to Acapulco rolls around.

Here are some easy things you can do to make sure that you don't fall victim to the "freshman 15:"

- Take advantage of your meal plan; even cafeteria food is better than pizza, take-out, or fast food.

- Get in the habit of eating several small meals a day with lots of fruit, vegetables, and grains. Imagine that mom is looking over your shoulder as you go down the cafeteria line.

- Keep fruit, bagels, popcorn (no butter), and other nutritious snacks in your dorm room for when you get the munchies, so you can avoid late-night trips to the vending machine.

- Reduce your reliance on sodas; if you have a dorm-room fridge, stock it with fruit juices and flavored water.

The most important tip of all: exercise regularly. You have so many options for physical activities on campus that you really have no excuse for not exercising. Take a physical education class (and take up a new sport). Join an intramural team. Avail yourself of on-campus athletic facilities like the gym, health club, weight room, pool, or tennis courts. Go for a walk or ride your bike around campus. Or take advantage of nearby recreational facilities, such as hiking trails or a lake. Many of these facilities are free to students (since your student fees have already paid for them).

Regular exercise has so many advantages besides keeping the weight off. As you already learned, exercise is a great stress-buster. It also gives you more energy for studying and keeping up with your classes. You'll meet new people who share your interest in a particular athletic ability. And you'll develop a good habit that lasts a lifetime.

Avoiding Problems with Drugs and Alcohol

For many, college is their first exposure to alcohol, cigarettes, and illegal drugs. Couple that with being on your own for the first time and the pressures of college life, and it's easy to understand why the college years are often associated with abuse of drugs and alcohol.

Alcohol is by far the most frequently abused drug on college campuses, which explains why so many schools have clamped down on alcohol abuse and mandated alcohol-free campuses, even for students who are over 21. But the policy at other colleges and universities is that students are adults,

Bright Idea
Before leaving home, get a checkup with your doctor, dentist, and optometrist. You'll be more comfortable getting these checkups with doctors you're already familiar with, and you'll feel better going off to school with a clean bill of health.

able to make their own decisions about drinking. The reality falls somewhere in between.

Sometime during your freshman year, and possibly even during the first night you're at school, you will be offered a drink. Here are just a few things to think about before you accept that drink (all of the following are true of illegal drugs, as well):

- Student drinking is the number-one health problem on college campuses. Binge drinking, in particular, has led to several student deaths due to alcohol poisoning.

- The consequences of drinking for women can be very severe; 90 percent of rapes of female college students occurred while either the victim or the perpetrator or both were under the influence of alcohol.

- Underage drinking has been linked to criminal activity, vandalism, fights, sexually transmitted diseases, car accidents, drownings, and suicide.

- Underage drinking is illegal. You could easily wind up in jail or getting kicked out of school.

- Alcohol abuse usually leads to skipping classes and lower GPAs. Researchers say that alcohol is a factor in 41 percent of academic problems and in 28 percent of student dropouts.

- Alcohol impairs skills vital to playing sports. If you belong to a major college sports team, depend on an athletic scholarship, or even just really enjoy playing a game, too much drinking can take that away from you.

- Developing a drinking habit is expensive, taking money that you could spend on more substantial things, like your tuition.

- Alcohol is often a gateway drug, leading to abuse of illegal drugs. In fact, 80 percent of young people who have used illegal drugs are heavy drinkers. Also, young people who consume alcohol are much more likely to smoke.

- If you party all the time, you'll miss out on many of the other benefits of college life, including developing meaningful relationships, taking advantage of new opportunities like study-abroad and internships, and even getting your degree.

- This isn't high school anymore; no one will think any less of you if you refuse a drink. If they do, you don't really want them as friends. There are plenty of other students who you could get to know. If you truly have problems saying "no" when offered a drink, avoid those situations—look for substance-free activities or organizations that you can join where you won't be tempted.

If you do find yourself developing a drinking, drug abuse, or smoking problem, there are plenty of resources you can turn to for help. Just talking to a good friend, roommate, or RA is a good start. Counseling and other health clinic services are right there on campus to give you good advice and to help solve your problem. Your school may also have a substance abuse prevention center, which can provide information, counseling, and alternatives to partying with drugs and alcohol.

The following resources can also help if you or someone you know develops a substance abuse problem:

- Alcohol Treatment Referral Hotline: 1 (800) ALCOHOL
- Alcoholics Anonymous: (212) 870-3400
- Cocaine Hotline: 1 (800) COCAINE
- Marijuana Anonymous: 1 (800) 766-6779
- Narcotics Anonymous: (818) 780-3951
- National Drug and Alcohol Treatment Referral Service: 1 (800) 662-HELP
- Smokers' Hotline: 1 (800) 638-0668

Staying Safe

College campuses attract a lot of crime, ranging from robbery to rape. All colleges and universities strive to provide a safe environment for their students, but you have to do your part too. A little common sense goes a long way toward helping you stay safe.

If you employ the following suggestions for protecting yourself and your stuff, you shouldn't have anything to worry about:

- Never leave a backpack or book bag unattended. Consider getting a fanny pack to keep your wallet and keys in.
- If you have a bike, invest in a good kryptonite-type lock, and always keep your bike locked up. Find out whether you can store your bike inside the dorm, instead of outside.
- If you have a car, park in well lit areas. Lock your doors at all times—while inside and outside the car.
- Avoid using the ATM at night or in isolated areas. Don't use the ATM if you notice someone lurking around the machine. Ask a friend to go to the ATM with you and stand guard. Never leave an ATM until the transaction has completely finished, and never put your ATM card in the machine for someone else.
- Always keep your dorm room locked. Obey dorm security procedures, no matter how annoying they are—they're in place for your protection. Never let anyone into the dorm who doesn't seem to belong there.
- When you go home for extended breaks, take your valuables with you. Don't leave expensive stereo or computer equipment in a dorm room during spring break or the holidays, when campus empties out.
- Never walk alone at night. If you have to stay late at the library or in the labs, study with a partner. Know where emergency phones are located

Watch Out!
Another heavily abused college drug—although a perfectly legal one—is caffeine. College students use coffee and sodas to socialize, stay awake to study, and get going in the morning. Caffeine is addictive and can lead to health problems. Limit your caffeine intake to one or two sodas or cups of coffee a day.

Moneysaver
Renter's insurance, even for a dorm room, protects expensive items like your computer and stereo, and it's very cheap. Keep records of all expensive property—receipts, model numbers and serial numbers, and photographs—in case you have to make a claim.

on campus. Most schools provide free transportation or walking services at night—use them.

- Find out from other students whether there are any dangerous areas in the neighborhoods around campus, and stay away from those places, especially on foot.

- Date rape is a big problem on college campuses. Get to know your dates well before putting yourself in a vulnerable situation. Have dates in public, well traveled places, or go out with a group. Don't drink while on a date. Don't go to a dorm room or apartment with someone who you don't know well. If you feel pressured to have sex, say "no" and mean it; try to get away as quickly as possible, and get help.

- If you notice any suspicious behavior, such as someone trying to get into a dorm who doesn't belong there, report it to campus security or to your residence hall director. Post the number for the campus police by the phone in your dorm room.

Bright Idea
Many colleges offer courses in self-defense. Consider taking one—you'll learn how to protect yourself and get some exercise at the same time.

College on a Budget

One of the biggest problems for college students is money. With the high cost of college tuition, you may have to live on precious little during your college years. At the same time, you have to learn how to manage money, create a budget and stick to it, and handle checking accounts and credit cards.

Developing a College Budget

Set up a budget before going off to school, so you can control spending from the start. Every college student needs a budget, whether you intend to work at a part-time job or rely on mom and dad for pocket money. But it's not enough to just come up with a budget—you also have to stick with it. If you spend your entire clothing allowance on one pair of jeans, that's it—no more clothes for the rest of the semester.

The first step is to determine where your income is coming from. Your financial aid package is one major source of income, as are any additional student loans that you or your parents took out. You may also count the balance of your savings account, income from a part-time job, and an allowance allocated to you by your parents.

The second step is to determine how much money to allocate to the major expenditures that must get paid, no matter what: tuition and fees, housing, meals, books, health insurance, renter's insurance, and travel or car expenses, if you plan to bring your car with you or attend a college far from home. You should have developed a fairly good estimate of what all of these expenses will cost based on your financial aid award letter, which outlines the cost of attendance, and from your discussions with insurance companies and travel agencies.

Finally, concentrate on the other essentials of life: clothing, personal items, laundry, monthly phone service and long-distance charges (if you

Moneysaver
If you buy your books the week before classes begin, you're more likely to find used books and avoid the rush. Save all your receipts, and don't write in your textbooks until you're sure that you'll use them for the class.

can have a phone in your dorm room), school supplies, public transportation, and entertainment. Since you've never lived on your own before, you may not have a clue what amounts to assign to these categories.

A good way to start is to take note of what you buy in the three months leading up to when school starts (excluding special one-time expenditures for college, of course). Go with your mom or dad to the grocery store, and mark down the costs of such basics as shampoo and toothpaste, plus how often you have to replace them. Do your own laundry at home, so you can determine how often you'll need to do it at school (figure on spending $3 per load of laundry). Pad in a little extra for unexpected expenses and emergencies.

Use the following worksheet to come up with your college budget. A software program like Quicken or Microsoft Money can help you fiddle with the figures and track spending more easily.

Note that the amount of income should exceed or equal your expenses. If your expenses total is higher, you need to re-evaluate your budget or cut spending in some areas.

During the first semester, keep good records of how much money you spend in each category (your checking account statements will help you). At the end of the semester, take a fresh look at your budget. Determine where you overspent and where you underspent, and adjust the figures accordingly. If you're spending too much in any one category, figure out ways to economize (you'll find some money-saving hints at the end of this chapter).

Getting a Checking Account

You will need to open a checking account at a bank near the school. You may also need a savings account to handle financial aid disbursements, if they aren't paid directly to your school. Start thinking about this early in the summer, so you can shop around for the best deals.

Checking accounts carry fees—fees for the checks you write, ATM fees, fees for bounced checks, overdraft protection, and penalty fees if your balance falls below a specified minimum. Ideally, you want to find a checking account that costs you as little as possible in terms of added fees. Many banks near colleges offer special deals just for students—ask about them.

A good summer exercise is to learn how to balance a checkbook (ask one of your parents to teach you). Get in the habit of balancing your checkbook each month. This will help you see where your money goes, so you know if you're staying within the confines of your budget.

A sure consequence of not balancing your chcckbook is bounced checks. Even if you don't mean to bounce a check, you will be held liable for the amount of the bad check, plus bank fees and merchant fees. One bounced check could end up costing you $40 or more. It's a whole lot cheaper to just keep track of how much money is in your checking account, and thus avoid writing bad checks to begin with.

Watch Out!
Don't get in the habit of writing checks or making ATM withdrawals and not recording them in your check register. Many new checking account holders think they can be pretty casual about their accounts, and "figure it all out" later. But if your account becomes too disordered, you'll probably have to ask your parents or a bank employee to help you straighten it out, and you may even bounce checks. You'll save yourself a lot of time, money, and embarrassment by avoiding either of those situations.

Projected Income

From parents:

From savings:

Part-time job:

Scholarships:

Grants:

Loans:

Other:

Total semester income:

Projected Expenses

Tuition and fees:

Lab fees:

Rent or housing:

Food:

Books:

Special supplies:

Health insurance:

Renter's insurance:

Car insurance:

Gas:

Maintenance:

Parking:

Travel expenses:

Public transportation:

Phone:

Clothing:

Laundry/dry cleaning:

Toiletries:

School supplies:

Entertainment:

Bank charges:

Other:

Total semester expenses:

Total income:

Total expenses:

Difference:

Timesaver
To find out how costs in your school's area compare to costs at home, use the cost-of-living calculator at http://nt. amo-mortgage.com/ amo-scripts/calcs/ costofliving.asp.

Bright Idea
If your school's
bookstore lets you
cash checks, you
won't need to use
the cash machine.
You'll save on ATM
fees, and your can-
celed check will
serve as a record of
your expenditure.

Your checking account will probably come with an ATM or debit card. Be careful how you use it. While convenient, these cards make it all too easy to overspend, and it's more difficult to track where the money goes.

Until you become an expert at managing your personal finances, the best idea is to make it as difficult to spend money as possible. Carry very little cash with you, and write a check whenever you can; the extra hassle will make you think twice about any purchases you make. If you do need to get cash from the ATM, withdraw a small amount each time, and never get the maximum amount allowed. It's a whole lot easier to spend cash that's burning a hole in your pocket, and once the money is gone, you may not have a clue where it disappeared to.

Getting a Credit Card

You may also want to get a credit card for emergencies, such as a costly car repair or unexpected school expenses. But be careful. College students are notorious for abusing credit cards and winding up with a lot of debt that they can't afford to pay off. Often, they can't even remember what they spent all that money on.

When you arrive at school, you will be inundated with credit card offers—when you buy your books, outside the student union, in your mail. Throw all of these offers away. Credit cards aimed at college students are all too easy to obtain, but they carry high interest rates and exorbitant annual fees.

It's a much better idea to get a card jointly with your parents so they can monitor your spending. (I know you want to be independent, but you can wait to get your own credit card after you graduate and get a job—believe me, when you see all your friends drowning under credit card debt, you'll be glad you waited.) Also, your parents will qualify for cards with better terms, like no annual fee and a lower interest rate. Apply for a card with a relatively low credit limit, between $500 and $1500, so if you do go crazy, you won't get into too much trouble.

Reserve your credit card for emergencies only—a trip to the mall doesn't qualify. Hide your card where you won't see it every time you open your wallet. Pull it out only when you truly have no alternative way to pay, and when whatever you're purchasing is a true necessity. Never use your credit card to get a cash advance, to pay for essential living expenses like groceries, or to treat the gang to pizza—even if your friends do pay you back, you probably won't use the cash to pay off your credit card bill.

Saving Money on Room and Board

Some families try to save money by having the student live at home. This option saves dorm or apartment rental costs and looks very attractive on the surface. Yet, there are a number of hidden costs to staying at home—not the least of which is losing out on a major part of the college social experience by not being at the center of things. Commuting costs alone can eat away at the money that living at home saves.

Another reason why staying at home is more expensive than it looks is the cost of food. The student who stays at home won't be able to eat all meals there; students' odd hours often keep them away from home at mealtimes. So, commuter students tend to spend a lot of money in campus-area eateries, while students living in dorms buy a relatively inexpensive meal plan. (Meal plans may be available for non-dormers and are worth looking into.) Also, most parents won't stand for the poverty chic that can make student dollars stretch so far, and so will spend more money on clothing than the student would spend on his or her own.

While I recommend living in the dorm as an underclassman, once you get to be a junior or senior, you may consider moving out on your own. Splitting the rent and utilities of an apartment or house among three, four, or more roommates can be considerably cheaper than the costs of a dorm room, and you get a lot more space to boot. If you learn how to make nutritious, low-cost meals like pasta and stir-fries, you can save quite a bit on your grocery bill, as well.

But there are some important issues to consider if you decide to move off campus. The first is how you will get to classes. If you decide to bring your car to school, you'll have to pay for upkeep, gas, and on-campus parking. If you take a bus or subway, you'll have to pay the fares—invest in a semester- or year-long pass—and you may find yourself stranded if the buses stop running before the library closes. Depending on your school, you may find an apartment close enough that you can walk or ride a bike, which saves you money and provides daily exercise as a fringe benefit.

Another consideration is your roommates, who will share the responsibilities for paying the bills with you. Even if you are a wise money manager, your friends may not be. Settle issues like how the living space, bedrooms, bathroom use, and bills will be split up before you move in together, rather than waiting until problems develop. Tackle potential areas of contention before they arise; for instance, will boyfriends or girlfriends be allowed to stay over, and how often? Also decide whether you'll share groceries and cooking duties, which is often cheaper, or whether everyone must fend for themselves, which can be more convenient if you all have very different schedules.

Choose one responsible person to be in charge of paying the bills and collecting the other roommates' shares every month; this ensures that bills are paid consistently and on time. But remember that if one roommate can't pay his or her share of the power bill or the rent, you all will suffer. You may want to establish a secret emergency fund to cover these situations if they arise, so you won't have to deal with the hassle and fees involved with getting a utility turned back on.

A more upscale way to save money in college is to play the real estate game. Rather than giving money to a landlord, why not buy a campus-area condo or house? You can supplement your mortgage by renting out extra rooms to other students, and you can pay off a substantial amount of your

Watch Out!
While living off campus may be a good option for your junior or senior year, I don't recommend doing it as a freshman. Students who live off campus during their first year are more likely to have poor grades or drop out. It's much easier to meet people, get to class on time, and take part in campus activities if you live in the dorm.

Moneysaver
If you're married or have children, your school may offer married-student housing or family housing, which is usually a lot cheaper (and more convenient) than an apartment off campus.

college expenses if the property appreciates in value when you sell it. But the last point is a big "if." Despite the promises of real estate brokers, property values sometimes drop. There's no such thing as a no-risk deal. Still, if you have the money, owning your college home is a very attractive option. And if you can't afford it, maybe your parents can.

A very different alternative is cooperative housing. Many colleges offer this on-campus alternative to the dorms, which costs about half the price of a dorm room. What's the catch? You have to do a lot of the housework—cooking, washing dishes, cleaning—in exchange for the reduction in living expenses. Also, you will live with quite a few people in close quarters. But if your school offers it, co-op housing can combine the best of dorm living and off-campus living in one sweet deal.

Saving Money on Everything Else

Watch Out!
Don't buy school supplies or toiletries at the college store unless it's an emergency. The stores off campus—drug stores, grocery stores, Wal-Mart—usually have much lower prices.

Once you get to college, many ways to save money will present themselves that may not have been apparent at home. Students are famous for living in near-poverty. Unless you've joined a class-conscious clique, you may find that near-poverty can be quite genteel.

There are many easy ways to cut the costs of going to college:

- Go to the campus health clinic before going to a private doctor, dentist, or optometrist.

- Buying used books not only saves money, it can give you a head start on underlining your texts.

- If you buy a prepaid meal plan, stick to it instead of going out to eat.

- Stop eating out; cooking your own meals is a lot more cost-effective.

- Buying food from organizations like food co-ops saves a dollar here and there.

- Become an expert at finding free food. Attend free meals sponsored by on-campus vegetarian, cooking, and cultural clubs. Go to art gallery openings, lectures, and other events where you can snack freely. And swing by the grocery store on Saturdays when all the free samples are put out.

- When you go shopping, buy only what you need, and look for generic or sale items; consider joining a price club and buying certain items, such as toilet paper and sodas, in bulk.

- Check the Sunday newspaper for coupons on toiletries and other essentials.

- Well worn clothes and classy Goodwill castoffs can give a certain cachet and save money that you would otherwise spend on a costlier wardrobe.

- Need to spruce up your dorm room? Spend a Saturday afternoon hitting the thrift shops and yard sales (check your local paper) for cheap furnishings and kitschy decorations.

- Make long-distance calls only at night, or cut them out altogether—take up the lost art of letter-writing, or make judicious use of the school's Internet connection to send e-mail to your friends and family.

- Sell your car and buy a bicycle; most college campuses are so self-contained that you don't really need a car anyway, and think of what you'll save in upkeep, gas, and insurance.

- Sell your TV and VCR (you'll probably also see your grades improve, as you spend your free time studying instead of watching the tube).

- Go to the library a lot; besides studying, you can read magazines and newspapers and watch videotapes, all for free.

- Take advantage of free, on-campus entertainment, such as parties, movies, concerts, games, dances, and plays.

- Check out free activities—art galleries, museums, parks, wildlife preserves, lakes, lectures, and book readings, to name a few. A lot of these activities take place on or near campus.

- Don't join a health club; use the on-campus athletic facilities (you've already paid for them with your student fees).

- Take advantage of student discounts—at the movies, when traveling, wherever you go. Remember to carry your student ID with you at all times; you never know when a store or restaurant will offer a special deal to students.

- Quit smoking; you'll save money now (on cigarettes) and later (on health care).

Just the Facts

- It's not easy keeping track of everything it takes to survive a semester at college; plan ahead, so that you can buy what you need at home, where the prices are often cheaper and you're familiar with the stores.

- College life requires a lot of adjustments, and one of the biggest is getting used to living in a dorm and sharing your space with a roommate; it's best to set ground rules before any problems develop.

- You will have to take a certain number and kind of core courses in the major academic disciplines to fulfill graduation requirements, but the subject areas are very broad, so don't be afraid to explore—after all, college is the perfect place to learn something new.

- Academic life at college is very different than at high school; you will have to be more disciplined, develop good study habits, and learn how to manage your time to fit in both studying and social activities.

- College freshmen out on their own for the first time experience some common problems—stress, weight gain, and substance abuse are the biggies; remember that your college has a wide support network in

Moneysaver
If you're a female student with small children, find out whether your school offers free or low-cost daycare. The school of social work often provides this service, which means enthusiastic, careful attention. In any case, the expenses associated with raising kids should be reflected in your financial need, which could get you more aid.

place, including your professors, RA, academic advisor, and health clinic, to help you if you encounter problems.

- You can go to college on a budget if you learn how to manage your money and avoid common traps, such as easy credit; you may even have fun trying to find new and creative ways to economize.

GET THE SCOOP ON...
Deciding whether you need an advanced degree ▪ Graduate and
professional school options ▪ Choosing a college with grad school in
mind ▪ Planning a pre-grad school curriculum ▪ Making the transition from work to graduate school ▪ Choosing a graduate school ▪
How to pay for graduate school

Going on to Graduate School

Many high school students going through the college application process are already thinking ahead—to what they want to do after college. Because you have so many options when it comes to earning a higher degree, and so many choices of universities where you can get that degree, you need to devote a lot of thought and research to your choice of graduate or professional school.

Many college students don't even begin considering graduate or professional school until they've already started coursework in their major. But as an entering freshman, you may already be aware that your field of interest requires a higher degree for you to succeed. If you want to pursue a career in medicine, law, scientific research, or teaching at the college level, you know that your schooling won't stop with a bachelor's degree. By planning now, before you even get to college, you'll be well ahead of the game when it comes time to apply to graduate or professional school.

Why Get an Advanced Degree?

It used to be that a higher degree, particularly a Ph.D., was considered a prerequisite to a college or university teaching career. Not any longer. Because jobs in academe are becoming so scarce (and so low-paying), more and more graduate students are using their degrees to prepare for jobs out in the real world.

Today, fewer than half of new Ph.D.s find permanent employment in academic settings. Wall Street firms recruit among Ph.D.s in math, finance, economics, and computer science. High-tech and management consulting firms search out students with doctorates in varied fields like literature, sociology, and psychology. Chemistry and physics Ph.D.s are regularly recruited to work in investment banking and management consulting, and drug and biotech companies seek out biologists. These companies recognize that individuals with higher degrees are trained to solve problems and function independently.

Chapter 19

Unofficially...
Not every field
requires a higher
degree. Computer
science is one exam-
ple.; the job market
is so lucrative that
computer science
majors can get a
high-level, high-
paying job right out
of college.

Graduate programs have responded to this shift in purpose. More classes are taught by people in industry, rather than by professors. Class projects emphasize situations that students will encounter on the job. And more students are required to complete internships, which can eventually turn into full-time jobs. Graduate schools are also experimenting with interdisciplinary degree programs, because many real-world jobs require working knowledge of several different fields. Also, many graduate programs now require that their students acquire basic business and computer skills, no matter what degree they're pursuing; even medical doctors are learning business skills to help them deal with HMOs.

Another shift is that many graduate and professional schools are revamping their traditional programs to better prepare for today's jobs. For instance, business schools have designed new fields of concentration, like electronic commerce, health care, and brand management. And library science schools now prepare students for jobs in business intelligence, computer network design, and software development.

Therefore, most graduate students pursue a higher degree on the way to a better career. In many fields, a graduate degree leads to higher-level jobs with better paychecks, more responsibility, and more independence. And in some fields, you can't get far without a higher degree. Of course, a medical or law degree is required for all doctors and lawyers. But even engineers typically need to gain a master's degree to advance into management-level positions. Workers in many fields, including engineering, nursing, teaching, and business, often elect to go to graduate school after working for several years so that they can advance to a higher job level or otherwise improve their careers.

Graduate and professional schools don't just attract students looking for better jobs. Students who have discovered a real passion for their fields, and who want to discover new facts, explore new ideas, and contribute something worthwhile to that field, also find great rewards in earning a higher degree. Even retirees return to graduate school just for the love of learning or to pursue an interest in a particular subject.

But graduate school isn't for everyone. Unlike undergraduate education, graduate school focuses on a single field or specialty. Students pursue knowledge in that field at great depth. Therefore, earning a higher degree requires a great love for the subject, a tremendous commitment, and a lot of discipline.

It also requires enormous sacrifice. Graduate school requires a lot of hard work and a high level of discipline. Students who start graduate or professional school immediately after graduating from college delay for several years getting a real job and earning some real money. Graduate and professional school students earn little or no money while studying, and often graduate with both a higher degree and a huge debt load.

To determine whether graduate or professional school is right for you, you need to assess both your abilities—whether you can succeed in the rigorous academic world of graduate school—and the demand for higher degrees in your field. For instance, the demand for MBAs and for physics and chemistry Ph.D.s is great, even in fields tangential to the ones in which the students earned their degrees. But the demand for English Ph.D.s is not so great—a tenured professorship in a college or university is just not a guarantee anymore. Study the statistics to determine whether professionals in your field who hold master's and doctoral degrees routinely get better jobs and higher salaries than those who hold only a bachelor's degree.

Also, factor the cost of graduate or professional school into your decision. Don't forget that most graduate students must take out hefty loans to pay their tuitions and living expenses while they're studying. Will any gains in salary and position make up for these financial sacrifices?

To help you decide, take advantage of the resources at the college or university you attend as an undergraduate. Discuss your higher education plans with your academic advisor; he or she can help you determine whether you're academically qualified for graduate school and can help you plan a curriculum that will prepare you for graduate school work. Talk to graduate students and postdoctoral researchers at your university or to professors who have already earned their higher degrees to get a better idea of what graduate school is actually like. If you attend a university, sit in on a graduate-level class or two. Also, talk to people in the field—practicing lawyers, doctors, business executives, or engineers—to find out what it's like to have a career in that field, what sacrifices are involved, and what the rewards are.

It's not a good idea to decide on graduate or professional school just because you're unsure of what you want to do after college. Without clear goals to motivate you, you'll find it very difficult to make the sacrifices—both personal and financial—demanded by a graduate school education.

You do have time, though. There's no rule that says you have to start graduate or professional school immediately after graduating from college. In fact, many people put off earning a higher degree until they have a year or two of work experience under their belts, and a clearer idea of what they want to accomplish in their careers. The delay won't hurt your admissions prospects, and depending on what you do in the interval, it may actually help. For example, many business and nursing schools require work experience as a prerequisite. Going to work for a while before starting on that higher degree is also a good idea if you feel "burned out" by courses and tests, and you need a break from school for a while.

Just keep in mind that it can be very difficult to give up a good salary or a nice position to go back to school, and returning to the intensity of full-time study can be a struggle. In addition, many students find it easier to finance and devote the necessary time to graduate study when their lives aren't full of other obligations, such as a mortgage, a marriage, or children. But it's important to realize that you have options—just because you don't

Bright Idea
If you have Internet access, check out the newsgroup soc.college.grad, where you can chat with current graduate school students and get advice on whether graduate school is right for you.

Unofficially...
More than half of all graduate students are over 30 years old, and nearly a quarter are over 40. The average master's candidate is a working woman in her 30s who goes to school part-time.

Unofficially...
A popular new "hybrid" degree is the MD/Ph.D., which takes about three years more to earn than an MD does and provides training in research not offered in most MD programs.

start graduate school right out of college doesn't mean that you'll never earn a higher degree.

Your Graduate School Options

While you can earn a higher degree in pretty much any field and specialty, you have four broad options that determine what kind of degree you'll earn and what kind of graduate or professional school you'll attend:

- To earn a master's or Doctor of Philosophy (Ph.D.) degree in any of the academic disciplines, you must attend a graduate program in that field at a university.
- To earn a Master of Business Administration (MBA) degree, you must attend a business school.
- To earn a Doctor of Law (JD) degree and prepare yourself for taking the bar exam, you must attend a law school.
- To earn a Doctor of Medicine (MD) degree and become a medical doctor, you must attend a medical school.

There are big differences among these programs. Depending on which kind of higher degree you intend to earn, the courses you take in college, and even the college you attend, will be different. Getting admitted will require taking a different kind of standardized test for each program, and each kind of program has very different admissions standards—some highly value work and volunteer experience, others consider grades and personal statements to be the most important factors, and still others regard letters of recommendation as crucial. And the time and financial commitment required by each kind of program also varies greatly. This chapter will help you sort out the differences between your graduate and professional school options, so you can better prepare for the program of your choice.

Getting a Master's or Ph.D.

If your chosen field is in the arts, humanities, natural sciences, or social sciences, you'll pursue a master's and perhaps a Ph.D. in that field. Often you earn your degree in a specialty of your field.

A master's degree typically takes between one and three years to complete. During that time, you take a set curriculum in subjects in your field that aren't usually covered in undergraduate programs. Sometimes you also must write a thesis.

The master's degree is intended to prepare students to practice a profession or to continue on to more advanced study. While a master's degree is often earned on the way to a Ph.D., many students stop at this level. Getting a master's degree requires less time and commitment than getting a Ph.D., but it can often lead to careers with greater responsibility and higher pay than a Bachelor's degree alone. Having a master's degree is also useful for those students who want to teach at the high school or community college level.

Some master's degrees aren't intended to lead to doctoral study. These are called terminal master's, because they terminate at the master's level. Library science (MLS), architecture (M.Arch.) and fine arts (MFA) are examples of terminal master's. Terminal master's are highly valued in their fields and can help you earn a promotion or a higher salary. They can even lead to unexpected career paths. For example, a MLS is now seen as a stepping stone to a lucrative career in information technology. Similarly, an MFA can lead to a career in industrial design or computer graphics. Individuals who hold terminal master's are also qualified to teach at the college or university level in their fields.

One kind of terminal master's degree—called a professional master's—is highly valued in certain fields like social work, public health, engineering, nursing, microbiology, bioengineering, computer science, and environmental studies. These programs teach specific job-related skills like project management, complex problem-solving, counseling, and risk analysis. Internships or fieldwork often enhance the degree program. A professional master's may be the only way to advance to jobs with higher levels of responsibility and the higher salaries that go along with that.

If your goal is to perform scientific research or teach at the college and university level, or if the best jobs in your field require one, you might go on to earn a Ph.D. Ph.D.s also hold high-level jobs in major corporations, educational institutions, and state or federal government, and they serve as directors of museums and major libraries.

Doctoral programs last between three and eight years; five years is the average. The program is essentially an apprenticeship consisting of lecture and lab courses, seminars, exams, discussions, independent study, research, and teaching.

After passing departmental exams, the Ph.D. student enters candidacy under the supervision of a faculty advisor and dissertation committee. During candidacy, the student performs original research on a topic of his or her choice, writes a dissertation describing that research, and orally defends the dissertation before the faculty committee. Candidacy normally lasts two to four years, although this period has recently increased.

After earning a Ph.D., your schooling doesn't necessarily stop. In some fields like biology and chemistry, one or more years of postdoctoral experience are also required. This consists of a short-term appointment with a university, research institution, government agency, or corporation, in which the postdoctoral student gains in-depth research skills.

Obviously, you have many choices when it comes to deciding whether to pursue a master's or doctoral degree and what kind of degree to earn. You should spend a lot of time researching the options in your chosen field. If you'd like more information about pursuing a master's or Ph.D., the following organizations can provide it:

Bright Idea
Earning a master's degree can be a good way to change career directions completely. You can earn a master's degree in a completely different subject than the one you majored in during college and thus prepare yourself for an entirely new line of work. It may take you longer to earn the degree than it would if you already had a bachelor's degree in the subject, but it can be the ticket to a new life.

Unofficially...
Over a 40-year career, the average Ph.D. will earn $3 million, compared to $1.6 million for someone with a bachelor's degree.

- American Society for Engineering Education (ASEE): 1818 N Street NW, Suite 600, Washington, D.C. 20036-2479, (202) 331-3500, http://www.asee.org/

- Association for Library and Information Science Education (ALISE): PO Box 7640, Arlington, VA 22207, (703) 243-8040, http://www.alise.org/

- Association for Support of Graduate Students (ASGS): PO Box 4698, Incline Village, NV 89450-4698, (702) 831-1399, asgs@asgs.org, http://www.asgs.org/

- Association of Professional Schools of International Affairs (APSIA): Executive Office, 1400 K Street NW, Suite 650, Washington, D.C. 20005-2403, (202) 326-7828, apsia@erols.com, http://www.apsia.org/

- Council of Graduate Schools (CGS): One Dupont Circle NW, Suite 430, Washington, D.C. 20036-1173, (202) 223-3791, http://www.cgsnet.org/

- National Association of Graduate-Professional Students (NAGPS): 825 Green Bay Rd., Suite 270, Wilmette, IL 60091, 1 (888) 88-NAGPS, nagps@netcom.com, http://www.nagps.org/index_high.html

Going to Business School

The MBA is a professional master's degree, intended for students who plan to pursue careers in business and management at the managerial and executive levels. Getting an MBA is also relevant for preparation for management positions in government and in the public sector. Holders of MBAs have a better chance of being offered interesting positions and higher salaries than their colleagues with bachelor's degrees, especially when they combine their higher degrees with practical business achievements. MBA programs normally last two years, although in recent years the trend has been toward shorter programs with a more focused specialty.

A special kind of MBA called an Executive MBA (EMBA) has recently become a popular choice. This program enables experienced professionals to obtain an MBA in a way that minimizes disruption of work responsibilities. An EMBA program takes two years or less to complete and is usually fully sponsored by the student's employer. Typical candidates already hold managerial or executive positions and have at least 10 years of work experience.

Watch Out!
While one-year MBA courses cost less than a traditional two-year program, they are very intensive and are not widely offered in the United States. They also allow less time to study difficult business issues in-depth.

To obtain more information about business schools and earning an MBA, contact the following organizations:

- Graduate Management Admission Council (GMAC): 8300 Greensboro Dr., Suite 750, McLean, VA 22102, (703) 749-0131, gmacmail@gmac.com, http://www.gmat.org/

- International Association for Management Education: 600 Emerson Rd., Suite 300, St. Louis, MO 63141-6762, (314) 872-8481, http://www.aacsb.edu/

Going to Law School

It probably doesn't surprise you that the number-one reason most students go to law school is to become a lawyer. A degree from an American Bar Association-certified law school is required to be admitted to the bar in every state, and you must be a member of the bar to practice law. But a law degree is marketable in a variety of professions, not just the law—which is a good thing, because a glut of law school graduates has made it more difficult to establish a law practice or get a position with a good firm. In law school, you'll develop good analytic and communications skills, which are essential to every professional field.

If you'd like more information about getting a law degree, contact the following organizations:

- American Bar Association (ABA): 750 N Lake Shore Dr., Chicago, IL 60611, (312) 988-5000, legaled@abanet.org, http://www.abanet.org/legaled/

- Association of American Law Schools (AALS): 1201 Connecticut Ave. NW, Suite 800, Washington, D.C. 20036-2605, (202) 296-8851, aals@aals.org, http://www.aals.org/

- Law School Admission Council (LSAC): PO Box 40, Newtown, PA 18940, (215) 968-1001, LSACinfo@LSAC.org, http://www.lsac.org/

Going to Medical School

If you want to be a doctor of any specialty, you have to go to medical school—probably the most rigorous and expensive of all the professional schools. Most students decide to enter medical school directly after graduating from college, but that trend is changing. Increasingly, students are waiting until they receive some work experience or until they obtain a master's degree in a relevant field, such as bioengineering or nursing, before they tackle the grueling years of medical school.

If medical school isn't for you, you don't necessarily have to become a doctor to pursue a rewarding career in the health professions. You can get a higher degree in several health-related specialties, ranging from nursing to veterinary medicine to pharmacy.

If you'd like more information about taking the path to medical school, contact the following organizations:

- American Medical Association (AMA) Medical Student Section: 515 N State St., Chicago, IL 60610, (312) 464-5000, http://www.ama-assn.org/ama/pub/category/0,1120,14,FF.html

- American Medical Student Association (AMSA): 1902 Association Dr., Reston, VA 20191, (703) 620-6600, amsa@www.amsa.org, http://www.amsa.org/

- Association of American Medical Colleges (AAMC): 2450 N Street NW, Washington, D.C. 20037-1126, (202) 828-0400, amcas@aamc.org, http://www.aamc.org/

Unofficially...
Internal medicine is the most popular medical school concentration, with family practice coming in second.

Bright Idea
If you have Internet access, drop in on misc.education.medical, a newsgroup devoted to talking about medical school. You'll find a lot of good advice on choosing a medical school and getting in. Be sure to read the FAQ at http://www.stanford.edu/~epw/mem/faq/.

Selecting a Pre-Grad School College

If you already are fairly certain that you will want to attend graduate or professional school after getting your Bachelor's degree, then you're well ahead of your colleagues. You can look for colleges that offer strong preparatory courses in your field and send a large number of undergrads on to earn a higher degree. Then, when the time comes to apply for graduate school, your chances for admission will be improved because you attended a college that graduate and professional schools recruit from heavily.

While searching for colleges to apply to, look for schools that offer a strong academic program in the field that you intend to pursue all the way through to the graduate level. If you think you might go to law school or medical school, search out colleges that offer strong pre-law or pre-med curricula.

Another important characteristic of colleges to consider is the percentage of graduates that go on to pursue a higher degree. If the percentage rate is low, then that college's advising, reputation, curriculum, and student quality are lacking, which will make it more difficult for you to get accepted into graduate or professional school out of that college.

Don't just look at the raw numbers, though. Find out which specific graduate or professional programs most graduating students enter. Also, determine which universities and professional schools most graduates of the college attend. If the college's students consistently enter strong graduate programs, that means that the college has prepared them well for graduate school and that the best universities are recruiting students from that college.

Determine how much support the college gives to undergraduates who are on the graduate or professional school track. Does the college help undergraduates search for a graduate school, prepare for interviews and for writing personal statements, and study for the standardized tests? Are pre-law and pre-med advisors available to help you choose the right courses and groom yourself for being accepted into competitive schools?

Also consider the opportunities that you will get while attending the college. Graduate and professional schools value applicants with diverse experiences, both inside their fields and outside of them. If your college offers plenty of chances for research with professors, internships, study abroad, and volunteer experience, you can mold yourself into a better candidate for graduate or professional school.

Finally, think about the competition that you will encounter at that college. Graduate and professional schools won't accept all of their students from one college, no matter how many qualified applicants that college produces. Just like undergraduate admissions committees, they look for diversity when making up their classes. Therefore, a pre-med student at Harvard will have a lot of trouble standing out, because so many other highly qualified pre-med students go there, and competition for spots in

Watch Out!
Private colleges generally have more resources to offer students on the graduate school track than public schools do, especially for pre-law and pre-med students. Private schools often provide stronger advising support, for instance.

medical schools will be fierce. You may have an easier time getting into graduate school if you choose an undergraduate college where you know you'll be at the top of your class and won't be squeezed out by the competition.

Planning Your Undergrad Curriculum with Grad School in Mind

If you start college knowing that eventually you want to go to graduate or professional school, you're in a very good position. You can plan your curriculum and extracurricular activities to make yourself a more attractive candidate for the type of graduate or professional school that you want to attend. You can also use your undergraduate years to build contacts among your professors, employers, mentors, and fellow students that will help you garner recommendations for graduate school and will continue to be useful throughout your career.

During your undergraduate years, you have the best opportunity to take a broad selection of courses outside your chosen academic field that may be useful in your later career or if you want to pursue a higher degree. For example, a mathematics major who takes an accounting course or two is better equipped to do actuarial work. And an ecology major will gain perspective from courses in environmental engineering or environmental policy. Use your undergraduate years to explore different subjects and build a broad base for your later education. Graduate and professional schools value well rounded applicants, and you'll never have the chance again to take such a variety of courses. Sit down with your academic advisor to plan a well-rounded courseload that will best prepare you for graduate or professional school.

Your academic courses make up only part of your college life. Use this time to gain experience outside the classroom that will make you a better candidate for graduate or professional school. Choose extracurricular activities, volunteer service, internships, and part-time jobs that demonstrate your commitment to your chosen field and help you develop the qualities you need to succeed in that field. Establish relationships with your professors and the people you work with in your field; those are the people who you will call upon to write the impressive letters of recommendation you need to be accepted into graduate or professional school.

While anyone on the track to graduate or professional school should follow these suggestions, you can do other things during the undergraduate years depending on the type of higher degree program that you want to pursue. Those activities are described in the remainder of this section.

Preparing to Earn a Master's Degree or Ph.D.

While taking the right classes and earning high grades and test scores are certainly a big help in getting admitted to graduate school, they aren't as important as they were when you applied to college. One of the biggest

Unofficially...
Many of the country's leading universities are not among the top-ranked schools when it comes to sending their own undergraduates to graduate school. Small, private, liberal arts colleges are much more successful, including well known schools like Reed, Swarthmore, Oberlin, and Amherst and lesser-known schools like Wabash, Davidson, Occidental, and Birmingham-Southern.

Bright Idea
Join the student chapters of academic and professional societies in your field—these groups can provide valuable networking opportunities.

plusses for graduate school applicants is having solid research experience as an undergraduate. Another extremely important factor is a letter of recommendation from a professor who knows you well—ideally, a mentor who guided you in a lengthy research project.

As an undergraduate, choose research projects with the thought of how they will help you present yourself to graduate schools. Look for opportunities to perform research in your field. And get to know all of your professors very well, as they may be instrumental in leading you to research opportunities or writing letters of recommendation for you.

Graduate schools look for applicants who have demonstrated a commitment to their fields. The best way to do this is to gain practical experience as an undergraduate. Look for opportunities like part-time jobs, internships, and volunteer positions that are related in some way to the field you want to study as a graduate student.

The exceptions to this rule include graduate engineering programs, where test scores, recommendations, and especially the undergraduate GPA count more heavily than for other graduate programs. Also, many candidates for graduate engineering programs gain at least a couple of years of work experience before applying to graduate schools.

No matter what kind of graduate school program you apply to, you have to take the Graduate Record Exam (GRE) first. The GRE is like a super version of the SAT I; some graduate schools also require a GRE subject test in your field. For more information about registering for and taking the GRE, contact:

GRE-ETS
PO Box 6000
Princeton, NJ 08541-6000
(609) 771-7670
E-mail: gre-info@ets.org
http://www.gre.org/

Preparing for Business School

Business schools don't require a major in a specific subject. MBA students hold bachelor's degrees in a variety of fields—in the sciences, technical fields, social sciences, and humanities. But whatever your degree, a strong background in math is essential.

Business schools value high undergraduate GPAs and test scores. They also look for applicants with a diversity of experiences. Recommendations from many different people, including professors and employers, can be pivotal.

More than any other type of professional school, business schools value applicants with work experience. Very few applicants are accepted into an MBA program straight out of college. Instead, they must acquire at least two years (and usually more) of practical on-the-job experience.

Bright Idea
If you plan to go to graduate or professional school immediately after college, take the appropriate standardized test during your junior year. The result of your GRE (or other test), your GPA, and your advisor's opinion will help you decide whether you have the potential for graduate school.

Applicants for business schools take the Graduate Management Aptitude Test (GMAT). For more information about this standardized test, contact:

GMAT
Educational Testing Services
PO Box 6103
Princeton, NJ 08541-6103
1 (800) GMAT-NOW
E-mail: gmat@ets.org
http://www.gmat.org/gmat_frames.html

Preparing for Law School

When judging applicants, law schools look at the difficulty of the undergraduate courses that you take, your analytical and writing skills, and any out-of-class experiences that distinguish you from other applicants.

You don't have to major in any particular subject, but you should major in a field that helps you develop the skills that will be valuable to you as a law student—mainly reading, researching, writing, and critical analysis. Most pre-law students major in a field in the humanities or social sciences, such as history, English, political science, or philosophy. Choose a major that greatly interests you; if you have a great passion for the subject, you'll earn better grades in your major classes, and you'll make a more attractive candidate to law schools.

Most colleges don't have an established pre-law curriculum, so it's left up to you to choose the appropriate courses to prepare you for law school. To make yourself a better law school candidate, take courses in a wide variety of disciplines outside your major. Important subjects to take as an undergraduate include the following:

- Diversity courses, to gain an understanding of the diverse cultures in the US and global issues
- Economics—concentrating on microeconomics and public policy
- Ethics
- Finance—to learn how to analyze financial data
- History—concentrating on American history
- Mathematics
- Political science—concentrating on American politics
- Psychology—to gain a basic understanding of human behavior
- Sociology—to gain a basic understanding of social interaction

More and more students now take a year or more off before going on to law school. These students use the extra time to work in a law firm to get a sense of whether law school is right for them. At the same time, they earn money that they can use to help pay for law school and gain valuable work experience that will improve their chances for admission.

Timesaver
Many colleges offer pre-professional majors to help you prepare for entering a professional school, including pre-business, pre-law, pre-med, pre-vet, pre-nursing, pre-engineering, and pre-seminary curricula.

Unofficially...
Having work experience is particularly helpful to borderline grad school applicants. Someone with mediocre grades and accomplishments won't look very attractive to a law or engineering school. But if that same person works for a year as a paralegal or in a software company and gains the glowing recommendation of the boss, he or she will make a much better candidate.

Law schools rely heavily on the Law School Assessment Test (LSAT) to provide a level playing field for applicants from various colleges and from the workforce. Take the exam junior year to allow time for a retest if you need to improve your scores. For more information about the LSAT, contact:

LSAT
Law School Admission Council
PO Box 40
Newtown, PA 18940
(215) 968-1001
E-mail: LSACinfo@LSAC.org
http://www.lsac.org/lsac1.htm

Preparing for Medical School

Competition to get into medical school is fierce, so anything you can do as an undergraduate to make yourself stand out to admissions committees will greatly help your chances. Medical schools heavily weigh applicants' personal traits—traits like intelligence, curiosity, personal maturity, communication skills, and an ability to work with people.

They also look for an applicant's commitment to his or her chosen profession. Clinical work experience as an undergraduate can demonstrate this commitment. For example, you might volunteer several hours a week as a paramedic or in a hospital or clinic. Letters of recommendation from professors and from doctors and nurses that you work with will count heavily in your favor.

Pre-med is a major in itself, but since most colleges don't offer a pre-med major, it will be up to you to make certain that you have completed all the courses as an undergraduate that medical schools expect to see on your transcript. These courses include the following:

- Biology (at least one year)

- Chemistry (at least two years through organic chemistry, with labs)

- English composition (at least one year)

- Mathematics (at least one year)

- Physics (at least one year with a lab)

Bright Idea
Pre-law and pre-med students should major in something they particularly enjoy and that they can fall back on if they decide not to go on to professional school, or if they don't have the test scores and grades to get in.

Your major subject is left up to you. You don't have to major in a science, so choose a major that best fits your interests and where you'll earn the best grades. Medical schools care more about your GPA than about the subject that you majored in.

For those students majoring in biology, chemistry, or biochemistry, the pre-med requirements are integrated within your major's requirements (but don't forget to take physics!). Non-science majors must demonstrate that they can complete the scientific coursework required in medical school. It's a good idea to complete the required science courses as early as possible, so you can take the Medical College Admission Test (MCAT) well ahead of when you graduate.

For more information on the MCAT, contact the following:

MCAT Program Office
PO Box 4056
Iowa City, IA 52243
(319) 337-1357
http://www.aamc.org/stuapps/admiss/mcat/

Being a pre-med student is pretty grueling (but that's just a warm-up for medical school). Be prepared for difficult classes, long hours in the lab, and a lot of competition. Always remember to stay focused on your goal—getting accepted into a good medical school.

More students now take some time off before medical school. This gives them a breather from the rigors of study and an opportunity to beef up medical school applications by traveling, working, or volunteering in a health-related field. Taking time off also gives potential medical students the chance to figure out whether they really want to be doctors; some even go to law school or graduate school first before tackling medical school.

Preparing for Nursing School

The most important quality for nursing school applicants is what they have accomplished in the health-care field. Most master's programs in nursing require at least one year of prior clinical experience. Activities like community service also help an applicant to stand out. Finally, nursing school applicants need to demonstrate not only scientific knowledge, analytical ability, and practical know-how, but also compassion, dedication, and people skills.

Entering Graduate School from the Workplace

As I've stressed throughout this chapter, it has become a growing trend for college students to enter the workplace for several years before going after that higher degree. This path offers several advantages. You have more time to figure out what your career goals and interests are. You won't become burned out by too many years of continuous study. You can earn some money and save against the cost of graduate school. And you gain work experience that can, in many cases, improve your chances for admission into a graduate or professional school. As you've already learned, many graduate programs—including engineering, nursing, and business schools—actually require work experience and value it more highly than college grades and standardized test scores when making admission decisions.

But taking some time off between college and graduate school doesn't mean that you can slack off. Graduate school admissions officers will look closely at what you did during that time and will want to know why you are a better candidate for graduate school as a result of those activities.

If you join the workforce for a few years before applying to graduate school, use your work experience to make yourself look like a more valuable applicant. For example, many Internet and computer software companies hire employees right out of college. Spending a few years designing software or managing a website can make you a very attractive candidate for engineering, library science, computer science, or even business graduate programs.

But you don't necessarily have to hold down a traditional job during your time off. For instance, volunteering for organizations like the Peace Corps can be a good transition to medical school or a school of public affairs. Even your activities outside of work can reflect highly on you. For example, volunteering on a political campaign can boost your chances for admission to law school. If you pursue your interests passionately and use your time wisely, graduate schools will be impressed by your "real-world" accomplishments.

Choosing a Graduate School

You spent a lot of time selecting which colleges to apply to and where to go. You should spend even more time choosing a graduate program or professional school. While the specific steps of choosing a graduate school depend largely on your field of study, this section outlines some general tips that every potential graduate student should follow.

The following are the most important characteristics to search for in a graduate or professional school:

- *Quality:* At the graduate level, department reputation is extremely important. Find out who the faculty of the program are, what research they have done, and how their interests match yours. If you plan to attend a professional school, find out about the faculty members' work experience. Published guides to specific programs and search sites like the ones listed in Appendix B, "College Admissions Resource Guide," will help you locate the best programs in your field.

- *Job placement services:* The university's career center should provide statistics on what percentage of students find work in their fields, who hires them, and how much they get paid. Also, find out whether the career center regularly sends students job and internship announcements.

- *Cost:* Don't choose a program until you have received all financial aid offers. Find out whether the funding offered to you will be available every year you are in graduate or professional school.

- *Location:* Go to graduate or professional school in the area where you want to work. It will be easier for you to practice law in California if you graduate from a California law school, for instance. Also, consider whether the school is located in an urban or rural setting. While urban schools are often more expensive, they are also closer to major

Bright Idea
Many graduate school applications require a personal statement—an open-ended essay. If you took time off after college and did something unusual, the personal statement is the perfect opportunity to explain why you did it and what you learned from your unique experiences.

corporations and research centers where you will eventually want to seek work.

Paying for Graduate School

Finding the financial resources to go to graduate or professional school is not easy. It is difficult to hold down a full-time job while earning a higher degree. Therefore, graduate students must rely heavily on financial aid to pay not only their tuition costs, but all of their living expenses.

Graduate students are classified as independent students when applying for financial aid. That means that most students qualify for more need-based financial aid as graduate students than they did as undergraduates, because only their own incomes and assets are considered when calculating financial need (and their spouses', if they're married).

Unfortunately, grants and scholarships aren't widely available for graduate students, particularly from the federal government. Most graduate students rely heavily on loans to pay the way, counting on the higher salaries that they will earn once they get their degrees to pay back their debt. Depending on the type of graduate program you're entering, you may also gain financial assistance in the form of fellowships, grants, assistantships, and employer reimbursement.

The following are the major sources of financial aid for graduate students:

- *Federal Work-Study:* As at the undergraduate level, work-study awards are based on financial need. Your salary generally hovers around minimum wage.

- *Federal Perkins Loans:* Graduate students with exceptional financial need can borrow up to $40,000 total, less the amount they borrowed as undergraduates. Repayment begins nine months after graduation, and the interest rate is five percent.

- *Subsidized Stafford Loans:* These loans are awarded based on financial need. The government pays interest charges while you earn your degree, at a maximum interest rate of 8.25 percent. As a graduate student, you may borrow up to $8500 per year to a maximum of $65,500, less whatever you borrowed as an undergrad. Repayment begins six months after you receive your degree.

- *Unsubsidized Federal Stafford Loans:* Graduate students can borrow up to $10,000 per year to a maximum of $73,000, regardless of financial need. Repayment begins 60 days after the loan is disbursed, but it may be deferred if you are a full-time student. Interest continues to accrue during the time of deferment. The maximum interest rate is 8.25 percent.

- *State aid:* While many states offer grants and loans to graduate students, most aid programs are limited only to certain kinds of graduate programs, such as medical school and the other health professions, or are

Bright Idea
Ask your college professors to recommend graduate programs and professors in your field. Your college career center can also help.

Unofficially...
Financial support for graduate school is most abundant for students in the hard sciences. The National Science Foundation, for example, awards 1000 fellowships worth $15,000 each year.

aimed solely at women and minorities. To receive this aid, you must usually remain in your home state for graduate school. Check with your state's financial aid agency to learn more (see Appendix D, Important Addresses").

- *Research and teaching assistantships:* Assistantships are most commonly given to Ph.D. students and can pay for the cost of tuition plus a small stipend.

- *Departmental grants:* These awards are controlled by the chair of the academic department where you will complete your graduate school program, rather than by the university's financial aid office.

- *Internships:* Your professor may hook you up with a short-term job at a major corporation, with good pay and even better experience.

- *Employee benefits:* Your current employer may subsidize your graduate-level education to groom you for a higher-level position with the company.

- *Cooperative education:* These programs are just like undergraduate cooperative education programs, but at the graduate level. For more information, contact the National Commission for Cooperative Education at 360 Huntington Ave., 384CP, Boston, MA 02115-5096, ncce@lynx.neu.edu, http://www.co-op.edu/.

Moneysaver
Graduate students can deduct some of the interest they pay on education loans. The maximum deduction will be $2000 in the year 2000 and $2500 in 2001.

Many students attend graduate school part-time and work to help pay the way. Besides helping to pay the bills, working can also be a valuable way to gain practical experience in your field while earning your degree. For example, the majority of doctoral candidates receive assistantships that allow them to teach or perform research while earning a Ph.D. Graduate assistantships also are commonly available in many master's programs. And many professional master's programs, such as nursing, engineering, and business programs, offer flexible class schedules that enable students to keep on working while getting the degree.

But if you do go to graduate school part-time, it will take you longer to earn your degree, and it may be difficult to get some kinds of financial aid. Also, be aware that some types of graduate work, particularly at the highest levels, require a full-time commitment. Some graduate programs won't even accept part-time students. If you go to law school or medical school, maintaining an outside job—indeed a life of any kind—is pretty much impossible. For those programs, it makes more sense to borrow the money that you need to pay tuition and to live on, and pay your debt back later from the increased earnings that you'll receive with a higher degree.

The costs of graduate and professional school, and the available sources of financial aid, differ greatly depending on what kind of higher degree you're pursuing. The rest of this section describes in general the major sources of financial aid for each kind of graduate program. Before applying to graduate school, thoroughly research the costs of the particular degree program that you want to pursue and the financial aid resources available for that particular program.

Paying for a Master's or Ph.D.

Financial aid is scarce for terminal master's candidates. If you go back to school from the workforce or work part-time while getting your degree, your employer may assist with paying for your education, particularly in fields like engineering. Stafford loans and private loans are another major source of support for terminal master's candidates.

Much more financial support is available for doctoral candidates. Very few Ph.D. candidates pay the full cost of graduate school. The majority—75 percent—work as research or teaching assistants at their universities, which pays for tuition plus a stipend of between $8000 and $16,000 per year. Assistantships are awarded by the graduate program that you attend, and the amount of money awarded depends largely on the graduate program's funding. Because assistantships pay so little, many doctoral candidates end up taking out an education loan to help pay the bills.

Other common sources of financial aid for both master's and Ph.D. candidates include the following:

- Fellowships from private foundations

- Paid summer internships

- Tuition reimbursement from your future employer

- Loan forgiveness programs for degree-holders entering underserved areas, public service, or needed professions

Paying for Business School

Business school is expensive—$25,000 or more a year, on average. Most MBA students finance their degrees through a combination of personal savings, scholarships, and loans.

Business schools offer many scholarships, but they tend to go only to the top students and to students from diverse backgrounds. Other sources of scholarships are employers and private foundations.

Two-thirds of MBA students require loans to pay their way. They borrow Stafford loans, state-sponsored loans, and low-interest loans sponsored by the Graduate Management Admission Council. Several private lenders also offer loans that are customized to the needs of MBA students, including the Access Group, Citibank, Key Education Resources, Nellie Mae, Sallie Mae, and The Education Resources Institute (refer back to Chapter 16, "Looking Elsewhere for Aid," for contact information).

Paying for Law School

Law students typically spend more than $125,000 total for their degrees. The vast majority of law students—around 75 percent—rely on loans, especially federal Stafford loans. Law school loans are also available from several private lenders, including the Access Group, Key Education Resources,

Moneysaver
If you go to graduate school immediately after graduating from college, you can defer repaying your federal student loans while you're earning a higher degree. Most private education loans also allow you to defer repayment while you attend graduate school, as well.

Unofficially...
A strong graduate program is more likely to receive research grants and to pass that money on to students in the form of assistantships.

Moneysaver
The Consortium for Graduate Study in Management is a group of 11 universities offering 180 full-tuition fellowships yearly to African-American, Hispanic American, and Native American students pursuing MBAs. For more information, contact the Consortium at 1 (888) 658-6814 or at http://www.cgsm.wustl.edu:8010/.

Nellie Mae, Sallie Mae, and The Education Resources Institute (refer back to Chapter 16 for contact information).

There isn't a lot of additional financial aid money available for law students. Law schools do have some grant and scholarship money to give, but these awards typically go to the top students and to students who bring diversity to their classes. Some law schools have also established loan repayment or forgiveness programs for graduates who enter public service.

Paying for Medical School

Medical school is not cheap. Tuition and fees for first-year medical students average $11,000 per year at public, in-state medical schools and $27,000 per year at private medical schools. Also, medical schools do not have a lot of financial aid funds to award, so students must look to outside sources for support.

Medical students rely heavily on loans—both federal and private—to pay for their medical degrees. Besides the Stafford Loan program, the federal government offers Health Profession Student Loans (HPSL), a need-based loan program that enables medical students to borrow tuition plus $2500 a year at five percent interest. Medical students can also turn to low-interest loan programs like the MEDLOANS Alternative Loan Program, sponsored by the American Association of Medical Colleges, or to private lenders like the Access Group, Citibank, Education Funding Services, IHELP, Key Education Resources, MEDFUNDS, Nellie Mae, Sallie Mae, and The Education Resources Institute.

Grants and scholarships are scarce for medical students. If you develop clear-cut career goals, you may be able to win some awards from professional associations in your specialty.

As for nursing school and the other health professions, these programs have attracted a wide range of federal, state, and private funds to ensure that enough people are trained to meet the growing demand. For example, the National Health Service Corps offers competitive scholarships—full tuition plus a stipend—in return for service in an underserved area.

Just the Facts

- Graduate degrees aren't just for professors, lawyers, and doctors anymore; in many diverse fields, a higher degree leads to a better-paying job that carries more responsibility and independence.

- There are four broad kinds of graduate programs: programs that lead to a master's or doctoral degree; MBA programs; law schools; and medical schools.

- If you already know that you want to attend graduate or professional school after graduating from college, start off on the right foot by choosing a college that sends a large percentage of undergraduates to prestigious programs in your chosen field and that will adequately prepare you for earning a higher degree.

- As an undergraduate, you can improve your chances for admission to graduate or professional school by taking challenging courses in a wide range of subjects, gaining volunteer and work experience in your field, and developing relationships with your professors and employers.

- More people take time off to work or volunteer before going to graduate or professional school; this real-world experience often helps them present themselves as more attractive applicants.

- When selecting a graduate program or professional school, the reputations of the department and its faculty are the most important criteria.

- Getting a higher degree requires a financial sacrifice; while some grant, scholarship, and assistantship money is available for graduate students, most students rely heavily on loans to pay for tuition and living expenses while they're earning their degrees.

Glossary of College Admissions Terms

4-1-4 or 4-4-1 calendar   Academic calendar used by some schools, consisting of two semesters of four months, with a one-month-long semester between or following them.

academic advisor   College faculty member who assists undergraduate students in selecting academic courses and programs, and who often provides general counseling, as well.

academic calendar   The period that makes up the school year, usually divided into two terms (semesters), three terms (trimesters), or four terms (quarters).

academic probation   The status of a college student whose grades have fallen below the college's minimum acceptable standard; during this period, the student must maintain a certain GPA, or the student may be expelled.

academic year   Period of study usually consisting of two semesters or three quarters or trimesters, each with a certain amount of credit hours, which determines a student's classification as freshman, sophomore, junior, or senior.

accelerated degree program   Program offered by some colleges that allows students to earn a bachelor's or higher degree in fewer years than it would normally take to complete the course of study.

accreditation   Seal of approval by a general regional accrediting agency or a specific academic-area accrediting agency, indicating that an institution of higher learning has been recognized as providing an adequate education.

ACT   See *American College Testing Assessment*.

admission requirements   Standards set by a college or university, including high school courses, GPA, and standardized test scores, that applicants must meet to be considered for admission.

admissions committee   The group of admissions officers who collectively read applications and makes acceptance decisions for a school.

admissions officer   Member of a college's admissions staff who recruits potential students, reads applications, and helps decide which applicants are admitted.

admissions plans   All the options offered by a college or university to students for how to apply; admissions plans include regular admission, early decision, early action, and rolling admission.

Advanced Placement (AP)   Refers to college freshman-level courses taken during high school and the exams administered by the College Board that are given to students after they complete such a course. Colleges use AP exam scores to exempt students from required courses.

Affidavit of Support   Certification from a bank that an international student has sufficient funds to pay the entire tuition and living expenses while attending college in the United States. An Affidavit of Support may be required before a college will admit a foreign applicant or before the American Consulate will issue a student visa.

alternative loan   See *private loan.*

American College Testing (ACT) Assessment   A national standardized college admission exam, widely given in the West and Midwest.

AP   See *advanced placement.*

application   Form that students fill out to request admission to colleges and universities and all supporting materials, including transcripts, test scores, essays, and letters of recommendation.

application fee   The fee charged to cover the cost of processing a college application. Typical application fees range from $30 to $50. Many colleges waive the fee for students who can demonstrate financial need.

assistantship   Financial aid awarded to graduate students that pays tuition and a stipend in exchange for research or teaching work.

associate's degree   Degree granted after completing a two-year program—generally a technical or vocational program—at a community college.

audit   To sit in on a class without earning credit for the course.

award letter   The official document issued by the financial aid office that lists all of the financial aid that has been awarded to a student. The letter breaks down the aid package by the amount, source, and type of aid, includes the terms and conditions of granting the aid, and notes the total Cost of Attendance.

award year   The academic year for which financial aid is requested.

BA   See *bachelor's degree.*

bachelor's degree   Degree awarded by a college upon successful completion of a four- or five-year program of study in the liberal arts, sciences, or professional areas. Depending on their majors, college graduates earn either a Bachelor of Arts (BA) or Bachelor of Science (BS) degree.

base year Twelve-month period ending on December 31 preceding the year for which financial aid is sought. The financial aid award is based on earnings and assets reported to the IRS for the base year.

block plan Academic calendar under which students take one class at a time; classes generally last three-and-a-half weeks.

BS See *bachelor's degree.*

bursar Office responsible for accepting tuition payments and disbursing emergency loans, financial aid checks, and refunds.

business school Graduate-level professional school that awards students an MBA degree.

campus-based program Federal Supplemental Educational Opportunity Grants, Federal Work-Study, and Federal Perkins Loan programs. These programs are called "campus-based" because the financial aid office at the school administers them from a fixed pool of federal funds.

candidacy Period during which a doctoral candidate performs original research and writes a dissertation.

candidate notification date Date by which a school notifies an applicant of its acceptance decision.

candidate reply date Date by which students must notify colleges that have accepted them whether they will attend that school in the fall; for most colleges, this date is May 1.

capitalization Postponement of paying accrued interest on an education loan; the interest is added to the principal amount to be repaid later. Every time a loan is capitalized, the amount that will have to be repaid increases.

CEEB code See *College Entrance Examination Board code.*

certificate program Non-degree program, usually lasting six months to a year, that trains and certifies students in a specific field.

class rank A student's standing in his or her high school graduating class relative to his or her peers. Class rank may be expressed as a raw number or as a rough percentile.

CLEP See *College Level Examination Program.*

COA See *Cost of Attendance.*

college Institution of higher learning that grants Bachelor's degrees.

College Board Nonprofit organization of universities, colleges, and other educational institutions that administers the SAT I, SAT II Subject Tests, AP exams, and CLEP exams.

College Entrance Examination Board (CEEB) code A high school's six-digit code that enables colleges to request an applicant's test scores, grades, and transcript.

college fair Event held at high schools or in the community where students can meet with several college representatives and learn about different colleges.

College Level Examination Program (CLEP)   Exam program administered by the College Board that awards college credit for nontraditional college-level education, including independent study, correspondence, work, and on-the-job or military training.

college-prep curriculum   Courses taken in English, math, the social sciences, the natural sciences, foreign languages, and the arts during high school to prepare for college-level work. All colleges and universities require applicants to have completed a certain number of courses in each academic area to be eligible for admission, but these requirements vary from school to school.

College Scholarship Service (CSS) Financial Aid PROFILE   Centralized financial aid application service operated by the College Scholarship Service of the College Board. This financial aid form is required by many private colleges and universities, and uses the Institutional Methodology to calculate financial need.

combined score   The total score given on the SAT I, equal to the score on the Verbal section plus the score on the Math section.

Common Application   A generic application form that is accepted by many private colleges and universities.

community college   A two-year college; community colleges generally offer a transfer curriculum, in which credits can be transferred toward a bachelor's degree at a four-year college, and a vocational or technical curriculum that prepares students for a particular field of employment. Also called a junior college.

commuter student   A student who doesn't live on campus; typically refers to a student who lives at home with his or her parents while attending college.

composite score   The overall score given on the ACT, obtained by averaging the scores on each of the four test sections.

concurrent enrollment   Program in which high school students attend a nearby college and earn college credits while completing their high school work.

conditional acceptance   Admission offered to some students on the condition that the student successfully complete specified academic requirements, such as attending summer school, taking remedial courses, or maintaining a certain GPA during the first college semester.

Congressional Methodology   See *Federal Methodology*.

consolidation loan   A new, single loan issued by a private lender for the entire amount of two or more education loans. Consolidation generally results in a lower, more manageable monthly payment, but it often extends repayment terms and the overall amount to be repaid.

consortium   Agreement between institutions for sharing programs, faculties, and/or facilities.

cooperative education   Program in which a student alternates going to college with periods of work experience related to his or her field of study.

core curriculum   Specified courses that an institution requires of all its students to earn a degree.

co-requisite   A course that must be taken during the same semester as another course.

correspondence course   Class where students receive lessons and return completed assignments to instructors via the mail.

cost of attendance (COA)   The total amount it costs a student to go to college, usually expressed as a yearly figure. The COA is determined according to rules established by Congress and includes the following: tuition and fees; on-campus room and board or a housing and food allowance for off-campus students; and allowances for books, supplies, transportation, loan fees, costs related to a disability, and miscellaneous expenses.

credit hour   How a college course is measured. To earn one credit hour, the student must attend class for one classroom hour (usually 50 minutes) per week. College courses are offered in one- to five-credit hour increments.

CSS/Financial Aid PROFILE   See *College Scholarship Service (CSS) Financial Aid PROFILE.*

Dean of Admissions   Person in charge of the admissions office who chairs the committee that makes admission decisions.

default   Failure to repay a loan according to the agreed-upon terms.

deferment   Agreement with the lender of a student loan where payments are temporarily suspended. If the loan is subsidized, the government pays interest charges during this time, but if it unsubsidized, interest continues to accrue.

deferred admission   Admissions plan under which students are admitted to a college but delay enrollment for a semester or a year because of special circumstances.

dependency status   A student's status as dependent or independent determines whether the student's parents' financial resources are counted toward the student's ability to pay for higher education. Independent student status is granted only under very strict guidelines.

dependent student   See *dependency status.*

direct exchange program   Agreement between an American college or university and a university in another country, in which students may attend the foreign institution at little or no cost.

Direct Loan   See *Federal Direct Student Loan Program.*

disbursement   The release of student loan funds to the school or borrower to pay for tuition and other school-related expenses.

distance learning   Classes taken through the Internet, via videotapes and CD-ROMs, by correspondence, and over the television.

doctorate   See *Ph.D.*

double major   A college academic plan in which you simultaneously complete the requirements for two majors and receive degrees in both majors upon graduation.

drop/add   Period of time during which students can adjust their class schedules by dropping or adding courses without academic or financial penalty.

early action   Admissions program offered primarily by highly selective schools in which a student may apply to one college and receive an answer well before the regular admission deadline. The student is not obligated to attend the college if accepted and may wait until the regular notification deadline in late spring to decide whether to attend the school.

early admission   Admissions program in which exceptionally bright students enroll in college after their sophomore or junior years without receiving their high school diplomas. Also called early entrance.

early decision   Admissions program in which a student may apply to one college under the early decision plan and receive an answer well before the regular admission deadline. If accepted (and if the financial aid offer is adequate), the student is obligated to attend the college and must withdraw any regular admission plan applications he or she has made.

early entrance   See *early admission.*

education loan   See *student loan.*

education IRA   IRA account that enables the holder to contribute a certain amount each year against higher education expenses for a child and which is generally exempt from taxation.

Educational Testing Service (ETS)   Nonprofit organization that produces and administers several standardized tests, including the ACT and the TOEFL.

EFC   See *Expected Family Contribution.*

electronic application   A college application form that can be filed via computer disk or over the Internet.

eligible program   Course of study that leads to a degree or certificate and meets the U.S. Department of Education's requirements. Students must be enrolled in an eligible program to receive federal financial aid.

EMBA   See *Executive MBA.*

endowment   Funds owned by a college or university and invested to produce income. Many institutions devote a portion of this income to financial aid.

English as a Second Language (ESL)   Program for students whose native language is not English.

entitlement program   Program that awards financial aid to *all* qualified applicants, such as the Pell Grant program.

equating section Section of the SAT I that does not count toward the final score. This section is used to ensure that the test is fair and to test new question types.

ESL See *English as a Second Language*.

ETS See *Educational Testing Service*.

Executive MBA (EMBA) Type of MBA degree that is typically awarded to professionals with 10 years or more of work experience. The EMBA program is designed to cause as few work disruptions as possible.

ExPAN Computer program available at some schools, libraries, and community centers that enables students to search for and apply to colleges electronically.

expected family contribution (EFC) Figure that indicates how much of the family's financial resources should be used to help pay for higher education. This number is subtracted from the COA (cost of attendance) to determine financial need and eligibility for campus-based programs.

extracurricular Any activity, such as clubs, work, sports, or volunteer service, that is performed outside of class.

FAFSA See *Free Application for Federal Student Aid*.

Federal Direct Student Loan Program Part of the Stafford Loan program, a type of federally guaranteed student loan that's administered directly by the government. Both subsidized and unsubsidized student Direct Loans are available. Not all schools participate in this program. (Often shortened to Direct Loan.)

Federal Family Education Loan (FFEL) Program Part of the Stafford Loan program, a type of federally guaranteed student loan that's administered by a private institution, such as a bank or credit union. Both subsidized and unsubsidized FFEL loans are available.

Federal Methodology Needs assessment formula used by the federal government to determine the EFC. Also called the *Congressional Methodology*.

Federal Perkins Loan Campus-based program that provides subsidized student loans to students with exceptional financial need. Perkins Loans have the lowest interest rate of any education loan.

Federal Supplemental Educational Opportunity Grant (FSEOG) Campus-based program that distributes grants to students with exceptional need. To qualify, the student must also be the recipient of a Pell Grant.

Federal Work-Study (FWS) Campus-based program that provides needy students with part-time employment to help pay school costs.

fellowship A stipend based on merit that is typically awarded to graduate students.

FFEL Loan See *Federal Family Education Loan Program*.

financial aid The money provided to a college student to help him or her pay the costs of higher education. Major forms of financial aid include loans, grants, scholarships, and work-study. Financial aid comes from many sources, including federal and state government, the schools, and private organizations like companies, associations, and foundations.

financial aid officer   Person at the college who administers financial aid packages and determines how much aid to award to each student.

financial aid package   The total amount of financial aid that a student receives, including federal, state, college, and private aid.

financial need   The difference between the COA (cost of attendance) of a particular college and a student's EFC (estimated family contribution). Financial aid awards are based on this amount.

first-choice plan   The most common type of early decision plan, in which applicants can apply early decision to one school, and can apply to any number of other schools under their regular admissions plans. If the student is accepted under the early decision plan, he or she must withdraw all other college applications.

forbearance   Period of time during which the lender agrees to temporarily postpone or reduce loan payments due to special circumstances. Interest continues to accrue during this period.

fraternity   Organized group of people sharing a common interest. Academic or business fraternities may be co-ed, but social fraternities are usually for men only.

Free Application for Federal Student Aid (FAFSA)   Form used to apply for Pell Grants and other federal need-based financial aid programs.

freshman orientation   Program offered by the college during the summer or in the week before classes start to enable new students to meet with an academic advisor, pre-register for classes, take placement tests, and learn about the school. Freshmen are often required to attend an orientation program.

FSEOG   See *Federal Supplemental Educational Opportunity Grant.*

full-time enrollment   Refers to students who enroll in 12 or more credit hours per semester.

FWS   See *Federal Work-Study.*

GED   See *General Education Development Certificate.*

General Education Development (GED) Certificate   Certificate received by students who pass a pre-approved high school equivalency test. Students without a high school diploma, such as home-schooled students, may need to obtain a GED to be eligible for financial aid and to attend some colleges and universities.

GMAT   See *Graduate Management Aptitude Test.*

GPA   See *Grade Point Average.*

grace period   Period between when a student leaves school or drops below half-time status and when the student must begin repaying an education loan—usually six to nine months.

grade point average (GPA)   System of scoring student achievement. A student's GPA is computed by multiplying the numerical grade received in each course by the number of credits offered for each course, and then dividing by the total number of credit hours studied.

Graduate Management Aptitude Test (GMAT) Standardized test required for admission to an MBA program.

graduate school Collection of programs offered by a university to students pursuing master's and doctoral degrees.

graduate student A student who has obtained a bachelor's degree and is continuing further study for a professional, master's, or doctoral degree.

graduation rate The percentage of entering freshmen who graduate within a certain period of time (usually four or five years).

Graduate Record Exam (GRE) Standardized exam that tests verbal and math skills and is used as part of the admissions process for graduate school.

grant Type of need-based financial aid that the recipient doesn't have to repay. Grant awards are typically based on financial need.

GRE See *Graduate Record Exam.*

Greek organizations On-campus organizations named by Greek letters that engage in social and charity events. Members frequently live together in a Greek house.

guaranty agency Organization that administers FFEL loans for state residents. Although the federal government sets loan limits and interest rates, each state is free to set its own additional limitations within federal guidelines.

half-time enrollment Required for eligibility for the Stafford Loan programs. At schools measuring progress by credit hours and semesters, trimesters, or quarters, half-time enrollment is at least six semester or quarter hours per term. At schools measuring progress by credit hours but not using semesters, trimesters, or quarters, half-time enrollment is at least 12 semester hours or 18 quarter hours per year. At schools measuring progress by clock hours, half-time enrollment is at least 12 hours per week. Some schools set higher minimums than these.

HBCU See *Historically Black Colleges and Universities.*

Historically Black Colleges and Universities (HBCU) Schools that were founded when African-Americans were denied access to most other colleges and universities. HBCUs typically have more African-American students and faculty than other schools.

honors program Advanced program of study offered by some colleges and universities to students with high academic qualifications.

HOPE Scholarship Tax credit intended to enable all students to afford two years of postsecondary education. Eligible families can deduct up to $1500 of tuition costs during the first two years of higher education.

I-20 Certificate of Eligibility Form issued by an American college or university to an accepted international student, enabling the student to obtain a student visa.

independent student   See *dependency status.*

independent study   Research and reading outside the classroom that earns course credit.

in-state student   Student who meets the residency requirements to qualify for decreased tuition at a public college or university.

Institutional Methodology   Formula to determine financial need that was developed and used by the colleges for allocating the schools' own funds.

intensive English program   Short-term program that teaches international students to read, speak, and understand English at a level at which they can attend college classes.

international student   Any applicant to an American college or university who is not a citizen of the United States. International students may have to complete supplemental application forms, take the TOEFL, and submit additional documentation to be considered for admission.

internship   Supervised work experience related to a student's field of interest for which degree credit is granted.

intramural sports   Organized athletic activities between the students within a school.

Ivy League   Group of scholastically prestigious private colleges and universities in the Northeast, including Brown, Columbia, Cornell, Dartmouth, Harvard, Radcliffe, Princeton, Yale, and the University of Pennsylvania.

January term calendar   Academic calendar consisting of two long semesters and one short, intervening term in January.

JD   Degree received after graduation from a law school.

junior college   See *community college.*

law school   Graduate-level professional school that students attend to earn a law degree.

Law School Admissions Test (LSAT)   Standardized test that applicants to law school must take.

legacy   A college or university applicant whose relative—typically a parent—is an alumnus or alumna of the school.

liberal arts college   College that offers a broad base of cultural education in the arts, humanities, natural sciences, and social sciences.

Lifetime Learning Credit   Tax credit that enables qualified families to deduct a certain percentage of some of the cost of tuition. This credit is available for juniors and seniors in college, graduate students, and adults returning to school.

LSAT   See *Law School Admissions Test.*

major   Academic area in which a student chooses to concentrate study when earning a bachelor's degree.

matriculate   To enroll as a student at a college or university.

master's degree   Degree received after one or two years of study following a bachelor's degree.

Master of Business Administration (MBA) Degree received after graduation from a business school.

MBA See *Master of Business Administration.*

MCAT See *Medical College Admission Test.*

MD Degree received after graduation from a medical school.

Medical College Admission Test (MCAT) Standardized test that applicants to medical school must take.

medical school Graduate-level professional school that students attend to earn a medical degree.

MELAB See *Michigan English Language Assessment Battery.*

merit-based aid Financial aid—typically a scholarship—awarded based on academic, artistic, or athletic merit, rather than on financial need.

Michigan English Language Assessment Battery (MELAB) Alternative to the TOEFL that is required by a few colleges and universities of non-English-speaking international applicants.

minor Officially recognized secondary concentration of study in a subject area.

National Collegiate Athletic Association (NCAA) Organization that regulates athletic programs at the majority of colleges and universities. The NCAA establishes rules for athletic eligibility, recruiting, and financial aid awards.

National Merit Scholarship National scholarship program awarded based on PSAT/NMSQT scores. National Merit finalists can receive scholarships from the National Merit Scholarship Corporation, which sponsors the program, or from a participating college or corporate sponsor.

NCAA See *National Collegiate Athletic Association.*

need-aware admission Admissions policy under which the college or university takes into account the applicant's ability to pay when making admission decisions.

need-based aid Financial aid based primarily on a student's financial need. All federal aid and most state aid is need-based.

need-blind admission Admissions policy under which the school does not consider an applicant's ability to pay when deciding whether to admit that applicant.

needs assessment Process of determining a student's financial need by analyzing the information provided on a financial aid application form according to a standardized formula, such as the Federal or Institutional Methodology.

non-need-based aid Broad category of financial aid that encompasses all aid awarded based on criteria other than financial need, including merit-based aid and aid based on a student's ethnicity, gender, religion, or affiliation with a group.

open admission Admissions program offered by some four-year colleges and most community colleges in which all students who apply and who have a high school diploma are admitted.

origination fee   Fee charged by the federal government on Stafford Loans and deducted from the loan before disbursement to partially offset administrative costs.

out-of-state student   Student who does not meet state residency requirements and must pay a higher tuition to attend one of the state's public colleges or universities.

outside scholarship   A scholarship not awarded by the school that the student is attending.

Parent Loans for Undergraduate Students (PLUS)   Federal education loans that are available to the parents of dependent students and may be used to pay the EFC. Qualification for a PLUS loan is not based on financial need. PLUS loans can be given under both the Direct Loan and FFEL loan programs.

part-time enrollment   Refers to students who enroll in fewer than 12 credit hours per semester.

Pell Grant   Federal program that awards grants to students with exceptional financial need. Most other financial aid awards are based on the application for the Pell Grant.

percentile score   Score received on the SAT that compares a student's performance to the performance of other high school students who took the test. The score refers to the percentage of students who scored lower.

Ph.D.   The highest university degree.

placement tests   Tests given to college freshmen before classes start to determine students' levels of achievement in English, writing, math, and foreign languages, and to place students in the correct college-level courses for their levels of achievement.

PLAN   Preliminary test typically taken by students during the sophomore year of high school that prepares students for taking the ACT and helps them identify career interests and abilities.

PLUS   See *Parent Loans for Undergraduate Students*.

preliminary application   Application form required of international students by some colleges and universities that is used to determine whether the applicant is compatible with the school. If so, the international student may continue with the regular application procedures.

Preliminary Scholastic Assessment Test/National Merit Scholarship Qualifying Test (PSAT/NMSQT)   National standardized test, typically taken during the junior year of high school, that prepares the student for taking the SAT I. The score on this test determines the student's eligibility for a National Merit Scholarship.

pre-professional program   Undergraduate curriculum that prepares students for entry to a professional school, including—but not limited to—pre-law, pre-med, pre-business, pre-engineering, pre-dentistry, pre-veterinary, and pre-pharmacy programs.

prerequisite   Course or qualification required before a student may take an advanced course or declare a major in a specific area.

private aid   Financial aid that originates from private sources, such as colleges and universities, foundations, associations, companies, and organizations.

private loan   Education loan provided by a private lender, rather than by the federal government, state government, or school. Private loans are typically given to parents and are based on creditworthiness rather than financial need. Also called an alternative loan or supplemental loan.

private school   College or university that was founded by a private group or benefactor, such as a religious denomination, and that is funded by tuition and alumni donations.

professional judgment   The financial aid officer's power, delegated by the federal government, to adjust a student's EFC, COA, or dependency status when a student can demonstrate unusual or changed financial circumstances.

professional master's   Category of master's programs designed to teach students specific job-related skills.

professional school   Graduate-level school that awards a professional degree, such as a business, law, or medical degree.

PSAT/NMSQT   See *Preliminary Scholastic Assessment Test/National Merit Scholarship Qualifying Test.*

public aid   Financial aid that originates from publicly funded sources, such as federal, state, and local government.

public school   College or university that was founded by the state and is funded partly or fully by tax money. Public schools often give preference for admittance to in-state applicants.

quarter   Class term that generally lasts 12 weeks. Schools on the quarter system have four class terms during the academic year.

RA   See *Resident Assistant.*

raw score   Standardized test score that is simply the sum of all questions answered correctly, minus the guessing penalty on some tests.

reach school   A college where an applicant may not necessarily meet admission standards, hence making it a "reach" for that applicant to gain admittance.

registrar   Office responsible for registration for classes and academic records.

regular admission   A college or university's primary admissions plan, under which applications must be received by a certain date and students are notified of admission decisions in the spring.

regular student   Student who is enrolled in an institution of higher learning to obtain a degree or certificate. Only regular students are eligible for federal financial aid.

remedial course   College course that carries no credit but is required of certain students who do not score high enough on placement exams before they can start college-level work in English, math, or the sciences.

Renewal FAFSA   Form that can be completed by students whose financial circumstances have not greatly changed in the past year when reapplying for financial aid.

research assistant   Graduate student who assists a professor in the lab or with other research. Research assistants receive a stipend and reduced tuition.

Reserve Officers' Training Corps (ROTC)   On-campus extracurricular program that trains students to be officers in a branch of the Armed Forces. Participants earn a small stipend as upperclassmen, and they often receive scholarships; in return, students are expected to fulfill a service commitment after college.

resident assistant (RA)   Trained upper-class student who coordinates dorm activities and helps other dorm residents with problems.

retention rate   Percentage of entering freshmen who remain at the school to graduate.

rolling admission   Admission program in which students can apply at any time and are notified of acceptance or denial as soon as their applications have been processed.

ROTC   See *Reserve Officers' Training Corps.*

safety school   A school for which an applicant is overqualified and is therefore well assured of admission; also refers to a school where the applicant knows he or she can afford the tuition.

SAI   See *Student Aid Index.*

SAR   See *Student Aid Report.*

SAT I   See *Scholastic Assessment Test.*

SAT II subject tests   Standardized tests administered by the College Board that measure a student's ability in one particular subject and are usually taken when the student has completed that course.

satisfactory academic progress   A college's or university's standard of academic achievement that a student must maintain in order to be eligible to receive federal financial aid.

scaled score   The final score that a student receives on a standardized test, calculated by plugging the raw score into a scoring formula.

scholarship   Form of financial aid that doesn't have to be repaid and is typically awarded on the basis of merit or some other qualification instead of financial need.

Scholastic Assessment Test (SAT I)   National standardized college admissions test, widely given in the East and South.

school report   Form that the high school must return to colleges to report an applicant's transcript and other information about the applicant. The school report is usually included with the college's application form.

score report Report containing a student's scores and other information about how well the student performed on a standardized test that is sent to the student and specified colleges after taking the test.

selectivity Percentage of applicants who are accepted to a college or university—the lower the percentage, the higher the school's selectivity. The most selective schools often have the highest admissions standards and receive applications from top students.

semester Class term that generally lasts 15 to 18 weeks. Schools on the semester system have two semesters during the academic year, plus one or more summer sessions.

service academy Four-year college that offers a bachelor's degree and an officer's commission in a branch of the Armed Forces. Service academies charge no tuition, but they are highly selective, and applicants must be nominated by their Congressional Representatives to apply.

service-learning College course or program where students learn while performing volunteer or community service.

servicer Organization that tracks education loans and collects payments on behalf of the lender.

single-choice plan A rare type of early decision plan under which students can apply to only one school—the school where the student applied early decision.

sorority Women's social organization often identified by Greek letters.

specialized school Four-year college that emphasizes study for a particular career in engineering, the arts, education, business, or some other specialized field. Also called technical schools.

SSIG See *State Student Incentive Grant.*

Stafford Loan Federal education loan program that encompasses both Direct Loans and FFEL loans.

standard error of measurement Estimate of the amount of errors in measuring standardized test scores.

standardized tests Any of a number of preformatted exams that all applicants to college, graduate school, and professional school must take. The PSAT/NMSQT, PLAN, SAT, ACT, AP exams, CLEP exams, TOEFL, GRE, MCAT, and LSAT are all examples of standardized tests. These tests are intended to enable colleges and graduate schools to equally compare applicants from all areas of the country.

State Student Incentive Grant (SSIG) State-run, need-based grant program for in-state residents. Although the state administers the program, the federal government helps fund it.

Student Aid Index (SAI) The number that appears on the Student Aid Report, indicating Pell Grant eligibility.

Student Aid Report (SAR) The report that is returned after a student applies for federal financial aid, indicating the student's Pell Grant eligibility and EFC. The student must provide a copy of this report to the school's financial aid officer so that the school can put together a financial aid package.

student loan Type of financial aid that must be repaid with interest. Also called an education loan.

student visa Formal permission granted to an international student by an American Consulate to study at a college or university in the United States. Student visas are typically granted to international students only after they have been admitted to a college and if they can produce evidence of sufficient funds to pay for their schooling.

study abroad Program in which a student spends a semester or year at a school in a foreign country.

subsidized loan A federally guaranteed loan, such as the Federal Perkins Loan or the subsidized Stafford Loan, that is awarded to students based on financial need. The federal government pays the interest charges that accrue while the student is in school.

summer session Courses offered by a college or university during the summer term. These courses are typically shorter, more intensive, and less expensive than courses offered during the regular academic year.

subject score The score received on one section of the ACT. This score isn't as important as the overall composite score.

supplemental loan See *private loan*.

syllabus A course outline that lists all the assignments, exams, and lecture topics for that course.

TA See *teaching assistant*.

teaching assistant (TA) Graduate student, usually a doctoral assistant, who teaches introductory undergraduate courses in exchange for a stipend and reduced tuition.

technical school See *specialized school*.

territory manager Admissions officer who oversees a particular geographic region, recruiting applicants and reviewing applications from that region.

Test of English as a Foreign Language (TOEFL) Standardized test to demonstrate acceptable proficiency in English, given to college applicants for whom English is not their native language.

test-prep course A course, usually offered by a regional or national company, that prepares students for taking a standardized test like the ACT or SAT I.

tipper A small detail that may tip the balance in admissions decisions. Tippers can include ethnicity, gender, home state, legacy status, or a special talent.

Title IV School Codes Codes entered on the FAFSA to specify which colleges and universities receive the financial aid application information.

TOEFL See *Test of English as a Foreign Language*.

transcript The official record of a student's academic work.

transfer student A student who has completed one or more years of college-level education at another community college or four-year school, and who has transferred enrollment and earned college credits to a new school.

trimester Class term that generally lasts 17 weeks. Schools on the trimester system have three class terms during the academic year.

tuition The cost of a college education and required institutional fees for services provided by the college.

tuition equalization Program adopted by some states that equalizes the tuition of in-state private and public schools for state residents.

tuition savings plan Private, state, or college plan that enables families to save for college over the long term. The savings are guaranteed to increase at the same rate as college tuition. State-sponsored plans are also exempt from state taxes.

undergraduate A bachelor's degree candidate at a college or university.

university Institution of higher education that encompasses a liberal arts college, several professional programs, and various graduate programs and graduate professional schools.

unmet need Any demonstrated financial need that is not met by a school's financial aid package.

unsubsidized loan A Stafford loan that is not awarded based on need and thus may be used to help pay the EFC. The student must pay all of the interest charges that accrue on the loan.

verification Review process during which a financial aid officer verifies all of the information provided on a financial aid application. Depending on the school, one-third to all of the financial aid applications submitted may be randomly selected for verification. The financial aid officer may also select any application that seems suspicious for verification.

wait list List of applicants who were not initially accepted by a college but who may be accepted if space becomes available.

woman's college College whose enrollment is limited to female students.

work-study Type of financial aid that gives the student a part-time job, usually on campus. The student's paycheck is used to help pay college costs.

College Admissions Resource Guide

Internet Resources

These selected Internet resources will help you with all aspects of the college admissions process. Relevant Internet sites are also listed in every chapter of this book.

Career Search

College Board's Career Search	http://www.collegeboard.org/career/bin/career.pl
Explore Careers and Majors at CollegeEdge	http://www.collegeedge.com/college/cm/
Occupational Outlook Handbook	http://stats.bls.gov:80/ocohome.htm

General College Admissions Resources

American College Entrance Directory	http://www.aaced.com/
College and University Admissions	http://collegeapps.About.com/
College Board Online	http://www.collegeboard.org/
College Compass	http://www.edonline.com/collegecompass/main.htm
College Is Possible	http://www.collegeispossible.org/
CollegeXpress	http://www.collegexpress.com/
Fishnet	http://www.jayi.com/
GoCollege	http://www.gocollege.com/

Peterson's The College   http://www.petersons.com/ugrad/
Channel

Power Students Network   http://www.powerstudents.com/

Think College   http://www.ed.gov/thinkcollege/

College Rankings

America's 100 Most Wired   http://www.zdnet.com/yil/
Colleges   content/college/

Critical Comparisons of   http://www.memex-press.com/cc/
American Colleges and
Universities

Money's Value Rankings   http://www.pathfinder.com/
                                 money/colleges98/article/
                                 rankindx.html

U.S.News Rankings   http://www.usnews.com/usnews/
                                 edu/college/cohome.htm

College Search

College and University   http://www.mit.edu:8001/people/
Home Pages   cdemello/univ.html

CollegeEdge   http://www.collegeedge.com/
                                 Default.asp

CollegeLink   http://www.collegelink.com/

CollegeNET   http://www.collegenet.com/

College Opportunities   http://nces.ed.gov/ipeds/cool/
On-Line

CollegeView College Search   http://www.collegeview.com/
                                 collegesearch/index.epl

Historically Black Colleges   http://www.webcom.com/~cjcook/
and Universities   SDBP/hbcu.html

Homeschool-Friendly Colleges   http://rsts.net/colleges/index.html

Yahoo! College Search   http://features.yahoo.com/
                                 college/search.html

College Preparation Services

ABC's of College Prep   http://www.abc-collegeprep.com/

Black Excel: The College   http://cnct.com/home/ijblack/
Help Network   BlackExcel.shtml

College Foundation Planners   http://www.cfpi.com/

CollegeGate   http://www.collegegate.com/

IvyBound College Consulting   http://www.ivybound.com/

MyEssay.Com	http://www.myessay.com/
Sample College Application Essays	http://www.bignerds.com/ce/cbooks.shtml
Your Virtual Interview	http://www.bergen.org/AAST/Projects/CollegePrep/interview.html

Standardized Tests

ACT Assessment	http://www.act.org/
Advanced Placement Program	http://www.collegeboard.org/ap/students/index.html
CLEP Exams	http://www.collegeboard.org/clep/students/study/html/testl000.html
Educational Testing Service	http://www.ets.org/
Kaplan	http://www1.kaplan.com/
PSAT/NMSQT	http://www.collegeboard.org/psat/student/html/indx001.html
Princeton Review	http://www.review.com/
SAT I and SAT II Subject Tests	http://www.collegeboard.org/sat/html/students/indx001.html
TOEFL	http://www.toefl.org/

Financial Aid

FinAid	http://www.finaid.org/
Financial Aid Calculators	http://www.collegeboard.org/finaid/fastud/html/fincalc/fcintro.html
Financial Aid Home Page by U.S.News	http://www.usnews.com/usnews/edu/dollars/dshome.htm
National Financial Services Network	http://www.nfsn.com/Educatio.htm
Office of Postsecondary Education	http://www.ed.gov/offices/OPE/Students/index.html
Project EASI	http://easi.ed.gov/

College Athletics

Athlete's Edge	http://www.athletesedge.com/
CollegeBound.Net Sports	http://www.cbnet.com/sports/index.html
College Recruiting Resource	http://www.crrathlon.com/

Online Scouting Network	http://www.osn.com/
Recruit Zone	http://www.recruitzone.com/
Yahoo! College and University Sports	http://dir.yahoo.com/Recreation/Sports/College_and_University/

College Life

Bolt College Planner	http://www.bolt.com/College/
CampusSafety.Org	http://campussafety.org/
College and Universities Chats	http://events.yahoo.com/Net_Events/Education/Colleges_and_Universities/Chat_Rooms/
College 101	http://www.geocities.com/~college101/
College Bound	http://www.cbnet.com/
College Life	http://collegelife.about.com/
College Press Network	http://www.cpnet.com/
CollegePride.Com	http://www.collegepride.com/
Colleges.Com	http://www.colleges.com/
CollegeTownUSA.Com	http://www.collegetownusa.com/
Drinking: A Student's Guide	http://www.glness.com/ndhs/
GreekNet	http://www.greeknet.net/
Savvy Student	http://www.savvystudent.com/
Study Abroad Directory	http://www.studyabroad.com/
Real World University	http://www.rwuniversity.com/
Tap Online: Campus	http://www.taponline.com/campus/

Academic Help and Reference

Basic Guide to Essay Writing	http://members.tripod.com/~lklivingston/essay/
Elements of Style	http://www.columbia.edu/acis/bartleby/strunk/
OneLook Dictionaries	http://www.onelook.com/
Research It!	http://www.iTools.com/research-it/research-it.html
Roget's Thesaurus	http://www.thesaurus.com/
Study Skills Help Page	http://www.mtsu.edu/~studskl/
A Word a Day	http://www.wordsmith.org/awad/index.html

Textbooks and Other College Stuff You Can Buy

BigWords	http://bigwords.com/store/
BookSwap	http://www.bookswap.com/bookswap/index.cfm?
CollegeDepot.Com	http://www.collegedepot.com/
Student Market	http://www.studentmarket.com/
VarsityBooks.Com	http://www.varsitybooks.com/

Graduate and Professional School

America's Best Graduate Schools (U.S.News)	http://www.usnews.com/usnews/edu/beyond/bchome.htm
Bschool.Com	http://www.bschool.com/
CollegeEdge for Graduate School	http://grad.collegeedge.com/
CollegeEdge for Professional Schools	http://pro.collegeedge.com/Default.asp
GradSchools.Com	http://www.gradschools.com/
Graduate School Survival Guide	http://www-smi.stanford.edu/people/pratt/smi/advice.html
LawSchool.Com	http://www.lawschool.com/
Law Student and Pre-Law	http://www.usc.edu/dept/Student Resourceslaw-lib/law-center/law-students.html
MBA Explorer	http://www.gmat.org/
MBAinfo	http://www.mbainfo.com/
Medical School Admissions	http://www.medicalstudent.net/
Official MBA Guide	http://unicorn.us.com/guide/
Peterson's Graduate and Professional Study	http://www.petersons.com/graduate/gsector.html
Pre-Med Site	http://www.uspremeds.com/
Pre-Medical Curriculum and Medical School Admissions Guide	http://www.bol.ucla.edu/~ericwang/index.html

Usenet Newsgroups

soc.college	General college discussion
soc.college.admissions	College admissions discussion
soc.college.financial-aid	Financial aid discussion
soc.college.grad	Graduate school discussion

Software

Higher Score for the SAT/ACT. Kaplan $29.95 (http://www.kaplan.com/). Windows.

Inside the SAT, PSAT, and ACT '99. Princeton Review (http://www. review.com/). $24.95. Windows and Macintosh.

One-on-One With the SAT. The College Board (1 (800) 323-7155 or http://cbweb2.collegeboard.org/shopping/). $29.95. Windows.

Student Organizer. Centaur Academic Media (http://www.studentquad. com/). $23.95. Windows.

Word Command. Lexio (http://www.lexio.com/). $39.95. Windows.

VHS Video

ABCs of Eligibility for College-Bound Student Athletes. The College Board (1 (800) 323-7155 or http://cbweb2.collegeboard.org/shopping/). $49.95.

AP: Pathway to Success. The College Board (1 (800) 323-7155 or http://cbweb2.collegeboard.org/shopping/). $15.00.

College Freshman Survival Guide. Octameron Associates ((703) 836-5480 or http://www.octameron.com/). $30.00.

How to Pay for College. Octameron Associates ((703) 836-5480 or http://www.octameron.com/). $30.00.

Look Inside the SAT I: Test Prep from the Test Makers. The College Board (1 (800) 323-7155 or http://cbweb2.collegeboard.org/shopping/). $10.00.

The Road to College. National Association for College Admission Counseling ((703) 836-2222). $29.95.

Think Before You Punch: Using Calculators on the SAT I and PSAT/NMSQT. The College Board (1 (800) 323-7155 or http://cbweb2.collegeboard.org/ shopping/). $30.00.

Recommended Reading

This bibliography lists other books and pamphlets that I recommend to help you with every step of the college search and application process. Where applicable, I have provided direct ordering information (phone and online), but the majority of these publications should be available for sale in your favorite local or Web-based bookstore.

College Guides

General Guides

The Best 311 Colleges. Princeton Review, 1998. $20.00.

Facts About American Colleges. National Association for College Admissions Counseling. $6.00. To order: (703) 836-2222.

Field Guide to Colleges. By Shannon R. Turlington. Arco, 1999. $24.95

The Fiske Guide to Colleges. By Edward B. Fiske. Times Books, 1998. $20.00.

The Insider's Guide to the Colleges. Griffin Trade, 1998. $16.99.

Internet Guide for College-Bound Students. By Kenneth E. Hartman. The College Board, 1999. $14.95. To order: 1 (800) 323-7155 or http://cbweb2.collegeboard.org/shopping/.

Peterson's Competitive Colleges. Peterson's, 1999. $18.95. To order: 1 (800) 338-3282 or http://www.petersons.com/.

Specialized Guides

The African-American Student's Guide to College. Princeton Review, 1998. $17.95.

America's 100 Best College Buys. John Culler & Sons, 1998. $19.95.

Barron's Best Buys in College Education. By Lucia Solorzano. Barron's Educational Series, 1998. $14.95.

The Campus Life Guide to Christian Colleges and Universities. Broadman & Holman, 1998. $14.99.

Christian Colleges & Universities. Peterson's, 1998. $14.95. To order: 1 (800) 338-3282 or http://www.petersons.com/.

The College Board Guide to 150 Popular College Majors. The College Board. $16.00. To order: 1 (800) 323-7155 or http://cbweb2.collegeboard.org/shopping/.

The College Majors Handbook: The Actual Jobs, Earnings, and Trends for Graduates of 60 College Majors. By Paul E. Harrington, Thomas F. Harrington, and Neeta Fogg. Jist Works, 1999. $24.95.

The Complete Book of Catholic Colleges. By Edward Custard and Dan Saraceno. Princeton Review, 1998. $21.00

Directory of Undergraduate Nursing Schools. Jones and Bartlett, 1999. $26.95. To order: (978) 443-5000 or http://www.jbpub.com/.

Historically Black Colleges and Universities. Arco, 1995. $16.95

K&W Guide to Colleges for the Learning Disabled. By Marybeth Karvets and Imy Wax. Princeton Review, 1997. $25.00.

The 100 Best Colleges for African-American Students. By Erlene B. Wilson. Plume Books, 1998. $14.95.

The Performing Art Major's College Guide. By Carole J. Everett. Arco, 1998. $19.95.

Peterson's Two-Year Colleges. Peterson's, 1998. $24.95. To order: 1 (800) 338-3282 or http://www.petersons.com/.

Professional Degree Programs in the Visual and Performing Arts. Peterson's, 1998. $26.95. To order: 1 (800) 338-3282 or http://www.petersons.com/.

Recommendations on the Colleges. Edited by Frederick E. Rugg. Rugg's Recommendations, 1999. $20.95. (A guide to majors.)

Top Colleges for Science. Peterson's, 1998. $24.95. To order: 1 (800) 338-3282 or http://www.petersons.com/.

Getting In

General Guides

50 Things You Can Do to Get Into the College of Your Choice. By O'Neal Turner. Arco, 1997. $11.95.

And What About College? How Homeschooling Can Lead to Admissions to the Best Colleges and Universities. By Cafi Cohen. Holt Associates, 1997. $18.95.

Behind the Scenes: An Inside Look at the Selective College Admission Process. By Edward B. Wall. Octameron Associates, 1998. $5.00. To order: (703) 836-5480 or http://www.octameron.com/.

College Admissions: A Crash Course for Panicked Parents. By Sally Rubenstone and Sidonia Dalby. Arco, 1997. $12.95.

The College Guide for Parents. The College Board. $14.00. To order: 1 (800) 323-7155 or http://cbweb2.collegeboard.org/shopping/.

Get Into Any College: Secrets of Harvard Students. By Jim Good and Lisa Lee. 101 Publishing, 1998. $16.95.

Going Back to School. Arco, 1998. $12.95

Guide to the College Admission Process. National Association for College Admissions Counseling. $6.00. To order: (703) 836-2222.

I Am Somebody: College Knowledge for the First-Generation Campus Bound. By Anna Leider. Octameron Associates, 1998. $7.00. To order: (703) 836-5480 or http://www.octameron.com/.

Reading Lists For College Bound Students. Arco. $11.95.

Preparing the Application

College Applications and Essays. By Susan D. Van Ralte. Arco, 1997. $9.95.

Do-It Write: How to Prepare a Great College Application. By G. Gary Ripple. Octameron Associates, 1997. To order: (703) 836-5480 or http://www.octameron.com/.

Perfect Personal Statements. Arco, 1995. $9.95

Ten Minute Guide to Applying to Graduate School. Arco, 1996. $10.95.

Your College Application. By Scott Gelband, Catherine Kubale, and Eric Schorr. The College Board. $9.95. To order: 1 (800) 323-7155 or http://cbweb2.collegeboard.org/shopping/.

Essay-Writing Help

100 Successful College Application Essays. By Christopher J. Georges. Mentor Books, 1991. $6.99.

The Best College Admission Essays. By Mark Alan Stewart. Arco, 1997. $9.95.

The College Application Essay. By Sarah Myers McGinty. The College Board. $12.95. To order: 1 (800) 323-7155 or http://cbweb2.collegeboard.org/shopping/.

How to Write a Winning College Application Essay. By Michael Mason. Prima Publishing, 1997. $14.00.

Test-Prep

10 Real SATs. The College Board. $17.95. To order: 1 (800) 323-7155 or http://cbweb2.collegeboard.org/shopping/.

AP Calculus Student Guide. The College Board, 1999. $12.00. To order: 1 (800) 323-7155 or http://cbweb2.collegeboard.org/shopping/.

AP English Student Guide. The College Board, 1999. $12.00. To order: 1 (800) 323-7155 or http://cbweb2.collegeboard.org/shopping/.

Arco Teach Yourself the ACT in 24 Hours. By Nicholas Falletta. Arco, 1999. $14.95.

Arco Teach Yourself the SAT in 24 Hours. By Nicholas Falletta. Arco, 1999. $14.95.

CLEP Success. Peterson's, 1999. $16.95. To order: 1 (800) 338-3282 or http://www.petersons.com/.

Everything You Need to Score on the SAT II: Writing. Arco, 1998. $12.95.

Hot Words for the SAT I. Barron's Educational Series, 1998. $8.95.

Master the ACT. Arco, 1999. $13.95.

Master the SAT and PSAT. Arco, 1999. $12.95.

The Official Study Guide for the CLEP Examinations. The College Board, 1999. $18.00. To order: 1 (800) 323-7155 or http://cbweb2.collegeboard.org/shopping/.

Peterson's Success With Words. By Joan Carris. Peterson's, 1998. $12.95. To order: 1 (800) 338-3282 or http://www.petersons.com/.

Preparation for the CLEP: The 5 General Examinations. Arco, 1999. $13.95.

Real SAT II: Subject Tests. The College Board. $17.95. To order: 1 (800) 323-7155 or http://cbweb2.collegeboard.org/shopping/.

SAT Math Workbook. Kaplan, 1999. $14.00. To order: 1 (800) KAP-ITEM or http://www.kaplan.com/.

SAT Verbal Workbook. Kaplan, 1998. $14.00. To order: 1 (800) KAP-ITEM or http://www.kaplan.com/.

The Unofficial Guide to the ACT. By Karl Weber. Arco, 1999. $16.95.

The Unofficial Guide to the SAT. By Karl Weber. Arco, 1999. $16.95.

Financial Aid

General Guides

The Best Way to Save for College: A Comprehensive Guide to State-Sponsored College Savings Plans and Prepaid Tuition Contracts. By Joseph F. Hurley. Bonacom Publications, 1999. $22.95.

College Savings Rx: Investment Prescriptions for a Healthy College Fund. By David G. Speck. Octameron Associates, 1998. $8.00. To order: (703) 836-5480 or http://www.octameron.com/.

Don't Miss Out: The Ambitious Student's Guide to Financial Aid. By Anna and Robert Leider. Octameron Associates, 1998. $8.00. To order: (703) 836-5480 or http://www.octameron.com/.

Financial Aid FinAncer: Expert Answers to College Financing Questions. By Joseph M. Re. Octameron Associates, 1998. $6.00. To order: (703) 836-5480 or http://www.octameron.com/.

Financial Aid Officers: What They Do—To You and For You. By Donald Moore. Octameron Associates, 1998. $5.00. To order: (703) 836-5480 or http://www.ocatmeron.com/.

Financing College: How to Use Savings, Financial Aid, Scholarships, and Loans to Afford the School of Your Choice. By Kristin Davis. Kiplinger Books, 1998. $17.95.

The Student Guide to Financial Aid. U.S. Department of Education. Free. To order: 1 (800) 4-FED-AID or http://www.ed.gov/offices/OPE/.

The Parents' Guide to Paying for College. The College Board. $14.95. To order: 1 (800) 323-7155 or http://cbweb2.collegeboard.org/shopping/.

The Unofficial Guide to Financing A College Education. By Shannon R. Turlington. Arco, 1999. $16.95.

General Scholarship Guides

The A's and B's of Academic Scholarships. By Anna Leider. Octameron Associates, 1998. $8.00. To order: (703) 836-5480 or http://www.octameron.com/.

College Student's Guide to Merit and Other No-Need Funding. By Gail A. Schlachter and R. David Weber. Reference Service Press, 1998. $32.00. To order: (916) 939-9620 or http://www.rspfunding.com/.

Financial Aid for Veterans, Military Personnel, and Their Dependents. By Gail A. Schlachter and R. David Weber. Reference Service Press, 1998. $40.00. To order: (916) 939-9620 or http://www.rspfunding.com/.

Peterson's Scholarships, Grants, and Prizes. Peterson's, 1998. $26.95. To order: 1 (800) 338-3282 or http://www.petersons.com/.

The Scholarship Advisor. By Christopher Vuturo. Princeton Review, 1998. $23.00.

The Scholarship Book. By Daniel J. Cassidy. Prentice Hall Press, 1999. $25.00. To order: 1 (800) 428-5331 or http://www.superlibrary.com/.

The Scholarship Handbook. The College Board, 1999. $24.95. To order: 1 (800) 323-7155 or http://cbweb2.collegeboard.org/shopping/.

Scholarship Guides—Specific Fields

Dollars for College—Art, Music, Drama. Garrett Park Press, 1999. $6.95. To order: (301) 946-2553.

Dollars for College—Business and Related Fields. Garrett Park Press. $6.95. To order: (301) 946-2553.

Dollars for College—Education. Garrett Park Press. $6.95. To order: (301) 946-2553.

Dollars for College—Engineering. Garrett Park Press. $6.95. To order: (301) 946-2553.

Dollars for College—Journalism and Mass Communications. Garrett Park Press. $6.95. To order: (301) 946-2553.

Dollars for College—Law. Garrett Park Press. $6.95. To order: (301) 946-2553.

Dollars for College—Liberal Arts: Humanities and Social Science. Garrett Park Press. $6.95. To order: (301) 946-2553.

Dollars for College—Medicine, Dentistry, and Related Fields. Garrett Park Press. $6.95. To order: (301) 946-2553.

Dollars for College—Nursing and Other Health Fields. Garrett Park Press. $6.95. To order: (301) 946-2553.

Dollars for College—Science. Garrett Park Press. $6.95. To order: (301) 946-2553.

The Journalist's Road to Success: A Career and Scholarship Guide. Dow Jones Newspaper Fund. $3.00. To order: DJNF, PO Box 300, Princeton, NJ 08543-0300.

Music, Dance, and Theater Scholarships: A Guide to Undergraduate Awards. Conway Greene, 1998. $24.95.

RSP Funding for Nursing Students and Nurses. By Gail A. Schlachter and R. David Weber. Reference Service Press, 1998. $25.00. To order: (916) 939-9620 or http://www.rspfunding.com/.

Scholarship Guides—Athletes

The Athletic Recruiting and Scholarship Guide. By Wayne Mazzoni. Mazz Marketing, 1998. $19.95.

Athletic Scholarships: A Complete Guide. Conway Greene, 1998. $23.95.

Scholarship Guides—Minorities

The Black Student's Guide to Scholarships. Madison Books, 1999. $17.95.

Directory of Financial Aids for Women. By Gail A. Schlachter. Reference Service Press, 1997. $45.00. To order: (916) 939-9620 or http://www.rspfunding.com/.

Dollars for College—Students With Disabilities. Garrett Park Press. $6.95. To order: (301) 946-2553.

Dollars for College—Women in All Fields. Garrett Park Press. $6.95. To order: (301) 946-2553.

Financial Aid for African-Americans. By Gail A. Schlachter and R. David Weber. Reference Service Press, 1997. $37.50. To order: (916) 939-9620 or http://www.rspfunding.com/.

Financial Aid for Asian Americans. By Gail A. Schlachter and R. David Weber. Reference Service Press, 1997. $32.50. To order: (916) 939-9620 or http://www.rspfunding.com/.

Financial Aid for Hispanic Americans. By Gail A. Schlachter and R. David Weber. Reference Service Press, 1997. $35.00. To order: (916) 939-9620 or http://www.rspfunding.com/.

Financial Aid for Minorities in... Awards Open to Students With Any Major. Garrett Park Press. $5.95. To order: (301) 946-2553.

Financial Aid for Minorities in Business and Law. Garrett Park Press. $5.95. To order: (301) 946-2553.

Financial Aid for Minorities in Education. Garrett Park Press. $5.95. To order: (301) 946-2553.

Financial Aid for Minorities in Engineering and Science. Garrett Park Press. $5.95. To order: (301) 946-2553.

Financial Aid for Minorities in Journalism and Mass Communications. Garrett Park Press. $5.95. To order: (301) 946-2553.

Financial Aid for Minorities in Health Fields. Garrett Park Press. $5.95. To order: (301) 946-2553.

Financial Aid for the Disabled and Their Families. By Gail A. Schlachter and R. David Weber. Reference Service Press, 1998. $40.00. To order: (916) 939-9620 or http://www.rspfunding.com/.

Funding for Persons With Visual Impairments. Reference Service Press. $30.00. To order: (916) 939-9620 or http://www.rspfunding.com/.

The Minority and Women's Complete Scholarship Book. Sourcebooks, 1998. $18.95.

Working Your Way Through School

The College Board Guide to Going to College While Working. By Gene R. Hawes. The College Board. $9.95. To order: 1 (800) 323-7155 or http://cbweb2. collegeboard.org/shopping/.

Earn and Learn: The Complete Guide to Cooperative Education. By Joseph M. Re. Octameron Associates, 1997. $5.00. To order: (703) 836-5480 or http:// www.octameron.com/.

The Internship Bible. By Mark Oldman and Samer Hamadeh. Princeton Review, 1998. $25.00.

International Students

Colleges and Universities in the USA. Peterson's, 1998. $24.95. To order: 1 (800) 338-3282 or http://www.petersons.com/.

English Language Programs. Peterson's, 1998. $21.95. To order: 1 (800) 338-3282 or http://www.petersons.com/.

International Student Handbook of U.S. Colleges. The College Board, 1999. $21.95. To order: 1 (800) 323-7155 or http://cbweb2.collegeboard.org/ shopping/.

Preparation for the TOEFL Test, 2000 edition. Arco, 1999. $16.95.

Scholarships for Study in the USA and Canada. Peterson's 1998. $21.95. To order: 1 (800) 338-3282 or http://www.petersons.com/.

TOEFL Grammar Workbook: Everything You Need to Score High. Arco, 1998. $11.95.

TOEFL Preparation Kit, 2000 edition. Arco, 1999. $29.95.

Alternatives to College

Bears' Guide to Earning Degrees Nontraditionally. By Mariah and John B. Bear. Ten Speed Press, 1999. $29.95.

But What If I Don't Want to Go to College? A Guide to Success Through Alternative Education. By Harlow G. Unger. Checkmark Books, 1998. $12.95.

College Degrees By Mail and Modem. By John and Mariah Bear. Ten Speed Press, 1998. $12.95.

Distance Learning Programs. Peterson's, 1998. $26.95. To order: 1 (800) 338-3282 or http://www.petersons.com/.

How to Get a College Degree Via the Internet. By Sam Atieh. Prima Publishing, 1998. $16.00.

The Independent Study Catalog. Peterson's, 1998. $21.95. To order: 1 (800) 338-3282 or http://www.petersons.com/.

Surviving at College

101 Things a College Guy Should Know. By Stephen Edwards. Andrews McMeel, 1998. $5.95.

Black College Student's Survival Guide. By Jawanza Kunjufu. African American Images, 1998. $14.95.

Campus Health Guide: The College Student's Handbook for Healthy Living. By Carol L. Otis, MD, and Roger Goldingay. The College Board. $14.95. To order: 1 (800) 323-7155 or http://cbweb2.collegeboard.org/shopping/.

Campus Daze: Easing the Transition From High School to College. By George Gibbs. Octameron Associates, 1998. $5.00. To order: (703) 836-5480 or http://www.octameron.com/.

College Bound: The Student's Handbook for Getting Ready, Moving In, and Succeeding on Campus. By Evelyn Kaye and Janet Gardner. The College Board. $9.95. To order: 1 (800) 323-7155 or http://cbweb2.collegeboard.org/shopping/.

College Survival. By Greg Gottesman. Arco, 1999. $10.95

Coping With Stress at College. By Mark Rowh. The College Board. $9.95. To order: 1 (800) 323-7155 or http://cbweb2.collegeboard.org/shopping/.

Dollars and Sense for College Students: How Not to Run Out of Money by Midterms. By Ellen Braitman. Princeton Review, 1998. $10.95.

The Ultimate College Survival Guide. Peterson's, 1998. $14.95. To order: 1 (800) 338-3282 or http://www.petersons.com/.

The Unofficial Guide to Study Abroad. Arco, 1999. $14.95.

Important Addresses

The following organizations can provide useful information and resources to help you with all aspects of searching for, applying to, and going to college. I have provided the mailing address, phone number, and where available, Internet addresses for each organization.

Contact information for important organizations is also given in several chapters of this book. Return to the following chapters to find them:

Chapter 6: organizations and resources for international students

Chapter 15: various scholarship programs and college athletic organizations

Chapter 16: private education lenders

Chapter 19: organizations for potential graduate and professional school students

General College-Related Resources

General information about higher education:

American Council on Education (ACE)
One Dupont Circle, NW
Washington, D.C. 20036
(202) 939-9300
E-mail: web@ace.nche.edu
http://www.ACENET.edu/

Information about accredited schools and academic programs:

Council for Higher Education Accreditation (CHEA)
One Dupont Circle NW, Suite 854
Washington, D.C. 20036
(202) 955-6126

Information about community colleges:

> American Association of Community Colleges (AACC)
> One Dupont Circle NW, Suite 410
> Washington, D.C. 20036
> (202) 728-0200
> http://www.aacc.nche.edu/

General information about college admissions:

> National Association for College Admission Counseling (NACAC)
> 1631 Prince Street
> Alexandria, VA 22314-2818
> 1 (800) 822-6285
> http://www.nacac.com/index.html

Information about the Honor Society, the Common Application, scholarships, and contests:

> National Association of Secondary School Principals (NASSP)
> 1904 Association Drive
> Reston, VA 20191-1537
> (703) 860-0200
> E-mail: nassp@nassp.org
> http://www.nassp.org/

Standardized Testing

Information about the PSAT program:

> PSAT/NMSQT Office
> PO Box 6720
> Princeton, NJ 08541-6720
> (609) 771-7070
> E-mail: psat@collegeboard.org
> http://www.collegeboard.org/psat/student/html/indx001.html

Information about the SAT program:

> SAT Program
> PO Box 6228
> Princeton, NJ 08541-6228
> (609) 771-7600
> http://www.collegeboard.org/sat/html/students/indx001.html

Information about the AP program and AP exams:

> AP Services
> PO Box 6671
> Princeton, NJ 08541-6671
> 1 (888) CALL-4-AP
> E-mail: apexams@ets.org
> http://www.collegeboard.org/ap/index.html

Information about CLEP colleges and exams:

> CLEP
> PO Box 6601
> Princeton, NJ 08541-6601
> (609) 771-7865
> E-mail: clep@ets.org
> http://www.collegeboard.org/clep/students/study/html/
> testl000.html

Information about the ACT Assessment:

> ACT National Office
> 2201 North Dodge Street
> PO Box 168
> Iowa City, IA 52243-0168
> (319) 337-1000
> http://www.act.org/

Information about fairness in standardized testing:

> FairTest
> 342 Broadway
> Cambridge, MA 02139
> (617) 864-4810
> E-mail: Info@fairtest.org
> http://www.fairtest.org/

Financial Aid

Federal Sources of Financial Aid

Information about the FAFSA and federal financial aid:

> Federal Student Aid Information Center
> PO Box 84
> Washington, D.C. 20044-0084
> 1 (800) 4-FED-AID
> http://www.ed.gov/offices/OSFAP/Students/

Information about financial aid for members of the military, veterans, and their dependents:

> U.S. Department of Veterans Affairs
> Education Service
> 810 Vermont Avenue, NW
> Washington, D.C. 20420
> 1 (888) GI-BILL-1
> http://www.va.gov/education/

Information about the FFEL program, FFEL lenders, and state loan guaranty agencies:

> Coalition for Student Loan Reform (CSLR)
> 1156 Fifteenth NW, Suite 302
> Washington, D.C. 20005
> (202) 872-0559
> E-mail: info@cslr.org
> http://www.cslr.org

State Financial Aid Agencies

For information about all of the financial aid programs administered by your state, contact your state's aid agency. This agency can also put you in touch with your state's loan guaranty agency, for information about FFEL student and parent loans.

The following lists the state offices for these agencies in alphabetic order by state:

Alabama:

> Alabama Commission on Higher Education (ACHE)
> PO Box 302000
> Montgomery, AL 36130-2000
> (334) 242-1998
> http://www.ache.state.al.us/

Alaska:

> Alaska Commission on Postsecondary Education (ACPE)
> 3030 Vintage Boulevard
> Juneau, AK 99810-7109
> 1 (800) 441-2962
> E-mail: custsvc@educ.state.ak.us
> http://www.state.ak.us/acpe/

American Samoa:

> American Samoa Community College
> Board of Higher Education
> PO Box 2609
> Pago Pago, American Samoa 96799-2609
> (684) 699-9155

Arizona:

> Arizona Commission for Postsecondary Education (ACPE)
> 2020 North Central Avenue, Suite 275
> Phoenix, AZ 85004-4503
> (602) 229-2591
> E-mail: toni@www.acpe.asu.edu
> http://www.acpe.asu.edu/

Arkansas:

> Arkansas Department of Higher Education
> 114 East Capitol
> Little Rock, AR 72201
> 1 (800) 54-STUDY
> E-mail: finaid@adhe.arknet.edu
> http://www.adhe.arknet.edu/

California:

> California Student Aid Commission
> PO Box 419026
> Rancho Cordova, CA 95741-9026
> (916) 526-7590
> http://www.csac.ca.gov/

Colorado:

> Colorado Commission on Higher Education (CCHE)
> 1300 Broadway, Second Floor
> Denver, CO 80203
> (303) 866-2723
> E-mail: CCHE@state.co.us
> http://www.state.co.us/cche_dir/hecche.html

Connecticut:

> Connecticut Department of Higher Education
> 61 Woodland Street
> Hartford, CT 06105-2326
> (860) 947-1800
> http://ctdhe.commnet.edu/dheweb/default.htm

Delaware:

> Delaware Higher Education Commission
> Carvel State Office Building
> 820 North French Street
> Wilmington, DE 19801
> (302) 577-3240
> E-mail: mlaffey@state.de.us
> http://www.doe.state.de.us/high-ed/index.htm

District of Columbia:

> District of Columbia Department of Human Services
> Office of Postsecondary Education, Research and Assistance
> 2100 Martin Luther King Jr. Avenue SE, Suite 401
> Washington, D.C. 20020
> (202) 727-3685

Florida:

> Florida Department of Education
> Office of Student Financial Assistance
> 255 Collins Building
> 325 West Gaines Street
> Tallahassee, FL 32399-0400
> 1 (888) 827-2004
> E-mail: osfa@mail.doe.state.fl.us
> http://www.firn.edu/doe/bin00065/home0065.htm

Georgia:

> Georgia Student Finance Commission
> 2082 East Exchange Place
> Tucker, GA 30084
> (770) 414-3000
> E-mail: info@mail.gsfc.state.ga.us
> http://www.gsfc.org/

Guam:

> University of Guam
> 303 University Drive
> Mangilao, Guam 96923
> (671) 734-4469

Hawaii:

> Hawaii State Postsecondary Education Commission
> 2444 Dole Street, Room 202
> Honolulu, HI 96822-2394
> (808) 956-8213

Idaho:

> Idaho Board of Education
> PO Box 83720
> Boise, ID 83720-0037
> (208) 334-2270
> http://www.sde.state.id.us/osbe/board.htm

Illinois:

> Illinois Student Assistance Commission (ISAC)
> 1755 Lake Cook Road
> Deerfield, IL 60015-5209
> 1 (800) 899-ISAC
> E-mail: isac@wwa.com
> http://www.isac1.org/

Indiana:

State Student Assistance Commission of Indiana (SSACI)
150 West Market Street, Suite 500
Indianapolis, IN 46204
(317) 232-2350
E-mail: grants@ssaci.state.in.us
http://www.ai.org/ssaci/

Iowa:

Iowa College Student Aid Commission
200 10th Street, 4th Floor
Des Moines, IA 50309-2036
(515) 281-3501
E-mail: icsac@max.state.ia.us
http://www.state.ia.us/government/icsac/index.htm

Kansas:

Kansas Board of Regents
700 SW Harrison, Suite 1410
Topeka, KS 66603
(785) 296-3421
E-mail: Barb@kbor.state.ks.us
http://www.ukans.edu/~kbor/index.html

Kentucky:

Kentucky Higher Education Assistance Authority (KHEAA)
1050 U.S. 127 South
Frankfort, KY 40601-4323
(502) 696-7393
http://www.kheaa.com/

Louisiana:

Louisiana Office of Student Financial Assistance
PO Box 91202
Baton Rouge, LA 70821-9202
1 (800) 259-LOAN
http://www.osfa.state.la.us/

Maine:

Finance Authority of Maine (FAME)
PO Box 949
83 Western Avenue
Augusta, ME 04332-0949
(207) 623-3263
E-mail: info@famemaine.com
http://www.famemaine.com/

Maryland:

Maryland Higher Education Commission
16 Francis Street
Annapolis, MD 21401
1 (800) 974-1024
E-mail: ssamail@mhec.state.md.us
http://www.mhec.state.md.us/

Massachusetts:

Massachusetts Board of Higher Education
One Ashburton Place, Room 1401
Boston, MA 02108-1696
(617) 727-7785
E-mail: bhe@bhe.mass.edu
http://www.mass.edu/

Michigan:

Michigan Higher Education Assistance Authority (MHEAA)
Office of Scholarships and Grants
PO Box 30462
Lansing, MI 48909-7962
1 (877) FA-FACTS
http://www.treas.state.mi.us/college/mheaa.htm

Minnesota:

Minnesota Higher Education Services Office (MHESO)
1450 Energy Park Drive, Suite 350
St. Paul, MN 55108-5227
(651) 642-0567
http://www.mheso.state.mn.us/cfdocs/webdirectory/index.cfm

Mississippi:

Mississippi Postsecondary Education Financial Assistance Board
3825 Ridgewood Road
Jackson, MS 39211-6453
(601) 982-6663

Missouri:

Missouri Department of Higher Education
Student Assistance Division
3515 Amazonas Drive
Jefferson City, MO 65109-5717
1 (800) 473-6757
http://www.mocbhe.gov/mostars/finmenu.htm

Montana:

Montana Guaranteed Student Loan Program (MGSLP)
2500 East Broadway
PO Box 203101
Helena, MT 59620-3101
(406) 444-6570
E-mail: custserv@mgslp.state.mt.us
http://www.mgslp.state.mt.us/

Nebraska:

Coordinating Commission for Postsecondary Education
PO Box 95005
Lincoln, NE 68509-5005
(402) 471-2847
E-mail: ccpe01@nol.org
http://nol.org/NEpostsecondaryed/

Nevada:

Nevada Department of Education
Student Financial Services
400 West King Street
Capitol Complex
Carson City, NV 89710
(702) 687-5915

New Hampshire:

New Hampshire Postsecondary Education Commission
2 Industrial Park Drive
Concord, NH 03301-8512
(603) 271-2555
http://www.state.nh.us/postsecondary/

New Jersey:

New Jersey Higher Education Student Assistance Authority
(NJHESAA)
PO Box 540
Trenton, NJ 08625
1 (800) 792-8670
E-mail: osacs@osa.state.nj.us
http://www.state.nj.us/treasury/osa/

New Mexico:

New Mexico Commission on Higher Education
1068 Cerrillos Road
Santa Fe, NM 87501
(505) 827-7383
E-mail: highered@che.state.nm.us
http://www.nmche.org/index.html

New York:

New York State Student Aid
Higher Education Services Corporation (HESC)
Student Information
Albany, NY 12255
1 (800) NYSHESC
http://www.hesc.state.ny.us/

North Carolina:

North Carolina State Education Assistance Authority
PO Box 2688
Chapel Hill, NC 27515-2688
(919) 549-8614
E-mail: information@ncseaa.edu
http://www.ncseaa.edu/

North Dakota:

Student Financial Assistance Program
North Dakota University System
600 East Boulevard Avenue
Bismarck, ND 58505-0230
(701) 224-4114

Northern Mariana Islands:

Northern Marianas College
PO Box 1250
Saipan, Northern Mariana Islands 96950
(670) 234-6128

Ohio:

Ohio Board of Regents
State Grants and Scholarships
PO Box 182452
Columbus, OH 43218-2452
1 (888) 833-1133
E-mail: regents@regents.state.oh.us
http://www.bor.ohio.gov/

Oklahoma:

Oklahoma State Regents for Higher Education
500 Education Building
State Capitol Complex
Oklahoma City, OK 73105
(405) 524-9100
E-mail: tsimonton@osrhe.edu
http://www.okhighered.org/

Oregon:

Oregon State Scholarship Commission
Valley River Office Park
1500 Valley River Drive, Suite 100
Eugene, OR 97401
(541) 687-7400
E-mail: ag57500dv@www.state.or.us
http://www.ossc.state.or.us/

Pennsylvania:

Pennsylvania Higher Education Assistance Agency (PHEAA)
1200 North Seventh Street
Harrisburg, PA 17102
1 (800) 692-7392
http://www.pheaa.org/

Puerto Rico:

Council on Higher Education
Box 23305—UPR Station
Rio Piedras, PR 00931
(809) 758-3350

Rhode Island:

Rhode Island Higher Education Assistance Authority
560 Jefferson Boulevard
Warwick, RI 02886
1 (800) 922-9855

South Carolina:

South Carolina Commission on Higher Education
1333 Main Street, Suite 200
Columbia, SC 29201
(803) 737-2260
http://che400.state.sc.us/

South Dakota:

South Dakota Department of Education and Cultural Affairs
Kneip Building, 3rd Floor
700 Governor's Drive
Pierre, SD 57501-2291
(605) 773-3134
E-mail: janelle.toman@state.sd.us
http://www.state.sd.us/state/executive/deca/

Tennessee:

Tennessee Student Assistance Corporation (TSAC)

404 James Robertson Parkway

Suite 1950, Parkway Towers

Nashville, TN 37243-0820

(615) 741-1346

http://www.state.tn.us/tsac/

Texas:

Texas Higher Education Coordinating Board

PO Box 12788

Austin, TX 78711-2788

(512) 483-6101

http://www.thecb.state.tx.us/

Utah:

Utah Higher Education Assistance Authority (UHEAA)

PO Box 45202

Salt Lake City, UT 84145-0202

1 (800) 418-8757

E-mail: uheaa@utahsbr.edu

http://www.utah-student-assist.org/

Vermont:

Vermont Student Assistance Corporation (VSAC)

PO Box 2000

Champlain Mill, 4th Floor

Winooski, VT 05404

1 (800) 642-3177

E-mail: info@vsac.org

http://www.vsac.org/

Virgin Islands:

Virgin Islands Joint Boards of Education

Charlotte Amalie, PO Box 11900

St. Thomas, Virgin Islands 00801

(809) 774-4546

Virginia:

State Council of Higher Education for Virginia (SCHEV)

James Monroe Building, 9th Floor

101 North 14th Street

Richmond, VA 23219

(804) 225-2317

http://www.schev.edu/

Washington:

Washington State Higher Education Coordinating Board
917 Lakeridge Way
PO Box 43430
Olympia, WA 98504-3430
(360) 753-7800
E-mail: info@hecb.wa.gov
http://www.hecb.wa.gov/index.html

West Virginia:

Student Services
Central Office, State College and University Systems of West Virginia
1018 Kanawaha Boulevard East, Suite 700
Charleston, WV 25301
(304) 558-2101
http://www.scusco.wvnet.edu/www/stserv/finaid.htm

Wisconsin:

Wisconsin Higher Educational Aids Board
PO Box 7885
Madison, WI 53707-7885
(608) 267-2206
E-mail: HEABmail@heab.state.wi.us
http://www.heab.state.wi.us/

Wyoming:

Wyoming Department of Education
2300 Capitol Avenue
Hathaway Building, 2nd Floor
Cheyenne, WY 82002-0050
(307) 777-7675
http://www.k12.wy.us/wdehome.html

State Prepaid Tuition Programs

Alabama PrePaid Affordable College Tuition (PACT): for more information, contact the Office of the State Treasurer at 1 (800) ALA-PACT

Alaska Advance College Tuition (ACT): for more information, call 1 (888) 966-6358

Arizona Family College Savings Program: for more information, contact the Arizona Commission for Postsecondary Education at (602) 229-2591

Golden State Scholarshare Trust (California): for more information, call (916) 526-3027

Colorado Prepaid Tuition Fund: for more information, call 1 (800) 478-5651 or go to http://www.prepaidtuition.org/

Connecticut Higher Education Trust (CHET): for more information, call 1 (888) 799-CHET or go to http://www.aboutchet.com/

Delaware Family Account for College Tomorrow (FACT): for more information, call 1 (800) 544-1655

National Capitol College Savings Trust (District of Columbia): for more information, call (202) 727-6055

Florida Prepaid College Tuition Program: for more information, call 1 (800) 552-4723 or go to http://fsba.state.fl.us/prepaid/

College Illinois! Prepaid Tuition Program: for more information, call 1 (877) 877-3724 or go to http://www.collegeillinois.com/

Indiana Family College Savings Plan: for more information, call 1 (888) 814-6800 or go to http://www.che.state.in.us/ifcsp/

Kentucky: for more information, call 1 (800) 338-0318

Louisiana START Saving Program: for more information, call 1 (800) 259-5626 ext. 1012 or go to http://www.osfa.state.la.us/START.htm

Maryland Prepaid College Trust: for more information, call 1 (888) 4MD-GRAD or go to http://www.prepaid.usmd.edu/

Massachusetts College Saving Program: for more information, call 1 (800) 449-MEFA

Michigan Education Trust (MET): for more information, call 1 (800) MET-4KID

Mississippi Prepaid Affordable College Tuition Program (MPACT): for more information, contact the Mississippi Treasury Department at 1 (800) 987-4450 or at http://www.treasury.state.ms.us/mpact.htm

Montana Family Education Savings Program: for more information, call 1 (800) 888-2723 or go to http://montana.collegesavings.com/

Nevada Prepaid Tuition Program: for more information, call 1 (888) 477-2667

UNIQUE College Investing Plan (New Hampshire): for more information, call 1 (800) 544-1722 or go to http://personal111.fidelity.com:80/planning/college/content/unique.html.tvsr

New Jersey Better Educational Savings Trust (NJBEST): for more information, contact the Office of Student Assistance at 1 (800) 792-8670 or at http://www.state.nj.us/treasury/osa/

New York College Choice Tuition Savings Program: for more information, call 1 (877) NYSAVES or go to http://www.nysaves.org/

North Carolina College Vision Fund: for more information, contact the College Foundation at 1 (888) CFI-6400 or go to http://www.collegevisionfund.org/

Ohio Tuition Trust Authority (OTTA): for more information, call 1 (800) AFFORD-IT or go to http://www.prepaid-tuition.state.oh.us/

Pennsylvania Tuition Account Program (TAP): for more information, contact 1 (800) 440-4000 or go to http://www.patap.org/

Rhode Island Higher Education Savings Trust: for more information, call 1 (877) 4-RIHEST or go to http://www.rihest.com/

South Carolina: for more information, call (803) 253-6217

Tennessee BEST: for more information, contact the State of Tennessee Treasury Department at 1 (888) 486-BEST or at http://www.state.tn.us/treasury/best.htm

Texas Tomorrow Fund: for more information, call 1 (800) 445-GRAD or go to http://www.window.state.tx.us/comptrol/ttf/ttfmain.html

Utah Educational Savings Plan Trust: for more information, call 1 (800) 418-2551 or send e-mail to gpetersen@utahsbr.edu

Vermont Higher Education Savings Plan: for more information, contact the Vermont Student Assistance Corporation at 1 (800) 642-3177

Virginia Prepaid Education Program: for more information, call 1 (888) 567-0540 or go to http://www.vpep.state.va.us/

Guaranteed Education Tuition (Washington): for more information, call 1 (877) GET-TUIT or go to http://www.get.wa.gov/

West Virginia Prepaid College Plan: for more information, call 1 (800) 307-4701 or go to http://www.wvtreasury.com/prepaid.htm

Wisconsin Education Investment Program (EdVest WI): for more information, call 1 (888) EDVESTWI or go to http://edvest.state.wi.us/

Wyoming Advance Payment of Higher Education Costs: for more information, call (307) 766-3214

Colleges and Universities That Accept Common or Electronic Applications

Directory of Schools That Accept the Common Application

The directory in Table E.1 lists the schools that use the Common Application. It also indicates which schools accept the electronic version of the Common Application and which schools request a supplemental form in addition to the Common Application (supplemental forms must be obtained directly from the college—either write off for the form or download it from the school's website).

TABLE E.1: SCHOOLS THAT ACCEPT
THE COMMON APPLICATION

School	Supplemental Form Required	Electronic Version Accepted
Adelphi University (Garden City, NY)	No	Yes
Agnes Scott College (Decatur, GA)	No	No
Albertson College (Caldwell, ID)	No	No
Albion College (Albion, MI)	No	Yes
Albright College (Reading, PA)	No	No
Alfred University (Alfred, NY)	No	Yes
Allegheny College (Philadelphia, PA)	Yes	No
American University (Washington, D.C.)	No	No
Amherst College (Amherst, MA)	Yes	No
Antioch College (Yellow Springs, OH)	Yes	No
Assumption College (Worcester, MA)	No	No
Babson College (Babson Park, MA)	Yes	Yes
Bard College (Annandale-on-Hudson, NY)	Yes	No
Barnard College (New York, NY)	No	No
Bates College (Lewiston, ME)	Yes	No
Beaver College (Glenside, PA)	No	No
Beloit College (Beloit, WI)	Yes	No
Bennington College (Bennington, VT)	No	No
Bentley College (Waltham, MA)	Yes	No
Birmingham-Southern College (Birmingham, AL)	Yes	Yes
Boston College (Chestnut Hill, MA)	No	No
Boston University (Boston, MA)	No	Yes
Bowdoin College (Brunswick, ME)	Yes	No
Brandeis University (Waltham, MA)	No	No
Bryant College (Smithfield, RI)	Yes	No
Bryn Mawr College (Bryn Mawr, PA)	Yes	Yes
Bucknell University (Lewisburg, PA)	No	No
Butler University (Indianapolis, IN)	No	No
Carleton College (Northfield, MN)	No	Yes
Case Western Reserve University (Cleveland, OH)	No	No
Centenary College of Louisiana (Shreveport, LA)	No	No

School	Supplemental Form Required	Electronic Version Accepted
Centre College (Danville, KY)	No	No
Claremont McKenna College (Claremont, CA)	Yes	No
Clark University (Worcester, MA)	Yes	No
Coe College (Cedar Rapids, IA)	No	No
Colby College (Waterville, ME)	No	Yes
Colby-Sawyer College (New London, NH)	Yes	Yes
Colgate University (Hamilton, NY)	Yes	Yes
College of the Holy Cross (Worcester, MA)	No	Yes
College of St. Benedict (St. Joseph, MN)	No	Yes
College of Wooster (Wooster, OH)	No	Yes
Colorado College (Colorado Springs, CO)	Yes	Yes
Connecticut College (New London, CT)	No	No
Cornell College (Mount Vernon, IA)	No	No
Dartmouth College (Hanover, NH)	Yes	Yes
Davidson College (Davidson, NC)	Yes	No
Denison University (Granville, OH)	No	No
DePauw University (Greencastle, IN)	Yes	No
Dickinson College (Carlisle, PA)	Yes	No
Drew University (Madison, NJ)	No	No
Duke University (Durham, NC)	No	No
Earlham College (Richmond, IN)	No	No
Eckerd College (St. Petersburg, FL)	No	Yes
Elizabethtown College (Elizabethtown, PA)	No	Yes
Elmira College (Elmira, NY)	No	No
Embry-Riddle Aeronautical University (Arizona and Florida campuses)	No	No
Emory University (Atlanta, GA)	Yes	Yes
Eugene Lang College (New York, NY)	Yes	No
Fairfield University (Fairfield, CT)	Yes	No
Fisk University (Nashville, TN)	No	No
Fordham University (New York, NY)	Yes	No
Franklin & Marshall College (Lancaster, PA)	Yes	Yes

TABLE E.1: SCHOOLS THAT ACCEPT
THE COMMON APPLICATION (CONT.)

School	Supplemental Form Required	Electronic Version Accepted
Furman University (Greenville, SC)	Yes	No
George Washington University (Washington, D.C.)	Yes	No
Gettysburg College (Gettysburg, PA)	No	No
Gonzaga University (Spokane, WA)	Yes	Yes
Goucher College (Baltimore, MD)	Yes	Yes
Grinnell College (Grinnell, IA)	Yes	No
Guilford College (Greensboro, NC)	No	Yes
Gustavus Adolphus College (St. Peter, MN)	Yes	No
Hamilton College (Clinton, NY)	Yes	Yes
Hampden-Sydney College (Hampden-Sydney, VA)	No	No
Hanover College (Hanover, IN)	No	No
Hartwick College (Oneonta, NY)	No	No
Harvard University (Cambridge, MA)	Yes	No
Harvey Mudd College (Claremont, CA)	Yes	No
Haverford College (Haverford, PA)	Yes	No
Hendrix College (Conway, AR)	No	No
Hiram College (Hiram, OH)	No	Yes
Hobart and William Smith Colleges (Geneva, NY)	No	Yes
Hofstra University (Hempstead, NY)	No	No
Hollins University (Roanoke, VA)	Yes	No
Hood College (Frederick, MD)	No	No
Ithaca College (Ithaca, NY)	No	No
Johns Hopkins University (Baltimore, MD)	Yes	No
Juniata College (Huntingdon, PA)	No	No
Kalamazoo College (Kalamazoo, MI)	No	Yes
Kenyon College (Gambier, OH)	Yes	No
Knox College (Galesburg, IL)	No	No
Lafayette College (Easton, PA)	No	No
Lake Forest College (Lake Forest, IL)	Yes	Yes
Lawrence University (Appleton, WI)	Yes	Yes
Lehigh University (Bethlehem, PA)	Yes	Yes

School	Supplemental Form Required	Electronic Version Accepted
LeMoyne College (Syracuse, NY)	No	No
Lewis & Clark College (Portland, OR)	Yes	Yes
Linfield College (McMinnville, OR)	No	No
Loyola College (Baltimore, MD)	Yes	No
Loyola University (New Orleans, LA)	No	Yes
Lynchburg College (Lynchburg, VA)	No	Yes
Macalester College (St. Paul, MN)	Yes	Yes
Manhattan College (Riverdale, NY)	Yes	No
Manhattanville College (Purchase, NY)	No	Yes
Marietta College (Marietta, OH)	No	No
Marquette University (Milwaukee, WI)	No	No
Middlebury College (Middlebury, VT)	No	Yes
Mills College (Oakland, CA)	Yes	Yes
Millsaps College (Jackson, MS)	No	No
Moravian College (Bethlehem, PA)	Yes	No
Morehouse College (Atlanta, GA)	No	No
Mount Holyoke College (South Hadley, MA)	Yes	No
Muhlenberg College (Allentown, PA)	No	No
New York University (New York, NY)	No	No
Oberlin College (Oberlin, OH)	Yes	Yes
Occidental College (Los Angeles, CA)	Yes	No
Ohio Wesleyan University (Delaware, OH)	No	Yes
Pitzer College (Claremont, CA)	No	No
Pomona College (Claremont, CA)	Yes	No
Randolph-Macon College (Ashland, VA)	No	No
Randolph-Macon Woman's College (Lynchburg, VA)	Yes	Yes
Reed College (Portland, OR)	Yes	No
Regis College (Weston, MA)	No	Yes
Regis University (Denver, CO)	No	No
Rensselaer Polytechnic Institute (Troy, NY)	No	No
Rhodes College (Memphis, TN)	Yes	Yes
Rice University (Houston, TX)	Yes	Yes

TABLE E.1: SCHOOLS THAT ACCEPT
THE COMMON APPLICATION (CONT.)

School	Supplemental Form Required	Electronic Version Accepted
Ripon College (Ripon, WI)	No	No
Rochester Institute of Technology (Rochester, NY)	No	No
Roger Williams University (Bristol, RI)	No	Yes
Rollins College (Winter Park, FL)	No	No
Salem College (Winston-Salem, NC)	No	Yes
Santa Clara University (Santa Clara, CA)	Yes	No
Sarah Lawrence College (Bronxville, NY)	Yes	No
Scripps College (Claremont, CA)	No	Yes
Seattle University (Seattle, WA)	No	No
Simmons College (Boston, MA)	Yes	No
Skidmore College (Saratoga Springs, NY)	No	Yes
Smith College (Northampton, MA)	Yes	No
Southern Methodist University (Dallas, TX)	No	No
Southwestern University (Georgetown, TX)	No	No
Spelman College (Atlanta, GA)	Yes	No
St. John's University (Collegeville, MN)	No	Yes
St. Joseph's University (Philadelphia, PA)	No	No
St. Lawrence University (Canton, NY)	No	No
St. Louis University (St. Louis, MO)	No	No
St. Michael's College (Colchester, VT)	No	Yes
St. Norbert College (DePere, WI)	No	No
St. Olaf College (Northfield, MN)	Yes	No
Stetson University (DeLand, FL)	No	No
Stonehill College (Easton, MA)	No	No
Suffolk University (Boston, MA)	No	Yes
Susquehanna University (Selinsgrove, PA)	No	Yes
Swarthmore College (Swarthmore, PA)	Yes	No
Syracuse University (Syracuse, NY)	Yes	No
Texas Christian University (Fort Worth, TX)	No	No
Trinity College (Hartford, CT)	No	No
Trinity University (San Antonio, TX)	No	Yes

School	Supplemental Form Required	Electronic Version Accepted
Tufts University (Medford, MA)	Yes	Yes
Tulane University (New Orleans, LA)	No	No
Union College (Schenectady, NY)	Yes	No
University of Dallas (Dallas, TX)	No	No
University of Denver (Denver, CO)	No	No
University of Miami (Miami, FL)	No	Yes
University of the Pacific (Stockton, CA)	No	No
University of Portland (Portland, OR)	No	No
University of Puget Sound (Tacoma, WA)	No	Yes
University of Redlands (Redlands, CA)	Yes	No
University of Richmond (Richmond, VA)	Yes	No
University of Rochester (Rochester, NY)	Yes	No
University of Scranton (Scranton, PA)	No	No
University of the South (Sewanee, TN)	Yes	No
University of Tulsa (Tulsa, OK)	No	No
Ursinus College (Collegeville, PA)	Yes	No
Utica College (Utica, NY)	No	No
Valparaiso University (Valparaiso, IN)	No	No
Vanderbilt University (Nashville, TN)	Yes	No
Vassar College (Poughkeepsie, NY)	No	No
Wabash College (Crawfordsville, IN)	Yes	No
Wagner College (Staten Island, NY)	Yes	Yes
Wake Forest University (Winston-Salem, NC)	Yes	No
Washington and Lee University (Lexington, VA)	No	No
Washington College (Chestertown, MD)	No	Yes
Washington University (St. Louis, MO)	No	No
Wellesley College (Wellesley, MA)	Yes	No
Wells College (Aurora, NY)	No	No
Wesleyan University (Middletown, CT)	No	Yes
Westminster College (New Wilmington, PA)	No	No
Wheaton College (Norton, MA)	Yes	No
Whitman College (Walla Walla, WA)	Yes	Yes

TABLE E.1: SCHOOLS THAT ACCEPT
THE COMMON APPLICATION (CONT.)

School	Supplemental Form Required	Electronic Version Accepted
Whittier College (Whittier, CA)	No	No
Widener University (Chester, PA)	No	Yes
Willamette University (Salem, OR)	Yes	No
Williams College (Williamstown, MA)	No	No
Wittenberg University (Springfield, OH)	No	No
Worcester Polytechnic Institute (Worcester, MA)	No	No

Directory of Schools that Accept Electronic Applications

The directory in Table E.2 lists most of the colleges and universities that enable you to fill out and submit applications over the Internet, along with the Web addresses of their electronic applications. This list excludes schools that solely accept the electronic version of the Common Application (listed in the preceding table) or that accept electronic applications only via an application service (see Table 4.2 in Chapter 4, "The Lowdown on the Application Process").

Important note: For the most part, the Web addresses in this list link directly to the application for full-time, undergraduate admissions. If you're a graduate school applicant, a transfer student, an international student, a nontraditional student, or if you're applying for part-time admission, check for a different application form or special instructions. You should find all the information you need in the school website's "Admissions" or "For Prospective Students" section.

TABLE E.2: SCHOOLS THAT ACCEPT
ELECTRONIC APPLICATIONS

School	Electronic Application Address
Adrian College (Adrian, MI)	http://www.adrian.edu/applicat.htm
Alabama A&M University (Normal, AL)	http://www.aamu.edu/admit.html
Alaska Pacific University (Anchorage, AK)	http://www.alaskapacific.edu/forms/polyform.dll/app
Albertson College (Caldwell, ID)	http://artemis.acofi.edu/admisap.htm
Albion College (Albion, MI)	http://www.albion.edu/admiss/admissions/onlineapp.html
Albright College (Reading, PA)	http://www.alb.edu/admission/online-app.html

School	Electronic Application Address
Alcorn State University (Lorman, MS)	http://www.alcorn.edu/admissions/firstpg_adm.htm
Alfred University (Alfred, NY)	http://www.alfred.edu/admissions/html/freshapp.html
Allentown College of St. Francis de Sales (Center Valley, PA)	http://www4.allencol.edu/~admiss/form.html
Alvernia College (Reading, PA)	http://www.alvernia.edu/appday.htm
Anderson University (Anderson, IN)	http://www.anderson.edu/admissions/application/onlineapp.html
Aquinas College (Grand Rapids, MI)	http://www.aquinas.edu/undergraduate/applying/applicat.htm
Arkansas Tech University (Russellville, AR)	http://www.atu.edu/acad/admission/Forms/admform.htm
Asbury College (Wilmore, KY)	http://www.asbury.edu/admiss/apply.htm
Ashland University (Ashland, OH)	http://www.ashland.edu/appli.html
Assumption College (Worcester, MA)	http://www.assumption.edu/admiss/freshman.html
Averett College (Danville, VA)	http://www.averett.edu/special/apply.html
Barry University (Miami Shores, FL)	http://www2.barry.edu/vpaa-admissions/esuginf1.html
Bay Path College (Longmeadow, MA)	http://www.baypath.edu/RegApplication.html
Baylor University (Waco, TX)	https://www.baylor.edu/~Admissions/UndergraduateApplication.html
Beaver College (Glenside, PA)	http://www.beaver.edu/admiss/applypt1.htm
Bellarmine College (Louisville, KY)	http://www.bellarmine.edu/public/admiss/webforms/underapp/admission.asp
Beloit College (Beloit, WI)	http://admiss.beloit.edu/applying/applications3.html
Bethany College (Scotts Valley, CA)	http://www.bethany.edu/Admissions/Application
Bethany College (Bethany, WI)	http://www.bethanywv.edu/Admissions/applications.html
Bethel College (Mishawaka, IN)	http://www.bethel-in.edu/adm/admapp.htm

TABLE E.2: SCHOOLS THAT ACCEPT
ELECTRONIC APPLICATIONS (CONT.)

School	Electronic Application Address
Bethel College (McKenzie, TN)	http://www.bethel-college.edu/admissions/application.htm
Biola University (La Mirada, CA)	http://www.biola.edu/admin/admissions/apply/
Bloomsburg University (Bloomsburg, PA)	http://www.bloomu.edu/admin/form/ungrad.htm
Boise State University (Boise, ID)	http://admissions.boisestate.edu/applicat.htm
Bowling Green State University (Bowling Green, OH)	http://www.bgsu.edu/welcome/appintro.html
Bradford College (Haverhill, MA)	http://www.bradford.edu/cgi-bin/admissions/pass_check.pl?1
Bradley University (Peoria, IL)	http://www.bradley.edu/admissions/application.html
Brewton-Parker College (Mt. Vernon, GA)	http://www.bigdigital.com/bpc/application.html
Bridgewater College (Bridgewater, VA)	http://www.bridgewater.edu/departments/admissions/applic.html
Brigham Young University (Provo, UT)	http://ar.byu.edu/admissions/apply_electronically/
Bryan College (Dayton, TN)	http://www.bryan.edu/Admissions/Apply%20for%20Admission.htm
Bryant College (Smithfield, RI)	http://www.bryant.edu/
Bryn Athyn College of the New Church (Bryn Athyn, PA)	http://www.newchurch.edu/college/catalog/application/index.html
Buena Vista University (Storm Lake, IA)	http://www.bvu.edu/~admis/application.html
Caldwell College (Caldwell, NJ)	http://www.caldwell.edu/admissions/udrgrad_app.html
California Lutheran University (Thousand Oaks, CA)	http://callutheran.edu/htdocs/instruction.html
Cameron University (Lawton, OK)	http://www.cameron.edu/student_affairs/admissions/application.html
Canisius College (Buffalo, NY)	http://www.canisius.edu/canhp/departments/admissions/
Capital University (Columbus, OH)	http://www.capital.edu/admissio/admfrapp.htm

School	Electronic Application Address
Capitol College (Laurel, MD)	http://www.capitol-college.edu/Visitors/adm/apply/fulltimeapp.htm
Carleton College (Northfield, MN)	http://www.carleton.edu/admissions/application/
Carnegie Mellon University (Pittsburgh, PA)	http://www.cmu.edu/enrollment/admission/process/apply.html
Carroll College (Waukesha, WI)	http://www.cc.edu/admissions/app.html
Carthage College (Kenosha, WI)	http://www.carthage.edu/admissions/carthapp.html
Catawba College (Salisbury, NC)	http://www.catawba.edu/admisfrm.htm?
Cedar Crest College (Allentown, PA)	http://www.cedarcrest.edu/admissions/appform.html
Cedarville College (Cedarville, OH)	http://www.cedarville.edu/dept/adm/application.htm
Centenary College (Hackettstown, NJ)	http://www.centenarycollege.edu/adapp.htm
Central Connecticut State University (New Britian, CT)	http://interact.ccsu.edu/admission/applform.htm
Central Methodist College (Fayette, MO)	http://www.cmc.edu/admissionsweb/Admission_App.html
Central Washington University (Ellensburg, WA)	https://www.cwu.edu/~cts/adm_appform_part1.htmlx
Chaminade University of Honolulu (Honolulu, HI)	http://www.chaminade.edu/apply1.html
Chapman University (Orange, CA)	http://www.chapman.edu/admission/
Chowan College (Murfreesboro, NC)	http://www.chowan.edu/admis/appli.htm
Christendom College (Front Royal, VA)	http://www.christendom.edu/undergrd.html
Christian Brothers University (Memphis, TN)	http://www.cbu.edu/Admissions/Day/ugapp.html
Christopher Newport University (Newport News, VA)	http://www.cnu.edu/admin/admit/forms/ug/UngrdApp.html
Clarke College (Dubuque, IA)	http://www.clarke.edu/admissions/NewViewbook/application.htm
Clarkson College (Omaha, NE)	http://www.clarksoncollege.edu/Applications/Undergraduate/Undergrad_Application.htm
Clarkson University (Potsdam, NY)	http://heron.tc.clarkson.edu/clarkson/admis/firsty.html

TABLE E.2: SCHOOLS THAT ACCEPT
ELECTRONIC APPLICATIONS (CONT.)

School	Electronic Application Address
Coe College (Cedar Rapids, IA)	http://www.coe.edu/admission/AdApp.html
College of the Atlantic (Bar Harbor, ME)	http://www.coa.edu/ADMISSIONS/admission_inst.html
College of New Jersey (Ewing, NJ)	https://tcnj6000.tcnj.edu/
College of St. Benedict and St. John's University (St. Joseph, MN)	https://www.csbsju.edu/prospective/admissions/application.htm
College of St. Mary (Omaha, NE)	http://www.csm.edu/html/appl.htm
College of Wooster (Wooster, OH)	http://www.wooster.edu/admissions/onlineapp/online.html
Colorado State University (Fort Collins, CO)	http://www.colostate.edu/~cwis116/uswel.html
Columbia International University (Columbia, SC)	http://209.196.158.90/cgi-bin/UndgApplyStart.cfm
Concordia College (Moorhead, MN)	http://www.cord.edu/dept/admissions/applicationform.html
Concordia University (River Forest, IL)	http://www.curf.edu/admis/appinfo.htx
Concordia University (St. Paul, MN)	http://www.csp.edu/admissions/applicat.htm
Converse College (Spartanburg, SC)	http://www.converse.edu/olform.htm
Creighton University (Omaha, NE)	http://www.creighton.edu/ADM/frm.html
Culver-Stockton College (Canton, MO)	http://www.culver.edu/~admissions/apppage1.htm
Dakota State University (Madison, SD)	http://www.dsu.edu/departments/admissions/application-form.html
Dana College (Blair, NE)	http://www.dana.edu/admissions/admiapp2.html
Davis & Elkins College (Elkins, WV)	http://dne.edu/deadm.htm
Delta State University (Cleveland, MS)	http://www.deltast.edu/cgi-bin/adm_appl
DePaul University (Chicago, IL)	http://emu.depaul.edu/admission/freshpass.asp
Dickinson College (Carlisle, PA)	http://delta.dickinson.edu/ColleagueWeb/apply.html
Dowling College (Oakdale, NY)	http://www.dowling.edu/applying/applying/undergra.htm

School	Electronic Application Address
Drexel University (Philadelphia, PA)	http://apply.admissions.drexel.edu/
East Carolina University (Greenville, NC)	https://admissions.eastnet.ecu.edu/
East Tennessee State University (Johnson City, TN)	http://www2.etsu.edu/adm/ mwaam_master.htm
Eastern Connecticut State University (Willimantic, CT)	http://nutmeg.ctstateu.edu/ admis/admission_form.html
Eastern Mennonite University (Harrisonburg, VA)	http://www.emu.edu/admiss/ forms/app_intr.htm
Eastern New Mexico University (Portales, NM)	http://www.enmu.edu/admissions/ apply/application.html
Eastern Washington University (Cheney, WA)	http://www.ewu.edu/StudentServ/ HowTo/forms/FMADM.HTM
Elizabethtown College (Elizabethtown, PA)	http://www.etown.edu/~admiss/
Embry-Riddle Aeronautical University (Arizona and Florida campuses)	https://secure.embryriddle.edu/ admissions/undergrad/application.html
Emory & Henry College (Emory, VA)	http://www.ehc.edu/web/admiss/ ehapp.html
Emporia State University (Emporia, KS)	http://www.emporia.edu/admiss/ app/app.htm
Erskine College (Due West, SC)	http://www.erskine.edu/application1. html
Faulkner University (Montgomery, AL)	http://www.faulkner.edu/admissions/ undergrad/index.htm
Ferris State University (Big Rapids, MI)	http://www.ferris.edu/htmls/admision/ application/homepage.htm
Fitchburg State College (Fitchburg, MA)	http://www.fsc.edu/www/ admissions_application_online.html
Florida Gulf Coast University (Ft. Myers, FL)	http://itech.fgcu.edu/online/
Florida Memorial College (Miami, FL)	http://www.fmc.edu/fmc_admissions1. html
Florida State University (Tallahassee, FL)	http://www.ais.fsu.edu:82/admissions/ step1.jhtml
Fort Hays State University (Hays, KS)	http://www.fhsu.edu/admissions/ ugform.html
Fort Lewis College (Durango, CO)	http://www.fortlewis.edu/ inst-adv/admiss/admisap1.html

TABLE E.2: SCHOOLS THAT ACCEPT
ELECTRONIC APPLICATIONS (CONT.)

School	Electronic Application Address
Franklin College (Franklin, IN)	http://www.franklincoll.edu/admweb/apply_gm.htm
Franklin Pierce College (Rindge, NH)	http://www.fpc.edu/cgibin/app.htm
Fresno Pacific University (Fresno, CA)	http://sunthree.fresno.edu/undergrad/new_students/admissions/online_application.html
Gardner-Webb University (Boiling Springs, NC)	http://www.gardner-webb.edu/GWU/main/admissions/app.html
Geneva College (Beaver Falls, PA)	http://www.geneva.edu/graphics/adm-fin/adm/adm-form.html
George Mason University (Fairfax, VA)	http://admissions.gmu.edu/apps/freshman.html
Georgia Institute of Technology (Atlanta, GA)	http://www.enrollment.gatech.edu/apply/option1.html
Georgia Southern University (Statesboro, GA)	http://www2.gasou.edu/sta/adm/forms/admis.html
Georgia Southwestern State University (Americus, GA)	http://www.gsw.edu/~gsw1/admissions/undergradapp.html
Gettysburg College (Gettysburg, PA)	http://www.gettysburg.edu/homepage/admissions/gusource.html
Gonzaga University (Spokane, WA)	http://www.gonzaga.edu/admissions/apply.html
Goshen College (Goshen, IN)	http://www.goshen.edu/admissions/vbapp.htm
Grace University (Omaha, NE)	http://www.graceu.edu/index2.html
Graceland College (Lamoni, IA)	http://www2.graceland.edu/potential/application/appform.html
Grand Valley State University (Allendale, MI)	http://www.gvsu.edu/college/apply.html
Green Mountain College (Poultney, VT)	http://www.greenmtn.edu/ApplicationExpress.htm
Greensboro College (Greensboro, NC)	http://www.gborocollege.edu/forms/admissapp.htm
Greenville College (Greenville, IL)	http://www.greenville.edu/Admissions/Application/instruct.htm
Gwynedd Mercy College (Gynedd Valley, PA)	http://www.gmc.edu/applygmc.htm
Hampden-Sydney College (Hampden-Sydney, VA)	http://www.hsc.edu/admis/apply/plans/

School	Electronic Application Address
Hawaii Pacific University (Honolulu, HI)	http://www.hpu.edu/forms/app-ugrd.html
Henderson State University (Arkadelphia, AR)	http://www.hsu.edu/dept/ura/application.html
Hofstra University (Hempstead, NY)	http://www.hofstra.edu/application
Hollins University (Roanoke, VA)	http://www.hollins.edu/html/application/apply.htm
Hood College (Frederick, MD)	http://www.hood.edu/admiss/application/intro.html
Illinois College (Jacksonville, IL)	http://www2.ic.edu/admis/application.html
Illinois Institute of Technology (Chicago, IL)	http://216.47.147.206/freshman/
Illinois Wesleyan University (Bloomington, IL)	http://star.iwu.edu/application/instructions.html
Indiana State University (Terre Haute, IN)	http://web.indstate.edu:80/admissions/instruct.htm
Indiana University (Bloomington, IN)	http://www.indiana.edu/~iuadmit/online/appl.html
Indiana University Northwest (Gary, IN)	http://www.iun.indiana.edu/admissions/Undergra.htm
Indiana University of Pennsylvania (Indiana, PA)	http://www.iup.edu/admiss/appl2.htmlx
Indiana University-Purdue University Indianapolis	http://www.iupui.edu/~admiss/
Indiana Wesleyan University (Marion, IN)	http://www.indwes.edu/Admissions/Application/FirstTime.html
Ithaca College (Ithaca, NY)	https://adminwww.ithaca.edu/admis/
Jackson State University (Jackson, MS)	http://ccaix.jsums.edu/~www/admis_form.htm
Jacksonville State University (Jacksonville, AL)	http://jsucc.jsu.edu/cgi-bin/apps/undergraduate
Jacksonville University (Jacksonville, FL)	http://www.ju.edu/admissions/application/appform.htm
Jamestown College (Jamestown, ND)	http://acc.jc.edu/Admissions/appform.htm
John Brown University (Siloam Springs, AR)	http://www.jbu.edu/apply_online/
Johns Hopkins University (Baltimore, MD)	http://apply.jhu.edu/action/admissions.nsf/pages/main_get

TABLE E.2: SCHOOLS THAT ACCEPT
ELECTRONIC APPLICATIONS (CONT.)

School	Electronic Application Address
Johnson C. Smith University (Charlotte, NC)	http://www.jcsu.edu/admiss/admission_main.htm
Kansas State University (Manhattan, KS)	http://www.ksu.edu/admit/application.html
Kent State University (Kent, OH)	http://secure.kent.edu/admissions/AppOnline.htm
Kentucky State University (Frankfort, KY)	http://www.kysu.edu/Admission/admitapp.html
Kettering University (Flint, MI)	http://www.kettering.edu/admin/corp-rel/admapp.htm
King College (Bristol, TN)	http://www.king.edu/admissions/app.htm
Kutztown University (Kutztown, PA)	http://www.kutztown.edu/admin/admission/application
Lasell College (Newton, MA)	http://www.lasell.edu/apply.htm
Lebanon Valley College (Annville, PA)	http://www.lvc.edu/www/admission/application_form.html
Lewis-Clark State College (Lewiston, ID)	http://www.lcsc.edu/admissions/adm/application.htm
Lincoln University (Lincoln University, PA)	http://www.lincoln.edu/pages/application/
Lock Haven University (Lock Haven, PA)	http://www.lhup.edu/admissions/application_form.html
Loyola University (New Orleans, LA)	http://www.loyno.edu/admissions/apply/freshapp.html
Luther College (Decorah, IA)	http://www.luther.edu/apply/admit.htm
Lycoming College (Williamsport, PA)	http://www.lycoming.edu/dept/admiss/admisapp.htm
Lynchburg College (Lynchburg, VA)	http://www3.lynchburg.edu/www/application.html
Lynn University (Boca Raton, FL)	http://www.lynn.edu/admissions/application/
Lyon College (Batesville, AR)	http://www.lyon.edu/HTML/FV/9APP1.htm
MacMurray College (Jacksonville, IL)	http://www.mac.edu/admissions/app_info.html
Mansfield University (Mansfield, PA)	http://www.mnsfld.edu/depts/admissns/app.html

School	Electronic Application Address
Marist College (Poughkeepsie, NY)	http://www.marist.edu/admissions/freshapp.html
Marlboro College (Marlboro, VT)	http://www.marlboro.edu/homepage/admissions/applications.html
Marquette University (Milwaukee, WI)	http://www.marquette.edu/apply@mu/app98-99/apply.html
Martin Methodist College (Pulaski, TN)	http://www.rackley.com/admission_form.html
Marycrest International University (Davenport, IA)	http://www.mcrest.edu/
Maryland Public Colleges and Universities	http://www.acaff.usmh.usmd.edu/umsapp/uindex.html
Marylhurst University (Marylhurst, OR)	https://www.marylhurst.edu/register/start/apply.html
Maryville College (Maryville, TN)	http://www.maryvillecollege.edu/Admissions/Online_Application/online_application.html
Maryville University (St. Louis, MO)	http://www.maryville.edu/admissions/Undergraduate%20Day%20Programs/Undergraduate_Application.html
Marywood University (Scranton, PA)	http://www.marywood.edu/ug_cat/admissions/applic.stm
Massachusetts College of Liberal Arts (North Adams, MA)	http://www.mcla.mass.edu/admissions/admform6b.htm?
McMurry University (Abilene, TX)	http://www.mcm.edu/mcminfo/admis/application.htm
Menlo College (Atherton, CA)	http://www.menlo.edu/application/application.html
Mercer University (Macon, GA)	http://www.mercer.edu/admissions/apply.html
Mercy College (Dobbs Ferry, NY)	http://merlin.mercynet.edu/admissions/application.html
Mesa State College (Grand Junction, CO)	https://mesaweb.mesastate.edu:1500/
Messiah College (Grantham, PA)	http://www.messiah.edu/mcinfo/admit/admiform.htm
Metropolitan State College of Denver (Denver, CO)	https://www.mscd.edu/enroll/admissions/application/index.htm
Michigan State University (East Lansing, MI)	https://www.welcome.msu.edu/AdmissionsApplications/LoginScreen.asp?ToApp=UN

TABLE E.2: SCHOOLS THAT ACCEPT
ELECTRONIC APPLICATIONS (CONT.)

School	Electronic Application Address
Millsaps College (Jackson, MS)	http://www.millsaps.edu/www/admiss/apply/online.htm
Milwaukee School of Engineering (Milwaukee, WI)	https://www.msoe.edu/admiss/app/undergrad/
Mississippi State University (Mississippi State, MS)	http://msuinfo.ur.msstate.edu/admissions/app_dom.htm
Monmouth College (Monmouth, IL)	http://www.monm.edu/admission/applyto/appli.htm
Monmouth University (West Long Branch, NJ)	http://www.monmouth.edu/~admissn/freshapp.htm
Montana State University at Bozeman	http://www.montana.edu/wwwrg/application.html
Moravian College (Bethlehem, PA)	http://www.moravian.edu/misc/docs/appcoll.htm
Morehead State University (Morehead, KY)	http://www.morehead-st.edu/prospects/web01.html
Morningside College (Sioux City, IA)	http://www.morningside.edu/prospectives/admissions/index.htm
Mount Ida College (Newton Centre, MA)	http://www.mountida.edu/Secure-Server-01/admissions/index.html
Mount Union College (Alliance, OH)	http://www.muc.edu/admissions/app3.htm
Mount Vernon Nazarene College (Mount Vernon, OH)	http://www.mvnc.edu/admissions/enrollment/application.html
National American University (Rapid City, SD)	http://www.national.edu/applyonline.html
Nebraska Wesleyan University (Lincoln, NE)	http://www.nebrwesleyan.edu/admisap.html
New Hampshire College (Manchester, NH)	http://www.nhc.edu/admissio/inquiry/index.htm
New Jersey Institute of Technology (Newark, NJ)	http://mis.njit.edu/cgi-bin/admn.exe
New Mexico Highlands University (Las Vegas, NM)	http://www.nmhu.edu/admissions/ugradadm.htm
New Mexico State University (Las Cruces, NM)	http://www.nmsu.edu/~admision/admit-form.html
New York Institute of Technology (Old Westbury, NY)	http://www.nyit.edu/applications/ug_app.html

School	Electronic Application Address
Norfolk State University (Norfolk, VA)	http://www.nsu.edu/admissions/app.htm
North Dakota Public University System	http://www.rdb.und.nodak.edu/owa_ea/owa/ea_home
North Georgia College and State University (Dahlonega, GA)	http://www.ngc.peachnet.edu/admiss/applic.htm
Northern Arizona University (Flagstaff, AZ)	https://www.nau.edu/undadm/application/
Northern Michigan University (Marquette, MI)	http://www.nmu.edu/flexmail2/flex-admapp.html
Northern State University (Aberdeen, SD)	http://www.northern.edu/apply.html
Northwest Missouri State University (Maryville, MO)	http://www.nwmissouri.edu/admissions/UNDERGRAD_APPL.HTML
Northwest Nazarene College (Nampa, ID)	http://www.nnc.edu/
Northwestern College (Orange City, IA)	http://www.nwciowa.edu/apply.html
Norwich University (Northfield, VT)	http://www.norwich.edu/admiss/undergraduate/application/online.html
Oakland University (Rochester, MI)	http://www.oakland.edu/admissions/admis.htm
Oglethorpe University (Atlanta, GA)	http://www.oglethorpe.edu/admission/applying.htm
Olivet Nazarene University (Olivet, MI)	http://www.olivet.edu/Departments/Admissions/
Oregon Institute of Technology (Klamath Falls, OR)	http://wwwcset.oit.osshe.edu/cgi-bin/part1a.exe
Oregon State University (Corvallis, OR)	http://osu.orst.edu/admissions/adminfo.htm
Otterbein College (Westerville, OH)	http://www.otterbein.edu/admission/apapply.htm
Pace University (New York, NY)	http://apply.pace.edu/
Pacific Union College (Angwin, CA)	http://www.puc.edu/PUC/enrollment/application.html
Pacific University (Forest Grove, OR)	http://nellie.pacificu.edu/NetForms/admissions/app/app0.shtml
Park College (Parkville, MO)	http://www.park.edu/admit/admis.htm
Pennsylvania State University (University Park, PA)	http://www.psu.edu/dept/admissions/

TABLE E.2: SCHOOLS THAT ACCEPT
ELECTRONIC APPLICATIONS (CONT.)

School	Electronic Application Address
Peru State College (Peru, NE)	http://www.peru.edu/admissions/application.html
Pikeville College (Pikeville, KY)	http://www.pc.edu/
Pittsburg State University (Pittsburg, KS)	http://go.pittstate.edu/ug.admit.form.html
Plymouth State College (Plymouth, NH)	http://www.plymouth.edu/psc/admit/appform.htm
Polytechnic University (Brooklyn, NY)	http://www.poly.edu/undergradPrograms/application.html
Portland State University (Portland, OR)	http://banweb.pdx.edu/adm/
Presbyterian College (Clinton, SC)	http://www.presby.edu/admissions/application.htm
Purdue University (West Lafayette, IN)	http://wwwdev.adpc.purdue.edu/Admit/Welcome.html
Quincy University (Quincy, IL)	http://www.quincy.edu/admissions/online_app.html
Radford University (Radford, VA)	http://infolink.runet.edu:80/~ruadmiss/adminapp.html
Randolph-Macon College (Ashland, VA)	http://www.rmc.edu/getapplic.html
Roanoke College (Salem, VA)	http://www2.roanoke.edu/admissio/applform.htm
Rochester College (Rochester Hills, MI)	http://www.rc.edu/Admissions/applicat.htm
Rochester Institute of Technology (Rochester, NY)	https://www.rit.edu/~960www/application/undergraduate/
Rutgers University System (New Jersey)	http://clue.rutgers.edu/cgi-bin/admitp/ug_application_ceeb.ceeb_search1
Sacred Heart University (Fairfield, CT)	http://www.sacredheart.edu/admiss/ugapp.html
Shawnee State University (Portsmouth, OH)	http://online.shawnee.edu/admissions/usapp.htm
Shenandoah University (Winchester, VA)	http://www.su.edu/apps.htm
Shippensburg University (Shippensburg, PA)	http://www.ship.edu/admiss/app.html
Sierra Nevada College (Incline Village, NV)	http://www.sierranevada.edu/admissions/onlinapp.htm

School	Electronic Application Address
Slippery Rock University (Slippery Rock, PA)	http://www.sru.edu/depts/admissio/aplicati.htm
Southern Connecticut State University (New Haven, CT)	http://www.southernct.edu/application/
Southern Utah University (Cedar City, UT)	http://www.suu.edu/ss/admissions/suuapplyform.htm
Southwest Missouri State University (Springfield, MO)	https://www.secure.smsu.edu/application/freshmanapp.html
St. Ambrose University (Davenport, IA)	http://www.sau.edu/administration/newstudent/admit-form.htm
St. Cloud State University (St. Cloud, MN)	http://www.stcloudstate.edu/~scsu4u/fappl1.html
St. John Fisher College (Rochester, NY)	http://www.sjfc.edu/adm_info/freshman.html
St. Joseph's College (Rensselaer, IN)	http://www.saintjoe.edu/admissions/appform.php3
St. Leo College (St. Leo, FL)	http://www.saintleo.edu/admissions/application/98_fall_app.htm
St. Mary's College (Notre Dame, IN)	http://www.saintmarys.edu/Considering/Application/preapp.html
St. Norbert College (DePere, WI)	http://www.snc.edu/admit/appform1.htm
State University of West Georgia (Carrollton, GA)	http://www.westga.edu/~admiss/ap.html
Stephens College (Columbia, MO)	http://www.stephens.edu/www/PR/ADMISSION/ADMTRANSFER.HTML
Stetson University (DeLand, FL)	http://www.stetson.edu/admissions/appl.htm
Susquehanna University (Selinsgrove, PA)	http://www.susqu.edu/ad_depts/admissions/applications/startappnew.htm
Teikyo Post University (Waterbury, CT)	http://www.teikyopost.edu/
Tennessee Technological University (Cookeville, TN)	http://wserve.tntech.edu/webdocs/ahomepg1.htm
Texas Public Universities	http://www.applytexas.org/adappc/commonapp.html
Thomas College (Waterville, ME)	http://www.thomas.edu/admiss/app.htm
Thomas Edison State College (Trenton, NJ)	https://www.tesc.edu/public/f_colreg2.html

TABLE E.2: SCHOOLS THAT ACCEPT
ELECTRONIC APPLICATIONS (CONT.)

School	Electronic Application Address
Toccoa Falls College (Toccoa Falls, GA)	http://www.toccoafalls.edu/adm/undergrad_application.htm
Transylvania University (Lexington, KY)	http://www.transy.edu/new_app_application.html
Troy State University (Troy, AL)	http://www.troyst.edu/forms/newundergradapp.html
Tufts University (Medford, MA)	http://admissions.tufts.edu/indexb.htm
Union College (Barbourville, KY)	http://mars.unionky.edu/applic.htm
United States International University (San Diego, CA)	https://www.usiu.edu/Admissio/howapply.htm
University of Akron (Akron, OH)	https://www.uakron.edu/mvslink/admissions/admappl.html
University of Alaska at Fairbanks	https://www.uaf.edu/admrec/forms/index.html
University of Arizona (Tucson, AZ)	https://www.arizona.edu:9876/cgi-bin/admissions/application.pl
University of Arkansas at Little Rock	http://www.ualr.edu/~adminfo/apply.htm
University of Bridgeport (Bridgeport, CT)	http://www.bridgeport.edu/Indexhtml/Admissions/undergrad-appl.html
University of California System	http://www.ucop.edu/pathways/appctr.html
University of Central Arkansas (Conway, AR)	http://www.uca.edu/admissions/application.htm
University of Central Florida (Orlando, FL)	http://pegasus.cc.ucf.edu/~admissio/application/
University of Cincinnati (Cincinnati, OH)	http://129.137.76.132/pages/adm/adm-application.html
University of Colorado System	http://www.cusys.edu/~comapp/index.cgi
University of Dayton (Dayton, OH)	http://admission.udayton.edu/apply.asp
University of Delaware (Newark, DE)	http://www.udel.edu/admissions/application.html
University of Evansville (Evansville, IN)	http://www.evansville.edu/~admisweb/onlineapp/under/index.html
University of Findlay (Findlay, OH)	http://www.findlay.edu/
University of Florida (Gainesville, FL)	http://www.reg.ufl.edu/on-line/

School	Electronic Application Address
University of Georgia (Athens, GA)	http://www.admissions.uga.edu/99app.html
University of Hartford (Hartford, CT)	http://www.hartford.edu/onlinereg/regform.html
University of Hawaii at Hilo	http://www.uhh.hawaii.edu/UHHforms/admis/uhh_app.htm
University of Idaho (Moscow, ID)	http://www.uidaho.edu/admissions/ugrad/commonap.htm
University of Indianapolis (Indianapolis, IN)	http://admissions.uindy.edu/app.html
University of Iowa (Iowa City, IA)	http://www.uiowa.edu/admissions/Undergrad/apply/applications.html
University of Louisville (Louisville, KY)	http://www.louisville.edu/student/services/admissions/uapp/uapp.html
University of Maine at Augusta	http://www.uma.maine.edu/a%26r/ua&rapplicationinstructions.html
University of Maine at Farmington	http://www.umf.maine.edu/~admit/apply/apply.html
University of Maine at Fort Kent	http://www.umfk.maine.edu/admissions/apply.htm
University of Maine at Presque Isle	http://www.umpi.maine.edu/admis/app.htm
University of Massachusetts at Boston	http://www.umb.edu/admission_and_financial_aid/application_form.html
University of Massachusetts at Lowell	http://www.uml.edu/Admissions/Apply/Application_Form/application_form.html
University of Miami (Miami, FL)	http://www.miami.edu/admission-information/apply.html
University of Mississippi (University, MS)	http://www.olemiss.edu/admissions/undergrad.html
University of Missouri at Columbia	http://web.missouri.edu/~regwww/admission/US/Application_Form/Application_index.html
University of Missouri at Rolla	http://www.umr.edu/~cisapps/uapp.html
University of Missouri at St. Louis	http://www.umsl.edu/admission/underapp1.htm
University of Nebraska at Omaha	http://www.ses.unomaha.edu/admissions/ugapp2.html

TABLE E.2: SCHOOLS THAT ACCEPT
ELECTRONIC APPLICATIONS (CONT.)

School	Electronic Application Address
University of New Hampshire (Durham, NH)	https://webcat.unh.edu/prod/plsql/hwskalog.P_DispLoginNon
University of New Haven (West Haven, CT)	http://www.newhaven.edu/UNH/studentapp2.html
University of New Orleans (New Orleans, LA)	http://www.uno.edu/~admi/admission.html
University of New Mexico (Albuquerque, NM)	http://www.unm.edu/~apply/intro.htm
University of North Carolina at Asheville	http://tserve.unca.edu/
University of North Carolina at Chapel Hill	https://www-s2.ais.unc.edu/sis/adm/appcenter.html
University of North Carolina at Wilmington	https://tswww.mis.uncwil.edu/ahomepg.htm
University of Northern Colorado (Greeley, CO)	http://www.univnorthco.edu/admissions/adform.htm
University of Northern Iowa (Cedar Falls, IA)	http://access.uni.edu/stdt/ugapinst.htm
University of Notre Dame (Notre Dame, IN)	http://208.171.159.3/undergraduateadmissions/htdocs/onlineapplication/
University of Oregon (Eugene, OR)	http://admissions.uoregon.edu/~admit/apply/onlineapp.htm
University of Pittsburgh (Pittsburgh, PA)	http://www.pitt.edu/~oafa/freshman.html
University of Pittsburgh at Greensburg	http://www.pitt.edu/~upg/elecadm1.html
University of Pittsburgh at Johnstown	http://www.pitt.edu/~upjweb/admissions/application_notice.html
University of Puget Sound (Tacoma, WA)	http://www.ups.edu/admission/Apply_online.htm
University of Rhode Island (Kingston, RI)	https://web7.mis.uri.edu/ixpress/web7/srs$2dbook/Instructions
University of Rio Grande (Rio Grande, OH)	http://www.urgrgcc.edu/Admissions/admisapp.htm
University of Scranton (Scranton, PA)	https://www.uofs.edu/admissions/appinfo.html
University of South Carolina (Columbia, SC)	http://web.csd.sc.edu/app/ugrad_cola/

School	Electronic Application Address
University of South Carolina at Aiken	http://www.sc.edu/admissions/Aiken/aiken.html
University of South Dakota (Vermillion, SD)	http://www.usd.edu/admissions/
University of Southern California (Los Angeles, CA)	https://arr2.usc.edu/admapp/
University of Southern Mississippi (Hattiesburg, MS)	http://www.usm.edu/usmweb/admissions/admissions/applic.html
University of Virginia (Charlottesville, VA)	http://www.virginia.edu/%7Eadmiss/ugadmiss/applica.html
University of West Alabama (Livingston, AL)	http://www2.westal.edu/admiss/appform.htm
University of West Florida (Pensacola, FL)	http://www.uwf.edu/~admiss/uapf.htm
University of Wisconsin System	http://apply.wisconsin.edu/
University of Wyoming (Laramie, WY)	http://siswww.uwyo.edu/adm/adm_form/adm_index.htm
Ursuline College (Pepper Pike, OH)	http://www.ursuline.edu/admissions/application.htm
Utah State University (Logan, UT)	http://www.usu.edu/~registra/admrec/apply-usu.html
Valparaiso University (Valparaiso, IN)	http://www.valpo.edu/admissions/UndergradApp.html
Villanova University (Villanova, PA)	http://admission.villanova.edu/application/aplction.html
Virginia Intermont College (Bristol, VA)	http://www.vic.edu/admiss/application/index.html
Voorhees College (Denmark, SC)	http://www.voorhees.edu/admisfm.htm
Wabash College (Crawfordsville, IN)	http://www.wabash.edu/admissions/apply/webapp.htm
Wake Forest University (Winston-Salem, NC)	http://www.wfu.edu/admissions/online-app/introduction.html
Waldorf College (Forest City, IA)	http://www.waldorf.edu/application/applicat.htm
Walla Walla College (College Place, WA)	http://www.wwc.edu/admissions/apply/application.html
Warren Wilson College (Swannanoa, NC)	http://www.warren-wilson.edu/application/onlineapp.shtml
Washburn University (Topeka, KS)	http://www.washburn.edu/services/admissions/form/admission.html

TABLE E.2: SCHOOLS THAT ACCEPT
ELECTRONIC APPLICATIONS (CONT.)

School	Electronic Application Address
Washington and Jefferson College (Washington, PA)	http://www.vwadesign.com/wj/vb_app.html
Washington State University (Pullman, WA)	http://www.wsu.edu/admissions/help_fr1.html
Waynesburg College (Waynesburg, PA)	http://waynesburg.edu/Campus/Admit/App.html
Weber State University (Ogden, UT)	http://catsis.weber.edu/Admissions/
Wentworth Institute of Technology (Boston, MA)	http://www.wit.edu/Admissions/apply.html
West Chester University (West Chester, PA)	http://wwwscripts.wcupa.edu/cgi-win/adm/admform.exe
West Virginia Public Colleges and Universities	http://www.scusco.wvnet.edu/www/stserv/commapp/commonapp.htm
Western Baptist College (Salem, OR)	http://www.wbc.edu/admissions/online_application.htm
Western Connecticut State University (Danbury, CT)	http://www.wcsu.ctstateu.edu/admissions/applicationform.html
Western Illinois University (Macomb, IL)	http://wiuadm1.wiu.edu/cgi-win/miadm/dbApp.exe
Western International University (Phoenix, AZ)	http://www.wintu.edu/student.html
Western Maryland College (Westminster, MD)	http://www.wmc.car.md.us/HTMLpages/Admissions/APPWMC.html
Western Michigan University (Kalamazoo, MI)	http://www.wmich.edu/admi/undergradapp/undergrad-programs.html
Western Oregon University (Monmouth, OR)	http://www.wou.edu/studentaffairs/admissions/apply/
Western State College of Colorado (Gunnison, CO)	http://mail.western.edu/admolap/ola_inst.html
Western Washington University (Bellingham, WA)	http://www.ac.wwu.edu/~admit/UndergradApp.html
Westminster College (Fulton, MO)	https://www.westminster-mo.edu/application/instructions.html
Westminster College (Salt Lake City, UT)	http://www.wcslc.edu/admissions/undergraduate/applyonline.html
Whitman College (Walla Walla, WA)	http://www.whitman.edu/admission/app/app.html

School	Electronic Application Address
Wichita State University (Wichita, KS)	http://www.wichita.edu/online/admissions/onlineapp.asp
Wilberforce University (Wilberforce, OH)	http://www.wilberforce.edu/admit/packet/applic.htm
William Penn College (Oskaloosa, IA)	http://www.usmall.com/college/schools/wmpenn/appl.html
Williams Baptist College (Walnut Ridge, AR)	http://www.wbcoll.edu/Applicat.htm
Wilson College (Chambersburg, PA)	http://www.wilson.edu/
Wittenberg University (Springfield, OH)	http://www.wittenberg.edu/admit/app/appinstr.shtml
Wofford College (Spartanburg, SC)	http://www.wofford.edu/admissions/index.htm
Worcester Polytechnic Institute (Worcester, MA)	http://www.wpi.edu/Admin/AO/application.html
Worcester State College (Worcester, MA)	https://magic.worc.mass.edu/apply.html
York College (York, PA)	http://www.ycp.edu/admissions/html/application_intro.html